"The Presentation of the Augsburg Confession," from the flyleaf of
Concordia: Pia et Unanimi consensu Repetita Confessio fidei et doctrinae . . .
(Leipzig: Johann Gross, 1677).

LUTHERAN QUARTERLY BOOKS

Editor

Paul Rorem, *Princeton Theological Seminary*

Associate Editors

Timothy J. Wengert, *United Lutheran Seminary, Philadelphia*
Mary Jane Haemig, *Luther Seminary, Saint Paul*
Mark C. Mattes, *Grand View University, Des Moines, Iowa*

Lutheran Quarterly Books will advance the same aims as *Lutheran Quarterly* itself, aims repeated by Theodore G. Tappert when he was editor fifty years ago and renewed by Oliver K. Olson when he revived the publication in 1987. The original four aims continue to grace the front matter and to guide the contents of every issue, and can now also indicate the goals of *Lutheran Quarterly Books:* "to provide a forum (1) for the discussion of Christian faith and life on the basis of the Lutheran confession; (2) for the application of the principles of the Lutheran church to the changing problems of religion and society; (3) for the fostering of world Lutheranism; and (4) for the promotion of understanding between Lutherans and other Christians."

For further information, see www.lutheranquarterly.com.

The symbol and motto of *Lutheran Quarterly,* VDMA for *Verbum Domini Manet in Aeternum* (1 Peter 1:25), was adopted as a motto by Luther's sovereign, Frederick the Wise, and his successors. The original "Protestant" princes walking out of the imperial Diet of Speyer in 1529, unruly peasants following Thomas Müntzer, and from 1531 to 1547 the coins, medals, flags, and guns of the Smalcaldic League all bore the most famous Reformation slogan, the first Evangelical confession: The Word of the Lord remains forever.

For the complete list of *Lutheran Quarterly Books*, please see the final pages of this work.

THE AUGSBURG CONFESSION

RENEWING LUTHERAN FAITH AND PRACTICE

TIMOTHY J. WENGERT

Fortress Press
Minneapolis

THE AUGSBURG CONFESSION
Renewing Lutheran Faith and Practice

Cover design: Laurie Ingram

Print ISBN: 978-1-5064-3294-6
eBook ISBN: 978-1-5064-3295-3

CONTENTS

Contents

Abbreviations

TAL	*The Annotated Luther.* Ed. Hans Hillerbrand, et al. 6 vols. Minneapolis: Fortress, 2015–2017
Ap	Apology of the Augsburg Confession
CA	Augsburg Confession [*Confessio Augustana*]
CR	*Corpus Reformatorum: Philippi Melanthonis opera quae supersunt omnia.* Edited by Karl Bretschneider and Heinrich Bindseil. 28 vols. Halle/Braunschweig: A. Schwetschke & Sons, 1834–1860
Ep	Epitome of the Formula of Concord
FC	Formula of Concord
LC	Large Catechism
LW	*Luther's Works* [American edition], 55+ vols. Philadelphia: Fortress and St. Louis: Concordia, 1955–
MBW *Regesten* and MBW *Texte*	*Melanchthons Briefwechsel*, ed. Heinz Scheible, et al. Stuttgart-Cannstatt: Frommann-Holzboog, 1978–
NIV	*New International Version* of the Bible
SA	Smalcald Articles
SC	Small Catechism
SD	Solid Declaration of the Formula of Concord
WA	*Luthers Werke: Kritische Gesamtausgabe* [*Schriften*], 65 vols. (Weimar: H. Böhlau, 1883–1993)
WA DB	*Luthers Werke: Kritische Gesamtausgabe: Bibel*, 12 vols. (Weimar: H. Böhlau, 1906–1961)
WA Br	*Luthers Werke: Kritische Gesamtausgabe: Briefwechsel*, 18 vols. (Weimar: H. Böhlau, 1930–1985)
WA TR	Luthers Werke: *Kritische Gesamtausgabe: Tischreden*, 6 vols. (Weimar: H. Böhlau, 1912–1921)

FOREWORD

The Augsburg Confession is quite an inadequate document—as a dogmatics textbook, or as a handbook for pastoral care. The Augsburg Confession is a perfectly adequate document as a demonstration of the faithfulness to the biblical message and the catholic tradition, its original intention, and it also serves well as a summary of the insights of Luther, Melanchthon, and their Wittenberg colleagues. As such, it also functions well as a springboard for teaching the essential contents of Holy Scripture. In addition, its last seven articles address problems in practice as a kind of model for applying the message of Scripture to the life of the church. Thus, as Timothy Wengert demonstrates in this volume, not only those articles but all the Confession's articles speak to pastoral questions and deal with practical aspects of the life of Christians individually and in the course of their working and worshiping together in their congregations.

Wengert offers readers here a commentary on the text of the Augsburg Confession with the special focus on the living voice of the gospel and its application in the world in which believers experience the blessings of God. He is not the first to write a commentary on the Confession. Philip Melanchthon, its drafter, wrote the first such commentary, within a year of the Confession's presentation on June 25, 1530. He entitled this commentary *Apologia*, a title he had originally intended for the Confession itself. His "defense" of the Confession that he had placed in the mouths of the seven princes and two town councils won widespread use as well. A generation later a group of Melanchthon's and Luther's followers composed the Formula of Concord as a commentary on vital issues of the day, with the intention to clarify certain teachings of the Confession that had been, in the view of the Formula's authors and sponsors, misrepresented and undermined by some who claimed to be its adherents.

Wengert's commentary on the content of the Confession and his application of its teaching to contemporary questions and concerns of the twenty-first century church focus on the value that Melanchthon's insights have for

Christian living today. The theology of the Wittenberg Reformers developed in the context of concerns for the proper care and consolation of Christian consciences raised by the crisis of pastoral care of the fifteenth century. Luther's fresh approach to delivering the message of Scripture developed not only in his intensive study of the Bible, especially in preparation for his lectures in the cloister and the university during the 1510s, but his approach also arose out of his own exercise of pastoral duties, especially preaching and hearing confessions, which his vows as an Augustinian friar imposed upon him. Melanchthon never served as a congregational pastor or assumed such pastoral roles as those Luther practiced. Nonetheless, he was keenly sensitive to how the proclamation of the biblical message would bring sinners to repentance and bring comfort to the repentant. He publicly opposed the ignorance and misimpressions of late medieval popular piety. He criticized the subjection of catholic tradition to non-biblical authorities, such as Aristotle (whom Melanchthon could use for certain purposes, of course), by contemporary theologians and bishops. Melanchthon and his family lived, worshiped, shopped, and gossiped with their neighbors in little Wittenberg, and he knew the kinds of joys and sorrows that filled their daily lives.

The theological enterprise in which he had been engaged for a decade by 1530 had cultivated in his own exegetical work a sensitivity to the pedagogical and pastoral challenges of parish life. Theological study and instruction flowed naturally for him into preaching and pastoral care. Therefore, it is no wonder that his Confession of what he believed and taught, though designed for other purposes, functions effectively as a foundation for the practice of the faith and ministry to the faithful.

Tim Wengert and I have been friends since 1978. We do not always agree, but we have both drunk deeply from the wells of the fresh waters our families gave us, drawn from Luther's Small Catechism. Few whom I know have been more sensitive to the pastoral dilemmas imposed by North American cultures upon Christian life, for both believers as individuals and in their congregations. Few have Wengert's command of Melanchthon's own way of thinking and the expression of his faith, as well as those of his colleagues, as he drew it together in the Augsburg Confession. In this volume he demonstrates how the rich resources offered by the Wittenberg theologians can give powerful support for pastors and people in their confession of our faith in Jesus Christ. This volume clearly shows that this Confession continues to offer effective aid for conveying the promise that Christ's death and resurrection have won for his people, and offer effective support for applying the Word of God to the predicaments and problems encountered by them day in and day out.

Robert Kolb

Acknowledgments

Many people have contributed to the writing of this book. Although I cannot possibly name them all, here are some of the ones that matter. First, there were my many teachers: At the University Freiburg, where I spent my junior year, Gottfried Schramm, from whom I first heard lecture on the Reformation in 1970, and Heinz Holeczek, who taught German history; at the University of Michigan, James A. Vann, my MA advisor, and John O'Malley, S.J., who as guest professor lectured on the Reformation; at Luther Seminary, Charles Anderson, who taught Lutheran Confessions, and Gerhard Forde, who taught Lutheran theology in that special blend of history and dogmatics reflected in these pages; at Duke University, David C. Steinmetz, my thesis advisor, who taught a love for historical texts and the history of biblical interpretation, and Robert C. Gregg, who opened up the patristic literature, and Winfred Hudson, who embodied American religious history; and at the University of Tübingen, where I spent a research year, the incomparable Heiko A. Oberman. Then there are all of those friends and colleagues: Richard Muller, Susan Schreiner, John Thompson, Irving Sandberg, Robert Moore, James Estes, Irene Dingel, Gordon Lathrop, Gail Ramshaw, Susan Wood, SCL, Mary Jane Haemig, Paul Rorem (who accepted this book in the "Lutheran Quarterly Books" series), Scott Tunseth, Roy Riley, Michael Möller, and all those long-suffering colleagues at Mt. Airy, to say nothing of all those students, especially Luka Ilic, Martin Lohrmann, and Derek Cooper. Special mention must be made of Robert Kolb, in whose clearings through the woods of Lutheranism I have happily sown and harvested, and whose foreword graces this book. Then there is my family, including my late wife Barbara, my children Emily and David, my grandchildren, Alexandra and Juliette, my parents, Norman and Janet, my siblings, Eugene and Christine, and my dearest Ingrid, the best working pastor and companion I could have, to whom, along with all her colleagues in ministry, I dedicate this work.

Introducing the Augsburg Confession

According to Martin Luther, on 25 June 1530 one of Jesus's prophecies was fulfilled. It was not the first time this prophecy would have been fulfilled, but for Luther it was by far one of the most important. In Matthew 10:18 we read: "And you will be dragged before governors and kings because of me, as a testimony to them and the Gentiles." Here Jesus was simply paraphrasing Psalm 119:46: "I will also speak of your decrees before kings, and shall not be put to shame." In a letter to Conrad Cordatus dated 6 July 1530, Luther first connected Psalm 119 (and, by extension, Jesus's subsequent prophecy) to the public reading of the Augsburg Confession as he reflected on what had happened on that fateful day, 25 June 1530.[1] While German printings of the CA did not include this text, Latin editions of 1530 and beyond put it boldly on the title page.[2] By citing this text, Luther put readers on notice that the real point of the Augsburg Confession was not simply stating correct doctrine or compelling compliance to such doctrine—despite the ways in which churches later may have used the CA—but rather was a moment of confessing.[3]

This also warns modern-day readers that, into whatever ecclesiastical service they may press the CA, its real life and deepest meaning come about when they, too, are driven to confess their faith. That, after all, is what Jesus himself anticipates in Matthew: standing before the powerful of the world

---

1. WA Br 5: 441–42; LW 49:353–56.
2. The German versions of 1530 called the CA an "Attestation and Confession of Faith and Doctrine That the Appellant Estates Delivered to His Imperial Majesty at Augsburg Recently." For the 1531 copy of the first edition of the Augsburg Confession and Apology with Melanchthon's request for corrections from Luther and Luther's own handwritten notes, see https://digital .slub-dresden.de/werkansicht/dlf/162007/5/0/, accessed 8 April 2019.
3. For a far more extensive examination of Evangelical Lutheran confessing, see Robert Kolb, *Confessing the Faith: Reformers Define the Church, 1530-1580* (St. Louis: Concordia, 1991), especially 13–42.

with only a word, a confession. Thus, a remarkable weakness lies at the very heart of the Christian faith confessed not just in Augsburg but throughout the history of the Christian church. The claim in CA IV of justification without works echoes every act of confessing Christ. Such confessing cannot occur in the safety of a fortress or from the security of one's study; it cannot simply be lip service to an ecclesiastical party line ("Gottes Wort und Luthers Lehr' vergehen nun und nimmermehr"—God's Word and Luther's teaching will never, ever pass away). It is precisely what happens when everything is on the line or, rather, when it becomes truly a matter of death and life.[4] In a peaceful, bourgeois society, many Christians can scarcely conceive what it means to stand up and say, "I believe." For example, what looks to faithful pastors like a failure of their pedagogical prowess—namely, when children seem rather bored with catechesis and the ancient creeds—has little to do with pastoral failings and far more to do with Jesus's prophecy or, rather, with an absence of such a confessing moment. Such confessing cannot be manufactured but comes instead as a fearsome gift, knocking over all pretense and forcing the believer to cry out to God for help. That help comes at the very moment of confessing. Even the halting tones of the desperate father in Mark 9:24 ("I believe; help my unbelief!") point to that moment and its grace-filled center. This means that confessing and justification by faith alone are two sides of the same coin.

Jesus's prophecy and Psalm 119 are all the more remarkable in that they are both promises: this will happen. You will confess! *And*: you will not be put to shame! Imagine that! The point of confessing is not to stir up feelings of inadequacy and guilt but, to the contrary, confessing always eliminates shame. In the immediate wake of the 1521 imperial diet held in Worms, Luther and his supporters published the *Acta et res gestae . . . in Comitiis Principum Wormaciae* [*The Records and Actions . . . in the Assembly of Princes at Worms*], describing the back and forth not only of Luther's hearing before the emperor but also of subsequent interviews, especially with the Archbishop of Trier. As is now widely accepted, the most famous line from the published Latin account (and the only one in German), "Hier stehe ich; ich kann nicht anders!" (Here I stand, I cannot do otherwise), was not a part of what Luther actually said but was instead placed into printed accounts published in 1521.[5] But that does not make it any less important for understanding what Luther and his colleagues insisted was going on: Luther confessing his faith before the most powerful man in Europe between Charlemagne and Napoleon. In 1536,

---

4. Gerhard Forde, *Justification: A Matter of Death and Life* (Philadelphia: Fortress, 1982).
5. The debate over these words rages on, especially given the coming anniversary in 1521. Still one of the most helpful summaries of positions of the various scholars up to 1896 is in Adolf Wrede, ed., *Deutsche Reichstagsakten, Jüngere Reihe*. Vol. 2 (Gotha: Perthes, 1896), 555–57, n. 1. See also LW 32:101–31.

Luther will use the same language to conclude the Smalcald Articles, marking another moment of confessing—this time before God (as a theological last will and testament) and before pope and council.[6]

These confessing moments have shaped the chapters in this book, each of which addresses a separate article of the Augsburg Confession: beginning with a vignette or history, continuing with a citation of the source and explanation of the text, and concluding with an application titled "We Teach and Confess," paraphrasing a similar phrase in the Formula of Concord.

History

The history of the Augsburg Confession began on 31 October 1517, when Luther wrote a letter to Archbishop Albrecht of Mainz to which he enclosed a copy of the *95 Theses.*[7] Thus, from the very beginning of the Reformation, Luther insisted that church authorities needed to hear his plea for reform—not of church practices and structures but of the preaching of the gospel. This appeal fell on deaf ears as first Tetzel and Conrad Wimpina in January 1518, then Johann Eck by mid-year, and finally Tommaso de Vio (Cardinal Cajetan) in October (along with many others) took issue not simply with Luther's theology but also with his attempt to instruct the church and its leaders. In the years leading up to the Diet held in Worms in 1521, a mixture of threats and negotiations failed to prevent Luther from, first, defending his position and then expanding his criticisms to include both the sacramental system and the papal structure of the church.[8]

With the papal condemnation of Luther as a heretic in January 1521 and his subsequent outlawing at the Diet in April, the stage was set for a different kind of negotiation, as (in the absence of Emperor Charles V) subsequent diets struggled to come to terms with the spread of Luther's and Wittenberg's teaching and the deepening intransigence among the Evangelical[9] princes and estates, especially after the less clearly committed Elector Frederick the Wise was succeeded by his convinced Evangelical brother, Elector John the Steadfast, in 1525 and the Landgrave Philip of Hesse came over to the Evangelical side. This struggle broke into the open in the decision of the 1526 Diet of Speyer, where the assembled estates promised to act in matters of religion as

---

6. SA III.iii.15 (BC, 326): "These are the articles on which I must stand and on which I intend to stand, God willing, until my death. I can neither change nor concede anything in them."

7. See Timothy J. Wengert, ed., *Martin Luther's 95 Theses: With Introduction, Commentary, and Study Guide* (Minneapolis: Fortress, 2015) and TAL 1:13–46.

8. Scott Hendrix, *Luther and the Papacy: Stages in a Reformation Conflict* (Philadelphia: Fortress, 1981).

9. Throughout this work, the word "Evangelical" (capitalized) will be used for what was later called "Lutheran." That is, followers of Luther who represented the "Wittenberg way" of doing theology.

they could defend before God and the emperor. In other words, when the imperial cat's away (fighting the French), the Saxon and Hessian mice, along with their allies, will play. In 1529, at the second Diet of Speyer, the now victorious emperor though absent was able to impose his will on the estates through a particularly harsh decree regarding the empire's religious unrest, which the Evangelicals immediately appealed to the Imperial High Court (*Reichskammergericht*)—an appeal technically called a *protestatio* (whence the later, mistakenly used term *Protestant*).

Then these appellants were blindsided by an imperial summons issued in January 1530 to a new diet to be held in Augsburg and in the presence of the emperor, newly crowned by the pope as Holy Roman Emperor. More than that, the summons demanded not only support for fighting the Turkish sultan, whose troops had in 1529 reached the gates of Vienna, but also an accounting of the faith and practices of the Evangelicals, with a view toward resolving once and for all the religious division in the empire.

But why were the imperial powers involved at all in religious affairs? Answering this question places the historical origins of the CA into the fifteenth century and the successful and unsuccessful attempts to solve problems of the late-medieval church through church councils held within the boundaries of the Holy Roman Empire. Whereas the Council of Constance (1414–1418) had resolved (more or less successfully) the papal schism with the election of Pope Martin V and had dealt (albeit harshly) with the problem of the Bohemian "heresy" by burning Jan Hus and Jerome of Prague at the stake, subsequent councils, especially the Council of Basel, championed a kind of conciliarism that forcefully challenged papal authority. At the same time, subsequent imperial diets often included official *gravamina*, appeals for specific reforms of the church "in head [the papacy] and members [the clerics]."[10] Imperial diets in Worms (1521) and Augsburg (1530) attempted to employ imperial authority in assisting the church to overcome Luther's challenge to church teaching and practice.

The anxiety that the summons to Augsburg evoked in the Saxon camp may be seen in the behavior of some of the participants as the party made its way south from Wittenberg to Augsburg. Already before they left Saxony, Elector John had summoned his theologians to the Castle Torgau (the electorate's chief administrative center), where they had fashioned a series of memoranda (incorrectly labeled "articles" in the nineteenth century) that defended changes in religious practice.[11] Philip Melanchthon assumed that he and the

---

10. Luther even used this literary form to shape his 1520 *Address to Christian Nobility*. See the introduction by James Estes in TAL 1:369–75.
11. Robert Kolb and James A. Nestingen, eds., *Sources and Contexts of the Book of Concord* (Minneapolis: Fortress, 2001), 93–104. The material that goes back to Philip Melanchthon has now been more definitively dated and edited by the editors of *Melanchthons Briefwechsel.* See MBW

other theologians might even die a martyr's death in Augsburg, as had John Hus at the Council of Constance a century earlier. Martin Luther, still an outlaw of the empire, could accompany the retinue only as far south as the Castle Coburg, where he remained throughout the Diet, only accessible by mail. Despite the tendency to paint Luther as an invincible theological hero, he, too, realized the momentous nature of the occasion.

Excursus: Martin Luther and the CA

On Holy Saturday 1530 (16 April), Luther preached a sermon to the departing company in which he expressly focused not on the benefits of Christ's death but on the cost of discipleship, using the familiar story of St. Christopher (whose fresco prominently graces a wall in the Augsburg Cathedral to this day) to illustrate what it meant to bear witness to Christ.[12] After attacking the "factious spirits" for choosing their own crosses and imagining that such crosses merit God's grace, Luther pointed out that Christian suffering is not self-chosen but instead works for the good of the believer, since Christ "will not only help us to bear this suffering but also turn and transform it to our advantage."[13] In any case, Luther advised his hearers to "give our greatest attention to the promise. . . . And this is precisely the thing that differentiates Christian's suffering and afflictions from that of all others. For other people . . . when they run into affliction and suffering . . . have nothing to comfort them, for they do not have the mighty promises and the confidence in God which Christians have."[14] Later he added, "For this is the Christian art [*Kunst*], which we must all learn, the art of looking to the Word and looking away from all the trouble and suffering that lies upon us and weighs us down."[15] For Luther, Christ, not the believer, bore the brunt of such suffering and evil. He also blamed the devil for suffering and then depicts a joust between Christ and the devil.

> So the two heroes meet, each doing as much as possible. The devil brews one calamity after another; for he is a mighty, malicious, and turbulent spirit. So it is time that our dear God be concerned about his honor; for

---

nos. 875 (dated Wittenberg, after 15 March 1530), 881 (dated Torgau, ca. 25 March 1530), 883 (dated ca. 27 March 1530), 894, and 895 (both dated ca. April 1530) in MBW *Regesten*, 1:372, 374–75, 378–79; and MBW *Texte* 4/1:77–82, 95–109, 134–40.

12. Luther, who recognized the fantastical nature of the legend, described how the giant Christopher [whose name means "Christ bearer"] would carry people across a dangerous river. When the Christ child asked him to do the same, the child became so heavy that Christopher's enormous staff broke under the weight. See LW 51:195–208 (WA 32:28–39).

13. LW 51:200.

14. LW 51:201.

15. LW 51:203.

the Word which we wield is a weak and miserable Word, and we who have and wield it are also weak and miserable, bearing the treasure as Paul says [2 Cor 4:7], in earthen vessels.... Then our Lord God looks on for a while and puts us in a tight place, so that we may learn from our own experience that the small, weak miserable Word is stronger than the devil and the gates of hell. They are to storm the castle, the devil and his cohorts. But let them storm; they will find something there that will make them sweat, and still they will not gain it; for it is a rock, as Christ calls it, which cannot be conquered.[16]

Armed with Luther's valedictory, the Saxon party then set out for Augsburg, leaving Luther and his companion, Veit Dietrich (later pastor in Nuremberg), at the Coburg. Luther and Melanchthon both felt frustrations over the distance between them and complained that the other was not paying attention to what they wrote or requested. Yet, in the end, Luther was exuberant at the Saxon party's opportunity to confess the faith. Two weeks after the public reading of the CA, he wrote to Elector John. He noted that Evangelical preaching had been banned by the emperor and his supporters, but added

[T]hese miserable people do not see that by the presentation of the written confession more has been preached than might have otherwise been done by perhaps ten preachers. Is it not deep wisdom and high irony that [the preachers] . . . have to be silent, while instead the Elector of Saxony, together with other sovereigns and lords, comes on stage with the written confession and preaches unhindered before [His] Imperial Majesty [Charles V] and the whole Empire, right under our opponents' noses, so that they have to listen to it and are unable to say anything against it?[17]

Already on 3 July, Luther wrote to Melanchthon expressing his great pleasure with his *Defense* [of the faith; i.e., the CA] and called him in the salutation "a servant and confessor of Christ."[18] Even earlier, in mid-May, Luther

---

16. LW 51:206–7. The fact that Luther delivered this sermon at the Castle Coburg makes the analogy all the more poignant.

17. LW 49:362, letter to Elector John dated 9 July 1530. He expresses a similar point in a letter from the same day written to Justus Jonas, his Wittenberg colleague at the Diet. See LW 49:368.

18. LW 49:342. The subtle irony of the rest of Luther's letter (WA Br 5:435-36; MBW 951 [*Texte* 4/1:316–19]) was lost even on some copyists, who thought Luther was referring to Melanchthon (a mistake followed by Gottfried Krodel in LW 49:345–47). The editors of Melanchthon's correspondence, by using as the basis of their edition a copy that goes back to Melanchthon's closest companion in Augsburg, Johannes Brenz, who had access to the original, makes it clear that it is the CA that "errs and sins." But what Luther is doing here is voicing the opinion of opponents, described by Christ in Luke 19:14 as rejecting his rule. Thus, it is a "double negative." The CA

expressed (to Elector John) his satisfaction with an earlier version of "Master Philip's *Apologia* [defense, i.e., the CA], which pleases me very much; I know nothing to improve or change in it, nor would this be appropriate, since I cannot step so softly and quietly. May Christ, our Lord, help [the Confession] bear much and great fruit, as we hope and pray."[19]

The Drafters in Augsburg

Although even at the time it was being written Martin Luther and others associated Philip Melanchthon with the text of the CA, he did not work alone but rather as the chief drafter for a team of theologians.[20] The inner circle included Johannes Brenz, pastor in Schwäbisch Hall and theological advisor to Margrave Georg of Brandenburg-Ansbach, one of the CA's signers. Brenz and Melanchthon were in his quarters while the CA was being read aloud at the Diet, in tears. Johann Agricola, who was supposed to have been a preacher for the Evangelicals at the Diet until Charles V banned all preaching, was rector of the Latin school in Eisleben, a former student of Luther, and a close acquaintance of Melanchthon since 1518. Even though the two had recently had a dustup over the role of the law in theology, they were back on good terms.[21] Justus Jonas had been Melanchthon's colleague at the University of Wittenberg since the early 1520s, when he was hired to teach canon law [ecclesiastical law]. (He lectured on the Bible—including the acts of the apostles—instead.) Georg Spalatin, former advisor to Elector Frederick on educational and religious matters in the electorate, was by 1530 superintendent in Altenburg, and from the very beginning of the Reformation a close friend and supporter of Luther. We know of several memoranda written for Elector John, one of which bore the names of core members of the Saxon theological advisors: Jonas,

---

sins by not following Christ's description of those who reject him but rather by confessing Christ alone. The same goes for the reference to the opponents as builders who reject Christ, the cornerstone. The CA "errs" by *not* rejecting Christ.

19. LW 49: 297–98, dated 15 May 1530. He uses the term *leisetreten* [actually "sanfft und leise nicht tretten"]. As Heinz Scheible has pointed out ("Luther and Melanchthon," *Lutheran Quarterly*, 4 [1990]: 317–39), this use of the verb rather than the noun does not carry the same negative connotations as the English "pussyfooting around." Indeed, the use of two adverbs (softly and quietly) also points to a far more positive construal (since there is no such verb as "sanfttreten" and "sanft gehen" can mean "sneak about"), one that hearkened back to Luther's preface to the 1529 German translation by Justus Jonas of Melanchthon's *Scholia on Colossians*, where he contrasted Luther the gruff woodsman to Melanchthon the happy farmer. See LW 59:250. David Chytraeus rendered the text of the letter in Latin as "in such a moderate and smooth style."

20. For an exhaustive study of Luther and Melanchthon's collaborators, see Robert Kolb, *Luther's Wittenberg World: The Reformer's Family, Friends, Followers and Foes* (Minneapolis: Fortress, 2019).

21. Timothy J. Wengert, *Law and Gospel: Philip Melanchthon's Debate with John Agricola of Eisleben over "Poenitentia"* (Grand Rapids: Baker, 1997).

Agricola, Melanchthon, and, according to the editors of Melanchthon's correspondence, the unnamed Georg Spalatin.[22]

But there were others as well. Urbanus Rhegius, the Evangelical pastor in Augsburg and soon to be superintendent in Lüneburg at the invitation of Duke Ernest (another signer of the CA), recounted to Luther about the daily meetings in Augsburg that included Melanchthon, Jonas, Spalatin, Agricola, and himself.[23] Andreas Osiander, at the time a Nuremberg pastor, in later life insisted (contrary to fact) that he had helped Melanchthon formulate the CA, improving Philip's weak theology. A Nuremberg patrician and former student of Luther and Melanchthon in Wittenberg, Jerome Baumgartner, also was involved in some discussions and sent an early version of the CA to the Nuremberg city fathers. Erhard Schnepf, advisor to the Landgrave Philip of Hesse and highly regarded by Melanchthon, had arrived in Augsburg already on 4 May 1530 and may also have played a role in the deliberations.[24] Political advisors to the Saxon party, Gregor Brück and Christian Beyer, the latter of whom on 25 June 1530 read aloud the German version of the CA to the Diet, were also involved in negotiations, especially the writing of the preface.

No question, however, that Philip Melanchthon, whose literary skills were legendary, was in charge, not least because he also had Luther's imprimatur. In 1497 Melanchthon was born Philip Schwartzerdt in Bretten, a town in southwest German on the edge of the principalities of Baden and Württemberg. After his father's untimely death, he was sent to Latin school in nearby Pforzheim where he began avidly studying Greek, earning him the Greek version of his name (Schwartz=black; Erdt=earth), *melan-chthon*. After receiving his bachelor of arts degree at Heidelberg, he transferred to Tübingen, where he earned a master of arts. When the University of Wittenberg approached Johannes Reuchlin, a famous humanist and Melanchthon's relative by marriage, to recommend someone for their newly created Greek professorship, he recommended Melanchthon, who arrived in Wittenberg in August 1518. In addition to teaching in the arts faculty, where he held courses not only in Greek but also in rhetoric and logic—the core courses in any arts faculty of the time—Melanchthon studied theology with Luther, earning the first theology degree (the so-called bachelor of Bible) in September 1519. This allowed him to lecture in the theology faculty on the content of the biblical books (and not just on the Greek text). He never received another theology degree but continued to lecture on the Bible throughout his career and by 1530 had published commentaries on Matthew, John, Romans, 1 and 2 Corinthians, Colossians, Proverbs, and (in 1529/30) a rhetorical outline of Romans. In 1527 he received a special professorship that allowed him to lecture in both the

---

22. MBW no. 961, dated 9 July 1530, *Texte* 4/1:342.
23. WA Br 5:334, 5–9.
24. See Melanchthon's letter to Luther, dated 4 May (MBW no. 899, in *Texte* 4/1:150–55, here 154).

arts and the theology faculties. In 1524 he revised the curriculum of the arts faculty along Reformation and Renaissance lines; in 1533 he did the same for the theology curriculum. He was, next to Luther, the most highly respected Wittenberg theologian, and his knowledge of Greek was equal to that of Erasmus of Rotterdam (the humanist who published the first printed edition of the Greek New Testament in 1516).

The Saxon party arrived in Augsburg on 2 May 1530, having taken nearly a month for the journey from the Torgau Castle.[25] Participants brought with them various documents that fed into their work. The Schwabach Articles, written in 1529 as the Saxon elector's confession of faith, were presented in Innsbruck to the emperor, who promptly rejected them—an action that led to their being substantially rewritten and forming the basis of the doctrinal articles (CA I–XIX). The Marburg Articles, written in 1529 for negotiations with Ulrich Zwingli and his Swiss and South German supporters, paralleled the Schwabach Articles.[26] The Torgau memoranda were hardly "articles," but they provided the basis for many of the disputed articles. The Schwabach Articles themselves show many parallels to Luther's own confession of faith appended to his 1528 *Confession Concerning Christ's Supper.*[27] Also fresh in the minds of the drafters were the *Instruction by the Visitors for the Parish Pastors in Electoral Saxony.*[28]

As soon as they arrived, the party began reworking these documents. For one thing, rolling off the presses in nearby Ingolstadt as they arrived was a work of their chief opponent, Johann Eck: *The 404 Articles,* accusing the Reformers and others of writing 386 heretical statements. Some of the charges needed to be answered with new articles (especially CA XX). For another thing, the emperor, still in Innsbruck, dismissed the Schwabach Articles, forcing the Evangelicals not only to rework the articles on practices under dispute (CA XXII–XXVIII) but also to revise the articles of faith, where articles sixteen through twenty-one dealt with specific theological disputes that had arisen in the 1520s.[29] Several manuscripts have survived that help us trace the

---

25. According to the MBW, *Regesten,* vol. 10: *Orte A-Z und Itinerar* (Stuttgart-Bad Cannstatt: Frommann-Holzboog, 1998), 383–84, 388–89, the trip took from 4 April to 2 May 1530, and went through Grimma, Altenburg, Eisenberg, Jena, Weimar, Saalfeld, Gräfenthal, Neustadt bei Coburg, Coburg (where they remained from 15–24 April), Bamberg, Forchheim, Nuremberg (26–28 April), Roth, Weißenburg, Donauwörth, and Gablingen. The return trip lasted from 23 September to 11 October and traced approximately the same itinerary.
26. For these texts, see *Sources and Contexts,* 83–92.
27. Kolb and Nestingen, *Sources and Contexts,* 93–104; LW 37:360–72.
28. LW 40:267–320. Among other things, this text, a joint effort by Luther, Melanchthon, and Johannes Bugenhagen, put to rest the dispute between Agricola and Melanchthon (in the latter's favor).
29. Secular authority (CA XVI), the return of Christ (CA XVII), free will and human culpability (CA XVIII, XIX), the relation of faith and works (CA XX), and prayer to saints (XXI).

development of the CA during discussions in Augsburg.[30] Because German was the official language of the empire and Latin the official language of the church, a version in each language was presented on 25 June 1530, with the German text being read aloud to the assembled diet by the Saxon chancellor, Christian Beyer. The originals were later both destroyed, so that efforts to reconstruct the original text rely on a variety of copies made at the time. After a rogue version was published in 1530, the Saxons produced an official version (the *editio priceps*) in 1531 combined with Melanchthon's Apology [Defense] of the CA. But Melanchthon continued to sharpen the texts already in the 1530s, and in 1540 and 1542 produced a text that reflected more accurately Wittenberg's approach to justification and included wording consonant with the 1536 "Wittenberg Concord" on the Lord's Supper agreed to by Martin Bucer and other South German theologians. These editions were nicknamed the *Variata* [the "altered" editions] and became themselves part of disputes over the Lord's Supper in the 1550s and beyond.[31]

The Style of the CA's Articles

Alongside these documents, the drafters of the CA possessed one other thing in common: a deep knowledge and experience with rhetoric, that is, with the basic rules for writing speeches and other documents, first codified by Cicero, compiled by Quintilian, and taught to every schoolboy in the Renaissance schools that dotted the Holy Roman Empire north of the Alps. Because these rules are no longer well known among twenty-first-century readers, it is necessary to point out the rhetorical side of the CA in more detail. The following year (1531) in a revised edition of his textbook on rhetoric, *Elementorum rhetorices libri duo* [*Two Books of the First Principles of Rhetoric*] Melanchthon expressed the conviction that it was appropriate in religious debates to use the rhetorical principles designed for legal arguments [the *genus iudiciale* or oratory in the law court]. There he wrote: "We teach these rules [regarding the *genus iudiciale*] for judging the speeches of others and for instructing the youth how to handle controversial matters in letters and in ecclesiastical matters. For ecclesiastical disputes have to a great extent similarities to legal contests."[32] Melanchthon first cautioned the students to pay attention to the heart of the matter under dispute, pointing out that it often takes the rules of logic to determine this central point, which is either the conclusion of a logical

---

30. For details, see Wilhelm Maurer, *Historical Commentary on the Augsburg Confession*, trans. H. George Anderson (Philadelphia: Fortress, 1986).

31. For an English translation of the *Variata*, see Henry E. Jacobs, ed., *Historical Introduction, Appendixes and Indexes to the Book of Concord* (Philadelphia: Frederick, 1883), 103–58.

32. Philip Melanchthon, *Elementa rhetorices/Grundbegriffe der Rhetorik*, ed. Volkhard Wels (Berlin: Weidler, 2001), 60.

syllogism or (less often) its major premise. Such a speech is then divided into six parts: the exordium [introduction], the narration [of the basic facts of the case], the proposition [the main point of argument], the confirmation [or proof of the proposition], the confutation [the rebuttal of the other side's objections], and the peroration [conclusion].

Armed with this outline, scholars have already examined portions of the Apology [Defense] of the Augsburg Confession, written and revised by Melanchthon at precisely the time his *Rhetoric* was being published.[33] But there are also important indications that Melanchthon also shaped at least some of the articles in the CA itself to the rules of rhetoric. With the exception of CA XX, the doctrinal articles (I–XXI) evince a consistent pattern (especially when the titles, which were added much later, are ignored). We find that, after an opening phrase that describes the topic ["concerning X"], basic thesis of the article is expounded, followed by reference to certain biblical and ecclesiastical authorities and ending with a rejection of false teaching. At times one or more of these elements is lacking or, in the case of CA IV–V and CA VII–VIII, the rejection of false teaching is placed in the second article, or, in the case of CA IV–VI, the final authority (in CA VI "Ambrose") supports the arguments in all three articles. CA XX and the disputed articles (CA XXII–XXVIII) are lengthier and represent clear defenses of Evangelical theology and practice. Here we can identify how Melanchthon employed certain aspects of the *genus iudiciale* [courtroom speech]. Although the exordium (the appeal to the hearer or reader to listen) may be missing, other parts in their proper order—especially a clear statement of the proposition being debated, the proof of that proposition, and the refutation of counter-arguments—are clearly present. Recognizing these rhetorical elements may help the reader appreciate better the way in which Melanchthon and his team were prosecuting their arguments in what was an extremely volatile situation.

We Teach and Confess

What is the Augsburg Confession? If we reduce it to a catalog of orthodox teaching, we may lose its confessional context. If we reduce it to an act of confession, we may lose its unique, confessional content. When the princes and estates added to the preface the words, "as well as of our faith," they raised

---

33. The two versions of the Apology appeared in May and September/October 1531; the *Elementa* appeared on 26 September 1531, although the manuscript may have been completed much earlier, perhaps in late 1530. For this work see Timothy J. Wengert, "Philip Melanchthon's Last Word to Cardinal Lorenzo Campeggio, Papal Legate at the 1530 Diet of Augsburg," in *Dona Melanchthoniana: Festgabe für Heinz Scheible zum 70. Geburtstag*, ed. Johanna Loehr (Stuttgart-Bad Cannstatt: Frommann-Holzboog, 2001), 457–83; and Charles Arand, "Melanchthon's Rhetorical Argument for *Sola Fide* in the Apology," *Lutheran Quarterly* 14 (2000): 281–308.

the stakes so that a proper use of this confession cannot simply involve others ("our pastors and preachers") but must finally involve one's self. Theological theory and historical accuracy are no replacements for the act of confessing the faith alongside the saints—and not just any faith but precisely one that rests squarely and exclusively in the grace and mercy of God in Christ. To present and confess just such a faith is the goal of what follows in this book.

THE PREFACE:
OBEDIENT DISOBEDIENCE

When writing a book, one always writes the preface last. The Augsburg Confession was no exception, as the princes, imperial cities, and their theologians tried to match up the emperor's expectations to their point of view. As a result the preface and the Confession attached to it had two very distinct goals: to confess the faith of the subscribing princes and cities and defend changes in practice, on the one hand, and to shield that very faith and those alterations from political charges of sedition on the other.

A quick search of the internet and a glance at recent printed copies of the CA reveals that this preface often gets dropped, as if the Augsburg Confession, shorn of its historical context, sprang like Athena full-grown from the head of Zeus. To ignore or downplay the historical context so idealizes this Confession that it loses its ability to speak meaningfully to the church today, where the twin tasks of confessing the faith and rejecting the political distortions of Christianity still define the church's chief duties.

Melanchthon made several attempts at writing a preface, the first being quite friendly toward Charles V and the second sounding much harsher, given the imperial rejection of the Schwabach Articles. In the end, however, the Saxon court produced the present preface, one that again extended an olive branch to Charles while at the same time defending the Evangelicals and calling for a general council, a topic that Philip of Hesse especially demanded be a part of the document to guarantee he would sign it. The published version of the Augsburg Confession also included a brief preface to the reader, the sharp tone of which reflected the situation in 1531, when the emperor had accepted the *Confutation* (the article-by-article rejection of the CA)[1] as the law of the land, the adversaries had begun attacking the CA in print, and Melanchthon

---

1. For this text, see *Sources and Contexts*, 105–39.

had produced his defense, the Apology.[2] As interesting as these other documents may be, the preface that finally prevailed shows quite clearly the historical and theological context for the entire CA, as the Reformers and their princes struggled to balance their confession of faith and changes in practice with obedience to the emperor and the unity of the church.

The Text

Preface to Emperor Charles V[3]

Most serene, most mighty, invincible Emperor, most gracious Lord. A short time ago, Your Imperial Majesty graciously summoned an imperial diet to convene here in Augsburg. The summons indicated an earnest desire, first, to deliberate concerning matters pertaining to "the Turks, that hereditary foe of ours and of the Christian name," and how this foe "might be effectively resisted with unwavering help"; and second, to deliberate "and diligently to consider how we may act concerning the dissension in the holy faith and Christian religion and to hear, understand, and consider with love and graciousness everyone's judgment, opinion, and beliefs among us, to unite the same in agreement on one Christian truth, and to lay aside whatever may not have been rightly interpreted or treated by either side, so that all of us can accept and preserve a single, true religion. Inasmuch as we are all enlisted under one Christ, we are all to live together in one communion and in one church." Because we, the undersigned elector and princes, including our associates as well as other electors, princes, and estates, have been summoned for these purposes, we have complied and can say, without boasting, that we were among the first to arrive.

As hinted at above, "graciously summoned" rather obscures the fact that, after the 1529 Diet in Speyer, the Evangelicals were shocked to be called back to a diet, this time in the emperor's presence. Rather than use their own words to summarize the emperor's intention, the Evangelicals cite his summons. This small fact, indicated by the quotation marks in the English text, helps the readers to understand the unusual (by Evangelical standards) references to the Turkish invasion of Eastern Europe. The Evangelicals hoped to use the emperor's desire to defeat this "hereditary foe," which in 1529 had besieged Vienna, as a way of gaining a fair hearing regarding the second reason he had

---

2. See BC, 29, n. 1.

3. This heading comes from the Latin version of 1530; it is omitted in early German versions.

called the Diet: to resolve the religious crisis of disunity gripping the Holy Roman Empire. The very length of this citation demonstrates how seriously the Evangelicals took this issue.

> Moreover, Your Imperial Majesty graciously, most diligently, and earnestly desired, in reference to the most humble compliance with the summons and in conformity to it, as well as in the matters pertaining to the faith, that each of the electors, princes, and estates should commit to writing, in German and Latin, his judgments, opinions, and beliefs concerning said errors, dissensions, and abuses, etc. Accordingly, after due consideration and counsel, it was proposed to Your Imperial Majesty last Wednesday that, in keeping with Your Majesty's wish, we should present our case in German and Latin today, Friday. Wherefore, in most humble obedience to Your Imperial Majesty, we offer and present a confession of our pastors' and preachers' teachings as well as of our faith, setting forth on the basis of the divine Holy Scripture what and in what manner they preach, teach, believe, and give instruction in our lands, principalities, dominions, cities, and territories.

The language of diplomacy, employed not only in princely courts but also in many other sixteenth-century venues, may strike today's readers as overblown puffery. Here the Evangelical princes and other estates wanted to show their humble obedience, when the background revealed a very different situation. The Augsburg Confession had been in the works for well over a month, especially with the rejection of the Schwabach Articles by the emperor, and it went back to confessional documents of 1529 and memoranda formulated at the Torgau Castle in early 1530. This was hardly a ten-day exercise (from last Wednesday to this Friday—although the Confession was not actually read aloud [in German] until the next day, Saturday).

What the Evangelical princes and estates say they are doing is twofold: presenting a description of their teachers' instruction *and their own faith*. It is this other side to the CA that defines it most sharply in Luther's mind, as we have seen in the previous chapter. The other subtlety comes with the mention, almost in passing, of scriptural authority. At first it might appear that the emperor would be in for a lot of proof texting. But the first half of the CA (art. I–XXI) contains relatively few biblical citations and certainly lacks sophisticated interpretive arguments. Yet we know from the Reformers' other writings that the citations were hardly arbitrary but arose out of more than a decade of intense theological and exegetical debate.

By emphasizing their obedience, the Evangelicals were also painting their own ecclesiastical *dis*obedience in the best possible light. When reading the CA, one must always reckon on these two goals: defending and confessing faith on the one hand and defending civil disobedience on the other. The crisis for the Holy Roman Empire was not exclusively a theological debate. The Middle Ages had seen plenty of debates over a wide variety of theological and practical issues without rupture. But now the Evangelicals had not only changed the center of Western Christian theology but, far more scandalously, had altered practices that were also matters of church and imperial law. This preface was designed to portray them as "obedient rebels."[4]

> If the other electors, princes, and estates also submit a similar written statement of their judgments and opinions, in both Latin and German, we are quite willing, in complete obedience to Your Imperial Majesty, our most gracious Lord, to discuss with them and their associates—as far as this can be done in fairness—such practical and equitable ways as may unite us. Thus, the matters at issue between the parties may be presented in writing on both sides; they may be negotiated charitably and amicably; and these same differences may be so explained as to unite us in one, true religion, since we are all enlisted under one Christ and should confess Christ. All of this may be done in consequence of Your Imperial Majesty's aforementioned summons and in accord with divine truth. We, therefore, invoke God Almighty in deepest humility and pray for the gift of his divine grace to this end. Amen!

What follows is a clever though completely unattainable proposal. By the time this final preface was being drafted, the Evangelicals either knew for certain or strongly suspected that their opponents were not planning to present their own confession of faith. This imbalance foreshadowed the collapse of negotiations before they could begin. Indeed, when their opponents finally presented the *Confutation*, it made matters much worse, since it expressly dismissed of every teaching that the Evangelicals held dearest. Here Heiko Oberman rightly suspected that the break in the Western church occurred not with the presentation of the Augsburg Confession but rather with the *Confutation* and its refusal to discuss Evangelical doctrine except to condemn it.[5] It also demonstrates the Evangelical side's faith in conversation and dialogue. The very mildness of the CA, noted by several of the participants at the time and enshrined in Martin Luther's famous *compliment* of Melanchthon's ability to "tread softly," marked a way of doing theology—by conversation and not fiat—that Lutherans today sometimes reject in favor of bombast and decrees from on high.

---

4. The phrase comes from Jaroslav Pelikan, *Obedient Rebels: Catholic Substance and Protestant Principle in Luther's Reformation* (New York: Harper & Row, 1964).
5. Heiko A. Oberman, "Truth and Fiction: The Reformation in the Light of the Confutatio," in *The Reformation: Roots and Ramifications* (London: T & T Clark, 1994), 167–78.

If, however, our lords, friends, and associates who represent the electors, princes, and estates of the other party, do not comply with the procedure intended by Your Imperial Majesty's summons, so that no charitable and amicable negotiations take place among us, and if they are not fruitful, we on our part shall not have failed in anything that can or may serve the cause of Christian unity, as far as God and conscience allow. Your Imperial Majesty as well as our aforementioned friends, the electors, princes, estates, and every lover of the Christian religion who is concerned about these matters, will be graciously and sufficiently assured of this by what follows in the confession which we and our people submit.

In the 1960s and '70s, some Lutheran theologians proposed calling the CA an ecumenical proposal to the church catholic, and a few even lobbied for Rome itself to accept the document. Although these positions may overstate the case, nevertheless the preface underscores an aspect of the CA sometimes overlooked: that it was written to "serve the cause of Christian unity." To be sure, Christian unity in the sixteenth century was light years away from what sometimes passes for ecumenism in the American religious scene: a toleration of almost anything, "as long as one is sincere." There were limits that the confessors in Augsburg felt constrained to mention: "as far as God and conscience allow." An appeal to conscience, already an important part of Luther's earliest conversations with Rome through Cardinal Tommaso de Vio (Cajetan) in 1518 and invoked by Luther standing before the emperor in 1521, points to an important aspect of medieval theology and practice that the Reformers never hesitated to invoke. But the reference to God raises the stakes even higher. This appeal will appear in CA XVI, where the political ramifications of the Augsburg Confession appear most clearly expressed. Following Peter in Acts 5:29 ("We ought to obey God rather than mortals"), the Evangelicals derive permission to disobey political authorities over matters that they insist are clearly defined in Scripture. Not only the conscience but also God prevents unthinking and unbelieving adherence to the emperor.

In the past, Your Imperial Majesty graciously intimated to the electors, princes, and estates of the empire, especially in a public instruction at the diet of Speyer in the year 1526, that, for reasons there stated, Your Imperial Majesty was not disposed to render a decision in matters pertaining to our holy faith, but would urge the pope to call a council. Again, by means of a written instruction at the last diet in Speyer a year ago, the electors, princes, and estates were, among other things, informed and notified by Your Imperial Majesty's viceroy, His Royal Majesty of Hungary and Bohemia, etc., and by Your Imperial Majesty's orator and appointed commissioners, "that Your Imperial Majesty's viceroy, deputy, and councilors of the imperial government, together with representatives of the absent electors, princes and estates who were assembled at the diet convened at Regensburg, had considered the proposal for a general council and acknowledged that it would be fruitful to have one called." Since, then, the negotiations between Your Imperial Majesty and the pope resulted in a good, Christian understanding, so that Your Imperial Majesty was certain that the pope would not refuse to call such a council, Your Imperial Majesty graciously offered to promote and arrange for the calling of such a general council by the pope, along with Your Imperial Majesty, at the earliest opportunity without putting any obstacles in the way.

At this point, Landgrave Philip of Hesse "enters the room," so to speak. While initially skeptical of the Saxon position and openly courting the Swiss and south German churches, Philip changed his mind and entered into negotiations with Elector John and his theologians. The text of the CA was almost completely settled, but Philip insisted that the preface had to refer to what, at the Diets of Speyer (1526 and 1529) and at the poorly attended diet in Regensburg (1527), had been a major aspect of the Evangelicals' defense for changes in practice: the calling of a general council of the church. It was, of course, not always clear whether this appeal to a council was to be taken seriously or whether it was simply a ploy to delay an inevitable condemnation. Certainly, the Evangelical party knew that the pope himself was very resistant to such a council, so that a first official summons to a council to be held in Mantua did not come until 1536 and then from Pope Paul III, with the actual council not beginning until 1545 but then in Trent.

Already in 1518 Luther had also appealed to a council over against Leo X's decision not to change the church's practice regarding indulgences. Unfortunately for him, his papal opponents insisted that, according to canon law, any appeal to a council over a papal decision was itself a sure sign of heresy. Nevertheless, Luther continued to include such an appeal in his subsequent writings.[6] The preface to the CA, however, carefully avoids any reference to an appeal of papal decisions but describes it instead as Emperor Charles V's own idea, supported by the imperial diet and Charles's brother, Ferdinand. By quoting a statement from the second Diet of Speyer, once again the princes showed their respect for the political realities and could make it seem as if their interest in a council simply matched the concerns of the imperial court. Not too subtly, the Evangelicals also hint at papal intransigence in this regard. By including this call here, the Evangelicals could kill two birds with one stone. On the one hand, they expected that the pope would continue to resist

---

6. See Christopher Spehr, *Luther und das Konzil: Zur Entwicklung eines zentralen Themas in der Reformationszeit* (Tübingen: Mohr Siebeck, 2010).

the calling of a council, and thus they were buying time. On the other hand, by citing this decree, they could also undermine any claims by the emperor to settle the matter directly. Thus, as actually happened, when Charles V accepted the *Confutation* of the Augsburg Confession as the religious law of the land, the Evangelicals could continue to resist any attempts to force them back into the Roman fold.

> In this case, therefore, we offer in full obedience to Your Imperial Majesty even beyond what is required: to participate in such a general, free, Christian council, as the electors, princes, and estates have requested, with high and noble motives, in all the diets of the empire that have been held during Your Imperial Majesty's reign. We also have, following legal form and procedure, called upon and appealed to such a council and to Your Imperial Majesty at various times concerning these most important matters. We now once again adhere to these actions, and neither these nor any subsequent negotiations shall make us waver (unless the matters in dissension are in a charitable and friendly manner finally heard, considered, settled, and result in Christian unity, according to Your Imperial Majesty's summons), as we herewith make public witness and appeal. This is our confession and that of our people, article by article, as follows.

This final paragraph summarizes the Hessian (and Saxon) position on the matter, again clothing it in almost obsequious language ("full obedience" and "beyond what is required"). Here, however, they define the contours of such a council without any reference to the pope. A "general, free, Christian council" is exactly what the pope would resist. At first, the Evangelicals were peremptorily excluded from Trent. In the aftermath of the Smalcald War of 1547, some Evangelicals including Johannes Brenz actually attended. Philip Melanchthon, representing the now victorious new elector of Saxony, Moritz, made his way south as far as Nuremberg before the Revolt of the Princes (1552) rendered his participation at Trent moot. In two cases (Saxony and Württemberg), the Evangelicals wrote new confessions of faith in order to stake out their positions vis-à-vis their Roman opponents in Trent.[7] What recent

---

7. From Saxony, drafted primarily by Melanchthon, came *Confessio Doctrinae Saxonicarum Ecclesiarum scripta Anno Domini MDLI, ut Synodo Trinentinae exhiberetur* [Confession of the teaching of the Saxon churches written in the year 1551 for presentation at the Council of Trent] (Leipzig: Papst, 1553); from Württemberg, drafted by Brenz, *Confessio piae doctrinae, quae nomine illustrissimi principis ac Domini D. Christophori Ducis Wirtenbergensis . . . per legatos eius die XXIIII. Mensis Ianuarii, anno M.D.LII. congregationi Tridentini Concilii propositae est* [Confession of the godly teaching which was submitted in the name of the illustrious prince and lord, Lord Christopher, duke of Württemberg through his delegates on 24 January 1552 to the assembly of the Tridentine Council] (Tübingen: Morhard, 1552).

research has again made clear, there were voices at Trent far more sympathetic to Evangelical concerns than many scholars have imagined.[8] This appeal to a council also had effects much later, as the Vatican II council insisted on inviting observers from a variety of Protestant and Orthodox churches and also took up some of the Reformation's church-dividing issues. One might even go so far as to say that the 1999 Joint Declaration on the Doctrine of Justification between the Lutheran World Federation and the Roman Catholic Church could not have come into being without this clear call for unity through conciliar conversations.

The Saxon party, however, had taken a different tack and had hoped that the emperor might allow a very different kind of solution to the problem of disunity. Thus, in this final paragraph both the Hessian and the Saxon positions—the appeal to a council and openness to an imperial solution—appear side-by-side. Indeed, one can imagine that the Saxon party insisted that the parenthetical phrase ("unless the matters in dissension are in a charitable and friendly manner finally heard, considered, settled, and result in Christian unity, according to Your Imperial Majesty's summons") were written to modify Hessian hopes. Neither proposal bore fruit in the short term, so that Charles finally called upon his military strength to resolve the matter. That, too, failed, and the resultant breech in visible church unity remains to this day.

We Teach and Confess

"We believe in one, holy, catholic, and apostolic church." Despite the plea for unity and a fair hearing, the events in Augsburg—especially the emperor's rejection of the CA and acceptance of its opponents' refutation—signaled a break in the visible unity of the Western church. Although the gift of unity wrought by the Holy Spirit through Word and sacrament remains untouched, the visible disunity of the various churches that arose out of the Reformation—Lutheran, Reformed, Anabaptist, *and* Roman Catholic—means we are still divided.

Yet the CA rests on the very cusp of that dissolution. It offers the churches even today a way forward toward agreement in Word and sacrament. In the sixteenth century, especially among Reformed churches,[9] the CA became the model for their own confessions of faith. Certain aspects of the CA were positively received by the Council of Trent and certainly shaped how Trent

---

8. John O'Malley, *Trent: What Happened at the Council* (Cambridge, MA: Belknap, 2013).

9. This would include the ancestors of the Presbyterians, Reformed Church in America, the Church of the Prussian Union and other union churches, the Anglican and Episcopalian churches, the Methodist and Wesleyan churches, the various Baptist churches, and the Dutch Reformed church.

expressed what it rejected.[10] More recently, as mentioned above, some even suggested that the Vatican accept the Augsburg Confession (at least its doctrinal articles) as a way forward in the ecumenical relations with Lutherans. Although Leif Grane may be correct in saying that too much water has gone over the dam to presume that by moving back to 25 June 1530 the subsequent problems in ecumenical relations could be resolved, nevertheless such suggestions at least point to the unique vantage point that the CA holds.

In this sense, the preface to the CA offers insight both into the attitudes and expectations of the princes, cities, and theologians who offered this confession of faith and into a possible way forward in ecumenical relations. Despite the high tension among the various groups assembled in Augsburg—which included charges and counter-charges of heresy and how to eradicate it "with fire and iron" (that is, burning the teachers at the stake and subduing their supporters with the sword)—the Evangelical princes and cities stressed their obedience to governmental powers, while at the same time defining in no uncertain terms both their confession of faith and their willingness to converse (at a future, free council). That conversation, even in the darkest moments since 25 June 1530, has not really ceased (even when marked almost exclusively by polemic). And, through a series of political accidents, political enforcement of the Christian faith has disappeared. This new situation makes room for a new appreciation of the CA, and it provides a starting point for conversations about trusting God's mercy in Christ at this end of the ages—a mercy that alone brings unity, holiness, catholicity, and apostolicity for all believers.

---

10. For the most recent and best account of Trent, see O'Malley, *Trent.*

PART ONE

CONFESSING THE FAITH
(THE DOCTRINAL ARTICLES)

1

"WE ALL BELIEVE IN ONE TRUE GOD"

The rural congregation loved the "new" song their pastor had taught them: Martin Luther's hymned version of the Nicene Creed set to music from the 1970s composed by Art Gorman for his "Chicago Folk Mass." With their pastor on sabbatical and Trinity Sunday approaching, the worship committee was only too eager to sing that "old favorite"—except that they could not read music and the new organist knew nothing of Gorman's setting. Instead, she dutifully played the somewhat somber tones of Luther's original, modal melody. The result was predictable: looks shot across the room during the introduction; those few who could read music tried nobly for half the first verse; in the end the congregation was reduced to standing silently while the final two-and-a-half verses droned on out of the organ. There were plenty of comments and laughter over coffee an hour later. Somehow the congregation had been robbed of lustily commemorating the only feast in the church calendar celebrating a doctrine: the Feast of the Holy Trinity.

This robbery happens more often than one might imagine and involves not simply songs of praise and confession but the teaching itself—the central, distinctive doctrine of the entire Christian church: found in St. Paul's letters (2 Cor 13:13; 1 Cor 12:4–6); on the lips of Jesus (Matt 28:19); in the earliest baptismal creeds (the Old Roman Creed that continues in the Western church as the Apostles' Creed); and most notably in the Nicene Creed (of 325 and 381). Since the eighteenth century, theologians of various stripes have expressed varying degrees of discomfort with such a blatantly Christian teaching. Yet there it is: Christians confess the Trinity—Father, Son, and Holy Spirit. Not only does the *Book of Concord* include the three "ecumenical creeds" confessing the Trinity, but five Lutheran Confessions contained in the book also include expositions of this doctrine. Rather than being seen as an embarrassment or a remnant of an all-too-philosophical Christian past, the Augsburg Confession confesses the Trinity as revealing the very heart of God and the ground of all Christian unity.

CA I

[German]

[Latin]

In the first place, it is with one accord taught and held, following the decree of the Council of Nicaea, that there is one divine essence which is named God and truly is God. But there are three persons in the same one essence, equally powerful, equally eternal: God, the Father, God the Son, and God the Holy Spirit. All three are one divine essence, eternal, undivided, unending, of immeasurable power, wisdom, and goodness, the creator and preserver of all visible and invisible things. What is understood by the word "person" is not a part nor a quality in another but that which exists by itself, as the Fathers once used the word concerning this issue.

Rejected, therefore, are all the heresies that are opposed to this article, such as the Manichaeans, who posited two gods, one good and one evil; the Valentinians, the Arians, the Eunomians, the Mohammedans, and all others like them; also the Samosatenians, old and new, who hold that there is only one person and create a deceitful sophistry about the other two, the Word and the Holy Spirit, by saying that the two need not be two distinct persons since "word" means an external word or voice and the "Holy Spirit" is a created motion in all creatures.

The churches among us teach with complete unanimity that the decree of the Council of Nicaea concerning the unity of the divine essence and concerning the three persons is true and is to be believed without any doubt. That is to say, there is one divine essence which is called God and is God: eternal, incorporeal, indivisible, of immeasurable power, wisdom and goodness, the creator and preserver of all things, visible and invisible. Yet, there are three persons, coeternal and of the same essence and power: the Father, the Son, and the Holy Spirit. And the term "person" is used for that meaning which the church's authors used in this case: to signify not a part or a quality in another but that which subsists in itself.

They condemn all heresies that have arisen against this article, such as that of the Manichaeans, who posited two principles, one good and the other evil; likewise, those of the Valentinians, Arians, Eunomians, Mohammedans, and all others like them. They also condemn the Samosatenians, old and new, who contend that there is only one person and cleverly and impiously argue that the Word and the Holy Spirit are not distinct persons but that "Word" signifies a spoken word and "Spirit" a created movement in things.

Reflections

Who is speaking in the CA? The signers of the Augsburg Confession were not the theologians who drafted it but rather the princes and cities that were confessing it before Emperor Charles V at the Diet of Augsburg in 1530. But in both the German and Latin editions, they do not present simply their own personal confession but either (as in the German) use the passive voice to include all citizens in their territories or (as in the Latin) specify "the churches among us." Confession of faith is not, strictly speaking, solely the responsibility of the prince or burgomaster but of all in the Christian church. As much as Americans may hanker after individualism in Christianity, the facts are that there is no such thing as the solitary believer but only the Christian assembly, gathered around Word and sacrament (CA VII).

The basis of Christian unity. Many outsiders, when viewing the variety of churches, denominations, and sects among Christians may sometimes wonder what ever happened to Jesus's prayer to the Father in John 17 "that they [his disciples] may be one." Yet here the CA echoes one of the most remarkable aspects of Christianity down to the present day: the sheer number of different Christian bodies that confess the Nicene Creed: "with one accord" (CA I, German) or "with complete unanimity." While many of the articles of the CA may seem to distinguish Lutherans from other Christians, this article in particular unites them. The point of the entire CA is not to divide the church but to unite it in confession around the Triune God. This first article refutes the false notion of beginning an account of one's faith with what divides one group of believers from another instead of what unites all Christians.

One God ... Three Persons. This article's basic point, explained far more fully in the Nicene and Athanasian creeds, is a simple one: Christians worship one God in three persons. As much as this was hardly under dispute between Lutherans and Roman Catholics in the sixteenth century, still the stakes for this article are high, so that the Latin version insists that this "is true and is to be believed without any doubt." Notice that this article is not describing individual faith and doubts—that will come in CA II—but our commonly held faith. Such strong language demonstrates just how crucial this faith is for the whole Christian church. But the word "without doubt" also points to another side of the Christian faith: that faith itself is the gift and work of the Holy Spirit, not an action of the human being's pusillanimous will (see CA V). Thus, "without doubt" not only reveals our weakness but also God's strength in overcoming our doubts.

Yet the article does not stop with the slogan ("one God in three persons") but explains more fully who this God is, using a slew of attributes (in the Latin): "That is to say, there is one divine essence which is called God and is God: eternal, incorporeal, indivisible, of immeasurable power, wisdom and goodness, the creator and preserver of all things, visible and invisible. Yet, there are three persons, coeternal and of the same essence and power: the Father, the Son, and the Holy Spirit." Christians share many parts of this description of the Godhead with other, non-Christian religions, especially with adherents of Judaism and Islam. The "almighty creator," confessed in the first article of the Apostles' and Nicene creeds, does not, however, encompass all that Christians have to say about God. For that readers will have to wait especially for CA III, where the scandal of the incarnation comes to light.

"**What is understood by the word** *person*?" Why add this note? Here a history lesson comes in handy. Just as Martin Luther, Philip Melanchthon, and their compatriots were preparing to confess their faith before the emperor, a man arrived in Wittenberg claiming new insights into the nature of God. The Wittenbergers were horrified by what they heard. Johannes Campanus claimed that only the Father is truly God and that the Son and the Holy Spirit are lesser beings, so that "person" in the phrase "three persons" describes simply a quality of relationship and not a true, distinct, co-equal hypostasis. With this shocking encounter fresh in their minds, Philip Melanchthon and his fellow drafters insisted that the word person "is not a part nor a quality in another but that which exists by itself, as the Fathers once used the word concerning this issue." The Latin even employs the technical term: subsistence. The Wittenberg Reformers and their collaborators assembled in Augsburg refused to abandon the ancient church's confession ("of one being with the Father"): not simply out of respect for ancient church authorities but more importantly because if Christ is less than God, then salvation itself comes into question (see CA III).

"**Rejected therefore**" (German) and "**They [the teachers] condemn**" (**Latin**). Twenty-first-century Christians may imagine that they can define their own faith without excluding other options. In many cases, this kind of deception demonstrates either a lack of seriousness about one's own beliefs or a refusal to realize that claiming to believe one thing excludes its opposite. Indeed, condemnations are a key factor in Christian faith, going back to St. Paul (Gal 1:8–9) and including decrees of the ancient councils, including the Council of Nicaea in 325, where the bishops condemned followers of Arius who claimed that when it came to the Son of God, Jesus Christ, "there was [a point] when he was not." These rejections, then, function as a well-defined border between Christian, Trinitarian faith and its opposite—not simply hearkening back to ancient times but always addressing contemporary threats to the Christian confession. For us to read the list that follows as bygone history misses entirely the point of confessing the Trinity.

Manichaeans and Valentinians: These Gnostic groups (the former opposed by Augustine and the latter by Irenaeus) had one thing in common: they understood that the world was governed *not* by a single God but by two competing principles: one good and spiritual, and the other evil and fleshly. Both groups constructed elaborate myths describing how in the spiritual world, a fall occurred that trapped shards of spiritual light in the darkness of matter and flesh. Salvation involved an escape from this materialistic god and a return of the light to its origin. One cannot but think of modern spiritual movements (such as the New Age), where once again the point of reflection and renewal is an escape from this world into the pure world of thought and spirit. In the face of the twenty-first century's addiction to spirituality, Luther and his colleagues confess a robust carnality by focusing on Christ's incarnation (enfleshment!) and on Christians' callings *in* this world not out of it.

Arians and Eunomians: The Nicene Creed addressed the christological heresy named here. Arius, a priest in Alexandria, Egypt, gained notoriety by teaching about Christ that "there was when he was not." By emphasizing the sovereignty of the Father, he allowed (especially in the view of his opponents, chief among them Athanasius, Alexandria's bishop) the Son of God to be something of a god of second rank—like or of a similar substance to God the Father. Many historians have concentrated their descriptions of this "Arian controversy" in the Church on political matters (the role of Emperor Constantine in calling the council of Nicea to maintain religious peace among the newly recognized Christians) or on philosophical matters (especially the role of philosophy in Christian theology). But this minimizes the central soteriological nature of the debate. Christians, Arius thought, could far more easily imitate Christ as a divine being closer to human creatureliness than as a distant Father.[1] Athanasius, on the contrary, viewed Christ's equality with the Father as insuring that Christ alone could rescue a humanity enthralled to sin, death, and the devil and completely unable to save itself. No wonder when Pelagians (who rejected Augustine's emphasis on grace and insisted that human beings had a role in their salvation; cf. CA II) looked for support among the empire's bishops, they found it among the semi-Arian bishops of the Eastern Empire. By mentioning Eunomius, who insisted that the Son was *unlike* the Father, the CA reminds the reader where Arianism finally leads.

Mohammedans. Today we may well ask, "What is Muhammad doing here?" Our knowledge of Islam has grown by leaps and bounds since Martin Luther and Philip Melanchthon first insisted upon allowing the printing of a Latin translation of the *Qur'an* in the 1530s.[2] But at this point, it is not at all clear what the Reformers knew of this religion, except that it was a

---

1. See especially Dennis Groh and Robert Gregg, *Early Arianism: A View of Salvation* (Philadelphia: Fortress, 1981).
2. For Luther and Melanchthon's role in the publication of the Qur'an in Latin, see J. Paul Rajashekar and Timothy J. Wengert, "Martin Luther, Philip Melanchthon, and the Publication of the Qur'an," *Lutheran Quarterly*, 16 (2002): 221–28, and the literature cited there.

motivating force behind the Turkish sultan's invasion of Europe, which had just culminated in the siege of Vienna in 1529. But, relying on medieval reports, the Reformers assumed that Islam was a kind of christological heresy, where Jesus was understood as a good teacher and a "son of God" but not in any way "of one being with the Father," let alone Allah. Under this misapprehension, Christians simply labeled "Mohammedans" as another example of an Arian-like heresy, where Jesus Christ is not divine.

In an era of toleration, it may be hard to imagine why someone would condemn another religion. But sometimes our good intentions regarding other religions can result in undermining our own confession of faith in Christ. Indeed, the Augsburg Confession is precisely a *confessional* document, which means that as Christians and together with other Lutherans throughout the last five hundred years, we confess these specific things about Christ, about our standing before God, about the church and about the Christian life in the world. Making positive statements about our faith, however, will always imply—whether intended or not—certain negative statements: we believe X and therefore not Y. Even the Creed of Nicea included originally anathemas, directed at Arians (e.g., the belief that "There was when he [Christ] was not"). Since this negative side of confessing always turns up, Christians must take great pains not to downplay *whether* they disagree with others, as if we could just all get along. Even that sentiment, after all, implies a negative, namely, those people are wrong who defend any exclusive statements of faith. Instead, it is much more honest simply to confess what one believes to be true. The real problem that arose in the sixteenth century and continues today is when our confession turns into coercion: "You must believe this, or else!" For Christians, who confess that their relation to God depends upon God's mercy, this reveals a terrible contradiction, to which Lutherans, too, have sometimes fallen prey.

"Also the Samosatenians, old and new." Melanchthon now turns to a third group of Trinitarian heresies. It is worth noting that in no case does he name names. Nevertheless, we know whom he intended by the phrase "old and new." "Old Samosatenians" designated a group that denied full divinity to the Son and the Holy Spirit and insisted that God the Father was the only true God from all eternity and that the Son and the Holy Spirit were lesser divine beings or even simply further aspects of the Father. When in John's Gospel we read, "And the Word was God," it meant rather a spoken word coming from God but not the true God. Moreover, the Holy Spirit is simply God in action and not a separate person of the Trinity. But Melanchthon's real quarrel was with quite new Samosatenians, especially Johann Campanus, who had appeared in Wittenberg touting a new approach to the Trinity gleaned from his own idiosyncratic reading of the biblical texts. When he showed up in Wittenberg, the theologians soon set him packing, and when he popped up in the duchy of Jülich, they begged the prince there to prevent him from teaching.

We encounter a similar approach to God most vividly among Jehovah's Witnesses, who insist along with their Presbyterian-trained founder from the nineteenth century that Jesus is *a* god not *the* God and that the Holy Spirit is also not true God.[3] Does it really matter? Is the Bible really so clear that we can say for certain who Christ really is and why he came? The Reformers would emphatically answer, "Yes!" And, as with the Arians, what one confesses about Christ's *nature* impacts directly how one understands Christ's *function* as savior and Lord. When the ancient church's theologians insisted that "God became a human being so that human beings might become divine," they were banking on this connection. Our teaching about God matters! Not only does the church's confession of faith insist upon the unity of God, as confessed in Hebrew Scriptures, but it also takes seriously the fact that already the earliest Christians confessed Jesus as Lord and God.

To capture this intimate relation between who God is and what God has done for us, the English theologian J. B. Philipps once wrote, referring to the incarnation, "We live on a visited planet,"[4] visited by God himself in the flesh. A seventeenth-century German poet, Johannes Klaj, put it this way in his poem on Jesus's cry from the cross, "My God, my God, why have you forsaken me?": "Es riß sich Gott von Gott" (God is ripping God's very self apart).[5] And the Reformed theologian Jürgen Moltmann could even title his book on Christology *The Crucified God.*[6] Lutherans in Augsburg insisted upon traditional teachings about the Trinity both to show that they were orthodox Christians but also to underscore the unity of the Trinity in working "for us and for our salvation" as Father, Son, and Holy Spirit.

We Teach and Confess

This unity of who God is and what God does comes to full expression in Luther's hymned version of the Nicene Creed, which that rural Wisconsin congregation so much wanted to sing that Trinity Sunday, 1988.

---

3. A similar group is the much less well-known Christadelphians, who also mix apocalyptic thought with a "low" Christology.

4. John Bertram Phillips, *God Our Contemporary* (New York: Macmillan, 1960), 63.

5. Johannes Klaj, *Dem leidenden Christus zu Ehren*, "Vierte Handlung," cited in Anselm Steiger, "Zorn und Gericht in der poetischen Meditation der Passion Jesu Christi – insbesondere bei Johannes Klaj und Andreas Gryphius," in Udo Sträter, *Orthodoxie und Poesie* (Leipzig: Evangelische Verlagsanstalt, 2004), 92.

6. Jürgen Moltmann, *The Crucified God: The Cross of Christ as the Foundation and Criticism of Christian Theology* (Philadelphia: Fortress, 1973).

1) We all believe in one true God, Who created earth and heaven,
   The Father, who to us in love has the right of children given.
He in soul and body feeds us; all we need his hand provides us;
   Through all snares and perils leads us, Watching that no harm
   betide us.
He cares for us by day and night;
   All things are governed by His might.
2) We all believe in Jesus Christ, His own Son, our Lord, possessing
   An equal Godhead, throne, and might, Source of ev'ry grace and
   blessing;
Born of Mary, virgin mother, By the power of the Spirit,
   Word made flesh, our elder brother; That the lost might life
   inherit,
Was crucified for all our sin
   And raised by God to life again.
3) We all confess the Holy Ghost, Who, in highest heaven dwelling
   With God the Father and the Son, Comforts us beyond all
   telling;
Who the Church, His own creation, Keeps in unity of Spirit.
   Here forgiveness and salvation Daily come through Jesus' merit.
All flesh shall rise, and we shall be
   In bliss with God eternally.[7]

With each person of the Trinity, Luther moves seamlessly from who each is to what each chiefly does—parallel to his catechisms.[8] But the CA does this as well, catching us up in the "Dance of the Trinity," not for God's sake but for ours.[9]

---

7. *Evangelical Lutheran Worship* (Minneapolis: Augsburg Fortress, 2006), no. 411.
8. See Timothy J. Wengert, *Martin Luther's Catechisms: Forming the Faith* (Minneapolis: Fortress, 2009), 43–68.
9. See *Evangelical Lutheran Worship*, no. 412.

2

THE FALL "UPWARDS"

S he burst into my office, as the choir director always did when something
was on her mind. It was not about songs or choirs or music but something far more serious. "I ran into a classmate of mine from high school. We
were confirmed at the same Lutheran church. But now she'd joined some new
church outside town and had given her life to Jesus. 'You Lutherans,' she told
me. 'Always confessing that you're in bondage to sin! Well, since I've given
my life to Jesus, I am not in bondage to anything.'" And then my congregant
added, "Pastor, that confession has always given me such comfort. Why can't
she see that?"

The critic was correct. Lutherans, especially but not exclusively in North
America, regularly confess that they are "in bondage to sin" or "captive to
sin." To be sure, some "new" versions of the confession of sins that begin
Lutheran worship ignore such honest talk in favor of focusing on individual sins rather than the human condition that causes them. Perhaps in part
this reflects Lutheran embarrassment about its own teaching in favor of that
"born-again" detractor's point of view. But this startling confession of being
trapped in sin and helpless to get out, of being addicted to sin (and not just
individual sins), marks one of the most Lutheran aspects of our liturgy—one
that upsets all denials to the contrary and, in the end, provides realistic comfort to sinners like that Lutheran congregant.

CA II

[German]

Furthermore, it is taught among us that since the fall of Adam, all human beings who are born in the natural way are conceived and born in sin. This means that from birth they are full of evil lust and inclination and cannot by nature possess true fear of God and true faith in God. Moreover, this same innate disease and original sin is truly sin and condemns to God's eternal wrath all who are not in turn born anew through baptism and the Holy Spirit.

Rejected, then, are the Pelagians and others who do not regard original sin as sin in order to make human nature righteous through natural powers, thus insulting the suffering and merit of Christ.

[Latin]

Likewise, they teach that since the fall of Adam all human beings who are propagated according to nature are born with sin, that is, without fear of God, without trust in God, and with concupiscence. And they teach that this disease or original fault is truly sin, which even now damns and brings eternal death to those who are not born again through baptism and the Holy Spirit.

They condemn the Pelagians and others who deny that the original fault is sin and who, in order to diminish the glory of Christ's merits and benefits, argue that human beings can be justified before God by their own powers of reason.

Reflections

"Since the Fall of Adam." By over-historicizing the account in Genesis 2–3 and trying to get back to the garden, many Christians risk reducing the "Fall," as later Christians called it, to an unfortunate accident eons ago—one with which we are stuck with but about which we bear no direct responsibility. Others hope to balance the grim anthropology of Genesis 2–3 with the happier thought from Genesis 1 that human beings were created in "God's image," but they only end up making God over in their own image—itself a great indication for how far we have fallen. Either way, Christians miss the gravity of the human situation and end up "heavy in denial" about it.

The story in Genesis 3 itself labors under a misconstrual of a central object in the story: the tree of the knowledge of good and evil. As a child, I always took this story to be unfair, with Adam and Eve only discovering that what they did was wrong *after* they had eaten from the tree that was to enlighten them about right and wrong. Already in Genesis 4, however, the readers learn that "to know" (*yadah* in Hebrew) is clearly more than book knowledge, with the man "knowing" his wife and producing Cain and Abel. But the specific phrase, "knowledge of good and evil," occurs in two other instances in the Hebrew Scripture, where its meaning becomes clear. In the first instance, Barzillai (2 Sam 19:35), one of King David's counselors who wishes to retire, complains that he no longer knows good and evil—that is, he can no longer decide matters of state. In Isaiah 7:15–16 the prophet speaks of the time "before the child knows good and evil"—that is, before boy reaches what we call the age of accountability, when he is capable of making his own decisions. Perhaps the name of the tree in the garden could better be rendered the "I-can-decide-for-myself-what's-right-and-wrong" tree.

With this change, the problem with the human condition becomes crystal clear and the snake's "temptation" matches precisely our problem: "You shall not die; you shall be like gods deciding good and evil." Then it is clear that the "Fall" is not down from the knowledge and perfection (something that our minds associate with the divine and toward which we must aspire) but "upward," so to speak, usurping as our own the thing that rightly belongs to God alone: giving creation its life and deciding good and evil for all creation.[1] Then, boasting in our divine image or reducing our problem to blemishes that we should be able to clear up with just the right face cream becomes part of the cover-up, the denial of our hankering after the divine.

"Born in the natural way." Jesus Christ breaks the rule of sin in human lives. Although article three will deal with the person of Christ, the CA makes clear that there is one exception to the rule of sin, one "true human," who trusted God right to the end, namely Jesus Christ. This allusion to natural propagation hints at a long theological tradition, beginning with Tertullian (c. 155–c. 240) and Augustine (354–430), which had connected sin with the lustful act of sexual intercourse, through which the human soul was bent and the human being was "sinner from the mother's womb" (Ps 51:5, KJV). The CA, however, seems rather uninterested in such theories and simply wants to describe the human condition in such a way that no one is exempt.[2] Sin may be something we get better at with age, but we do not simply sin because of others' examples (Pelagius) or because of an inclination of human nature that life's ambiguities exploit. We are sick unto death from the very get-go!

"That is, without fear of God, without trust in God, and with concupiscence." The Latin text here explains what the drafters meant by the German text's "full of evil lust and inclination." Medieval theologians focused their understanding of original sin on concupiscence, that propensity toward selfish desire (self-centeredness) that infects all human beings. On this point

---

1. See Gerhard Forde, *Where God Meets Man: Luther's Down-to-Earth Approach to the Gospel* (Minneapolis: Augsburg, 1972), 50–55.
2. For example, in the second edition of the *Loci communes* (CR 21:287), Philip Melanchthon mentioned propagation as the place from which original sin spreads to the human race, but again he does not speculate about it any further.

Lutherans and their opponents in Augsburg were in agreement. But the other phrase ("without fear of God, without trust in God") revealed the gap between the two parties. The authors of the *Confutation* rejected out of hand mixing fear and trust with original sin, insisting that these things were its consequences: discrete actions of the will.[3]

This objection demarcates the deep divide between the parties. For the Reformers "fear of God" and "trust in God" described the original relationship with God destroyed by sin. For their opponents fear and trust were the result of the disorder wrought by the fall and its loss of original righteousness and stabilizing grace. Not until the Joint Declaration on the Doctrine of Justification (signed by the Vatican and representatives of the Lutheran World Federation in 1999) would these vastly different definitions begin to get sorted out.[4] Luther made his readers aware of this difference in the very first words of the Latin version of his 1520 tract, *Freedom of a Christian*. "Many people view Christian faith as something easy, and quite a few people even count it as if it were related to the virtues. They do this because they have not judged faith in light of any experience, nor have they ever tasted its great power."[5] Once faith becomes a result of human action, a virtue cooked up by human beings, then it remains under human control—a virtue that we concoct through our own understanding and effort. In CA XX Melanchthon himself defines faith not as a human work but as a relationship established by God's grace: "the word 'faith' is to be understood not as knowledge, such as the ungodly have, but as trust that consoles and encourages terrified minds."[6]

The CA does not reduce the human condition before God to problems solved by human effort but to a broken relationship (lack of fear and trust). A year earlier, Luther had done the same thing in the Large Catechism, where he associates the first commandment's demand ("You shall have no other gods") to trust, which makes both God and idol.[7] In both the Catechism and

---

3. *The Confutation of the Augsburg Confession*, Pt. 1, art. 2, in *Sources and Contexts of the Book of Concord*, ed. Robert Kolb and James A. Nestingen (Minneapolis: Fortress, 2000), 107.

4. See *Joint Declaration on the Doctrine of Justification: English Language Edition* (Grand Rapids: Eerdmans, 2001), p. 24, par. 36: "Catholics can share the concern of the Reformers to ground faith in the objective reality of Christ's promise, to look away from one's own experience, and to trust in Christ's forgiving word alone (cf. Mt 16:19; 18:18). With the Second Vatican Council, Catholics state: to have faith is to entrust oneself totally to God, who liberates us from the darkness of sin and death and a wakens us to eternal life."

5. TAL 1:487.

6. CA (Latin) XX.26 (BC, 57).

7. LC, Ten Commandments, par. 2 (BC, 386). Later editions of the CA drop the references to fear and trust in order to respect the position of the church fathers, especially Augustine, and to demonstrate sensitivity to their opponents' position. See Apology II.3 (BC, 112): "This passage testifies that we deny to those conceived and born according to the course of nature not only the act of fearing and trusting God, but also the ability or gifts needed to produce such fear and

the Confession, the human problem lies in trusting ourselves to decide right and wrong.

"This same innate disease and original sin is truly sin and condemns to God's eternal wrath." Human creatures, addicted to divine immortality and to taking matters into their own hands, cannot stand this assertion about sin and wrath. Sin is a disease, a cancer, not just affecting some lower part of the human soul but targeting the very best humanity has to offer. Here the language of Alcoholics' Anonymous helps enormously. The worst part of addiction is not just the damage it does to addicts and those around them but that it fosters a kind of ignorance and denial of the actual problem, the elephant in the room. The less serious human beings can make sin, the more they can remain in control and trust themselves—the very heart of the disease in the first place—to eradicate sin. Thus, to hear about God's wrath disconcerts the "Old Adam and Eve," because it spells the end to all myths of control and power and may even make a person angry at God for the perceived unfairness about the entire mess the person is in. Still, the only cure for this illness consists in stripping us of all control over ourselves and our destiny before God. The sinner must finally die to sin, lose control, and be subject to God alone.

"All who are not in turn born anew through baptism and the Holy Spirit." There is a way of turning this statement into a threat to others rather than a confession of faith. The point is *not* to separate one set of sinners from another, thereby making Christians into a higher (or at least luckier) type of human being. Instead, this statement shows how little control we really have (birth or rebirth being the most passive of metaphors) and how much we rely upon God alone for rescue. Unless God acts, we are doomed. This sentence also hints at the Reformers' conviction of the centrality of baptism for the life of a Christian. One can imagine that the drafters had Luther's remarkable words in the Large Catechism, published just the year before, rattling around in their heads.

> These two parts, being dipped under the water and emerging from it, point to the power and effect of Baptism, which is nothing else than the slaying of the old Adam and the resurrection of the new creature, both of which must continue in us our whole life long. Thus a Christian life is nothing else than a daily Baptism, begun once and continuing ever after. For we must keep at it without ceasing, always purging whatever pertains to the old Adam, so that whatever belongs to the new creature may come forth.[8]

---

trust. For we say that those who have been born in this way have concupiscence and are unable to produce true fear and trust in God."

8. LC, Baptism, 65 (BC, 465).

"They condemn the Pelagians and others." One of the most important aspects of the Augsburg Confession, which we have already seen in CA I, involves its use of the ancient church. The Reformers never imagined that they had caused a split in the church but rather insisted that they were witnessing to the heart of the Christian gospel proclaimed by the church in every age. For this article and the ones that follow the Pelagian heresy played a central role. Pelagius was a British monk with a very optimistic view of human nature and its abilities for improvement. When he arrived in Rome, he discovered people reading Augustine's *Confessions,* which contained this (for Pelagius) shocking prayer to God: "Give what you command and command what you will."[9] This upset the poor man, since the words implied that fulfilling God's commandments rested *not* with the individual exercise of the free will but with God's mercy. This is not to say that Pelagius and his followers denied that God was gracious. However, in Augustine's eyes they had reduced God's grace to the giving of the commandments and to the exercise of human freedom in fulfilling them.

This reduction of grace to the giving of the law and the human creature's free choice occurs in every age of the church's existence. Thus, the phrase "and others" points to the Reformers' opponents, especially those who followed the likes of the fifteenth-century theologian Gabriel Biel, who argued that, given human freedom, "to those who do what is in them, God will not deny grace" and who insisted that the chief effect of original sin was ignorance of God's will and not any real bondage to sin. The same is true today. For example, the popular TV evangelist Joel Osteen, while noting that Christ unconditionally forgave the woman caught in adultery before sending her out with the words, "Go and sin no more," moved immediately to an appeal to the viewers to commit their lives to Christ. But liberal theologians, too, get caught in the same trap, insisting that the heart of Christianity is not God's grace but human response.

"Who deny that the original fault is sin and who, in order to diminish the glory of Christ's merits and benefits, argue that human beings can be justified before God by their own powers of reason." This final sentence in the Latin gets to the heart of the Lutherans' critique of works-centered theology in any age. The result of *any* claims of human power over against God always spells an end to Christ's saving power. The Latin version here states it even more strongly than the German by attributing to such errant teachers the intention of diminishing Christ's merits and benefits. This is always what happens. When the Old Creature gets wind of God's unconditional grace in Christ, it immediately sets about constructing something to do. "Of course, God is gracious, but we must cooperate with God, get serious about God, or

---

9. Augustine, *Confessions* X.29.

God's grace won't work." If that seems too much, then God's grace is turned into an offer, which the neutral observer (the Old Creature) can decide to accept. "Sure, God is gracious, but we need to unwrap the gift"—to which my twelve-year-old daughter, upon hearing this, blurted out, "But Dad, the gift comes unwrapped!" Finally, worried about losing all autonomy, the Old Creature whines, "But at least I can reject the gift!" to which the answer has to be, "Why in heaven's name would you want to do that?" This retort finally unmasks all the bluster and pretense and leaves a person confessing God's unlimited, unmerited, and unconditional mercy in Christ.

This last line also echoes one of the most remarkable phrases in Luther's Small Catechism. In paraphrasing the third article of the Creed ("I believe in the Holy Spirit"), Luther writes, "I believe that by my own understanding or strength I cannot believe in Jesus Christ my Lord or come to him, but instead the Holy Spirit has called me through the gospel, enlightened me with his gifts, made me holy and kept me in the true faith."[10] Our reason, with its claims to independence and freedom, is the real culprit here—always listening to the snake in the grass (cf. Gen 3:4–5): "You will not die; you will be like gods, deciding good and evil." On the contrary, St. Paul insists (1 Cor 1:27), "God chose what is weak and foolish to shame the strong," and Jesus says (John 15:16), "You did not choose me, but I chose you."

We Teach and Confess

By beginning with a description of the human condition, the CA underscores its commitment to the movement from law (CA II) to gospel (CA III–V) and, in baptismal terms, from death to life (CA XII). Moreover, by mentioning Pelagius, the CA places Lutheran theology squarely within the church's orthodox tradition against those who insist on undermining Christ's merit and mercy by appealing to the free will. Thus, from the very beginning the CA centers its witness on Christ and his grace, turning aside all appeals to human powers of understanding or effort. No wonder my congregational member found such comfort in confessing her bondage to sin, always followed in the liturgy by the amazing news of freedom and forgiveness in Christ: "I announce to you the entire forgiveness of all your sins."

---

10. SC, Creed, 6 (BC, 355). The phrase "understanding or strength" refers to the twin powers of the soul (intellect and will).

3

CHRIST ALWAYS AND ALONE

His wife had died six months earlier, and now the alcohol-induced liver cancer would take his life by the next day. As pastor, I was called to his bedside in the local hospital but with scarcely any sense of how to administer care in such a situation. "Well, I guess this is it, Ray," I mumbled incoherently. "I just want to go lie down next to Arlene," he replied, referring to his long-suffering wife whom we had placed in the grave only a short time before. "Well, God is with you," I muttered with less than any conviction at all. And he responded, "I just trust Jesus." His drinking buddies, huddled in the back of the funeral home during the service, wept when I recounted this scene. "I just trust Jesus!" I can only wish that the Holy Spirit would place such a remarkable confession of faith on my lips at the end of my life.

In the first edition of his introductory textbook for Wittenberg's theology, the *Loci communes theologici* [theological main themes], published in 1521, Philip Melanchthon insisted that "to know Christ is to know his benefits."[1] Two years later, in his introductory lecture to John's Gospel, Melanchthon made the same point by distinguishing two types of christological heresies. "Ebionites [a somewhat misleading label for those who claimed Christ was only son of God by adoption] are those who deny the divinity of the Son; but those are Ebionites twice over who, while confessing Christ's divinity, deny his benefits."[2] So, too, the third article of the CA paraphrases the Apostles' Creed, to be sure, but it also insists on certain aspects that

---

1. Philip Melanchthon, *Commonplaces: Loci communes 1521*, trans. Christian Preus (St. Louis: Concordia, 2014), 24.
2. Timothy J. Wengert, *Philip Melanchthon's 'Annotationes in Johannem' of 1523 in Relation to Its Predecessors and Contemporaries* (Geneva: Droz, 1987), 149.

would, if denied, undermine the Holy Spirit's work in distributing Christ's benefits. But this same emphasis on Christ's benefits also appears in Luther's Small Catechism, where the christological statement ("true God . . . and true human being") forms a dependent clause for his main point ("is my Lord who has redeemed me").[3]

CA III

[German]

Likewise, it is taught that God the Son became human, born of the pure virgin Mary, and that the two natures, the divine and the human, are so inseparably united in one person that there is one Christ. He is true God and true human being who truly "was born, suffered, was crucified, died, and was buried" in order both to be a sacrifice not only for original sin but also for all other sins and to conciliate God's wrath. Moreover, the same Christ "descended into hell, truly rose from the dead on the third day, ascended into heaven, is sitting at the right hand of God" in order to rule and reign forever over all creatures, so that through the Holy Spirit he may make holy, purify, strengthen, and comfort all who believe in him, also distribute to them life and various gifts and benefits, and shield and protect them against the devil and sin. Finally, the same Lord Christ "will come" in full view of all "to judge the living and the dead . . .," according to the Apostles' Creed.

Rejected are all heresies that are opposed to this article.

[Latin]

Likewise, they teach that the Word, that is, the Son of God, took upon himself human nature in the womb of the blessed virgin Mary so that there might be two natures, divine and human, inseparably conjoined in the unity of one person, one Christ, truly God and truly human being, "born of the virgin Mary," who truly "suffered, was crucified, died, and was buried" that he might reconcile the Father to us and be a sacrifice not only for original guilt but also for all actual sins of human beings. He also "descended into hell, and on the third day he was" truly "resurrected." Thereafter, "he ascended into heaven" in order to "sit at the right hand of the Father," and he will reign forever and have dominion over all creatures. He will sanctify those who believe in him by sending into their hearts the Holy Spirit, who will rule, console, and make them alive and defend them against the devil and the power of sin. The same Christ will publicly "return to judge the living and the dead . . .," according to the Apostles' Creed.

---

3. SC, "Creed," 4 (BC, 355).

Reflections

Earlier English translations of this article did not demarcate the CA's citation of the Apostles' Creed (referred to in the very last sentence) from the drafters' commentary on it. By using quotation marks (something only sporadically employed later in the sixteenth century), the English reader can easily determine what the Reformers deemed important enough from the Apostles' Creed to emphasize and explain. But the practical side of these comments will only become clear in the context of two important controversies involving the Lord's Supper.

"Likewise, it is taught that God the Son became human, born of the pure virgin Mary." The virginity of Mary, taken for granted by all the principle actors in the sixteenth century, seems anything but certain among many today. In part, this doctrine has links to an understanding of conception that made the woman a passive vessel for the man's "seed," which then grew in her womb. But here, as in the Apostles' Creed, the point was not explaining Mary's virginity but rather emphasizing Jesus's humanity. The fact that the CA includes the word "pure" indicates the Reformers' acceptance of Mary's special role in salvation. Already the early church confessed Mary as *theotokos* [bearer of God], a position challenged by the bishop Nestorius who believed Mary was only *christotokos* [bearer of Christ]. By the late Middle Ages, the Western church insisted upon Mary's purity, including her immaculate conception and her perpetual virginity. Lutherans, however, despite Luther's own belief in Mary's perpetual virginity, did not insist upon this doctrine. It was enough to adhere to the biblical witness (Matthew 1; Luke 1) and insist on both the humanity and divinity of Christ.

Of course, our reason wants explanations on *how* Jesus could be both, but such explanations inevitably obscure the biblical message and the ancient church's witness. Jesus Christ is truly 100 percent human being. In fights over just how "human" Jesus was, the ancient church's slogan helps express what is at stake: "What he [Christ] has not assumed, he has not healed." Thus, Christ did not just assume a human body as a kind of cloak, while *really* being only divine. Nor did he replace a human soul or spirit with a divine one. When we encounter Jesus, we meet a true, complete human being, who truly was born, lived, and died.

At the same time, he is true God. Judged by our own distorted views of reality and philosophy, this seems an impossibility—so much so that people are forever trying to "explain" how this could be, using certain biblical passages to make Jesus a little less than God. Then another ancient slogan may draw us up short: "God became a human being so that human beings might become divine." Insofar as our adoption as God's children is at stake, Jesus must be God. Anything less and we are left to deal with our weaknesses and sin on our own—yet another example of how ancient doctrines of the Trinity and Christology directly connect to salvation. The Nicene Creed is especially clear in this regard, introducing its account of the incarnation with the words, "who for us and for our salvation . . ."

And that the two natures, the divine and the human, are so insepara-bly united in one person that there is one Christ. After hundreds of years of debate over the natures of Christ, the Council of Chalcedon resolved the disputes (for most Christians of the day) by insisting on a "both . . . and" approach: "acknowledged in two natures without confusion, without change, without division, without separation." The wording of the Augsburg Confession echoes the formula of Chalcedon, not simply to demonstrate Lutheran christological "orthodoxy" but instead to reject any doctrine that seemed to separate the two natures.

This was not simply a theoretical matter but involved a quite real fight over the nature of the Lord's Supper. In early October 1529, Martin Luther, Philip Melanchthon, and others who supported Wittenberg's position of Christ's real presence in the bread and wine met in Marburg with and argued against Ulrich Zwingli, Johannes Oecolampadius, and other supporters of the Swiss approach to the Supper, which insisted that the Supper was a memorial in which Christ was at best spiritually present, so that the bread and wine only signified Christ's body and blood. They also held that Christ in his humanity could not be present in the bread and wine with his body and blood precisely in part because that humanity was seated at the right hand of God in heaven, which they defined as a specific place. For Luther, not only was God's right hand clearly a metaphor for God's power (and, thus, not a place), but also the Swiss position divided the two natures of Christ, with some adherents later arguing that, although Christ's *divinity* was present everywhere, his humanity was not.

Far from being an esoteric battle over competing Christologies, for Luther and his colleagues the unity of Christ's natures went to the very heart of salvation itself. No wonder Martin Luther could opine at table, "Whoever wants to know God and look upon God without danger should look in the manger."[4] The God we encounter outside the incarnation is always inscrutable and threatening. Of course, we can say that God is in a rainbow or a beautiful mountain scene. But is the God encountered there for us or against us? The rainbow could follow a destructive tornado or precede a flood, and the mountain could be Mt. St. Helens, just before it blows its top. Our lives may be filled with vestiges of God's presence, but each of them contains a certain ambiguity of God's actual disposition toward humanity. To encounter Christ's divinity in the Lord's Supper stripped of its humanity leaves that ambiguity intact. Only the incarnate one—the resurrected Christ who still

---

4. WA TR 6:38 (no. 6558). See also WA 33:123 and WA 49:287.

bears the print of the nails in his body—provides unambiguous assurance of God's saving grace.

He is true God and true human being who truly "was born, suffered, was crucified, died, and was buried" in order both to be a sacrifice not only for original sin but also for all other sins and to conciliate God's wrath. With this brief comment on the heart of the second article of the Creed, another opposing view of the Lord's Supper is questioned. As much as Lutherans and their opponents at Augsburg agreed in Christ's real presence in the Supper, so they disagreed about whether in that Supper the priest is offering up an "unbloodied" sacrifice to God for the sins of the assembled congregation or, in the case of Masses for the dead, for the sins of a dearly departed soul for whom the Mass is being said. Although modern Roman Catholic understanding of the Lord's Supper has shifted, in Luther's day most Western Christians understood that the Mass was a sacrifice that occurred when the priest elevated the bread and wine. Thus, the most important thing parishioners did in the Mass was to watch that sacrifice, sure that its benefits then applied to them.

Although a much more thorough examination follows in CA XXIV below, article three anticipates eliminating such "propitiatory" sacrifice from the Mass by insisting that Christ's incarnation, suffering, death, and burial reconciles us to God not only by removing the punishment for original sin (something that their opponents also confessed) but all sin. Only beginning in the twentieth century has it become clear that, whatever the Roman Catholic Church means by the sacrifice of the Mass, it does not intend to undermine the "once-for-all" nature of Christ's death (Heb 7:27).

But what is one to make of this talk about "God's wrath"? Here modern sensibilities get in the way of honesty. As a pastor, I can still recall several instances where a parishioner sat in my office and asked in tears, "Is God angry with me?" In our day, we can be quick to deny the reality of their pain and sense of abandonment—as well as the strong faith of such a sufferer! In the face of sorrow and despair, many may just resign themselves to "fate" and complain about the "luck of the draw." In feeling betrayed or punished by God, however, one puts one's fortune and faith where it belongs: in God's hands. Then, rather than try to fathom God's inner nature (Is God angry? Distant? Absent?), one places one's true feelings and experience right where they belong: in *God's* hands alone. Then, Jesus's suffering and death appear as the only faithful answer to the question of God's wrath. Jesus, fully human and divine, suffers *with* us, and thus God knows our own abandonment ("My God! My God! Why have you forsaken me?"), but this same Jesus suffers and dies *for* us, in our place, taking our well-deserved abandonment upon himself in the cross and swallowing it up in his resurrection. We cannot by our own reason or strength explain God's wrath away, instead Christ must intervene and take that very real wrath on his own shoulders for us.

The same Christ "... is sitting at the right hand of God" in order to rule and reign forever over all creatures. Given the earlier reference to the Lord's Supper controversy with the Swiss, it is not surprising that the Reformers add this small gloss to "sitting at the right hand of God." It is not a place but rather a description of Christ's coeternal reign with the Father and the Holy Spirit. As far as *how* the humanity of Christ can be both in heaven at God's right hand and on earth in the Supper and, according to Matthew 18:20, with the assembled believers, Luther in effect replied to this question when raised at the 1529 meeting in Marburg with the Swiss theologians Ulrich Zwingli and Johann Oecolampadius: "Stop asking mathematical questions."[5] The Latin version of CA III says it even more forcefully: "Thereafter, 'he ascended into heaven' in order to 'sit at the right hand of the Father,' and he will reign forever and have dominion over all creatures." It would almost seem that these words anticipate Handel's "Hallelujah Chorus" by two centuries: "And he shall reign forever and ever." But they actually echo the common source: Revelation (11:15).

He will sanctify those who believe in him by sending into their hearts the Holy Spirit, who will rule, console, and make them alive and defend them against the devil and the power of sin. The German version clearly links Christ's present reign with the work of the Holy Spirit by beginning the discussion of the Holy Spirit with the words, "so that."[6] The word *sanctify*, however, is often misunderstood to mean only our good works that follow salvation. But for the early Reformers, the word meant literally, "to make holy," and included the entire life of the Christian, which the CA goes on to describe *not* in terms of what Christian believers do for God but rather in terms of what the Holy Spirit effects in and through us. Look at the list of the Holy Spirit's actions: "rule, console, and make them alive and defend them against the devil and the power of sin." It almost sounds as if the drafters in Augsburg had read Luther's catechisms, published the previous year—which indeed they had! There Luther wrote:

> Neither you nor I could ever know anything about Christ, or believe in him and receive him as Lord, unless these were offered to us and bestowed on our hearts through the preaching of the gospel by the Holy Spirit. The work is finished and completed; Christ has acquired and won the treasure for us by his sufferings, death, and resurrection, etc. But if the work remained hidden so that no one knew of it, it would have been all in vain, all lost. In order that this treasure might not remain buried but put to use and enjoyed, God has caused the Word to be published and

---

5. *The Marburg Colloquy and the Marburg Articles* (1529), in LW 38:45, 67, 75.
6. German: "so that through the Holy Spirit he may make holy, purify, strengthen, and comfort all who believe in him, also distribute to them life and various gifts and benefits, and shield and protect them against the devil and sin."

proclaimed, in which he has given the Holy Spirit to offer and apply to us this treasure, this redemption. Therefore being made holy is nothing else than bringing us to the LORD Christ to receive this blessing, to which we could not have come by ourselves.[7]

Certain words here reflect Philip Melanchthon's own favorite expressions regarding the work of the Holy Spirit through the gospel, especially "console." In a new commentary on Romans, on which he was working before and after the Diet of Augsburg, Melanchthon noticed how Paul moves from a description of justification (Rom 3–4) to the effect of such justification (Rom 5:1: "Peace with God"). Thus, by mentioning comfort (along with all the other things), Melanchthon is anticipating arguments in CA IV and V (on justification) and CA XX (on faith and good works, where he cites Rom 5:1).

We Teach and Confess

CA III, combined with these words of Luther and Melanchthon, underscores the way in which Lutherans, more than perhaps most other Christians, could be called the "Holy Spirit church." Without the Holy Spirit, there is no rule of God, no consolation, no enlivening, and no defense against evil. Moreover, as becomes clear in CA V, there is also no faith. The point of the Holy Spirit is not simply to hand out snazzy spiritual gifts, about which many today seem only too glad to boast, but to apply to us the salvation won by Christ. When Luther writes in the Small Catechism, "I believe that by my own understanding or strength I cannot believe in Jesus Christ my LORD or come to him," he places our entire life, including faith itself, into the Holy Spirit's hands. Similarly, when he explains that in praying "Your kingdom come" we are praying for the Holy Spirit to bring us faith through the Word of God, then we know where to turn when experiencing God's wrath or God's absence: to God the Holy Spirit, begging the Spirit to give us faith in the midst of doubts, forgiveness in the midst of sin, and life in the face of death—that is, to make us holy until Christ's return, so that we, too, may confess: "I just trust Jesus."

---

7. LC, Creed, 38–39 (BC, 436).

4

THE CHRISTIAN'S TWO RELIGIONS

People who read this book are practicing two religions, not one. This may come as a surprise to a lot of Christians. Most forms of Christianity ascribe a "before and after" to the Christian faith. In Martin Luther's day, if you committed a mortal sin, you lost saving grace and were condemned to a state of sin until you availed yourself of the church's sacraments and, with the aid of the grace offered there, moved from a state of sin (the before) to a state of grace (the after). In our own day, Christians explain how they *used to be* sinners but since they committed their lives to Jesus they are now saved. And, when that first level of salvation (justification) falters, they then may go on to being sanctified, filled, baptized in the Spirit, and the like—but from beginning to end the process has a "before and after" to it: once a sinner; now saved.

But the Augsburg Confession insists that we have two religions, the first of which was described in CA II (chapter 2, above). Based upon the suggestions of other teachers before me, I nickname it "Up Religion": the attempts of human beings, who have fallen away from God, to get back up to God.[1] So human creatures are "ladder climbers," intent on working their way back into God's graces by the works they do, the rules or laws they follow, and the decisions they make. But the differences among such climbers is not so much in the climbing as in whom we run into at the top of the ladder: a god created by us and our work in our own image and likeness.

---

1. See Gerhard O. Forde, *Where God Meets Man: Luther's Down-to-Earth Approach to Theology* (Minneapolis: Augsburg, 1972), 7–17.

Thus, at the heart of "Up Religion" is the human quest for control of our lives, our destinies, and our relation with God. In their book *Lutheranism: The Theological Movement and Its Confessional Writings*, Eric Gritsch and Robert Jenson label this "If . . . then" religion, that is, a conditional religion that at some level or another depends on what we do and decisions we make.[2] "If you do X, God will do Y for you." In discussing how human beings break the first commandment, Luther describes this very thing.

> There is, moreover, another false worship. This is the greatest idolatry that we have practiced up until now, and it is still rampant in the world. . . . It involves only that conscience that seeks help, comfort, and salvation in its own works and presumes to wrest heaven from God. It keeps track of how often it has made endowments, fasted, celebrated mass, etc. It relies on such things and boasts of them, unwilling to receive anything as a gift of God, but desiring to earn everything by itself or to merit everything by works of supererogation, just as if God were in our service or debt and we were his liege lords. What is this but to have made God into an idol . . . and to have set ourselves up as God?[3]

One of the most important facets of this "religion" involves who the subject of the theological sentence is. It always devolves to an "If *I*" or "If *we*," "then God . . ." This is why CA II, in describing the heart of the human predicament, emphasizes our lack of fear of God and trust in God. Becoming the subject of the theological sentence has two related effects on us: pride and despair. We hear the pride in Luke 18:11, where the Pharisee boasts, "I thank you God that I am not like others . . . even that tax collector over there." But it is also reflected in those who may say, "*I* gave my life to Jesus, what's holding *you* back?" As if our decisions make any difference in our standing before God! Having disabused ourselves of such notions, of course, we insist on praying: "Lord, we thank you that we're not like that!" And so it goes!

But our "Up Religion" also results in despair. *If* we follow the rules, then God will truly love us, bless us. But, the despairing person cries, "Have I done enough?" "Was my decision truly from my heart?" "Have I truly prayed hard enough, committed deeply enough, followed closely enough?" This despair has two sides: true, it is honest enough to recognize one's own failure, but, as

---

2. Robert Jenson and Eric Gritsch, *Lutheranism: The Theological Movement and Its Confessional Writings* (Philadelphia: Fortress, 1976), 42–44.
3. LC, Ten Commandments, par. 22 (BC, 388–89).

a product of "Up Religion," it still assumes that our relation to God is up to us and our own work. We despair *because* we trust ourselves. One of the most insidious forms of this combination of pride and despair turns faith itself into a work. "If you believed," it says, "You would not be sick" or "God would have healed you." The overweening, spiritual pride of purveyors of "Up Religion" results in total despair.

Now, the good news is that Christians also live with a second religion, which I nickname (not surprisingly) "Down Religion." It is the remarkable message of the gospel that God the Son, "for us and for our salvation came down from heaven," as the Nicene Creed puts it. How far down? All the way into the flesh and death on the cross! Thus, Paul writes, quoting that remarkable Christ hymn of his Philippian correspondents (Phil 2:5–8): "Let the same mind be in you that was in Christ Jesus, who, though he was in the form of God, did not regard equality with God as something to be exploited, but emptied himself, taking the form of a slave, being born in human likeness. And being found in human form, he humbled himself and became obedient to the point of death—even death on a cross." Or, in John's Gospel (1:14) we read: "And the Word became flesh." But even before this, in the Hebrew Scriptures, we encounter this self-emptying God, bound to the children of Israel, despite their wanderings. In 2 Corinthians 5:21, Paul expresses this in writing: "God made Christ, who knew no sin, to be sin for us, so that in him we might become the righteousness of God." Or, in Galatians 3:13–14, Christ takes on the curse so that believers receive the blessing of God.

In Gritsch and Jenson's vocabulary, this is "Because . . . Therefore" religion, that is, it is unconditional, dependant upon God's disposition toward us and not anything we do for God. This makes the subject of the theological sentence not us but God: "Because God loved the world, therefore God sent the only Son." To say that God comes down to us means we live by God's grace (=mercy) alone because of Christ alone. *How* God comes down to us in Christ brings with it the confession that God comes to us by God's Word of gospel alone (see CA V). Moreover, we receive this God by faith alone. Here, however, we need to remember that faith is not a work we do but a work or relation that God establishes through that very Word (see CA V and XX).

Of course, "up" and "down" are just metaphors, pictures, for our relation to God. The Reformers, relying on biblical images, speak of salvation or, more specifically, justification: being declared and made righteous before God. In this light we can examine article four.

CA IV

[German]	[Latin]
Furthermore, it is taught that we cannot obtain forgiveness of sin and righteousness before God through our merit, work, or satisfactions, but that we receive forgiveness of sin and become righteous before God out of grace for Christ's sake through faith when we believe that Christ has suffered for us and that for his sake our sin is forgiven and righteousness and eternal life are given to us. For God will regard and reckon this faith as righteousness in his sight, as St. Paul says in Romans 3 and 4.	Likewise, they teach that human beings cannot be justified before God by their own powers, merits, or works. But they are justified as a gift on account of Christ through faith when they believe that they are received into grace and that their sins are forgiven on account of Christ, who by his death made satisfaction for our sins. God reckons this faith as righteousness (Romans 3 and 4).

Reflections

We cannot obtain forgiveness of sin and righteousness before God through our merit, work, or satisfactions. This single sentence rejects any and all forms of "Up Religion." Of course it is framed in the language of the sixteenth-century disputes, where "merit, work, or satisfactions" express the heart of the dispute with the opponents, who claimed that at some level human activity played some role, however slight, in one's relation to God ("before God"). The German text explains the Latin technical term, "justified," with "forgiveness . . . and righteousness." But all these terms simply portray the believer's relation to God. Most important is the use of the word "obtain." This very "getting" describes the heart of the problem: the human desire to be in control, to "obtain" something from God for something that we have done. The Latin slogan for such a mercantile relation to God is: *"Do ut des"* ("I give so that you may give"). This means either that God's grace bribes us into doing good ("I, God, give . . .") or that our actions obligate God to do something for us.

We receive forgiveness of sin and become righteous before God. "We *receive*." Our relation to God is, to use the apt phrase of the Reformation historian Berndt Hamm "a gift without reciprocity" ("Gabe ohne Gegengabe").[4] Of course, at this point the Old Creature, addicted as it is to being in charge,

---

4. Berndt Hamm, "Martin Luther's Revolutionary Theology of Pure Gift without Reciprocation," *Lutheran Quarterly* 29 (2015): 125–61. Hamm describes the *"do ut des"* mentality of late-medieval Christianity on p. 128–29.

begins to worry that we may really be in God's hands. "Surely faith is what I do!" it snorts. Or, when it discovers that faith is *not* a work, "At least we can reject, can't we?" To the former, CA V will talk about the work of the Holy Spirit, but to the latter, one must realize that this is an example of a fake theology, what Luther calls a *theologia illusoria*, an illusory theology. To such a question, one can simply ask, "Why would you want to do that?" To this, most people will respond, "Well, I wouldn't, but can't you?" Imagine being surprised by a master chef with your favorite meal and then saying, just before you sit down, "Well, I can reject it, can't I?" What a foolish thing to say and quite impossible in that situation! Or, if one's beloved asks for a kiss, who in their right mind would respond, "Do I *have* to?"

Out of grace for Christ's sake through faith. These three things succinctly outline "Down Religion." First it is "out of grace" or, as the Latin puts it *"gratis"* ("as a gift"). Between 1519 and 1521, Martin Luther's understanding of grace underwent a rather remarkable shift. Medieval theology had distinguished several different kinds of "grace" (Latin: *gratia*). Two stand out: first, the "grace given freely" (*gratia gratis data*), defined as God's call to the sinner (Bonaventure) or the gifts of law and free choice to human creatures (Gabriel Biel); second and most importantly, the grace that makes acceptable (*gratia gratum faciens*), defined as the infusion into the human soul of a disposition of love (*habitus charitatis*) that moves a person from a state of sin into a state of grace. Grace in this second definition is a force or power that changes something in the soul, making a sinner, who is unacceptable to God, acceptable.

In 1516, however, Erasmus of Rotterdam published for the first time the Greek New Testament, set in parallel columns with the Vulgate, along with his *Annotations* pointing out where the Latin text could be improved on the basis of the Greek. When he gets to the word *charis* in the Greek, Erasmus criticizes the Vulgate's use of the word *gratia* (given the ontological categories associated with the word by scholastic theologians) and proposes instead to translate it as *favor Dei* (God's favor). In his 1519 commentary on Galatians (Luther's first published commentary on a biblical book), Luther tries to split the difference by arguing that *charis* means both God's favor and the grace that makes acceptable. By 1521, however, probably under the influence of Wittenberg's Greek expert, Philip Melanchthon, Luther changes his tune and insists that *charis* and *gratia* should *only* be understood as God's favor or mercy. Thus in CA IV, while Melanchthon uses the German word for grace (*Gnade*), he uses in the Latin text *gratis* (freely or as a gift), so as to avoid any sense that we are talking about an infused disposition. Grace is God's undeserved love and mercy!

By saying "for Christ's sake" the CA refers us back to CA III and the centrality of the incarnation and, as we will see, especially the crucifixion. In many ways, this is the very center of this article, because by saying that we are made right before God because of Christ, we are at the same time saying that this is all a matter of God's mercy, which can only be received through faith.

"Through faith" is a tricky phrase in German, since one could translate "*durch den Glauben*" as either "by faith" or "through faith." Here, as editors of *The Book of Concord*, we relied on the Latin, which distinguishes between "*per fidem*" (through faith) and "*fide*" (by faith). If we say "through faith," then we understand faith as a kind of instrument for receiving God's grace; if we say "by faith," then faith becomes more clearly a direct description of God's relation to us as one of trust and consolation. For some reason, when some hear that they are justified through faith, they imagine that faith is something like a driver's license that we can keep in our pocket and pull out either when we need identification ("See? I am a Christian!") or when the police stop us. Yet others imagine that "by faith" indicates our control over the relation with God, as if faith were something we offer to God in return for grace.

When we believe that Christ has suffered for us, and that for his sake our sin is forgiven, and righteousness and eternal life are given to us. This line underscores the centrality of Christ and his suffering and death ("who for us and for our salvation came down") for establishing our relationship with God. The "when we believe" here is not "if we believe," as CA V will make clear. Instead, faith (alone) establishes a relation with God where, rather than trusting our own works or decisions, we only trust God. This sentence reveals another important aspect of our relation to God: it is *not* just about forgiveness of sin. Somewhere in the twentieth century, if not before, people began to imagine that the Reformation began with Luther's search for a merciful God and that modern life is no longer so obsessed with sin. For example, Paul Tillich, using his method of correlation, insisted that to appropriate Luther's theology one must shift from his search for a merciful God to the search for God per se.[5] Not only is the premise about the contrast between Luther and modern or postmodern sensibilities questionable (given our continued obsessions with guilt and shame), but Luther's "quest" has little basis in fact. According to oral tradition, Steven Ozment once said that everyone else in the sixteenth century was worried about whether they were a sheep or a goat (Matthew 25); Luther worried whether God was carnivorous or herbivorous! Indeed, from everything that Luther wrote in the earliest days of the Reformation, one discovers far broader concerns about one's relation to God than simply forgiveness of sin. In CA IV, too, we hear of three related results of God's mercy: forgiveness, righteousness, and eternal life. But the actual list is far longer! Everything that serves life and faith comes from God

---

5. Paul Tillich, *The Courage to Be* (New Haven: Yale University Press, 1952), 57–63.

alone. Indeed, if all we ask after is whether God exists, we will inevitably construct a god made in our image—a perfect reflection of our addiction to conditional religion. The God who is "for us" does not need our help in proving his existence—and any help we offer only leads to an encounter with the God who is against us.

For God will regard and reckon this faith as righteousness in his sight, as St. Paul says in Romans 3 and 4. How is this possible, given that faith is the very opposite of any work? How can God regard "faith" as "righteousness"? Here we come face-to-face with the two kinds of righteousness that inhabit our lives. The one kind truly is based upon our works and inheres in us. For example, an expert in antique guns, appearing on a show about a pawnshop in Las Vegas, declares an old Winchester to be a "righteous" rifle. That is, everything about it—from its firing mechanism to its age to its patina—accords to what the seller had claimed for it. Our human righteousness or, to use Luther's term, our proper righteousness similarly accords to our deeds, thoughts, and words. In this world, we are righteous because we do righteous things.

But before God "all our righteous deeds are like filthy cloth" (Isa 64:6), so that we have no claim or boast to make in God's presence. Instead, stripped of all such externals, knocked off of our ladders, we finally fall into the wounded hands of this righteous God. God must finally declare us to be righteous despite our works, decisions, thoughts, or words. Nothing inheres in us except Christ himself, so that our righteousness by faith is always an alien righteousness—never our own by right but only ours by faith in Christ and his righteousness alone.

Later Lutherans fought mightily over the "reckoning" spoken of here. It seems so cheap, as if it is merely a mental trick or a piece of fiction. God pretends we are righteous even though we are really not. In 1531, as he works on the Apology of the Augsburg Confession, Philip Melanchthon even gets tangled in a debate with his fellow Reformer and drafter of the CA, Johannes Brenz, who preferred to imagine that God declares us righteous in view of the future righteousness of our own deeds. In writing their joint response to Brenz, both Luther and Melanchthon object to their colleague's approach (popular among many Lutheran theologians today) in large part because it undermines our certainty in God's mercy and causes us, once again, to rely on our own righteousness. After all, if we see no progress in our lives, then how can we trust God is truly merciful to us? Thus, Luther's part of the letter reads:

> And I am accustomed, my Brenz, for the sake of understanding it better, to think of it in these terms: as if there is no quality in my heart that might be called "faith" or "love," but in that place I put Jesus Christ and say, "This is my righteousness; he is the quality and (as they say) formal righteousness," so that I may in this way set myself free and disentangle

myself from considering the law and works—even from considering that objective Christ, who is understood as teacher or giver. But I want him to be gift and teaching in himself, so that I may have all things in him.[6]

Around that time, Melanchthon was also working on a new commentary on Romans (having already published one in 1522 and another in 1530). For the first time, he goes into detail about the nature of being "reckoned" righteous. He calls it a Hebraism in Paul's language and then offers a well-known story from Roman history as an analogy. Scipio, the famous, victorious Roman general of the Punic Wars, was later caught embezzling money from Rome's coffers and ordered to appear before Rome's Senate, to face sure and swift (capital) punishment for his misdeeds. When the people of Rome heard it, they surrounded Scipio on his way to the Forum, shouting, "May every Roman mother have a son like Scipio!" That is, they declared crooked Scipio righteous and thereby prevented the Senate from executing him.

This example only makes sense if you and I *are* Scipio, not simply in theory but *really*! If, as became the prevailing view in later Lutheranism, such a declaration is merely hypothetical, it will more likely make us yawn rather than rejoice. But truly standing before God and facing our certain end, death, it immediately becomes a word of comfort and spiritual joy. Then, the simple declaration ("I announce to you the entire forgiveness of all your sins") does what it says: kills the Old Creature using God's faith-creating Word and raises a New Creature to life, clothed in Christ's righteousness alone.

We Teach and Confess

A former student of mine once told me how she became a Lutheran. As a fifteen-year-old Roman Catholic, she had gone to confession and received from the priest a list of things she needed to do to show her penitence. Because she never did them, she kept feeling guilty and stopped going to church altogether. In college, a friend invited her to come with him to his Lutheran church. At the beginning of the service, the congregation started with the general confession of sins, and all of her guilt came flooding back, reminding her why she had given up on religion. But then the pastor turned to the congregation and said, "As a called and ordained minister of the church of Christ and by his authority, I announce to you the entire forgiveness of all your sin." Shocked at what she was hearing, she burst out (loud enough for the entire congregation to hear), "Is that it?" Yes, that *is* it, not just for her but for all who

---

6. See Timothy J. Wengert, "Luther and Melanchthon—Melanchthon and Luther." *Luther-Jahrbuch* 66 (1999): 55–88, here p. 69, translating WA Br 6:100,49–101,55 (no. 1818), now also MBW no. 1151.

have ears to hear: Christ's righteousness is ours, and our sin belongs to Christ, once and for all.

Here is the way Luther put it in his 1520 tract, *Freedom of a Christian.*

The third incomparable benefit of faith is this: that it unites the soul with Christ, like a bride with a bridegroom. By this "mystery" (as Paul teaches) Christ and the soul are made one flesh. For if they are one flesh and if a true marriage—indeed by far the most perfect marriage of all—is culminated between them (since human marriages are but weak shadows of this one), then it follows that they come to hold all things, good and bad, in common. Accordingly, the faithful soul can both assume as its own whatever Christ has and glory in it, and whatever belongs to the soul Christ claims for himself as his own. . . . This is truly the most delightful drama, involving not only communion but also a saving war, victory, salvation and redemption. For Christ is God and a human being in one and the same person, who does not and cannot sin, die or be damned; and his righteousness, life, salvation are unconquerable, eternal and all-powerful. When, I say, such a person shares in common and, indeed, takes as his own the sins, death and hell of the bride on account of the wedding ring of faith, and when he regards them as if they were his own and as if he himself had sinned—suffering, dying and descending into hell—then, as he conquers them all and as sin, death and hell cannot devour him, they are devoured by him in an astounding duel. For his righteousness is superior to all sins, his life more powerful than death and his salvation more invincible than hell.[7]

---

7. TAL 1:499–501.

5

Means to the End

I came to seminary in 1973 a convinced "evangelical," having spent two years involved with a Roman Catholic charismatic community in Ann Arbor, Michigan. I was persuaded that if a person did not make a personal commitment to Christ, they were not truly Christian. And I came to seminary with the intention of converting all of my teachers to my point of view. Within a few months, I had identified the real culprit among the faculty members, Gerhard O. Forde, who seemed to be teaching just the opposite. Even though I did not have him for a course, I decided to take the bull by the horns and confront him. I made an appointment to see him in his office, showed up full of myself and my convictions, and left with a completely different point of view than the one I had arrived with just an hour earlier. Somehow in that brief time faith ceased being a decision I made and had become a work of the Holy Spirit through the Word.

In almost all forms of American Christianity, to say nothing of similar types around the world, there is plenty of talk about "amazing grace" and the love of Jesus. The Word of God is also deemed important. But when it comes to faith, many varieties of Christianity insist that faith is a decision we make, a commitment we undertake, in order to get into a right, saving relation with God. Underneath this insistence lies a commitment to humanity's free choice (something we will look at more closely in CA XVIII). But this widespread assumption cannot help but turn the unconditional nature of God's grace ("*because* God loves us, *therefore* . . .") into something that, in the end, depends upon us and what we do ("*if* I commit, *then* God will . . ."). When that happens, then all is lost, and we are thrust back upon ourselves and our work. In the face of this American religion, article 5 presents a completely different, counter-cultural way to view faith, where faith depends not on our working but God's speaking, for "faith comes from what is heard" (Rom 10:17), not from deciding or committing.

CA V

[German]

[Latin]

To obtain such faith God instituted the office of preaching, giving the gospel and the sacraments. Through these, as through means, he gives the Holy Spirit who produces faith, where and when he wills, in those who hear the gospel. It teaches that we have a gracious God, not through our merit but through Christ's merit, when we so believe. Condemned are the Anabaptists and others who teach that we obtain the Holy Spirit without the external word of the gospel through our own preparation, thoughts, and works.

So that we may obtain this faith, the ministry of teaching the gospel and administering the sacraments was instituted. For through the Word and the sacraments as through instruments the Holy Spirit is given, who effects faith where and when it pleases God in those who hear the gospel, that is to say, in those who hear that God, not on account of our own merits but on account of Christ, justifies those who believe that they are received into grace on account of Christ. Gal 3 [:14b]: "So that we might receive the promise of the Spirit through faith." They condemn the Anabaptists and others who think that the Holy Spirit comes to human beings without the external Word through their own preparations and works.

Reflections

"To obtain such faith, God . . ." Articles 4 and 5 are a matched set and are, rhetorically speaking, a single article. The "such faith" (Latin: ["this faith"]) referred to here is clearly the justifying faith spoken of in the previous article. This faith occurs "when we believe that Christ has suffered for us and that for his sake our sin is forgiven and righteousness and eternal life are given to us." This is hardly a theoretical faith or a belief in the "facts" of God's work but, as Melanchthon will explain more fully in CA XX, a relation with the one who alone saves us.

But look at who the subject of the verb is here. Not human beings but God! It is not, "to obtain faith *we* must commit" but rather "*God* must act." (Here the Latin version, by using the passive voice, only implies the divine activity that the German text states explicitly.) Indeed, whenever we reduce faith to human decisions, the very comfort of the gospel gets lost in one of two ways: pride or despair. Either we say (usually to others not as fortunate as we are), "Well, since *I* decided for Jesus, everything has worked out and I'm just filled with joy"; or, despairing, we can only see our doubts and inability to believe, made worse by those who seem to imply that such decisions are easy to make and keep. But since faith is *not* in our hands but God's, suddenly everything appears in a completely different light. When doubts come (and they will), we can cry out like the father in Mark 9:24: "Lord, I believe; help my unbelief." When our loved ones or neighbors show little or no faith despite the way we brought them up, then we need not browbeat them or (worse yet) consign them to hell, but we can actually pray God to act: sending the Word and the Holy Spirit to make believers out of them—something that Luther outlines in his Small Catechism's explanations to the first and second petition of the Lord's Prayer, where we pray first for faithful teaching of the Word and then for the Holy Spirit to give us faith to trust that Word. And, continually witnessing to God's grace for all people, we place our neighbors in God's merciful hands, not in their own hands or (worse yet) our judgmental hands.

"God instituted the office of preaching, giving the gospel and the sacraments." We will have other opportunities to examine the office of ministry, but it is important to notice that the CA introduces this office so early in the document and directly connects it to justification. The Latin version provides some added clarity when it talks about "the ministry of teaching the gospel and administering the sacraments." The word "ministry," as the Reformers used it, always pointed to a specific office in the church and *not* to the so-called "priesthood of all believers."[1] But note what kind of office this is! Late-medieval Christians understood clerical status as a path to saying the Mass, especially private Masses for the souls of the dead. Often separated at the altar from the laity behind a rood screen, these functionaries knew the proper prayers and actions used for the various rites and sacraments of the church. By the late fifteenth century, people even distinguished between pastors, who presided over all of the church's ceremonies (including preaching) and preachers, a separate category of priests who filled certain endowed pulpits in larger cities and towns and dedicated their time to preaching. By using the term "ministry" and "*ministerium*" for these people, the Reformers shifted the emphasis to service; by talking of the *Predigtamt* (preaching office) as a general designation for such ministers, they underscored the centrality of the proclamation of the Word of God at the center of a pastor's or preacher's office.

---

1. This corrects an erroneous note in the earlier translation from 1959. See Timothy J. Wengert, *Priesthood, Pastors, Bishops: Public Ministry for the Reformation & Today* (Minneapolis: Fortress, 2008), 33–40. To be sure, in a true emergency any baptized Christian could fill the public office temporarily, but never to undermine the vocation of the rightly called officeholders.

The slightly more cumbersome language in the German points to a second aspect of the phrase that explains why the CA connects this office with justification: "giving the gospel and sacraments." For the Reformers, the office of ministry is transparent, not calling attention to itself ("lest anyone should boast") but functioning as "ambassadors for Christ." This emphasis on the actions of the officeholder rather than on their status does not reduce ministers to functionaries. Instead, the office itself (as "preaching office" and "ministry of teaching and administering") defines the continuity and essence of the ministry. Unfortunately, one cannot speak clearly or simply enough that the Old Creature cannot find some way around God's mercy. In this case, "gospel and sacraments" focuses on what truly matters for the hearers—unlike what passes for preaching and teaching in our own day, where political and moralistic preaching and rigorous limiting or downplaying of the sacraments are the only food offered to weak and starving souls.

"Through these, as through means, [God] gives the Holy Spirit who produces faith, where and when he wills, in those who hear the gospel." With these words the decision theology of our age collapses. The gospel and sacraments are the means or (Latin) instruments through which the Holy Spirit produces faith. Just the year before this, Martin Luther had written in the explanation to the third article of the Apostles' Creed in his Small Catechism: "I believe that by my own understanding or strength I cannot believe in Jesus Christ my Lord or come to him, but instead the Holy Spirit has called me through the gospel, enlightened me with his gifts, made me holy and kept me in the true faith."[2]

This spells an end to all attempts by the Old Creature to manufacture faith. Faith is not ours to produce; only the Holy Spirit uses the means of grace to make us believers. "But at least we can say no," the Old Creature whines, to which, as mentioned above, one may respond in two ways. First, we are, on our own, *always* saying no—that is what it means to be a sinner, trusting our own understanding (human reason) and strength (the human will). And, second, such a question is purely theoretical so that if one asked such a whiner, "Why would you want to do that?" the answer is always, "Well, I wouldn't. But I could if I wanted, couldn't I?" Such is the Old Creature's desperation, that it finally makes things up to escape the truth of its bondage to sin and self. This is an example of the addictive nature of sin. Like the addict, the Old Creature always thinks it is able to get out from under its selfishness by relying on the self: "I can quit [am in charge] any time I want!"

The "where and when [the Spirit] wills" comes from John 3, where Jesus does his best to break Nicodemus's addiction to works. Jesus sees through the false praise Nicodemus heaps upon him as just another attempt to boast.

---

2. SC, Creed, 5 (BC, 355).

Instead, Jesus provides the most passive metaphor in the entire Bible (being born from above [Greek: *anothen*]), which Nicodemus immediately makes fun of by misunderstanding *"anothen"* as "again," foreshadowing the same mistake that those who trumpet being "born *again*" make. Something that only God can do became for Nicodemus a joke about crawling back in the mother's womb and, for those addicted to their own decisions, an excuse for making God's grace depend upon their own work. Having failed with that metaphor, Jesus tries another: again playing on the word for wind and Spirit (Greek: *pneuma*; Hebrew: *ruach*). "The wind [*pneuma*] blows where it wills . . . so it is with everyone born of the Spirit [*pneuma*]." CA V echoes this language, to make sure that all works are eliminated from faith.

The addition of the words "in those who hear the gospel" prevents us from separating God's work from God's Word. The use of means and "instruments" (Latin), arising out of the incarnation itself, eliminates all attempts to climb into God's heart through our own spiritual exercises separate and apart from any externals. This was an ancient heresy, called *en–thusiasmus* [belief in the god within (us)], where some monks in the ancient church thought that they had no more need of the external Word or sacraments but could manage with their own spiritual powers to reach God. For the CA this "mystical" path only empowers self-justifying persons into trusting themselves. Eight years later, in the published version of the Smalcald Articles, Luther could say much the same thing.

> In short: enthusiasm clings to Adam and his children from the beginning to the end of the world—fed and spread among them as poison by the old dragon. It is the source, power, and might of all the heresies. . . . Therefore we should and must insist that God does not want to deal with us human beings, except by means of his external Word and sacrament. Everything that boasts of being from the Spirit apart from such a Word and sacrament is of the devil.[3]

"That is to say, in those who hear that God, not on account of our own merits but on account of Christ, justifies those who believe that they are received into grace on account of Christ. Gal 3 [:14b]: 'So that we might receive the promise of the Spirit through faith.'" Here the Latin provides a fuller text and defines explicitly what this gospel is: that everything depends upon Christ's promise and not on us. For the first time in the Latin text, Melanchthon quotes a biblical passage. Having already referred more generally to Romans 3–4 in the previous article, here he turns to Galatians, which Martin Luther called his "Kätie von Bora" (after his wife). For the CA, the

---

3. SA III.viii.9–10 (BC, 323).

grace received from Christ is part and parcel of the work of the Holy Spirit, so that the text here moves easily back and forth between the three persons of the Trinity. Thus, the Trinitarian description in CA I receives further instantiation in CA III and now even more in CA V, where the goal of the Holy Trinity's work comes to expression. This article's distinction between Christ and merit comes up in other articles as well (CA II [German only], III–VI, XX, XXIV, XXVI–XXVIII) and reveals the origins of descriptions of Christ's atoning work as "satisfaction." For the Wittenberg Reformers, the point is not to roll out a theory of the atonement in which Christ satisfies God's justice so that God may fully love humankind (a la the medieval theologian Anselm) but rather that the third part of Penance, namely satisfaction through meritorious works, is erased. Whatever needs satisfying, Christ, not our merits, brings graciously to pass. But the verse from Galatians is also important in that it underscores the importance of the promise (given visibly and aurally through preaching and the sacraments) and faith in such a promise.

"Condemned are the Anabaptists and others who teach that we obtain the Holy Spirit without the external word of the gospel through our own preparation, thoughts, and works." The typical form of the articles of the CA move from an explication of the Reformers' teaching, followed by references to Scriptural, creedal, or patristic authorities and ending with condemnations. The fact that the condemnation here aims at both CA IV and V demonstrates that these articles form a single teaching.

But here again we may ask why there are condemnations at all. For a variety of reasons, modern Christians often shy away from explicit rejections of other points of view, imagining that it is impolite or unecumenical if not unchristian. Yet condemnations perform an important role in defining a church's teaching. Although in many respects these Lutherans and especially Luther truly enjoyed paradox and, hence, a kind of "both—and" approach to theology, from the very start of the Reformation they faced opponents who rejected the very teachings now being set forth in the CA. Thus, when the Reformers insist on condemnations, they are trying to draw a clear line between themselves and those who rejected their positions.

But these same opponents also tried to equate Wittenberg's theology with that of other groups, with whom the Reformers also disagreed. This was particularly fraught with danger regarding the charge of being Anabaptist! In 1529 the imperial diet meeting in Speyer reaffirmed ancient imperial rescripts condemning those who rebaptized and threatening such practitioners with capital punishment. When in April 1530 Johann Eck published his attack on the Reformers in the *404 Articles*, he included a wide range of thinkers, including so-called Anabaptists, within his condemnations and implied that they were, in the end, all related. Thus, as part of their argument that they were law-abiding citizens, the Saxon theologians and their allies insisted that they were *not* Anabaptists.

But there was also another aspect to these condemnations that the drafters hid under the word "and others." This allowed them to condemn their Roman opponents without naming names and associating them (rather than the Reformers) with the vilified Anabaptists. The specific condemnation here is precisely the problem that this chapter has addressed: imagining that there is some way to God outside the means and instruments that God uses to offer himself and his grace to us. But the wording itself collapses the denial of means (CA V: gospel and sacraments) with human addiction to works (CA IV). There is no difference in the end. Any insistence upon human works undermines both God's mercy and the very instruments with which God has chosen to work. It also implies that the only or at least most important instrument for our salvation is ourselves. But the CA has especially a specific strand of late-medieval theology, namely, that of Gabriel Biel, in mind. Biel had insisted that: "to those who do what is in them, God will not deny grace" (known more familiarly in American circles as: God helps them who help themselves). Thus, by exercising the spark of free choice that God preserved in human beings after the fall into sin, Biel argued, a person could "earn" God's grace and produce acts of loving God above all else and one's neighbor as oneself. Indeed, already in the very earliest comments of Luther in his lectures on Romans (where he calls such people *Sautheologen* [pig theologians]) and in his September 1517 theses against scholastic theology (to say nothing of the *Heidelberg Disputation*, the *Explanation of the 95 Theses*, and *Freedom of a Christian*), Luther condemned this approach to justification as contrary to the gospel.[4]

But here the drafters err in mentioning the Anabaptists. It turns out that only a handful of people who rejected infant baptism and supported instead believers' baptism denied the efficacy of God's Word as the means through which the Holy Spirit works. To be sure, the Reformers did not have the luxury of five hundred years of history writing (and especially of the last hundred years) to make clear distinctions among the various groups that the Reformers labeled Anabaptists.[5] But the fact that this blanket condemnation has distorted what, for example, today's Mennonites believe, means that

---

4. For the *Lectures on Romans* (1515–1516), see LW 25:261–62; for the *Disputation against Scholastic Theology* (1517), LW 31:9–16; for the *Heidelberg Disputation* (1518), TAL 1:81–105; for the *Explanation of the 95 Theses* (1518), LW 31:212–28; for the *Freedom of a Christian* (1520), e.g., TAL 1:493.

5. See, however, FC XII (BC, 520–23, 656–60), where Jakob Andreae, who already in 1568 had held a disputation attacking anti-Trinitarians, makes some distinctions among them. See Irene Dingel, ed., *Antitrinitarische Streitigkeiten*, vol. 9 of *Controversia et Confessio* (Göttingen: Vandenhoeck & Ruprecht, 2012), 560–82.

Lutherans cannot treat their own confessions as inerrant. Instead, relations among Christians must begin by listening to one another and learning to tell the history of the sixteenth century together. These errors and false generalizations do not undermine the CA's authority but enhance it by clarifying what the document is really all about: witnessing to the gospel, teaching the gospel, and gathering believers around that very witness and teaching. When condemnations like those in CA V result in persecution of those who disagree with them, as they did, Lutherans must face the weakness of their confessions and learn to practice the fruits of repentance.[6]

We Teach and Confess

Well, at least we can say "No!" can't we? Or at least we can stop resisting and become passive, right? These and other defenses that the Old Creature cooks up show just how desperate we are to remain in control of our relation to God at some level or another. We are not neutral; we are addicted to sin—that is, to fearing, loving, trusting ourselves first and foremost. And whether we claim that our free will or our passive will does it, our *self*-will stays in charge. Even Martin Luther took years before he finally discovered that it was not up to him *at all*. Some scholars think this shift in Luther's theology took place as he was working on his defense of the *95 Theses* in the spring of 1518.[7] In the early going, he tried to explain that the Christian had to empty him- or herself of all claims to merit God's grace. But by the time he comes to explain Thesis 62: "The true treasure of the church is the most holy gospel of the glory and grace of God," Luther places all the emphasis on God's work through the gospel.[8]

This breakthrough, to a confession of God's work through the spoken and visible Word, is nowhere better demonstrated than in Luther's 1522 "Invocavit" sermons. The background to these sermons is simple. After being condemned by the imperial diet, the Duke-Elector of Saxony, Frederick the Wise, arranged to have Luther smuggled to one of his fortresses, the Wartburg Castle, and placed under protective custody. This lasted until March 1522, when Luther, worried over reports of unrest in Wittenberg and convinced that his reforming colleagues were making a mess of things, left the elector's protection on his own and appeared again in Wittenberg's pulpit on the first Sunday in Lent, called in those days, "Invocavit Sunday." For eight days running he spoke *against* the reform measures his colleagues had undertaken with

---

6. See *Healing Memories: Reconciling in Christ: Report of the Lutheran–Mennonite International Study Commission* (Geneva: Lutheran World Federation, 2010), 75–76.

7. Oswald Bayer, *Promissio: Geschichte der reformatorischen Wende in Luthers Theologie* (Göttingen: Vandenhoeck & Ruprecht, 1971), forthcoming in English translation from "Lutheran Quarterly Books."

8. See below, chapter 12, for this quotation from Luther.

the approval of the city of Wittenberg—things with which, theoretically, he agreed but which, in his opinion, simply replaced one set of laws that believers must do with another. It was a classic case of works righteousness that denied that God's Holy Spirit working through the Word did it all. In the second sermon, Luther described his own experience with God's word this way:

> For the Word created heaven and earth and all things [Ps 33:6]; the Word must do this thing, and not we poor sinners. In short, I will preach it, teach it, write it, but I will constrain no one by force, for faith must come freely without compulsion. Take myself as an example. I opposed indulgences and all the papists, but never with force. I simply taught, preached, and wrote God's Word; otherwise I did nothing. And while I slept [cf. Mark 4:26–29], or drank beer with my friends Philip [Melanchthon] and [Nicholas von] Amsdorf, the Word so greatly weakened the papacy that no prince or emperor ever inflicted such losses upon it. I did nothing; the Word did everything.[9]

---

9. "The Second Sermon, March 10, 1522, Monday after Invocavit," in *Eight Sermons at Wittenberg, 1522* (LW 51:77).

6

THE FRUITS OF JUSTIFICATION

"Good trees bear good fruit." With this saying of Jesus, Martin Luther, already as early as 1520 in *The Freedom of a Christian*, answered the most pointed objection of his opponents to justification by faith alone.[1] Without necessarily realizing it, however, these opponents were actually paraphrasing an objection that St. Paul anticipated from his own moralistic adversaries in Romans 6: "Shall we sin the more that grace may more abound?" Paul's answer ("You have died!"), like Luther's, did not dismiss his previous arguments: that gospel is good news, not bad; that we are justified by faith not by any works at all; that we have peace with God. Instead, Paul pointed to God's action of putting to death and making alive.

If you have reached this place in this book and have finally asked this question (which, because of Paul's letter to the Romans, I call question number six), then you are exactly on the right track. Other forms of Christianity, with their emphasis on works, virtue, and the law, would never lead you to ask this question, since it is clear that their approach to whole enterprise depends, to some degree, upon works, not upon God's gracious word of forgiveness alone. But when you ask this question, then you're in league with Ed, from my parish in Wisconsin, whose wife and four rambunctious children had

---

1. TAL 1:514–15. The second half of *Freedom of a Christian* (cf. TAL 1:510–31, especially 510: "Here we will respond to all those people who are offended by the word of faith . . ."), often taken as a separate subject, is rhetorically speaking a "confutation," that is, an answer to anticipated questions from opponents. In this case, Luther already knows that his opponents thought his approach to the gospel of justification by grace through faith led only to licentiousness or even rebellion. That "Christians are servants of all" is the result of justification by faith alone *not* a separate subject.

just joined the congregation. Having come from a Roman Catholic congregation in Northern Wisconsin, he participated in a class instructing him in the Lutheran witness to the gospel. Having heard of "up and down" religion in the first session, he finally said: "So we're saved by grace alone, right?" "Yes," I responded, not without some pride in my ability to teach. "And there's nothing that we can do to earn God's love?" "Absolutely," I said to my brilliant student. "Well," he added, "Just don't tell the kids!" His comment demonstrates that Paul's objection in Romans 6 can only arise when *all* works are excluded from our relation to God.

The way we describe things in theology makes a difference. If we begin on the defensive, trying to answer the question of the relation of faith to works in such a way as to preserve good works at all costs ("We *have* to do something, don't we?"), then all is lost and the pictures we use to describe the relation of faith and works will always assume a "before and after" or an "if . . . then" in the Christian life: First we're saved by faith, and then we *have* to do works. Even the ubiquitous slogan of the Evangelical Lutheran Church in America ("God's work; our hands") could be used to support such coercion regarding works. But if we begin with another question: "What are you going to do now that you don't *have* to do anything?" then everything changes. Then the slogan, for example, would better be expressed as "God's work; our hands—so we don't get bored!"

Then, too, Jesus's saying about trees and fruit turns much of what passes for preaching (even among Lutherans) upside down, because another complaint I've often heard from pastors (who have never read Dietrich Bonhoeffer's very *Lutheran* comments on the subject but only use his statement to defend their own moralistic preaching)[2] is that justification by grace through faith alone is "cheap grace." And they usually add that they've tried preaching this way, but their congregation members take it as an occasion to do nothing. Of course, grace is neither cheap nor expensive; it's free—which frightens the works-righteous Old Creature to death. Moreover, if the problem is a lack of fruit, then according to Jesus's advice the solution is to plant trees, not to yell at them ("Bear fruit or else!"). Moreover, Luther thinks that what actually constitutes good works is precisely *not* our self-chosen spirituality and religiosity but our various callings in the world to love our neighbor (things like changing diapers, supporting pastors, or paying taxes to whom taxes are due). This means that very often the problem is *not* that we are not bearing good fruit but that we don't believe it. (This theme gets dealt with in CA XVI, XVIII, and XX.)

---

2. Dietrich Bonhoeffer, *The Cost of Discipleship*, 2nd ed., trans. R. H. Fuller (London: SCM, 1959), 35–47.

CA VI

[German]	[Latin]
It is also taught that such faith should yield good fruit and good works and that a person must do such good works as God has commanded for God's sake but not place trust in them as if thereby to earn grace before God. For we receive forgiveness of sin and righteousness through faith in Christ, as Christ himself says [Luke 17:10]: "When you have done all [things] . . . say, 'We are worthless slaves.'" The Fathers also teach the same thing. For Ambrose says: "It is determined by God that whoever believes in Christ shall be saved and have forgiveness of sins, not through works but through faith alone, without merit."	Likewise, they teach that this faith is bound to yield good fruits and that it ought to do good works commanded by God on account of God's will and not so that we may trust in these works to merit justification before God. For forgiveness of sins and justification are taken hold of by faith, as the saying of Christ also testifies [Luke 17:10]: "When you have done all [things] . . . say, 'We are worthless slaves.'" The authors of the ancient church teach the same. For Ambrose says: "It is established by God that whoever believes in Christ shall be saved without work, by faith alone, receiving the forgiveness of sins as a gift."

Reflections

"It is also taught that such faith should yield good fruit and good works and that a person must do such good works as God has commanded for God's sake but not place trust in them as if thereby to earn grace before God." The words "such faith" again remind us to connect this article to CA IV. The Latin text helps in two places to understand the "should" and "must" in the German version. In the first instance, we read: "this faith is bound to." This reflects one of the astounding points that Luther makes in *Freedom of a Christian*, that works come spontaneously. This spontaneity just *has* to happen—much like a person in love just *has* to freely love their beloved. If they didn't it wouldn't be love at all. The juxtaposition of spontaneity and necessity should surprise us all and undercut the favorite "shoulds" and "musts" of moralistic preaching. The doing of good works is a necessary result of justification by faith alone, not yet another threat from God. Good trees bear good fruit!

In the second instance, the Latin text reads, "it [such faith] ought to do good works." In fact, if it doesn't, then something is wrong with faith, not works. Indeed, Jesus's parable of the barren tree (Luke 13:6–9) may especially help us here (see below). The remarkable thing about this parable, of course, is that—when read aloud—the next year never comes, that is, the mercy of

71

"one more year" always strikes a person's ears anew, for "next year" is always a year away.

Both the German and Latin texts guard themselves against such moralistic approaches to the Christian life by adding "as God has commanded for God's sake but not place trust in them as if thereby to earn grace before God." When it comes to the neighbor, we love them not because they are loveable but precisely because God loved us, we who are equally as unloveable as our neighbor. It is rather like what happens when a person in love meets the future in-laws: he or she loves them for the sake of the beloved. But this same love eliminates earning grace, where once again the Latin is clearer ("trust in these works to merit justification before God"). The believer never has any claim to make before God. Were that to happen, then faith in God (here: "trust") becomes faith in ourselves and our works, so that even and especially regarding good works the Reformers refuse to abandon justification by faith alone but rather underscore it. Even when it comes to works, we are justified by faith alone!

"For we receive forgiveness of sin and righteousness through faith in Christ, as Christ himself says [Luke 17:10]: 'When you have done all [things] ... say, "We are worthless slaves."'" We will encounter this again in CA XX, but note how little time is spent talking about works: one sentence. Immediately, the CA returns to God's grace received through faith. This bespeaks the centrality of justification by faith to the entire Christian life. Luke 17 shows just how faith works. The parable that precedes it talks of the appropriate behavior of servants or slaves. Of course, Americans, used to boasting about the kingdom, the power, and the glory, will find this parable one of the hardest to swallow and will go off talking about an abundant (aka selfish) life, where God is at our beck and call. The drafters of the CA, however, have a completely different view of the Christian life. The "nothing in my hands I bring; simply to thy cross I cling" of the Reformed theologian Augustus Toplady hits the nail on the head, unless, of course, the Old Creature insists on turning "clinging" into a work. But servants (like good trees) have no alternative but to say, "We are worthless slaves." Indeed, in our world, where slavery exists but is universally banned, the outrageous metaphor of slavery is especially powerful in overturning any and all works righteousness. "Worthless slaves?" we snort. "But at least I try. Surely that counts for something, doesn't it?" No! There is no merit, only grace.

The Fathers also teach the same thing. For Ambrose says: "It is determined by God that whoever believes in Christ shall be saved and have forgiveness of sins, not through works but through faith alone, without merit." This cinches it for Melanchthon and his fellow drafters in Augsburg and shows once again that even in this article, later labeled "On Good Works," he simply repeats what we heard in CA IV (cf. the reference to "such faith").

The Christian life really is all about faith, and when we imagine otherwise we end up smuggling in works somewhere or another in our relation to God. But for the CA, even *talking* about works always leads us back to justification "by grace through faith on account of Christ."

But the citation of "Ambrose" invites us to consider how these Lutherans understood authority in the church. As Melanchthon writes in CA XX, the Fathers provide "*testimonia*," witness statements to the faith. This means that the oft-used phrase, *sola Scriptura*, is nowadays almost always completely misunderstood and misused. The very fact that in Luther's Latin writings "Scripture alone" occurs only eighteen times (half of which are instances where Luther insists he will *not* argue by Scripture alone) and never in Melanchthon's work, already indicates a problem. After all, were the phrase to be understood in a biblicistic manner, then why are you reading this book? No, Christians always have more authorities than just the Scripture (even the fundamentalist, when saying "the Bible says," often means "My pastor told me the Bible says"). It is not whether believers use other authorities but how they order them. Philip Melanchthon said that the Bible is the "*primum et verum*," the first and true authority. Later Lutherans similarly distinguished between biblical norm that sets the standard for all other authorities (the "*norma normans*"—the norming norm) and these secondary, normed authorities ("*norma normata*"—the normed norms).

The first witness that the CA invokes comes already in CA I with the Nicene Creed, followed in CA III by a citation and paraphrase of the Apostles' Creed. Here, as the culmination of the arguments in CA IV–VI, Melanchthon refers to St. Ambrose—except that it is *not* Ambrose at all, and Melanchthon probably knew it. Only a few years before, Erasmus of Rotterdam, as part of his commitment to providing the church with the oldest sources of its theology, had published the collected works of Ambrose, bishop of Milan. In it Erasmus argued that a Latin commentary on Paul's letters ascribed to Ambrose was not written by him at all. He even coined a name for this still anonymous author: Ambrosiaster—"somewhat like Ambrose." But Lutherans were not always interested in Erasmus's (or others') historical arguments.[3] The first question they asked was not who wrote something but how does it witness to the faith. Moreover, since they were addressing folks who also did not necessarily agree with Erasmus, they surely felt no compunction to obscure their point with unnecessary historical arguments.

This anonymous author from the fourth century, however, provided some remarkable support for the Evangelicals in Augsburg. Here was an author, centuries before the Reformation, who had insisted that salvation comes by

---

3. For a splendid study of this, see Irene Backus, *Historical Method and Confessional Identity in the Era of the Reformation (1378–1615)* (Leiden: Brill, 2003), 212–27.

faith *alone* without merit! Indeed, this is the very first time that we encounter the phrase "faith alone" in the CA, as if the drafters were saying, "Luther and his compatriots did not make this phrase up but were part of a centuries-old witness to the heart of the Christian message."

Sometimes, however, Lutherans imagine that using the words "faith alone" exclude other ways of speaking about justification. In Melanchthon's later discussions with Roman Catholics during the 1530s, he realized that they objected to the phrase "faith alone" because it was not in Scripture, so he introduced a helpful explanation. There were in Paul (and elsewhere in Scripture) certain "exclusive phrases" (*particulae exclusivae*), such as "not by works" or "by grace," which the Evangelical party summarized with the phrase "faith alone." Melanchthon's students also used the phrase, so that it even found its way into the Formula of Concord.[4]

We Teach and Confess

So, given that believers cannot or ought not do works on their own, where do they come from? Here, a phrase from the Formula of Concord provides another picture (beyond fruit-bearing and slavery). For believers as believers (not as sinners, out of whom God must drag good works) good works arise from "a free and merry spirit."[5] This phrase provides a great way to measure preaching. If a preacher talks about works in a sermon in such a way that people go out whistling, laughing, and dancing (generally signs of that "free and merry spirit"), then all is well. But if such preaching or teaching only results in more burdens heaped upon a captive audience, then all is lost.

The parable of Jesus about the fruitless tree (Luke 13:6–9) is especially illuminating. The owner, like many a moralistic preacher, cares only to chop the tree down, but the Good Gardner (like the Good Shepherd who foolishly leaves the ninety-nine to search for one lost sheep, and like the woman who sweeps the house for the lost coin, and the waiting father running to greet the lost and dead son), says what's needed is aeration and manure and one more year.[6] Of course, with this parable that year never comes. No matter when we hear it, the message is the same: "One more year!" To be sure, the moralizers and works-addicted may preach that that year of grace is finally over—and in so doing claim to be the owner (not fruitless trees!). But, no matter how we try, the words of Jesus refuse to end in judgment but stick with digging dirt and spreading manure.

---

4. Timothy J. Wengert, *A Formula for Parish Practice: Using the Formula of Concord in Congregations* (Minneapolis: Fortress Press, 2017), 58.

5. Solid Declaration VI.17 (BC, 590).

6. We often identify the "owner" with God, but frankly this mean-spirited, judgmental type is far more like the moralistic preachers who inhabit many pulpits.

One modern children's author, Arnold Lobel, put his finger on the surprise of good fruit in his *Frog and Toad* stories. In one called "The Garden," Toad wants to grow a garden but after planting the seeds insists on yelling at them to sprout and grow. When Frog warns him that he has frightened the seeds, Toad starts playing soothing music to them, which lulls him to sleep. When he awakes, his garden has sprouted (cf. Mark 4:26–29). When asked how he likes gardening, he complains about it being hard work. So, too, today's preachers and teachers! Instead of placing in their hearers' ears the promise of God's mercy and grace, they always have an agenda (a Latin participle for "things that must be done") and plain wear themselves and their hearers out shouting about works. But since "good trees bear good fruit," the same Holy Spirit, who uses the means of grace to create faith (CA V), spontaneously brings forth "fruits of the Spirit" to use Paul's phrase in Galatians, which he opposes to works of the flesh. These preachers may think such gardening is hard work, but only because they cannot trust the good seed or good tree to sprout and grow and bear fruit on its own.

7

The Characteristic Markings
of the Church Bird

What does the word "church" mean? In English, we use it in a variety of sometimes contradictory ways. "We'll be late for church, if you don't hurry, Tim!" a line I often heard from my father, who purposely set his watch five minutes fast so that I would get in the car and not miss *worship.* "This is my church," the pastor boasts, although he or she will most likely some day leave that *congregation* for another. "I taught in a seminary of the Evangelical Lutheran Church in America," the professor crows—although he really is speaking of a denomination. And, finally, there is the "church catholic," that is, the universal church, which different "churches" have also defined in very different ways. Luther seems to entry the fray when commenting in the Smalcald Articles: "God be praised, a seven-year-old child knows what the church is: holy believers and 'the little sheep who hear the voice of their shepherd [cf. John 10:3]."[1] A scholar in the 1950s reportedly quipped, "I'd like to meet that child."

Some help for defining this slippery term comes from an etymology of the word. Here Luther's discussion in the Large Catechism's explanation of the third article of the Creed turns out to be more accurate than nineteenth-century linguists gave him credit for.[2] The word "church" (cf. German: *Kirche*; Scottish: *kirk*; Swedish: *kyrka*) is related to the Greek term *kyriakos* and probably means "belonging to the Lord" (as opposed to being related to "circle" and thus similar to the political term "parish"). When combined with the Greek term for

---

1. SA III.xii.2 (BC, 324–25).
2. *Large Catechism*, Apostles' Creed, par. 47–48 (BC, 436–37).

church, *ekklesia*, which means those called out, it turns out that "church" provides a far stronger theological definition than most of the ways we use the term today. The church consists of the Christian assembly, a *con-gregation* (derived from the words *cum* [together] and *grex* [flock]) those called out who belong to the Lord—"the little sheep who hear the voice of their shepherd."

But how do we know whether the particular assembly we find ourselves in is the church or not? Here the fights of the Reformation help explain many specific features in CA VII, VIII, and XV. The earliest disputes of the Reformation first arose over indulgences (cf. the *95 Theses*) but quickly moved on to the question of papal authority. Although his opponents assumed that "church" was closely associated with respect for and connection to the bishop of Rome, Luther insisted that the true church was the (hidden) assembly of true believers. Thus, while popes or theologians might belong to the visible, external church, their unbelieving teaching and behavior left them far removed from the true church of believers, gathered from every time and place into Christ's body.

Luther's opponents immediately realized a serious problem in his argument. Luther insisted that faith came through the hearing of the sure and certain promises of God as brought into the heart by the Holy Spirit. But by defining the church as the assembly of believers (which could not be seen) he left the faithful uncertain whether they were truly in the church or not. Indeed, his opponents argued, Luther had simply turned the church into a "Platonic republic," that is, a utopia completely undetectable by believers struggling in this life for certainty about the gospel. By contrast, his opponents could point to real councils and a real succession of bishops that defined their "true" church.

In 1520, Luther addressed this challenge, since the certainty of faith in a sure Word of God hung in the balance. His solution, to some degree hinted at in Augustine and a few late-medieval writers, was unique and influenced discussions of ecclesiology for at least the next one hundred years—not only among Lutherans but also with some Roman Catholics. The church, Luther argued beginning in 1520, possesses certain visible signs to assure believers that they are in the right place. In a later writing he compared these signs to the characteristic markings in birds: the song and colors of their feathers. These markings were none other than the Word and sacraments. This definition was so important that ten years later in 1530 Philip Melanchthon used it in the CA VII and even more in the Apology VII/VIII.[3]

---

3. For an in-depth discussion of this development, see Gordon Lathrop and Timothy J. Wengert, *Christian Assembly: Marks of the Church in a Pluralistic Age* (Minneapolis: Fortress, 2004), 17–36.

CA VII

[German]

[Latin]

It is also taught that at all times there must be and remain one holy, Christian church. It is the assembly of all believers among whom the gospel is purely preached and the holy sacraments are administered according to the gospel. For this is enough for the true unity of the Christian church that there the gospel is preached harmoniously according to a pure understanding and the sacraments are administered in conformity with the divine Word. It is not necessary for the true unity of the Christian church that uniform ceremonies, instituted by human beings, be observed everywhere. As Paul says in Eph 4 [:4–5]: "There is one body and one Spirit, just as you were called to the one hope of your calling, one Lord, one faith, one baptism."

Likewise, they teach that one holy church will remain forever. The church is the assembly of saints in which the gospel is taught purely and the sacraments are administered rightly. And it is enough for the true unity of the church to agree concerning the teaching of the gospel and the administration of the sacraments. It is not necessary that human traditions, rites or ceremonies instituted by human beings be alike everywhere. As Paul says [Eph 4:5, 6]: "One faith, one baptism, one God and Father of all."

Reflections

"**It is also taught that at all times there must be and remain one holy, Christian church.**" With these words we discover that "church" will be defined separate and apart from individual congregations or denominations, and we learn that church has certain qualities, already laid out in the Nicene Creed ("one, holy, catholic and apostolic"). For the word "catholic," the Reformers use the word "Christian," *not* because they associated the "catholic church" with those in communion with Rome (as some Lutherans later alleged) but because already before the Reformation the standard German translation of the Nicene and Apostles' Creeds used the word "Christian" to translate ecclesiastical Latin's Greek loan word (*catholica*), which means universal. To express the term "universal church" in early modern new High German translators chose the term "Christian." (As we will see in the Latin version of CA XX, Melanchthon could use the word "catholic" in a completely positive sense.) First in the nineteenth century did the qualities described in the Nicene Creed become confused with the "marks of the church," especially among the Anglo-Catholic thinkers of the Oxford Movement in mid-nineteenth-century England.[4] Indeed, "one, holy, catholic and apostolic" cannot be visible marks for any individual church, since no one can successfully prove that these qualities exist *externally* in their assemblies (especially oneness, universality or holiness). Even "apostolic" is a term fraught with competing definitions.

Only when one realizes that the Holy Spirit (about whom the third article of the Creed speaks) bestows these qualities upon the church, can one escape boasting that "we are the true church, and you are not!" Indeed, this first sentence of CA VII indicates a remarkable starting point for Lutheran (and Christian) ecumenism: the church exists *at all times* and is always one, holy and catholic. It also indicates something often forgotten by Lutherans: that the Reformers insisted upon their continuity with the church of all ages. Lutheranism is not a sect that suddenly appeared on the scene in 1517, claiming apostolic roots but rejecting the post-apostolic church. As we already saw in CA VI, the Reformers remained in constant contact with the ancient and medieval church, insisting that they had not invented a new church but were in complete harmony with the church of all ages.

"It is the assembly of all believers among whom the gospel is purely preached and the holy sacraments are administered according to the gospel." The word "assembly" is a remarkable one. It contains within it the hint of a verb, the action of assembling, in this case assembling around the aural and visible Word of God. In the Latin of CA VII the word is *congregatio*, or, "the coming together of the flock." Thus, the single-most important insight of Lutheran ecclesiology is precisely that the church is not so much an institution or a building but rather an event (or, to use a term popular in the 1960s, a "happening"). It is an assembling of "believers" ("saints" in the Latin). This interchangeability of these two words, believers and saints, demonstrates how the Reformers understood the Christian life. Saints are not simply some small group of holier people but include *all* Christian believers, because what makes them holy and saint-like is not their works but faith itself, which clings not to one's own holiness but to God's holiness given in Christ to all who believe in, trust in, him. Moreover, the very thing around which believers assemble (the gospel and sacraments) are the means by which this faith is created and strengthened (CA V).

The gospel and the sacraments are the very visible signs of the church that Luther first associated with the true church's identification back in 1520. This insight into the nature of the Christian church gathered around the events of Word and Sacrament lies at the heart of Lutheran ecclesiology. These "signs," as Luther calls them, are not signs pointing away from themselves to some

---

4. For one example, see "Notes of the Church," in *The Oxford Dictionary of the Christian Church*, ed. F. L. Cross and E. A. Livingstone, 2nd ed. (Oxford: Oxford University Press, 1974), 982–83.

other reality, instead they are signs of life. Just as breathing and a heartbeat are signs of human life, so the gospel and sacraments are visible signs of the church's life of faith. As near as we can tell, Philip Melanchthon is the first to label these "signs" as "marks" (Latin: *notae*, "things that can be known"), and he does so in his defense of these articles in the Apology of the Augsburg Confession, published in 1531.

> However, the church is not only an association of external ties and rites as other civic organizations, but it is principally an association of faith and the Holy Spirit in the hearts of persons. It nevertheless has its external marks so that it can be recognized, namely, the pure teaching of the gospel and the administration of the sacraments in harmony with the gospel of Christ. . . . Nor indeed are we dreaming about some Platonic republic, as some have slanderously alleged. Instead, we teach that this church truly exists, consisting of true believing and righteous people scattered through the entire world. And we add its marks: the pure teaching of the gospel and the sacraments.[5]

But why does the CA say "*purely* preached" and "administered *according to the gospel*" (Latin: "rightly")? At first hearing these simple terms may sound as if they are reintroducing the very uncertainty Luther was trying to avoid by talking about external marks in the first place, since they make people wonder whether the Word is *purely* preached or the sacraments properly administered. But we may better interpret them as leaving the certainty in God's hands, not ours. Thus, Luther on occasion even observed that his Roman opponents were also the true church, since they read the gospel on Sunday mornings, baptized, and celebrated the Lord's Supper. (To be sure, at other times he insisted that his opponents' church had all the marks of the anti-Christian church!)[6] The modifying phrase for the sacraments may refer to the Reformers' insistence that the Lord's Supper includes distributing the elements (not just adoring them) consisting of both bread and wine and that baptism also includes children.

Using the word "purely" for the gospel, however, may seem even more problematic, especially when later Lutherans insisted that they truly knew what the pure gospel sounds like (namely, like the teaching of the Augsburg Confession) and were willing to punish those whose teaching and preaching did not measure up. Here a word from the next sentence in the German helps clarify the issue. The CA insists that such preaching take place "harmoniously," a word we already encountered in CA I. In Latin the same theme is

---

5. Ap VII/VIII.5, 20 (BC, 174, 177).
6. For more on this see Lathrop and Wengert, *Christian Assembly*, 81–112.

struck by the word *consentire* ("to agree" or even "to assert in a united fashion"). Thus, it is not a single person or even a single group of Christians who decide what the pure gospel constitutes but the entire body of believers, who confess their faith, among other places, in the church's creeds (as so-called rules of faith). The reason we can use the CA itself as a measure of the purity of the gospel comes precisely from its origins (in a confessing moment for the church) and in its remarkable acceptance (in part) by the Reformers' opponents in Augsburg.

But there may be an even more profound way to understand this word "purely." The word means something very different if viewed not so much from the contents of preaching and teaching as from their effect on the hearers. We experience these very effects when the instruction and proclamation actually lead us to faith, that is, to trusting God's mercy in Christ. Already in *Freedom of a Christian* from 1520, Luther criticizes preaching that only describes the heroic deeds of Christ, precisely because it only leaves the hearers with an example to follow. Instead, the preacher must lean over the pulpit, look folks in the eye, and proclaim, simply proclaim, that this Christ is "for you."[7] Pure teaching of the gospel, despite our human confusion, is not rocket science. It is the message of God's comfort in Christ to the terrified: "If God is for us, who can be against us?" It is the message of God's forgiveness in Christ to the sinner: "Which is easier to say, 'You are forgiven' or 'Take up your bed and walk'?" It is life to the dying: "I am the resurrection and the life." What both creates and unites the entire church of all times and places, then, are these "tidings of comfort and joy": "To you is born a savior!" It is pure grace!

"For this is enough for the true unity of the Christian church that there the gospel is preached harmoniously according to a pure understanding and the sacraments are administered in conformity with the divine Word." In the past fifty years or so, these words have been hotly contested in Lutheran circles, especially in North America, specifically in relation to ecumenical agreements with various churches. On one side, there are folks who insist that the "enough" (Latin: *satis*) here means that there must be full agreement in *all* matters of doctrine and sacramental practice. On another side, some criticize agreements with other churches that demand more than basic agreement on Word and sacraments—for example, insisting that particular forms of public ministry are also constitutive for true unity. Still others have insisted that the word "harmonious" or "agree" (Latin) presupposes a broader set of teachings and practices that make up Christian unity, or that some formal teaching authority in the church must determine these matters.

---

7. TAL 1:508.

Here much of the confusion lies in how one defines the word "church." All three positions assume that the church is not simply an event but also an institution and that the kind of unity described in CA VII has finally to do with institutional unity. But that is hardly what the Reformers were talking about here, as indicated by their use of the words "true" and "Christian."

"It is not necessary for the true unity of the Christian church that uniform ceremonies, instituted by human beings, be observed everywhere." This sentence has remained a conundrum to many Lutherans, who overlook the fact that this passage actually foreshadows CA XV, where such ceremonies are more fully defined. Indeed, one could look at CA VII, VIII, and XV as a single theological argument about the church, with what went before (CA I–VI on the Word) and after (CA IX–XIV, on the sacraments) as defining content for the marks of the church outlined here. Without CA XV the exact nature of these "unnecessary things" remains unclear, so we will delay discussion of this part of the definition of church until that chapter. It does, however, put the reader on notice that certain practices, as wholesome as they may be, do not constitute the church's true unity. Only hearing the Shepherd's voice unites us.

"As Paul says in Eph 4 [:4–5]: 'There is one body and one Spirit, just as you were called to the one hope of your calling, one Lord, one faith, one baptism.'" Here Melanchthon provides a remarkably ecumenical proof text for his entire argument. While today ecumenists often make much of John 17 and Jesus's prayer to the Father ("That they may be one"), the CA looks instead to the Pauline assertion that Christians (whether in the mixed Jewish and Gentile congregation of Ephesus or in the midst of the upheavals of the Reformation or in the even more culturally diverse world of the twenty-first century) *are* one by virtue *not* of their works but of the Holy Spirit's work through the means of grace (hope-filled calling, Lord, faith, baptism). From an argument of silence—Paul mentions no institutional unity tied to a particular person or place (Rome and its bishop or Wittenberg and its pastor, Johannes Bugenhagen)—the confessors in Augsburg insisted that, through the work of the Holy Spirit, they had not left the unity of the church as long as they continued to be nurtured by the true gospel and sacraments.

We Teach and Confess

My wife, a pastor of the Evangelical Lutheran Church in America, often asks new members why they joined her congregation. One time, a former member of another particularly rigid church in the area responded this way. "Why did I join this congregation, Pastor? Here, when I come to worship, I don't feel like I'm being beaten up." When we hear that church is the event of hearing the gospel preached rightly and the sacraments administered according to the gospel, we do better not to obsess over looking for a perfect, doctrinaire answer for finding the true church. Instead, we need only consider the effect the words and sacraments have on the participants. When sheep hear the Shepherd's voice, they are not beaten up but instead are comforted: picked up into the Savior's arms and carried to green pastures and streams of living water. *That* is truly church: those called who belong to the Lord and are marked by Word and sacrament.

8

WHAT HAPPENS WHEN
CHURCH LEADERS FAIL?

I was just into my second year of teaching in 1991 at the Lutheran Theological Seminary at Philadelphia when I received a call from a student on
a year-long internship in a nearby congregation. "What do I do?" she wanted
to know. "My supervisor, the pastor at this congregation, just ran off with the
church organist leaving his spouse behind, and people have been asking me
whether they need to have their children rebaptized, since he clearly was in an
adulterous relationship when he baptized their children." The "right answer"
was easy to give: "Read CA VIII to them!" But the pain of betrayal indicated
by their questions left an indelible mark on my teaching of this article.

The church first fought over the purity of its ministers in the fourth
and fifth centuries, especially in Northern Africa, where Augustine, the
bishop of Hippo, was surrounded by a group of purer Christian churches,
called Donatists after their lead bishop, Donatus. They rejected Augustine and his fellow "catholic" bishops and their congregations because in
the not-so-distant past a "catholic" bishop, suspected of handing over the
sacred books during a persecution (Latin: *traditor*, from which we get the
word *traitor*), participated in the ordinations of other bishops/pastors and
by that impurity had called into question all of the sacred actions of the
"catholics." Augustine took a far different tack. The purity and power of the
sacraments depend *not* on the minister but on God, who instituted them
and works through them—despite human weakness and sin. Putting a new
spin on Jesus's parables of the "Weeds and Wheat" (Matt 13:24–30, 36–43),

Augustine insisted that the church is a *corpus mixtum*, a mixed body of saints and sinners until the end, when God would finally sort things out and purify the church completely.

When Luther first began teaching that human beings are justified by grace through faith, some of his opponents wondered whether he was not picking up on some aspects of Donatism when he insisted that the true church was the assembly of believers and saints. In fact, nothing could have been further from Luther's mind, as CA VIII demonstrates. But the insistence on purity among a church's leaders (or even its members) found new adherents among the Puritans and later in many American forms of Christianity, where a person's (especially a parson's) own righteousness quickly became the standard by which to measure salvation and church affiliation. Indeed, many Protestant churches appear to be far more judgmental and legalistic than any of Luther's original opponents, so strong is the tendency to measure a person's relation to God by his or her own (self-) righteousness.

CA VIII

[German]

Likewise, although the Christian church is, properly speaking, nothing else than the assembly of all believers and saints, yet because in this life many false Christians, hypocrites, and even public sinners remain among the righteous, the sacraments—even though administered by unrighteous priests—are efficacious all the same. For as Christ himself indicates [Matt 23:2-3]: "The scribes and the Pharisees sit on Moses' seat...."

Condemned, therefore, are the Donatists and all others who hold a different view.

[Latin]

Although the church is, properly speaking, the assembly of saints and those who truly believe, nevertheless, because in this life many hypocrites and evil people are mixed in with them, a person may use the sacraments even when they are administered by evil people. This accords with the saying of Christ [Matt 23:2]: "The scribes and the Pharisees sit on Moses' seat...." Both the sacraments and the Word are efficacious because of the ordinance and command of Christ, even when offered by evil people.

They condemn the Donatists and others like them who have denied that the ministry of evil people may be used in the church and who have thought that the ministry of evil people is useless and ineffective.

Reflections

"Likewise, although the Christian church is, properly speaking, nothing else than the assembly of all believers [Latin: true believers] and saints, . . ." This is exactly what we heard already in CA VII, except that here the two terms (believers and saints) are put squarely together. CA IV insists that believers *are* saints, that is, are righteous, not because of what they have done but because of who God declares them to be. Thus, the confessors at Augsburg make clear in CA VIII that they will not answer the charge of Donatism by abandoning their definition of the church. Instead, they base their view of the church on the Holy Spirit's work through the Word and sacraments (CA V) to make believers righteous (CA IV). Note, too, that the church is an "assembly," what we called in chapter seven an ongoing event.

". . . [Y]et because in this life many false Christians, hypocrites, and even public sinners remain among [Latin: mixed in among] the righteous, . . ." This is simply the experience of every Christian and is why claims of holiness and righteousness are particularly demonic in Christian assemblies. This all goes back to the claim that the Christian life has a "before and after" to it, rather than a *simul*, that is, rather than insisting that (in the first of the *95 Theses*), "the *entire life* of a Christian is one of penitence." As Augustine had insisted, the church is a mixed body, a phrase alluded to in the Latin of CA VIII. As in the parable of the wheat and tares, this means that the burden of final judgment is lifted from our shoulders given that we live in a broken world. Of course, the church will have important *external* standards of behavior, to which its leaders and members must adhere, but in such cases the judgment can only occur for the sake of the "little sheep who hear the Shepherd's voice," and not as a means to enforce purity before God. And even the best external discipline will never root out sinners—not only because all are still sinners but also because many of the evilest people are also the most devious.

". . . [T]he sacraments—even though administered by unrighteous priests—are efficacious all the same." This rather long sentence now comes to its point, focusing here particularly on the sacraments, as had Augustine in his fights with the Donatists. But the German and Latin contain a delightful difference. The German version emphasizes that the sacraments are efficacious, that is, they really do what they have promised to do: make New Creatures; forgive sinners; strengthen the weak. The Latin, by contrast, states: "a person may use the sacraments." The very worry of those parishioners betrayed by their pastor's bad behavior is allayed with these words. It is fine. God is bigger than our sin, than our pastor's sin, than the sin of the whole world. In fact, as Luther says elsewhere, God spites the devil by using mortal, sinful creatures to overthrow sin and evil.[1] What blessed assurance to know that the sacraments, God's visible words of promise, cannot fail us even when others do.

"For as Christ himself indicates [Matt 23:2–3]: 'The scribes and the Pharisees sit on Moses' seat . . .'" What an interesting "proof" for the Reformers' claim! Rather than rely on a parable, which is open to a variety of interpretations, or on Augustine, they proffer Jesus's example. Jesus, who of all people could lay claim to his own purity over against all of his enemies, insisted instead that his opponents occupied legitimate offices. This had remarkable *ecumenical* implications for those early Lutherans. They could not simply dismiss the bishop of Rome or other bishops out of hand but had always to show where they strayed from the gospel, and they certainly could not set aside the offices of bishop or priest! The (especially American) addiction to walking out and founding new churches with no regard for the pastoral or episcopal office, is put to shame by Jesus himself, who had more reason than anyone to dismiss the religious officials in his day. Just before condemning them in the rest of Matthew 23, Jesus accepted their legitimate, official authority: "They sit in Moses' seat."

Latin: "Both the sacraments and the Word are efficacious because of the ordinance and command of Christ, even when offered by evil people." Here and in the next sentence we switch to the fuller Latin text. This is the first case (of several) where one text of the CA is longer than the other. I like to think of it as what happens when a new idea or expansion of an existing one pops into your head, and you think that adding certain words makes matters even clearer. The drafters were up against a deadline (25 June 1530), and one can imagine that at the very end certain comments only got into one version. Whatever else we do with the differences, we dare not play them off against one another, as if the authors were talking out of both sides of their mouths.

This sentence is revolutionary in that it expands Augustine's original answer to the Donatists regarding the sacraments to include now the Word. One of the last vestiges of a puritanical view of ministry rests with the preachers and pastors themselves, who in the pulpit sometimes worry over their own failings and weaknesses and unbelief and who go to great lengths to cover them up. But the Word's efficacy does not depend on how clever our words or how deep our faith. Instead, the Holy Spirit takes our words—despite all their weakness—and speaks the Word in the hearers' hearts. A simple example of this, common to many pastors, is when, after a particularly lifeless sermon, someone approaches the preacher after worship and exclaims, "Pastor, that's just what I needed to hear!" Despite the temptation to respond, "Well, then

---

1. See 1 John 3:20. For a translation of excerpts from Luther's 1544 sermon on the baptism of Jesus, see Gordon W. Lathrop and Timothy J. Wengert, *Christian Assembly: Marks of the Church in a Pluralistic Age* (Minneapolis: Fortress, 2004), 106–12, 153–58.

you must not have been listening," we can best thank God for using so miraculously the words of someone who is not only sinner but soon to be food for worms (or, Luther called himself, a *Madensack*—sack of maggots).

Latin: **"They condemn the Donatists and others like them who have denied that the ministry of evil people may be used in the church and who have thought that the ministry of evil people is useless and ineffective."** We know who the Donatists were, but here, as in CA V, one must ask who the "others" are. Most likely, the drafters of the CA had some actual people in mind. It could possibly be that they were trying to distance themselves somewhat from the medieval English theologian John Wycliffe or the Czech Hussites, who also emphasized the external character of the clergy.[2] Or, closer to home, they could have worried that some who rejected the Lutherans' understanding of the Lord's Supper also championed ministerial purity. A more likely target might be what the Reformers assumed the Anabaptists taught. Already in his tract *On Rebaptism* of 1528, Luther had worried about arguments against the validity of infant baptisms that rested upon the notion that because the pope was anti-Christ, all rites of the papal church were ineffective and invalid.[3] In the Large Catechism of 1529 he uses the shocking analogy that gold is still gold even if a prostitute wears it. So, too, baptism remains valid and effective, even if the officiant turned out to be in league with the devil![4]

We Teach and Confess

What is the attraction of insisting on a pure, holy clergy? It springs from the Old Creature's insistence that it alone is in charge, able to judge right from wrong, and fully capable of producing a holy life. "You shall be like gods, deciding right and wrong, good and evil." As with that couple in Eden, we want to place our certainty in ourselves and our abilities. But, in truth, our clergy and our congregations are filled with dying sinners. And there is nothing more comforting than to know that sin and death—in us or in others—do not block God's work, God's intent to declare us (sinners) what we are not (righteous) and, in the end, to make us children, "little sheep who hear the Shepherd's voice."

Nikolai Grundtvig, the renewer of the Danish Lutheran church in the nineteenth century, understood this aspect of Lutheran thought better than most. In one of his most famous hymns, "Built on a Rock, the Church Now Stands," he carefully outlines the contours of the Christian assembly. He begins by centering the Church on the Rock, Christ, and contrasting it to

---

2. The Roman Confutation mentions both. See *Sources and Contexts of the Book of Concord*, ed. Robert Kolb and James A. Nestingen (Minneapolis: Fortress, 2001), 111–12.
3. LW 40:231–34.
4. LC, Baptism, 59 (BC, 464).

the crumbling buildings that we confuse with the true church. In two verses missing from *Evangelical Lutheran Worship*, however, he underscores the foolish connection of God's presence now in last place we would expect, in those very crumbling buildings: "Now we may gather with our King; E'en in the lowliest dwelling; Praises to Him we there may bring, His wondrous mercy forth telling; Jesus His grace to us accords, Spirit and life are all His words, His truth doth hallow the temple." But then he turns to the Word and sacraments. "Here stands the font before our eyes Telling how God did receive us; Th'altar recalls Christ's sacrifice And what His table doth give us; Here sounds the word that doth proclaim Christ yesterday, today the same, Yea, and for aye our Redeemer."[5] As in many other instances, Grundtvig manages here to set a (by then) well-worn doctrine into simple poetry, both unmasking his own church leaders' inability or unwillingness to place the merciful Christ and his Word and sacraments at the center of their assemblies and leading the believers back to the gospel's comfort: "Jesus Christ, the same yesterday, today, and forever."

---

5. *The Lutheran Hymnary*, 2nd ed. (Minneapolis: Augsburg, 1935), no. 132.

9

Lutherans Are Pan-Baptists

Some people worry that infant baptism leads to all manner of evils in the church. They are only correct if the point of church is to make Pharisees, legalists, and moralists something that cannot occur if absolutely all are welcome at the font. Against such legalism and at the heart of our relation to God stands baptism: in my case, an action that I did not choose at an age when I couldn't even control my bowels, hold up my head, or think deep thoughts. A few years ago, my older brother found and sent to me a picture taken right after my baptism at the Lutheran Church in Bogota, New Jersey. My mother holding me and looking at me with such love; my eight-year-old brother playing the part of protector; my six-year-old sister holding her hands to her chest as if afraid that if she touches that little squirmy thing she'll break it. My father took the picture on 22 October 1950, with me wearing the same christening gown that my brother and sister wore along with all of our children and now grandchildren—except for the ones too chubby to fit into it or, in the case of my daughter's twins in January 2013—well, they're twins! So, yes, nostalgia, familial rite of passage, and all that jazz! But, this is what justification looks like—right before your eyes. Here is a sanctified, justified, glorified, saved little soul. When the author of 1 Peter wrote: "Baptism now saves us!" he had this very photograph in mind.

In 1521, as some began questioning infant baptism, Luther pronounced himself unsurprised. The one and only sacrament that, as he had announced in 1520, God had protected from the worst of medieval sacramental theology was now under attack. For him baptism was the central sacrament: a watery, visible sign and seal of God's promises to each and every person. By subsuming the medieval sacrament of penance under baptism (see CA XI and XII), he transformed penance into the sacrament of absolution (as he and other Lutherans love to call it) and baptism into the daily action of drowning and rising. Thus, in 1525 when the first adult believers' baptisms occurred in Zürich among erstwhile followers of Ulrich Zwingli, Luther already had in place his arguments against the practice. In 1528 at the request of some pastors, Luther published *On Rebaptism*, defending Wittenberg's commitment to what I would call "*pan*"-baptism [Greek for "all"] with arguments that also made it into the Large Catechism.[1] To be sure, Luther's contacts with Anabaptists were meager, including only the work of Balthasar Hubmeier and rumors and secondhand reports by others, but his commitment and that of his followers to this sacrament never wavered.

At issue in baptism is whether God does something for and to us there, or whether instead we are simply undertaking an act of public commitment before God (cf. CA XIII). Whenever baptism comes to us as a gift, the barriers we would put up to fence it (and God) in disappear. As a result, Lutherans (along with many other Christians) practice *pan*-baptism, that is, baptism for all people. This describes matters far more accurately than "pedo-baptism," which those who practice believers' baptism (as they call it) label it. As Jesus welcomed children, women, Gentiles, the weak, the sick and dying, so now he uses baptism to welcome us, no matter who we are or what we are like. *All* are welcome at the font!

In addition to the doctrine, there is also a political side to this article. At the imperial diet (i.e., parliament) in Speyer that met in 1529, as mentioned above, the authorities had revived an ancient imperial rescript that made rebaptism a capital offense. The Evangelicals' opponents in Augsburg, especially Johannes Eck in his *404 Articles* (see below, CA XX), simply lumped Lutherans and Anabaptists together. This made it all the more necessary for the evangelical party in Augsburg to differentiate their own position from that of Anabaptists, to show that they were law-abiding princes and subjects of the Holy Roman Empire, the political goal of the CA (cf. CA XVI).

Although in 1530 the Evangelicals were debating whether anyone should be put to death for religious reasons (Luther to some degree and Johannes Brenz to a far greater degree were against it), by 1535 Luther and Philip Melanchthon sent a memorandum to Landgrave Philip of Hesse in which they argued that blasphemy (and hence Anabaptist teaching) was a public crime punishable by death. Later, in the 1550s, the measure for blasphemous teaching became the Augsburg Confession itself. Although Lutheran princes were more reticent to exercise this "right" of capital punishment than their theologians were to defend it, these arguments resulted in executions and placed

---

1. For *On Rebaptism* (1528), see LW 40:225–62. For the similar arguments from 1529, see the Large Catechism, Holy Baptism, par. 47–63 (BC, 462–64).

a barrier between the two sides until 2010.[2] Such misuse of the CA actually should help sharpen our appreciation for its proper use: as a confession of faith in God's mercy, and it should redouble efforts to prevent this confession from being misused.

CA IX

[German]

Concerning baptism it is taught that it is necessary, that grace is offered through it, and that one should also baptize children, who through such baptism are entrusted to God and become pleasing to him.

Rejected, therefore, are the Anabaptists who teach that the baptism of children is not right.

[Latin]

Concerning baptism they teach that it is necessary for salvation, that the grace of God is offered through baptism, and that children should be baptized. They are received into the grace of God when they are offered to God through baptism.

They condemn the Anabaptists who disapprove of the baptism of children and assert that children are saved without baptism.

Reflections

"Concerning baptism it is taught that it is necessary, . . ." A single word added to the Latin ("for salvation") sometimes trips people up, since it then sounds that without baptism a person is damned. But there is another way to understand this language, helped by the omission of the word from the German text. To say baptism is necessary is to say that it *really* matters, that it is needed. This is not a matter of "take it or leave it," but a matter of utmost seriousness, especially in the face of those who seemed to question its validity for children. Indeed, the first argument in favor of pan-baptism is how much we all need baptism.

This is why some current arguments over whether baptism must always precede participation in the Lord's Supper can be so troubling. If someone were to receive the Supper before having been baptized, the response should never be, "To each, his or her own," or "Do what you like," but rather, "If you thought the Lord's Supper was cool, wait until I tell you about baptism!" Indeed, why would anyone who comes to the Lord's Table to receive "forgiveness of sins, life and salvation" not want God's gift of baptism, which is not limited to daily or weekly reception but remains with the believing sinner

---

2. See *Healing Memories: Reconciling in Christ: Report of the Lutheran–Mennonite International Study Commission* (Geneva: Lutheran World Federation, 2010), 42–72.

every moment of his or her life? If the person in question responded by saying, "Well, I'm not ready to make such a commitment," then the answer *has* to be: "Baptism is not so much about you doing something for God but far more about God's commitment to you, that is, what God does and will do for you."

"... [T]hat grace is offered through it, ..." Here the Latin text clears up the more ambiguous language of the German. CA IX is talking about the grace *of God*. But how do the Reformers define grace? As described above, starting in 1520 first Philip Melanchthon and then Martin Luther accepted the grammatical opinion on the matter by no less a Greek scholar than Erasmus of Rotterdam that the Greek word *charis* did not mean *gratia* (defined by medieval theologians as a "habit of love," an ontological disposition poured into the soul that made it acceptable to God), but rather that it meant *favor Dei*, God's favor or mercy. Understood in this way, baptism is not a magical rite that changes the nature of the human being as human being; instead, like every other sacrament (cf. CA XIII), it is a visible sign of God's mercy—no different from any other miracle in the Bible. God's mercy, revealed in the death and resurrection of Jesus Christ, is now poured out upon the baptized. This mercy stands at the heart of the New Testament's passive depictions of the baptism as new birth (John 3), a joining to Christ's death and resurrection (Romans 6), a dying and rising (Colossians 2–3), salvation in the ark (1 Pet 3:21–22), the disciple-making presence of the Trinity (Matthew 3 and 28), forgiveness (Acts 2), or a clothing in Christ (Gal 3:27).

That the drafters of the CA use the term "offered" hints at faith's role in the sacraments, a role that they first make clear in CA XIII, especially in an addition from 1531 that attacks the notion that sacraments are effective without faith by the mere performance of the rite (*ex opere operato*). For Lutherans, the goal of the sacrament is faith, so that however *valid* a sacrament may be, its effectiveness arises from and is received by faith alone. And yet, as CA IV and V made clear, faith is not a human work or decision but precisely the result of hearing the unconditional promise of God in Word and sacrament.

"... [A]nd that one should also baptize children, who through such baptism are entrusted to God and become pleasing to him." This forms the conclusion of the foregoing premises. Given baptism's necessity and its grace-filled character, Christians should not exclude children from this sacrament. Here the German provides a much clearer understanding of what the Evangelical confessors understand baptism to be. Baptism entrusts the baptized to God and makes them pleasing to God. To this day, this differentiates Lutherans (along with Roman Catholics, Orthodox, and Anglicans) from those who practice "believers' baptism," as they call it. Is baptism an act that we do for God or is it something God does to and for us? Again, CA XIII will investigate this question more fully for all sacraments. Believers' baptism, particularly as some churches practice it today, also implies a freedom of choice vis-à-vis

God where faith becomes a human act of the will, a position rejected in CA V and CA XVIII.

One of the striking images for baptism in the New Testament is that of being clothed with Christ. "As many as have been baptized into Christ have put on Christ," Paul writes in Galatians 3:27. This putting on Christ is reflected in the ancient practice of the baptismal gown. Through it, we enact the very thing to which Paul points. This "putting on Christ" implies that when God looks at us, God sees not us or our sin and weakness but only Christ. It puts in mind the hymn of Nicholas, count von Zinzendorf, "Jesus, Thy blood and righteousness, my beauty are, my glorious dress." But it also hearkens back to Luther's description of the "joyous exchange" between the bridegroom, Christ, and the Christian, where Christ takes on our sin and we receive his righteousness.[3]

But baptism also entrusts the baptized to God. Here another powerful biblical image comes into play: Jesus blessing the children from Mark 10. Starting in the 1530s, Lucas Cranach, Sr. and later his son, Lucas Cranach, Jr., began to produce paintings of this scene to be hung near or behind baptismal fonts in Evangelical churches. Each one shows women in sixteenth-century dress bringing their children to Jesus. The scene is touchingly chaotic, as the infants and children tug at Jesus's beard, crawl on his shoulder, clutch their dolls, and nurse at their mothers' breasts. In the corner stand some scowling old men, led by the Apostle Peter. This connection between Jesus's blessing and baptism was underscored in Luther's baptismal liturgy, which included reading this story—a practice first omitted from American Lutheran baptismal services in 1978.[4]

"Rejected, therefore, are the Anabaptists who teach that the baptism of children is not right." The German text is somewhat milder than the Latin, which reads: "They condemn the Anabaptists who disapprove of the baptism of children and assert that children are saved without baptism." First, the word "rejected" is far milder than "[our teachers] condemn." Second, in today's churches, not all of the successors to the Anabaptists teach what CA IX ascribes to them. Some congregations accept as members those baptized as children or infants; others do not. Third, the second part of the Latin text, which rejects claims that children are saved without baptism, points to the earlier arguments about necessity. It is one thing to wonder whether an unbaptized person is saved but quite another to insist that children have no need of baptism, as if we do not all participate in humanity's brokenness. As we have

---

3. See, for example, *Freedom of a Christian* (1520) in TAL 1:499–502.

4. It may still be possible to include reference to this story when introducing the baptismal rite: as Jesus blessed the children, so today Jesus takes this child into his arms, blesses and declares him or her to be God's child.

indicated, comments on necessity in CA IX address the second issue, not the first. Finally, only in the last forty years have Lutherans univocally rejected their predecessors' decision to measure public blasphemy by the CA or to use any confession of faith to justify judicial punishment against Anabaptists or others. Lutherans still reject arguments against infant baptism, but they have learned not confuse this rejection with political might. Confessing this sin of their predecessors has opened the way to far more fruitful conversations with the Mennonites and other present-day successors to the Anabaptists.

We Teach and Confess

Martin Luther concludes his hymn on the baptism of Jesus with this description of baptism: "All that the eye beholds is water as we pour it; before the eye of faith unfolds the power of Jesus' merit. For here it sees a crimson flood, to all the world brings healing: the power of his sacred blood, the love of God revealing, assuring his own pardon."[5] Baptisms of people of all ages are all foolishness when viewed through the eyes of reason. But faith sees Christ's blood and righteousness, God's love and mercy, and the Holy Spirit's holiness promising forgiveness, life, and salvation to everyone. Can you believe it?!

---

5. *Lutheran Book of Worship* (Minneapolis: Augsburg; Philadelphia: Board of Publication, 1978), no. 79.

10

"Here I Am for You!"

B ack in the 1980s in my rural Wisconsin congregation, we communed fifth graders. They were required to endure three sessions of teaching with the pastor, after which I would visit the children in their homes and talk with them about the Lord's Supper in the presence of their parents or guardians. Michelle, daughter of an oil hauler and a first-grade teacher, was a particularly bright student, who knew the answers almost before I asked them. Her parents sat on the couch in their living room proud as punch, until one question stumped her. "How do we *know* Christ is present in the Lord's Supper?" I asked. "Because Jesus promised to show up," came the immediate answer. But then the stumper: "*How* is Christ present?" Silence. "Come on, Michelle, this is important." Still silence, and her fair skin began to turn red. Her parents slumped in the cushions. "Pastor Tim, I don't know." "Right answer!" I exclaimed. "Oh, Pastor!" she sighed.

Lutherans insist absolutely that with the bread and wine Christ is truly present with his body and blood. Our certainty rests on the promise: "This is my body!" That is, "Here I am!" so that as close as the bread comes to your teeth and the wine to your lips, so close does Jesus himself come to you with his body and blood. In October 1529, when Ulrich Zwingli, the Reformer in Zürich, and Johannes Oecolampadius of Basel opposed Martin Luther face-to-face at a colloquy held at Landgrave Philip's castle in Marburg and insisted that the meal was a memorial feast at which the bread and wine at best only *signified* Christ's body and blood, much of the argument was over how to interpret Jesus's words, "This is my body." Luther, as a note to himself, wrote the Latin equivalent (*"Hoc est corpus meum"*) on the table in front of him, and later in the debate, flung the tablecloth back and announced, "Here is our text;

you have not yet taken it away from us." Of course, a person *could* interpret the word "is" in other ways; but his opponents had not proven to his satisfaction that one *must* define it as "signifies."

At the same debate, however, Zwingli pressed Luther to explain exactly *how* Christ could be present in or under or with the bread and wine, which Luther replied with the equivalent of the question, the answer which Michelle had forgotten, "Don't ask me mathematical questions!" That is, "I don't know!" It might be transubstantiation (although Luther criticized the importation of Aristotelian physics into theology and the multiplication of miracles)[1] or a host of other possibilities, but Lutherans refuse to try to explain the "how" of Christ's presence. Christ is really, truly, substantially present. God can work out the geometry.

In 1529 in his Large Catechism, Luther had already underscored Lutheran ignorance about the "how" question.

> With this Word you can strengthen your conscience and declare: "Let a hundred thousand devils, with all the fanatics, come forward and say, 'How can bread and wine be Christ's body and blood?' etc. Still I know that all the spirits and scholars put together have less wisdom than the divine Majesty has in his littlest finger. Here is Christ's word: 'Take, eat, this is my body.' 'Drink of this, all of you, this is the New Testament in my blood,' etc. Here we shall take our stand and see who dares to instruct Christ and alter what he has spoken."[2]

In other words: "I don't know." Despite later conflicts over the Lord's Supper among Lutherans,[3] they all remained stuck on Christ's remarkable promise: "Here I am!" In facing late-medieval interpretations of the Supper, they emphasize the "for you" (cf. CA XIII and XXIV). In the first instance, however, the focus is on Christ's unconditional promise to show up at his meal: "This is my body!"

---

1. This is his rather mild criticism already in the *Babylonian Captivity of the Church* from 1520 (LW 36:28–35). One has to believe that the accidents of bread remain while the substance changes before also believing that this is Christ's true body and blood. Of course, some opponents mocked the Lutheran position by labeling it "consubstantiation," but Luther and his followers rejected *any* importation of philosophical categories (in this case Aristotelian "accidents" [a thing's qualities] and substance [a thing's quiddity or essence]). Luther based his criticism in part on similar statements by medieval scholastic theologians, such as Pierre d'Ailly, who (using Occam's razor ["the simplest explanation is always best"]) defended the real presence without using the language of transubstantiation.
2. Large Catechism, Lord's Supper, par. 12, in BC, 468.
3. See Timothy J. Wengert, *A Formula for Parish Practice: Using the Formula of Concord in Congregations* (Minneapolis: Fortress Press, 2017), 104–9, 126–29.

CA X

[German]	[Latin]
Concerning the Lord's Supper it is taught that the true body and blood of Christ are truly present under the form of bread and wine in the Lord's Supper and are distributed and received there. Rejected, therefore, is also the contrary teaching.	Concerning the Lord's Supper they teach that the body and blood of Christ are truly present and are distributed to those who eat the Lord's Supper. They disapprove of those who teach otherwise.

Reflections

"Concerning the Lord's Supper it is taught that the true body and blood of Christ are truly present under the form of bread and wine in the Lord's Supper . . ." By refusing to answer the "how" question, Lutherans must resort to adjectives ("true") and adverbs ("truly") to make their case. Clearly, recent disagreement with the Swiss had left its mark on their language. Let God work out the geometry; Lutherans will stick with Jesus's promise. But, as a concession to their Roman opponents, at least the German text uses a phrase congruent to the doctrine of transubstantiation: "under the form," which, although absent from the Latin version of the CA, mimics the technical Latin phrase: "*sub specie.*" Thus, the Roman side had no trouble accepting this article. Later, in 1541 during a colloquy between the papal party and Lutherans, the papal legate, Cardinal Contarini, insisted that the Evangelicals had to confess transubstantiation, because the Lateran IV council in 1215 had defended Christ's presence using this phrase.[4] Only in the twentieth century, during the dialogues between Lutherans and Catholics, did scholars rediscover the fact that "transubstantiation," as it was first used in the twelfth century, did not so much rest upon the Aristotelian distinction of substance and accidents as it was seen to be a particularly trenchant way to reject mere symbolic interpretations of Christ's presence. Thus, today as in 1530 Lutherans and Roman Catholics are essentially agreed on the real presence of Christ with the elements of bread and wine in his meal.

Too much can be made of differences between the Latin and German versions of CA X. Both insist upon Christ's presence, but the Latin, with its "the body and blood of Christ are truly present . . . to those who eat the Lord's Supper," underscores even more sharply the Lutheran unwillingness to dabble in divine geometry. In 1543, a conflict arose among Lutherans in Eisleben about

---

4. Timothy J. Wengert, "The Day Philip Melanchthon Got Mad," *Lutheran Quarterly* 6 (1991): 419–33.

how to treat the leftover wine. Under normal circumstances, when confronted with a theological dispute, Wittenberg's theological faculty developed a single statement to help resolve such debates. In this case, however, Philip Melanchthon was in Bonn, helping to reform the archbishopric of Cologne, while Luther remained in Wittenberg. They each developed their own response, with Melanchthon worried about Christ getting trapped in the bread outside its use in the Supper and Luther worried that, if Christ were only present at the moment of reception, he would be more absent than present in his meal, lending support to the position of the Zwinglians. When shown Melanchthon's clearly different construal of the matter, Luther was forced to write a third memorandum reconciling the two: "Mr. Philip [Melanchthon] defines the sacramental action in relation to external things [*ad extram*]. . . . He does not divide that action inside itself [*intra se ipsum*] nor does he define it against itself." The result was to underscore Christ's presence within the entire action of the Supper (from the time the elements are taken to the altar until the benediction) but *not* outside its prescribed use. While some have tried to decipher the difference between the two (for example: Luther teaches a "real" presence and Melanchthon an "actual" presence), the Latin of CA X allows for both or, rather, refuses even to *imply* an answer to the "how" question.[5]

"... [Are truly present] ... and are distributed and received there." These three verbs summarize Christ's entire action in the Supper. Christ does not merely hover near the elements, but is present in the very distribution and eating. This also means that Christ's presence is a result not of our faith but of Christ's promise: "Take, eat, this is my body," where the three verbs in the Words of Institution match the CA's "are present" ("this is"), "distributed" ("take") and "received" ("eat"). The Latin text, while stated with an elegance typical of Renaissance Latin, also includes the same three elements, when it says: "truly present and are distributed to those who eat the Lord's Supper." Faith is the result of Christ's promise, not a cause. This, too, was vehemently debated between Zwingli's supporters and the Lutherans. If the meal is a sign of the Christian community and its members' faith, they argued, then only believers can participate in Christ. For Lutherans, this undermined the unconditional nature of Christ's promise and made faith into a work that validated Christ's promise.

In the 1550s, these three verbs would later be the subject of debate among Lutherans because of events in 1535 and 1540. In 1535, with both Zwingli and Oecolampadius having died in 1531, Martin Bucer, the chief Reformer in Strasbourg, who had stood with the two Swiss Reformers in Marburg, traveled to Wittenberg intent upon overcoming divisions among the Protestants on the Lord's Supper. The result was the Wittenberg Concord, in which both sides

---

5. Timothy J. Wengert, "Luther and Melanchthon on Consecrated Communion Wine (Eisleben 1542–43)," *Lutheran Quarterly* 15 (2001): 24–42, here 36; and Wengert, *A Formula for Parish Practice*, 125–36.

agreed that Christ was present *with* the bread (Latin: *cum pane*). In order to reflect this agreement (which did not completely resolve the question of the role of faith in the sacrament), Philip Melanchthon was commissioned to publish a revised version of the Augsburg Confession (later nicknamed the *Variata*) to be used in colloquies with their Roman opponents in the early 1540s. CA X was changed in the *Variata* to reflect the Wittenberg Concord, not least because Martin Bucer was one of the participants in Regensburg on the Evangelical side. It read: "Concerning the Lord's Supper, [our teachers] teach that with [*cum*] the bread and wine the Body and Blood of Christ are truly bestowed upon [*exhibeantur*] those who eat of the Lord's Supper." "With the bread and wine" clearly echoed the Wittenberg Concord. In the 1550s, however, the verb "exhibeantur" was interpreted as Melanchthon's attempt to distance himself from Luther's teaching about the real presence, since the verb could also be interpreted to mean simply "shown" (as in the English: "exhibit"). Thus, some argued that Christ appeared to be present but only in a spiritual way, not *really* (this despite the continued use of the adverb "truly" [*vere*]).[6]

"Rejected, therefore, is also the contrary teaching." The Latin reads: "They disapprove of those who teach otherwise." This mild language contrasts sharply with the much stronger rejection of the Anabaptists in the previous article. The reason was twofold. First, at the conclusion of the colloquy at Marburg, Luther and Melanchthon drew up a series of fifteen articles of faith (called the Marburg Articles), showing agreement between the Lutherans and their Swiss opponents on fourteen of fifteen articles. The fifteenth article on the Supper, despite agreements on the use of both elements and the rejection of the sacrifice of the Mass, outlined the remaining differences regarding the presence of Christ. Both sides subscribed to the articles and promised not to write against one another and to pray for one another. This very mild rejection reflected that agreement so that in the German version only the teaching and not the teachers are mentioned.

Second, the Saxon party expended much effort to get other Evangelical princes and cities to sign this confession, especially the Landgrave Philip of Hesse, who had sponsored the 1529 colloquy in the first place. But Martin Bucer had also arrived in Augsburg and was early on received warmly by Johannes Brenz, one of the CA's drafters. (Only after the Augsburg Confession had been presented, and then under pressure from Brenz and Lady Argula von Grumbach, did Melanchthon finally acquiesce and meet with Bucer in Augsburg.) In any case, this mild rejection actually paved the way for later discussions leading to the Wittenberg Concord.

---

6. For more on these debates, see Charles P. Arand, Robert Kolb, and James A. Nestingen, *The Lutheran Confessions: History and Theology of the Book of Concord* (Minneapolis: Fortress, 2012), 227–53; Wengert, *A Formula for Parish Practice*, 103–24; Gordon Jensen, *The Wittenberg Concord: Creating Space for Dialogue* (Minneapolis: Fortress, 2018).

We Teach and Confess

Nothing in the church more profoundly unites Christians and more profoundly divides them as the Lord's Supper. An initial, typically American response to this dilemma might be to insist that "It doesn't matter what you believe, as long as you're sincere" or some such thing. But that would so cheapen the deeply held convictions of our sixteenth-century brothers and sisters in the faith as to result in further divisions among the faithful. Instead, at least for Lutherans, it may be better to focus not so much on the doctrinal debates as on the deep consolation that the promise of Christ's real presence provides for us sinful mortals.

Consider the songs that have accompanied the liturgy of Holy Communion from the ancient church to this day—songs that Luther retained in his revisions for Wittenberg's worship precisely because in his opinion they were the very best parts of the service. The "Gloria in excelsis," begins with the angels' announcement to the shepherds (Luke 2), both because Christ's presence in the Supper parallels his incarnation and because "glory to God" and "peace on earth" are precisely the ways this incarnate One's sacrifice affects us all. Then comes the Nicene Creed, where, as Luther never tired of saying, we discover the heart of God and, to steal a phrase from the ancient church, the medicine of immortality: grace alone.[7] Then comes the *Sanctus*, so precious to Luther that he created his own German version of it (omitting the entry into Jerusalem and focusing instead on Isaiah's vision). But both halves of this song again underscore what is actually happening at the Table: with Isaiah we catch a glimpse of God's presence in the Temple on earth (Isaiah 6), and we cheer our lungs out in anticipation of the One who comes with the bread and wine in God's name: namely Christ, lowly and seated on a donkey (Mark 11). No wonder that Luther insisted that the elevation of the elements take place during that hymn. Next, the congregation sings the *Agnus Dei*, "Lamb of God, you take away the sin of the world, have mercy and grant us peace." This is not mere memory of a Lamb who came once upon a time but John the Baptist's remarkable proclamation from the fourth gospel (John 1 [cf. John 19]): "Behold the Lamb of God," right here, in the bread and wine. Finally, at least in Luther's rendition, comes the *Nunc dimittis*, old Simeon's song (Luke 2), intoned in a raspy old voice, as this tired prophet holds the infant Jesus in his hands. We, too, can die now in peace, because our hands have held the light of the nations and the glory of Israel, revealed under bread and wine. Once again, the incarnation comes to fulfillment for us, according to God's Word.

---

7. See Luther's "Foreword" to the *Little Prayer Book* (1522), TAL 4:167.

11

"TELLING THE TRUTH"

G erhard Forde and James Nestingen conclude their book on the Small
Catechism, *Free to Be*, with Luther's explanation of private confession—
virtually unknown to American Lutherans. They begin with the obvious question: "What has happened to private confession?" Answer: "The Old Adam
stole it from us."[1] Already in the sixteenth century, some Protestant churches
immediately did away with the practice, labeling it "non-biblical" and a remnant of "Romanism." In one instance, one of the counts of Mansfeld made fun
of Luther's retention of the rite, and John Calvin could even threaten those
who wanted to follow the Lutheran church more closely with the reinstitu-
tion of private confession. Still, the comment in *Free to Be* stands as a serious
reminder that the neglect of private confession is no gain but rather a deep
loss, precipitated by the old evil foe to rob Christians of the gospel's comfort.

Private confession, like its twin, public general confession, allows people
to hear the gospel addressed directly to their conscience. For the early Lutherans, especially according to an addition to Luther's Large Catechism, tacked
on to the second printing of 1529, confession was good news.

> Note, then, as I have often said, that confession consists of two parts.
> The first is our work and act, when I lament my sin and desire com-
> fort and restoration for my soul. The second is a work that God does,
> when he absolves me of my sins through the Word placed on the lips

---

1. Gerhard Forde and James Nestingen, *Free to Be: A Handbook to Luther's Small Catechism*
(Minneapolis: Augsburg, 1975), 199.

of another person. This is the surpassingly grand and noble thing that makes confession so wonderful and comforting.[2]

Some claim that whereas Luther was searching for a merciful God, today individuals are asking whether God exists at all. Not only is this a distortion of Luther's own spiritual struggles (which had far less to do with Luther's sinfulness than many imagine), but it also ignores the fact that many people today still struggle with guilt and shame—perhaps even more than Luther ever did. Thus, the neglect of this sacrament of absolution,[3] as the Reformers renamed it, truly has demonic overtones.

Of course, even where this sacrament remains, the devil is up to mischief. The demand to enumerate all sins and the concentration on the confession side of the equation, as well as the insistence on maintaining an Augustinian humility by doubting whether the absolution applied to the one confessing, were all parts of late-medieval piety. But during the early days of the Reformation, too, there were struggles to understand this sacrament. The most famous involved the church in Nuremberg in the 1530s, where one pastor, Andreas Osiander, objected to the general confession and absolution on the grounds both that hardened sinners might misuse forgiveness by imagining that the pronouncement of forgiveness gave them carte blanche to sin and that it undermined private confession. Veit Dietrich, a student of both Luther and Melanchthon, opposed Osiander, and the city council turned to Wittenberg's theology faculty for an official opinion. It sided with Dietrich, stating that preaching the gospel was itself always a form of general absolution and that hardened unbelievers would abuse Christian freedom in any and all cases anyway.[4] In later centuries, some Lutheran churches, heavily influenced by a certain brand of Pietism, turned confession back into a torture for souls. But even in Luther's day, private confession (what later became a perfunctory announcing for Holy Communion) was required before admitting people to the Lord's Supper, further fencing that sacrament from those who most needed its comfort.

Of course, the most terrible attack on this sacrament comes in the form of its neglect. About the only people who still demand private confession are addicts going through twelve-step programs. While the fifth step emphasizes a thorough-going examination of the sins that one's addiction has caused,

2. LC, Confession, 15 (BC, 478). See also his 1531 addition to the Small Catechism (Confession, 16 [BC, 360]): "Confession consists of two parts. One is that we confess our sins. The other is that we receive the absolution, that is, forgiveness, from the confessor as from God himself and by no means doubt but firmly believe that our sins are thereby forgiven before God in heaven."
3. For Lutheran inability to count the definitive number of sacraments, see CA XIII.
4. Ronald Rittgers, *The Reformation of the Keys: Confession, Conscience, and Authority in Sixteenth-Century Germany* (Cambridge, MA: Harvard University Press, 2004).

Lutheran pastors can still turn this toward the absolution by God without undermining the kind of reconciliation that still needs to take place in the addict's life.

CA XI

[German]	[Latin]
Concerning confession it is taught that private absolution should be retained and not abolished. However, it is not necessary to enumerate all misdeeds and sins, since it is not possible to do so. Ps 19[:12]: "But who can detect their errors?"	Concerning confession they teach that private absolution should be retained in the churches, although an enumeration of all faults in confession is not necessary. For this is impossible according to the psalm [19:12]: "But who can detect their errors?"

Reflections

"Concerning confession it is taught that private absolution should be retained and not abolished." Without directly raising the question of whether private confession and forgiveness should be seen as a sacrament, the drafters of the CA carefully place this article within the discussion of sacraments (CA IX–XIII), thus implying that it is a sacrament. Notice that the word they use to describe it is *not* confession (as was typical) but absolution, because (quoting Pastor Franklin Drews Fry) there is nothing absolute in life save the absolution. Indeed, that is the central thing, so that even people who had no particular sins to confess were urged in Luther's Small Catechism to confess generally so that they, too, could hear the absolution.

"However, it is not necessary to enumerate all misdeeds and sins, since it is impossible to do so." As much as the CA attempts to ameliorate differences between the two sides in Augsburg, here is one place where they insist upon emphasizing one of the central differences. The drafters knew from experience just how burdensome it had become for people to try to recall *all* their "mortal sins" (i.e., sins committed intentionally against God's commands). The confessional had become an instrument of torture, and the central point of the sacrament, namely absolution, had become completely obscured. Underneath this outward difference, however, lurked a far more profound issue: that the sacrament does not move a person from a state of sin into a state of grace but rather that one remains a sinner, to be sure a justified sinner, but a sinner nonetheless. We are *simul iustus et peccator*, at the same time a righteous person and a sinner. This claim, first made by Luther in his 1515–1516 lectures on Romans and often repeated by him and others (including Philip Melanchthon), strikingly resembles the twelve-step programs' insistence that one does not somehow graduate from being an addict—one may be a recovering addict, to be sure, but still an addict. Thus, the key to proper confession for Lutherans is to confess that one is a sinner and, at the same time, to hear the absolution and believe that it truly applies to the one confessing and makes them righteous.

In his Small Catechism, Luther stresses the importance of confessing those sins that truly are bothering a person's conscience. *That*, not a complete confession, is the point, because again it focuses on the absolution and on comfort for the sinner, not the sinner's "good work" of making a rigorous confession. By setting aside this requirement, the Reformers took aim at one of the most persistent pastoral problems in the late Middle Ages: *scrupulositas* (scruples). As we know from the *Table Talk*,[5] this was one of Luther's difficulties in private confession as a monk. Lifting the burden of such rigor helps all sensitive souls focus on what really matters: "I believe in the forgiveness of sins" (and not in my ability to recount them).

"Ps 19[:12]: 'But who can detect their errors?'" This is only the fifth (Latin: sixth) Bible passage cited in the first half of the CA. Like the others, it should not be construed as mere proof texting but rather as a reference to the much longer arguments using this text that we find in the Reformers' works (and which their opponents knew only too well).[6] In this case, Luther was expounding on this text in 1530, during his stay in the Castle Coburg, where he made clear how this text proved that believers are both righteous and sinners.[7] The use of this text in this manner also reveals an important part of Wittenberg's biblical interpretation, in which the speaker of the Psalms is not simply Christ (as the French humanist, Jacques Lefèvre d'Étaples insisted, echoing medieval and patristic sources) but included what James Samuel Preus's study of Luther's first lectures on the Psalms called "the faithful synagogue."[8] Although Luther never abandoned a christological reading of the Psalms, he also read them as pleas for mercy from believers. This allowed him to place the Psalms in the mouths of those in need, those in despair, those who exult, and those who trust. As he wrote in the introduction to the Psalms for his translation of the Bible:

---

5. Martin Luther, *Table Talk* (Spring 1533), LW 54:94–95 (no. 518).
6. The index to LW 1–54 (LW 55:374) lists thirty citations. See, for example, *Sermon on the Sacrament of Penance* (1519), TAL 1:199 and, for Philip Melanchthon, see his discussion of the power of the law in *Commonplaces: Loci Communes 1521*, trans. Christian Preus (St. Louis: Concordia, 2014), 104–5.
7. Martin Luther, *Die ersten 25 Psalmen auf der Koburg ausgelegt* (1530) in WA 31/1:344: "But it is beautiful to know that the righteous are still sinners."
8. James Samuel Preus, *From Shadow to Promise: Old Testament Interpretation from Augustine to the Young Luther* (Cambridge, MA: Harvard University Press, 1969).

The human heart is like a ship on a wild sea, driven by storm winds from the four corners of the world. Here it is struck with fear and worry about coming disaster; there comes grief and sorrow because of present evil. Here it floats on hope and anticipated good fortune; there blows confidence and joy in present blessings. . . . What is the greatest thing in the Psalter but this earnest speaking amid such storm winds of every kind?[9]

We Teach and Confess

As this new approach to the Sacrament of Absolution developed, the Wittenberg congregation experimented with various forms for the conversation between the confessor and the penitent. The one that Luther included in the 1531 edition of the Small Catechism became the standard, but before that several different forms were used. One in particular reflects Wittenberg's approach to private confession with striking language. For one thing, the one confessing actually demands absolution from the confessor. "I therefore ask that you, in God's stead would declare unto me my sins forgiven and comfort me with the word of God."[10] For another thing, since most confession occurred before the reception of Holy Communion, this early service included this exchange: "Why do you desire to receive the sacrament [of the Altar]? *Answer:* Because I desire to strengthen my soul with God's Word and sign and to obtain grace. But have you not found forgiveness of sins by absolution? *Answer:* So what! I want to add the sign of God to his Word. To receive God's Word in many ways is so much better."[11] Here the "So what?" (German: "*Was denn?*" [=*Was schadet das?* What's the harm?])[12] reveals the joyous heart of this sacrament (and of the Lord's Supper), a surfeit of God's grace and mercy, to which the believer could only respond: "The more, the merrier!"

---

9. TAL 6:209.
10. Martin Luther, "A Short Order of Confession" (1529), LW 53:117.
11. Martin Luther, "A Short Order of Confession" (1529), LW 53:118.
12. Cf. WA 30/1:345, n. 3.

12

LAW AND GOSPEL

This article gets to the very heart and initial cause of the Reformation: the sacrament of penance and the role of works in meriting forgiveness of sins. The *95 Theses* had proposed a debate over an aspect of this sacrament (indulgences), and the stormy reaction that ensued contributed to disunity in the church in the West. Medieval scholasticism had divided this sacrament into three parts: contrition (sorrow for sin out of love of God), confession (privately to a priest [cf. CA XI]), and satisfaction. Unlike the sacrament of baptism, which eliminated all of the consequences of sin (both guilt and punishment [*culpa et poena*]), the sacrament of penance, being repeatable, eliminated the guilt but only reduced the punishment from eternal punishment (the commission of mortal sins put a person in a state of mortal sin, headed for hell) to temporal punishment (according to the ancient church, seven years for every mortal sin). This punishment could then be reduced substantially or eliminated by performing the works outlined in the Sermon on the Mount: fasting, almsgiving, and prayer—and other religious activities derived from these three.[1] Whatever punishment was not satisfied before death could be satisfied afterwards in a place of purgation (purgatory), from which the purified soul then entered heaven.

Now, the church could be indulgent—either partially by causing a normal good work to satisfy far more punishment than normal or fully by offering satisfaction for the entire debt through a full or plenary indulgence. Until the fifteenth century, one received these plenary indulgences by participating in a crusade for religious reasons or visiting the tombs of the apostles in Rome

---

1. Luther refers to these three in his *Treatise on Good Works*, TAL 1:268.

(or St. James, Compostella) in a Jubilee Year (every twenty-five years starting in 1300). Then, in the 1400s believers could purchase letters of indulgence, which offered plenary satisfaction for those who financially supported a crusade or, in the case of the famous "Peter's Indulgence" of 1516 and following, supported the building of a new basilica in Rome over St. Peter's tomb. The late fifteenth century also saw an expansion of indulgences in another way, in that one could now purchase such letters for souls in purgatory. Indeed, in German-speaking lands, preachers of indulgences for the Jubilee indulgence of 1500 (offered in the following years), certainly could have agreed with Johann Tetzel's ditty: "As soon as money clinks in the chest and the cash bell rings, a soul flies out of Purgatory and sings."[2]

In the Latin *95 Theses*, which Luther sent off to Archbishop Albrecht of Mainz with a cover letter dated 31 October 1517, and even more in his March 1518 German *Sermon on Indulgences and Grace*, Luther reduced "indulgences" to their original, ecclesiastical, and pastoral purpose—a means of accepting back into the Christian community excommunicated members before their seven-year punishment for egregious, community-breaking, public sin was over (an ecclesial action completely separate from any divine consequences for sin). But Luther also began to define the sacrament of penance differently by eliminating satisfaction and works completely and concentrating instead upon God's Word of judgment and mercy. He continued to push for this reorientation of penance in his sermon on the subject published in 1519 and in the *Babylonian Captivity of the Church* from 1520.[3] In the *Loci communes theologici* of 1521, Philip Melanchthon followed suit. CA XII reflects this shift and shows the close relation between this sacrament and the Lutheran distinction between law and gospel.

Thus, this article offers the practical application of CA IV and V. Theology dare never reduce the doctrine of justification by grace through faith on account of Christ effected through the gospel to mere theory. Thus, CA XII demonstrates where believers experience justification in real life. Wherever uncertainty about one's relation to God exists, there the law and gospel work to destroy trust in ourselves by telling the truth about the human condition and to create faith in Christ as the savior of the world by telling the truth about God's unconditional mercy.

---

2. Berndt Hamm, *Ablass und Reformation: Erstaunliche Kohärenzen* (Tübingen: Mohr Siebeck, 2016), 55–62.
3. TAL 1:181–201 and 3:84–94.

CA XII

[German]   [Latin]

Concerning repentance it is taught that those who have sinned after baptism obtain forgiveness of sins whenever they come to repentance and that absolution should not be denied them by the church. Now properly speaking, true repentance is nothing else than to have contrition and sorrow, or terror about sin and yet at the same time to believe in the gospel and absolution that sin is forgiven and grace is obtained through Christ. Such faith, in turn, comforts the heart and puts it at peace. Then improvement should also follow, and a person should refrain from sins. For these should be the fruits of repentance, as John says in Matt 3 [:8]: "Bear fruit worthy of repentance."

Rejected here are those who teach that whoever has once become righteous cannot fall again.

However, also condemned are the Novatians, who denied absolution to those who had sinned after baptism.

Also rejected are those who do not teach that a person obtains forgiveness of sin through faith but through our own satisfactions.

Also rejected are those who teach that "canonical satisfactions" are necessary to pay for eternal torment or purgatory.

Concerning repentance they teach that those who have fallen after baptism can receive forgiveness of sins whenever they are brought to repentance and that the church should impart absolution to those who return to repentance. Now, properly speaking, repentance consists of two parts: one is contrition or the terrors that strike the conscience when sin is recognized; the other is faith, which is brought to life by the gospel or absolution. This faith believes that sins are forgiven on account of Christ, consoles the conscience, and liberates it from terrors. Thereupon, good works, which are the fruit of repentance, should follow.

They condemn both the Anabaptists, who deny that those who have once been justified can lose the Holy Spirit, and also those who contend that some may attain such perfection in this life that they cannot sin.

Also condemned are the Novatians who were unwilling to absolve those who had fallen and returned to repentance after baptism.

Also rejected are those who do not teach that forgiveness of sins comes through faith but command us to merit grace through our own satisfactions.

Also rejected are those who teach that canonical satisfactions are necessary to remit eternal punishment or the punishment of purgatory.

Reflections

"Concerning repentance it is taught that those who have sinned after baptism obtain forgiveness of sins whenever they come to repentance . . ." To begin with, there is an insoluble problem of translation into English here, since both the German word (*Buße*) and the Latin (*poenitentia*) have three equally good renderings in English: penance, penitence, and repentance. Thus, it would perhaps be better to translate the initial phrase, "Concerning Penance" (as in the sacrament of Penance). The Evangelicals' opponents in Augsburg read this article that way by accepting some sections of this article (where it touched on penitence) but rejecting what they viewed as a two-fold (instead of three-fold) division of [the sacrament of] penance.[4]

There is, however, a second weakness in the translation. The phrase "come to repentance" translates a phrase that literally means "whenever they are turned around [or converted; German: *bekehrt*; Latin: *convertuntur*]". While in the twenty-first century the phrase "converted" may bring to mind altar calls and conversion experiences, this was the furthest thing from the drafters' mind. This phrase may echo a sixteenth-century criticism of the Latin Vulgate and its translation of the Greek *metanoiete* in Matthew 3:2 and 4:17 that made its way into the 95 Theses. The Vulgate had translated the Greek as *poenitentiam agite* [do penance]. In the annotations on the New Testament, published in 1516 and expanded in 1519, 1522, and 1527, Erasmus of Rotterdam criticized this rendering, not only suggesting an alternative (*resipiscite*: come to your senses) but also blaming scholastic theologians for taking Augustine's comments about public discipline of sinners out of context and applying them to the sacrament of penance and private confession. In Luther's defense of the 95 Theses, the so-called *Explanation of the 95 Theses*, the Reformer reveals his dependence on Erasmus.[5] The phrase in CA XII also calls to mind the Hebrew *shuv*, which means "turn around." Perhaps most important, however, is that the verb is passive. Thus, it is not that the individual "comes" to repentance by exercising free choice but rather that God turns them around.

". . . [A]nd that absolution should not be denied them by the church." Here the CA uses the Reformers' favorite word for penance: *absolution*. Of course, one reason for including this phrase had to do with the ancient heresy of the Novatians, who withheld absolution from those who sinned after

---

4. *The Confutation of the Augsburg Confession*, art. 12, in *Sources and Contexts of the Book of Concord*, ed. Robert Kolb and James A. Nestingen (Minneapolis: Fortress, 2001), 113–14.
5. LW 31:83–85. By 1522, Erasmus began to back away from this rendering in Matt 3:2, while keeping it in Matt 4:17. The Luther Bible first renders the phrase in 1522 as "Bessert euch" [better yourselves] but by the mid-1520s already has changed back to "Tut Buße" [do penance; repent], one of many instances where the Latin translation influenced Luther's German one.

baptism. But the other reason for the Evangelicals had to do with the centrality of God's promise of forgiveness.

"Now properly speaking, true repentance is nothing else than to have contrition and sorrow, or terror about sin and yet at the same time to believe in the gospel and absolution . . ." Here the CA is picking a fight with their opponents or, rather, continuing Luther's battle with scholastic theology's insistence that the sacrament of penance had three parts. The Latin makes the point even more strongly: "Now, properly speaking, repentance [penance] consists of two parts: one is contrition or the terrors that strike the conscience when sin is recognized; the other is faith, which is brought to life by the gospel or absolution." The Latin also makes it clear that contrition is *not* a human work by defining it passively as "the terrors that strike the conscience when sin is recognized." Moreover, the Latin also avoids a perennial problem—not least of all among Lutherans—where contrition is objectified and reduced to recognition of sin. No! When sin is recognized, all hell breaks loose! Thus, both definitions describe this first part of *poenitentia* as terror, which breaks the pious notion that if one is sorry enough and sheds enough (crocodile) tears, all will be well. Terror is something that happens to individuals; it is not something they cook up on their own.

The second part of *poenitentia* is faith: "to believe in the gospel and absolution." Here "absolution" adds an important gloss to the word "gospel," so that we do not reduce the latter to information about Jesus. The German *darneben* rendered "at the same time" usually means "right next to" but is sometimes used, as here, in a temporal construct to mean simultaneously or "following on the heels of." Thus, the German text hints at the *simul iustus et peccator* (at the same time a righteous person and a sinner): God justifies sinners. The Latin passive construction again helps to underscore that faith is *not* a human work ("faith, which is brought to life"). As in CA V, the gospel is the means by which the Holy Spirit creates faith. Indeed, the sacrament of absolution (along with baptism and the Lord's Supper) is the practical, visible, and aural means through which God justifies.

". . . [T]hat sin is forgiven and grace is obtained through Christ. Such faith, in turn, comforts the heart and puts it at peace." The end of the preceding sentence in the German expresses what the Latin puts in the next sentence: "This faith believes that sins are forgiven on account of Christ, consoles the conscience, and liberates it from terrors." The point is simple: Christ obtains this forgiveness for us; we do not. Thus, these brief words recall CA IV and make clear that hearing the absolution *is* our justification before God through Christ. Most importantly, however, is the move from what the absolution *is* to what it *does*. As expressed in CA XX and in his commentary on Romans from 1532, Melanchthon even discovers this movement in St. Paul, who writes first about the nature of justification in Romans 3–4 and then expresses the effect of justification in 5:1: "Since we have been justified, we have peace with God." The law causes terror; the gospel brings comfort. This movement—from knowledge of sin to revelation of the savior, from terror to comfort, and from death of the Old Creature to the birth of the New— expresses the Reformers' true understanding of the distinction between law and gospel. These early Lutherans define the distinction of law and gospel not just on the basis of what law and gospel are (commands and promises; imperatives and indicatives) but far more based on what they do (terrify the comfortable and comfort the terrified). The drowning and rising of baptism live in the daily encounter with the law, which unmasks the human condition, and with the gospel, which reveals the heart of God's mercy in Christ. Without this experiential center, faith veers into either intellectualism or emotionalism. With the actual experience of the terrifying law and the comforting, peace-giving gospel, comes true freedom.

"Then improvement should also follow, and a person should refrain from sins. For these should be the fruits of repentance, as John says in Matt 3 [:8]: 'Bear fruit worthy of repentance.'" The structure of this article follows the argument in CA IV–VI and will receive an even more thorough treatment in CA XX. The Latin here is even clearer that good works are "the fruit of *poenitentia*" (understood as experiencing both contrition and faith [Law and Gospel]). Here the CA includes a "should" to such improving, refraining, and fruit bearing, which has two aspects. On the one hand, the necessity of fruit arises from the very nature of a good tree. One could almost say, "Good trees have no choice but to bear good fruit." On the other, the necessity also arises in the face of the believer who always remains a sinner. The gospel is not somehow a permission to sin (cf. Rom 6:1–4). Thus, as long as we are sinners, the law is there to restrain, to condemn, and to force us to do good works. In this way, good works are necessarily both free and not free: necessarily free insofar as they arise from faith; necessarily not free when they are wrung from the sinner's clenched fists.

Later Lutherans often seem to despise such teaching. Some treat believers as if they were bad trees, yelling at them to produce what, on the contrary, only comes freely and spontaneously, "from a free and merry spirit."[6] Others latch on to the description of good works as a way to import their own legalism into Christian teaching and preaching—again robbing people of the gospel's unconditional comfort. Many others simply become confused and ashamed of what appears to them to be Lutheranism's weak approach to the subject. What is always lacking with such teaching is faith in the gospel, which

---

6. Formula of Concord, Solid Declaration VI.17 (BC, 590). See the fuller discussion in Timothy J. Wengert, *A Formula for Parish Practice: Using the Formula of Concord in Congregations* (Minneapolis: Fortress Press, 2017), 90–102.

the Holy Spirit uses to make believers (good trees) capable of bearing good fruit. Moreover, quite often the preachers' lack of faith makes them blind to the actual good works that their hearers are doing all the time—good works that may also be hidden from the believers themselves ("When did we see you hungry . . . and feed you?" the sheep [who think they are goats] exclaim).

Latin: "They condemn both the Anabaptists, who deny that those who have once been justified can lose the Holy Spirit, and also those who contend that some may attain such perfection in this life that they cannot sin." This begins a series of condemnations, among the longest in the CA. The Latin gives a far fuller text and (like CA V in both versions) includes direct condemnation of "Anabaptists," a condemnation that applied to almost no one at the time. The German text does not directly connect a specific group to the teaching that someone cannot lose the Holy Spirit or can attain sinless perfection in this life. This mistaken attribution to Anabaptists in the Latin version of the CA, however, should not obscure the fact that over the ages some have indeed taught a kind of perfectionism that no longer admits to sin or the loss of the Holy Spirit. In fact, the opponents in Augsburg, by misconstruing the Evangelical definitions of contrition and faith, had even accused the Evangelicals of such a position. Thus, in part, the CA includes this condemnation to fend off any such attack. Dreams of such sinlessness haunt twenty-first-century Lutherans more than their forebears. The problem arises from a kind of circularity of thinking. To say that one can lose the Holy Spirit leads to the very uncertainty that will crush the weak and cause them to doubt God's mercy. To undermine God's promises, however, also occurs when one imagines that one can take possession of such promises in a way that has nothing to do with faith or trust and everything to do with hubris and self-centeredness.

Latin: "Also condemned are the Novatians who were unwilling to absolve those who had fallen and returned to repentance after baptism." The second group condemned here, the Novatians, were an otherwise obscure ancient heresy that obsessed over certain comments in Hebrews 10:26 and insisted that God would not allow any second chances. This notion, too, undermines God's mercy and makes it dependent upon one's own good behavior. It would not be too much of an exaggeration to say that the only ones not forgiven after baptism are those who insist that there is no forgiveness after baptism. The very legalism at the heart of this heresy is the very thing to which Jesus objects when he eats with sinners.

Latin: "Also rejected are those who do not teach that forgiveness of sins comes through faith but command us to merit grace through our own satisfactions." The third group gets directly to the heart of the original debate that sparked the Reformation: the nature of satisfaction and its relation to penance. While many of the attacks on opponents of Evangelicals in Augsburg up until this article have been more indirect, the drafters of the CA recognized that this was one place where the division between the sides was the widest. They had already laid the groundwork in CA IV, where they insisted "Christ has made satisfaction for our sin through his death." CA XII insists that God's mercy comes to us completely separate from any demand of merit on our part. No wonder that this claim garners the most complete refutation in the *Confutation*, where the authors cite all kinds of Bible passages and church fathers against this claim.[7]

Latin: *"Also rejected are those who teach that canonical satisfactions are necessary to remit eternal punishment or the punishment of purgatory."* The final condemnation, first added to the printed editions of the Augsburg Confession in 1531, again returns to the original fight over indulgences. Indeed, the CA here rejects what Luther had first pointed out in the fifth of the *95 Theses*, where he limited papal authority to lifting ecclesiastical, not divine punishments. When first examining the history of indulgences in 1517, Luther had uncovered the discrepancy between the ancient church's pastoral use of indulgence to shorten the discipline of blatant, public sinners under exigent circumstances and medieval, scholastic claims that such authority extended to God's chastisement of the Old Creature on earth and in purgatory. That the CA does not attack purgatory itself relates directly to CA IV, which states that Christ satisfies all punishment for sin. Once both our guilt and our punishment are laid at the foot of Christ's cross, the need for a place of purgation after death disappears. For all Lutherans know there may be a purgatory, but because of Christ's death it is empty!

This also helps put Lutheran usage of satisfaction language in proper perspective. That both Luther and Melanchthon speak of Christ's death making satisfaction for our sin or satisfying God's wrath against sin is for the most part unrelated to Anselm of Canterbury's satisfaction theory of the atonement—a theory that Christ as God-Man alone could satisfy God's honor, sullied because of human sin. Instead, they emphasize Christ's satisfaction over against late-medieval claims that this was humanity's responsibility. Early Evangelical theologians employed a host of images to describe the effects of Christ's death and resurrection, so that any reduction to a single explanation misses the complexities of their understanding.

---

7. This contrasts sharply to the 1999 *Joint Declaration on the Doctrine of Justification* (Grand Rapids: Eerdmans, 2000), 19, par. 25, where Catholics and Lutherans agree that *all* merit is excluded before and after justification: "We confess together that sinners are justified by faith in the saving action of God in Christ. . . . But whatever in the justified precedes or follows the free gift of faith is neither the basis of justification nor merits it." See also Ap XII.13–27 (BC, 190–91).

We Teach and Confess

She sat on her bed in Fairview Southdale Hospital, as I, a newly minted pastor, talked with her. A cancer from ten years ago had recurred, and the diagnosis was grim: she knew she was dying; and I knew; and she knew I knew. Somehow, after a lull in the conversation, she blurted out, "Pastor, I've tried to live a good life, but have I done enough?" There it was: the age-old feelings of inadequacy and the need to satisfy God with our works. At that moment in my young ministry, I suddenly realized that these old battles fought in the Reformation were not passé but the real-life experiences of people still oppressed by the law and unable to hear the gospel. "Have I done enough?" This question haunts all who have, one way or another, heard law and little or no gospel in their lives. Oppressive piety coupled with bad preaching concocts a nasty brew, extinguishing faith and making one's last days a living hell but also ruining all the days up until the last, as the need to satisfy the law extinguishes the joy of the gospel. The only antidote for such terror—and especially at the end of life—is a good dose of good news. Our God does not simply judge but forgives; does not simply bring down to Sheol but lifts up to heaven; does not simply put to death and crush the Old Creature but brings to life the New.

For Luther the distinction between law and gospel and the sacrament of absolution all spring from and return to baptism.

> Thus, we must regard Baptism and put it to use in such a way that we may draw strength and comfort from it when our sins or conscience oppress us and say: "But I am baptized! And if I have been baptized, I have the promise that I shall be saved and have eternal life, both in soul and body." . . . Here you see that Baptism, both by its power and by its signification, comprehends also the third sacrament, formerly called Penance, which is really nothing else than Baptism. What is repentance but an earnest attack on the old creature and an entering into a new life? If you live in repentance, therefore, you are walking in Baptism, which not only announces this new life but also produces, begins, and exercises it. In Baptism we are given the grace, Spirit, and strength to suppress the old creature so that the new may come forth and grow strong. Therefore Baptism remains forever. Even though someone falls from it and sins, we always have access to it so that we may again subdue the old creature.[8]

---

8. LC, Baptism, par. 44, 74–77 (BC, 462, 465–66).

13

GOD'S VISIBLE,
WORKING WORDS

N ecessity is the mother of poor similes. At least that was my experience as
a young professor when my students could not understand the distinction between *ex opere operantis* and *ex opere operato* in medieval explanations
of the sacraments. Unfortunately, I have still not figured out a better picture.
May those blessed with creativity please find one!

Once upon a time there was a queen who, people thought, was searching for just the right consort to share her love and her kingdom. Not surprisingly, her castle was filled with suitors. Now an evil sorcerer in the castle
had led them to believe that the queen was only attracted to the musky scent
of active men. As a result, the suitors divided themselves into two groups.
The one group (we can call them the *Operantis*), eager to achieve the proper
aroma, installed a treadmill in the basement of the castle and worked hard to
perspire. The other group (call them the *Operato*), noticing how exhausted
their competitors were, installed a special shower in the basement attached
to a vat of the perfect, musky perfume (so they thought). They designate
one of their lot to pull the chain as the others walked through, dousing
each with the desired odor. Only one suitor, who insisted on wearing a rain-
coat, got no benefit from the shower. Indeed, this second group could even
accommodate unconscious or dead suitors and make them acceptable to
the queen. In the end, however, neither group achieved any success, since
their approach to the queen was based upon the myth that *they* needed to
do something to make themselves acceptable to the queen. Instead, and
quite contrary to all expectations, the queen simply came off her throne

and embraced and kissed the chosen one, saying: "You're mine!" to which the completely unworthy fellow could only respond with trusting delight, "I'm yours."

In the twelfth century, Peter Lombard set about collecting the positions (*sententiae*) of the church fathers on a wide variety of theological topics into four books called the *Sentences*, which quickly became the standard textbook for medieval theology during the next four hundred years. All major theologians delivered lectures and wrote commentaries on the *Sentences*, and they accepted its basic distinctions. Lombard had noticed that in combating the Donatists in the late fourth and early fifth centuries, St. Augustine had distinguished between the Donatist claim that the sacraments were only effective when performed by virtuous, worthy people and the Catholic insistence that the sacraments mediated grace *not* based upon the work of the participants (thus *not* effective *ex opere operantis* [by the work of the one performing it]) but based instead upon the performance of the rite apart from any consideration of worthiness (*ex opere operato* [by the (mere) performance of the rite]). In the Old Testament, Lombard argued, the "sacraments" (i.e., circumcision and the animal sacrifices) were effective because of the faith and other virtues of the participants (and, hence, *ex opere operantis*). But in the New Testament a stronger grace obtained so that sacraments were effective regardless of what the officiant or the participants brought to them, that is, *ex opere operato* (by the [mere] performance of the rite). Only if one placed barriers (Latin: *obices*) in the way would one not receive the sacrament's benefits.

While the origins of this distinction helped strengthen the grace-filled nature of the sacraments, it resulted in a shift toward an almost magical understanding of grace and the sacraments, especially the Lord's Supper. The Mass could be performed on behalf of the dead souls in purgatory, and it became a commodity able to be bought and sold. The number of private Masses for such souls burgeoned, so that, for example, at the Castle Church in Wittenberg in 1518 there were over six thousand private Masses said for the souls of the ancestors of the Elector of Saxony. It is upon this backdrop that the drafters of the CA composed this article.

CA XIII

[German]	[Latin]
Concerning the use of sacraments it is taught that the sacraments are instituted not only to be signs by which people may recognize Christians outwardly, but also as signs and	Concerning the use of sacraments they teach that sacraments were instituted not only to be marks of profession among human beings but much more to be signs and testimonies of

testimonies of God's will toward us in order thereby to awaken and strengthen our faith. That is why they also require faith and are rightly used when received in faith for the strengthening of faith.

Rejected, therefore, are those who teach that the sacraments justify ex opere operato *without faith and who do not teach that this faith should be added so that the forgiveness of sin, which is obtained through faith and not through work, may be offered there.*

God's will towards us, intended to arouse and strengthen faith in those who use them. Accordingly, sacraments are to be used so that faith, which believes the promises offered and displayed through the sacraments, may increase.

Therefore they also condemn those who teach that the sacraments justify ex opere operato *and do not teach that faith, which believes that sins are forgiven, is required in the use of sacraments.*

Reflections

"**Concerning the use of sacraments it is taught that the sacraments are instituted not only to be signs by which people may recognize Christians outwardly . . .**" This article now concludes the section on the sacraments by moving from what the sacraments are (CA IX–XII) to what they do to us (CA XIII). This first phrase places the Evangelicals over against other sixteenth-century Christians, namely the Anabaptists and followers of Ulrich Zwingli. Even today, many who practice what they call "believers' baptism," insist that the sacraments are only demonstrations of faith for the world to see (in the case especially of baptism) or that they are signs of belonging to the Christian community (in the case especially of the Lord's Supper). Here, however, one must affirm with the CA that sacraments do function in this way. After all, by calling the Word and sacraments "marks of the church," Lutherans insist that sacraments are tangible, external signs of Christians in community. (The Latin even mentions "marks" [*notae*].) But that is not all they are. Otherwise, the sacraments would end up being effective by virtue of some quality that we bring to them—our commitment to Christ or our fellowship in the church—that is, *ex opere operantis* [by some work of the one participating in them]. When that is the case, the weak end up on the treadmill trying to improve and perfect their commitment to Christ and the community. In the modern American context, where faith has turned into a work we do or a commitment we undertake, the danger of the sacraments devolving into good works we do for God and community looms large.

This article also reveals an important aspect of Wittenberg's theology found in both Luther's and Melanchthon's works: the move from definition to effect. In the philosopher Aristotle's *Analytics*, he identifies ten questions that a person may pose to analyze an object, including such things as: whether a thing exists; what are its parts; what are its genus and species; and the like. For Wittenberg's Reformers, two questions were central: what a thing is (that is, its definition) and what its ultimate goal is (that is, what are its effects or uses). Here, CA IX–XII define the sacraments. CA XIII explains its effects: God gives the sacraments to embrace us, physical beings that we are, in his love and grace. Failing to ask God's intent in giving the sacraments misses their down-to-earth meaning completely.

"... [B]ut also as signs and testimonies of God's will toward us in order thereby to awaken and strengthen our faith." The CA now draws a sharp line between other Protestant Christian bodies (along with Anabaptists) and the Lutherans. The sacraments are really all about what God is doing for us, specifically what God's will is toward us. In baptism, God wills to declare us children; in the Supper, Christ wills to feed us with his body and blood for the forgiveness of sin; in absolution, the Holy Spirit continues our daily baptism by putting the Old Creature to death and raising up the New Creature of faith. At every turn, the sacraments rest unequivocally in what God has done, is doing, and will do for us and for our salvation. They embody the incarnation—God's drawing near to us so that we may draw near to God. Over and over again, we hear the sweet sounds of the savior's voice saying: "You're mine!" And faith is thereby awakened and strengthened, calling out in return, "I'm yours." Thus, this article repeats the assertion in CA V that "through these [Word and sacraments] as through means, the Holy Spirit works faith."

"That is why they also require faith and are rightly used when received in faith for the strengthening of faith." Once again, the notion of requirement will trip some readers up, so that this sentence is best read in the light of the Latin: "Accordingly, sacraments are to be used so that faith, which believes the promises offered and displayed through the sacraments, may increase." Although on a few occasions Luther claims that faith is a prerequisite and thus that sacraments may seem to be effective *ex opere operantis,* the "one working" here is not the individual recipient but precisely the Holy Spirit who uses the very sacraments to effect the faith that they demand. I suppose, continuing that rather weak example that started this chapter, one could say that receiving the queen's kiss requires puckering, not because it is a work that earns the lover's favor but rather because that's what kissing entails. Through God's gracious embrace, experienced in the sacraments, we fall in love.

"*Rejected, therefore, are those who teach that the sacraments justify* ex opere operato *without faith and who do not teach that this faith should be added so that the forgiveness of sin, which is obtained through faith and not through work, may be offered there.*" This sentence was added to the published edition of 1531 and served as a rebuke to the facile acceptance of this article by the *Confutation,* which only insisted that all seven sacraments be included here.[1] Because the sacraments only come to their true goal through faith, which is not a human work, they cannot be effective *ex opere operato* (by the [mere] performance of the rite). This results in a completely different understanding of the sacraments, so that believers have no need for private Masses (CA XXIV), while still insisting that God's grace alone gives the sacraments their true meaning.

In 1520, in the *Babylonian Captivity of the Church*, Luther frees both the Lord's Supper and baptism from any connection to an *ex opere operato*.[2] With the Lord's Supper he produces an entirely different framework for its meaning. No longer an unbloodied sacrifice that the priest performs on behalf of the living or dead, the Supper is Christ's [last will and] testament, where he promises to give himself (his body and blood) for us. Such a testament depends entirely on Christ's mercy and demands not works but faith, namely, trusting that the meal and its inheritance are truly "for us." Only unbelief, then, stands between us and this legacy of grace. If someone just refused to believe that Christ would do such a remarkable, selfless, gracious thing—rather like heirs who, because they are unworthy, just refuse to believe that an uncle's millions have been left to them—then, despite the validity of the will, unbelief blocks the way to receive the gift. But who in their right mind would do a foolish thing like that? Moreover, if they did, the solution to their unbelief could only be repeating the promise—perhaps with other words so that they might grasp it more clearly. But clearly the solution to unbelief does not rest merely in threats but in God's promised mercy.

Luther argues in a similar fashion about baptism. It is neither a virtuous work that we must do to earn God's grace (and thus effective *ex opere operantis*—by effort of the one doing the work) nor is it a kind of Christian "magic" (effective *ex opere operato*). Instead it consists of God's unconditional promise received in and creating faith, that is, trust in God's mercy. Like the Lord's Supper, it is a visible Word of God that shows us visibly (in water) what the words ("I baptize you in the name of the Father, Son, and Holy Spirit") tell us: we belong to Christ unconditionally. That is, baptism is God's way of

---

1. In Lombard's *Sentences*, he had listed seven sacraments: baptism, the Supper, penance, ordination, confirmation, extreme unction, and marriage. Already in 1520, Luther reduced the list to three (or two, if the sacrament of absolution was simply an extension of baptism). In the *Apology*, Melanchthon even imagines a way in which ordination can be defined as a sacrament. In the sixteenth century, no one understood the connection between confirmation and baptism in the ancient church (something first recovered in the twentieth century). Because marriage was a universal practice among all societies and had nothing directly to do with forgiveness of sins (being based upon a misreading of Eph 5:32), Lutherans never considered this a sacrament. Last rites were not among the actions that Christ commanded the church to do.
2. TAL 3:38–84.

revealing that God chooses to adopt us as sons and daughters, just as God announced at Jesus's baptism: "This is my beloved Son."

We Teach and Confess

Baptism seems like such a risky affair. You bring a child or adult to the font in front of the congregation and, no matter how much or how little water the baptizer uses, the action proclaims that this one—like the children whom Jesus blessed in Mark 10—belongs in God's embrace. "What are the chances," we wonder, "that this one will fall in love with the savior?" But Jesus was taking the same risk blessing those children! As Luther wrote: "All that the eye beholds is water as we pour it; before the eye of faith unfolds the power of Jesus' merit."[3]

The Lord's Supper seems so foolish: a morsel of bread and a sip of wine and it's over. Yet here, too, the action proclaims that Christ is truly present with his body and blood for the forgiveness of sins. "How is Christ present?" Luther and later Lutherans were asked. "Don't ask mathematical questions," Luther replied. The whole point rests upon the foolish announcement by Christ: "Take, eat, this is my Body. Drink of it, all of you, this is my blood of the New Testament."

And the sacrament of absolution? There, too, we see a weak, mortal sinner offering to an entire congregation of sinners the unconditional mercy of God in Christ: "You are forgiven!" And once again the voice of our souls' true love rings in our ears. The one whom the heavens cannot contain stoops to us and offers forgiveness, life, and salvation.

All three sacraments deliver God's unconditional promise of forgiveness, life, and salvation. There is no better news for the sinner, for the dying, or for the lost. As Philip Melanchthon had on his lips at the end of his life: "If God is for us, who can be against us?"

---

3. *Lutheran Book of Worship* (Philadelphia: Board of Publication; Minneapolis: Augsburg, 1978), no. 79.

14

Going Public with the Gospel

He or she does not look like much, standing up there on a Sunday morning: just another example of a mortal, sinful being from that group we call humanity. True, the pastor may wear fancy robes and assume a pulpit tone when preaching or may dress down and assume a folksy style. But he or she will eventually age like the rest of us, commit sins against God and the neighbor, and (perhaps worst of all) occasionally bore us to death in the sermon. That is the topic in CA XIV.

In January 1545, during a sermon on the baptism of Jesus, Luther reflected on the pastoral office as God's foolish instrument to spite the devil.

> Now, this proud spirit [the devil] is angered by the fact that he has to put up with the fact that I, a poor human being, condemn him, do you hear? "Devil, leave my soul in peace, for Christ has redeemed it." But whoever could believe that anyone has such authority, wouldn't he or she be just as happy to die as live? After all, what are you and I compared to this glorious power? We are mortal. There sit in the grave snakes and bugs and worms waiting to devour us—we are no better than that. And before that time there are lice, ticks, and fleas, which would love to find a host long before we may want to die. So what do we have in which to boast? Nevertheless, God shall with such a tongue and hand—soon to be the food for maggots—prove to spite the devil, so that they may trample him underfoot. No prophet, no apostle, is better than we are. Don't you think that makes the devil angry? It's not enough that a stinking hand does such a great work and had such a heavenly authority, but it is also sinful—in fact, the heart is full of sin and evil thoughts. Yet, it

shall humble that proud spirit, the devil! That one of God's own seeds, which he planted and brought forth from nature, should also be the one to restrain [the devil]! So God comes and says, "I am going to baptize with [such a creature], bathe, preach, and that one shall be my glory." Is it not a terrible shame when we do not preach the miraculous works of God but human traditions? And we who do preach or listen—should we not also believe, rejoice, thank God, and meditate on this?[1]

CA XIV

[German]

Concerning church government it is taught that no one should publicly teach, preach, or administer the sacraments without a proper call.

[Latin]

Concerning church order they teach that no one should teach publicly in the church or administer the sacraments unless properly called.

Reflections

Although this article is by far the shortest in the CA, it has engendered several controversies, as people wedded to later Lutheran positions try to glean support from the CA for their views of the public ministry. Some misapply the common priesthood shared by all believers to argue for the necessity of democratic governance in the church. Others insist that the Latin *rite vocatus*, translated here "properly called," could (because of the alternative meaning of *rite*) be translated "ritually called," thus supporting the necessity of ordination. As a result, we often find democratic authorization for the public ministry fighting against more hierarchically shaped views. While these debates are important, they regularly leave poor little CA XIV in the dust, struggling to make a much narrower point: that the church requires a regularly called public ministry.

"Concerning church government..." The Latin, which has "church order," carries the same general meaning. In the German of the sixteenth century, the word *Regiment* (=government) had the sense of the entire working order of a social entity, and in Latin the phrase *ordo ecclesiastica* makes the German even clearer: this is how things are organized in the church. What this phrase does not do is indicate biblical precedent for this position. Thus, the *Confutation*, while accepting CA XIV, assumes that it implies support for "canonical ordination," that is, ordination by bishops in communion with Rome. In the Ap XIV,

---

1. For a more thorough discussion and translation of this sermon, see Gordon Lathrop and Timothy J. Wengert, *Christian Assembly: Marks of the Church in a Pluralistic Age* (Minneapolis: Fortress, 2004), 106–12, 153–58.

Melanchthon realizes that the real problem revolves around not *whether* there is order in the church but whence that order's authority arises.

> Concerning this subject we have frequently testified in the assembly [i.e., at the Diet] that it is our greatest desire to retain the order of the church and the various ranks in the church—even though they were established by human authority. We know that church discipline in the manner described by the ancient canons was instituted by the Fathers for a good and useful purpose. However, the bishops compel our priests either to reject and to condemn the kind of doctrine that we have confessed, or by new and unheard cruelty they kill the unfortunate and innocent people. This prevents our priests from acknowledging such bishops. Thus the cruelty of the bishops is the reason for the abolition of canonical order in some places despite our earnest desire to retain it. Let the bishops ask themselves how they will give an answer to God for breaking up the church.[2]

This argument recurs in CA XXVIII, which discusses the office of bishop far more extensively. Thus, behind CA XIV lurks the insistence that the church's actual, visible order comes from human authority. God insists that there *must be* order as an antidote to the chaos engendered by human sin, but human beings are the ones who give that order its outward shape. This allows the Reformers to criticize church order while at the same time insisting that it is irreplaceable.

"... [I]t is taught that no one should publicly teach, preach, or administer the sacraments ..." The Latin subsumes the "teach and preach" of the German into a broader understanding of the word "teach." The German thus identifies three different activities related to the public ministry: teaching, preaching, and administering the sacraments. Many today are unaware that the late-medieval church in the Holy Roman Empire distinguished two separate callings in the church. The pastor (German: *Pfarrherr*, literally, lord of the parish) was responsible for all parish life and preached and presided at the sacraments. The preacher (German: *Prediger*), for whose financial support some cities even established separate foundations, had the narrower responsibility of preaching. There were, of course, other important offices: deacons (although this was often understood as simply a stepping-stone to full ordination as a priest), schoolteachers, university professors, and custodians of church property, to name a few. In direct relation to the gospel (cf. CA V), CA XIV mentions three: teacher, preacher, and presider at the sacraments.

As Heinz Scheible pointed out forty years ago, this article clears up the anachronistic and confusing language used by Melanchthon researchers, who

---

2. Ap XIV.1–2 (BC, 222).

label him a "lay theologian."[3] From 1527 he and Luther held extraordinary positions at the University of Wittenberg, which allowed them to teach whatever they wished (in Melanchthon's case in both the arts and the theology faculties). Melanchthon's entire theological existence arose out of a proper, public call. While in 1518 he arrived at Wittenberg with license to teach in the arts faculty as a Greek professor, in 1519 he received the first theological degree, the bachelor of Bible, which gave him leave to lecture on the Bible, which he did until his death in 1560 (with a minor interruption from 1523–1525 during which time, as rector of the university, he reformed the arts faculty's curriculum). To use the word "lay" in this setting imposes a late-medieval distinction between clergy and laity that the Reformation actually opposed.

"... **without a proper call** ..." One manuscript of the CA misread the word proper [*ordentlich*] as public [*offentlich*], accidentally reemphasizing the public nature of such calls. Here the drafters were objecting to those self-appointed Christian leaders who thought that the only call they needed to lead a Christian community came directly from God. This delusion affects many Christian groups today, where an alleged internal call of the Holy Spirit trumps any basis for accountability to the wider Christian church.[4] In contrast, early Lutherans consistently insisted upon oversight and proper public assessment of candidates for ministry. When asked how he could criticize the church of his day, Luther often referred to his own call as *doctor ecclesiae* (teacher of the church). Most of his colleagues had also been properly examined, called and ordained within the existing structures of the late-medieval church. Only in the 1530s, when relations with the bishops of the empire were on the verge of complete collapse, did the Wittenberg church begin regularly to perform its own ordinations. But even here, the ordinations themselves were most often done by the general superintendent of Saxony, Johannes Bugenhagen (Wittenberg's chief pastor), or, in his absence, by Martin Luther and involved strict examination of the candidates. Even when Luther ordained Georg von Anhalt as bishop of the diocese of Merseburg, this was done only as a last resort, after the bishop of Brandenburg (who was supportive of Evangelicals) died and the archbishop of Cologne, Hermann von Wied, lived too far away to participate.[5]

---

3. Erwin Iserloh, ed., *Confessio Augustana und Confutatio: Der Augsburger Reichstag 1530 und die Einheit der Kirche* (Aschendorff: Aschendorff Verlag, 1980), which records an exchange between Scheible and George Lindbeck.

4. Even within the Evangelical Lutheran Church in America some candidacy committees completely overemphasize an "internal call," forcing candidates to look inside themselves to manufacture the proper, "spiritual" feelings. Indeed, such an obsession is truly *en-thusiasmus*, a worshiping of the god within, and leads to the denigration of the church's responsibility as God's instrument to call candidates to public ministry in actuality.

5. See Timothy J. Wengert, "Certificate of Ordination (1545) for George von Anhalt, Coadjutor Bishop of Merseburg," *Lutheran Quarterly*, n. s., 16 (2002): 229–33.

The phrase "proper call" in German matches the Latin *rite vocatus*. Here Philip Melanchthon's own consistent usage of the Latin adverb, *rite*, as "properly" (as opposed to "ritually") should be enough to call into question later interpretations that tried to smuggle in an approval of a specific rite of ordination into this article. But the German here, *ordentlich*, also undermines a ritualistic interpretation of the phrase. This, however, is not to say that early Lutherans rejected ordination or its importance—their later behavior undermines that interpretation completely! Instead, it underscores that the question of ordination per se—first raised in the *Confutation*—was not initially at stake here.

In Ap XIII Melanchthon indirectly provides clarification for why CA XIV avoided talking about ordination. When commenting on the number of sacraments there, Melanchthon goes through the list of the Roman church's seven sacraments, providing arguments for why the Evangelicals accept or reject certain ones. Lutherans and Roman Catholics agreed that baptism, the Lord's Supper, and absolution were sacraments. Marriage, being a rite practiced outside the church and not directly connected to God's mercy in Christ, could not, according to the Apology, be a sacrament. Extreme unction and confirmation were both seen as lacking Christ's institution, and, although the latter quickly became a part of Lutheran practice (following the church in Strasbourg), neither was deemed a candidate for sacraments as Lutherans defined them.[6] But ordination, which clearly had scriptural sanction, posed another kind of problem: the purpose of ordination in the late-medieval church was chiefly to set aside people to say Masses, especially for the dead. In finding a place for ordination as a sacrament, Melanchthon argued this way:

> The opponents do not consider the priesthood as a ministry of the Word and of the sacraments administered to others. Instead, they consider it as a sacrificial office, as if there ought to be in the New Testament a priesthood, similar to the Levitical priesthood, which offers sacrifices for the people and merits the forgiveness of sins for other people. We teach that the sacrificial death of Christ on the cross was sufficient for the sins of the entire world and that there is no need for additional sacrifices, as though Christ's sacrifice was not sufficient for our sins. Therefore, human beings are justified not on account of any other sacrifice except the one sacrifice of Christ when they believe that they have been redeemed by that sacrifice. Thus priests are not called to offer sacrifices for the people as in Old Testament law so that through them they might merit the forgiveness of sins for the people; instead they are called to preach the gospel

---

6. Cf. Ap XIII.3 (BC, 219): "If we define the sacraments as rites, which have the command of God and to which the promise of grace has been added, it is easy to determine what the sacraments are, properly speaking."

and administer the sacraments to the people. We do not have another priesthood like the Levitical priesthood—as the epistle to the Hebrews [7–9] more than sufficiently teaches. But if ordination is understood with reference to the ministry of the Word, we have no objection to calling ordination a sacrament. For the ministry of the Word has the command of God and has magnificent promises like Romans 1[:16], the gospel "is the power of God for salvation to everyone who has faith." Likewise, Isaiah 55[:11], "so shall my word be that goes out from my mouth; it shall not return to me empty, but it shall accomplish that which I purpose. . . ." If ordination is understood in this way, we will not object to calling the laying on of hands a sacrament. For the church has the mandate to appoint ministers, which ought to please us greatly because we know that God approves this ministry and is present in it. Indeed, it is worthwhile to extol the ministry of the Word with every possible kind of praise against fanatics who imagine that the Holy Spirit is not given through the Word but is given on account of certain preparations of their own, for example, if they sit idle and silent in dark places while waiting for illumination—as the "Enthusiasts" formerly taught and the Anabaptists now teach.[7]

These arguments help clarify why CA XIV comes right *after* a discussion of the sacraments, namely, because Lutherans objected to their opponents' understanding of the priesthood and, thus, of ordination. Only when the priesthood abandons sacrificial presumptions and returns to its God-ordained goal—namely, serving the Christian assembly with God's aural and visible Word—could the laying on of hands once again take its rightful place among the sacraments. Until then, CA XIV could only address the "abuse" of *"Enthusiasten"* (where here again the mention of Anabaptists does not reflect their later position), that is, people who had reduced Christianity to the inward feelings of movements of the Holy Spirit without paying any attention to the external means of grace and the good order of the church. CA V, with its explicit mention of the *Predigtamt* (preaching office), had already linked the public ministry directly to the proclamation of the gospel and the proper administration of the sacraments. Here, too, as in the other articles, the gospel itself and its effect in the life of faith for individuals and in the Christian assembly provide the basis for the CA's understanding of public ministry.

We Teach and Confess

In April 1530, as the Saxon party was slowly wending its way south, leaving Luther at the Coburg Castle, Luther was in the process of composing a

---

7. Ap XIII.7–12 (BC, 220–21).

"mirror for princes" based upon his interpretation of Psalm 82. In it he identified three virtues of the good Christian prince: peacemaking, care for the poor by establishing just laws, and support of the pastor. In a country like the United States, this final support falls to members of congregations. But Luther's glowing description of the public office of ministry helps to focus CA XIV on what really matters: God's way of creating a new world. Contrasting the construction of glittering buildings to such care, he wrote:

> Even if a king could build a church of pure gold, or of emeralds and rubies, what would all these great and glorious things count for, compared with one true, pious, God-fearing pastor or preacher? He can help many thousands of souls, both in eternal life and in this life. . . . But who is such a prince? And where are the eyes that can see this virtue in a lord or prince? To support or protect a poor, pious pastor is an act that makes no show and looks like a small thing. But to build a marble church, to give it golden ornaments, and to serve dead stone and wood—that makes a show that glitters! That is a virtue of a king or prince! Well, let it make its show! Let it glitter! Meanwhile my pastor, who does not glitter, is practicing the virtue that increases God's kingdom, fills heaven with saints, plunders hell, robs the devil, wards off death, represses sin, instructs and comforts all people in the world according to their station in life, preserves peace and unity, raises fine young folk, and plants all kinds of virtue in people. In a word, he is making a new world! He builds not a poor, temporary house, but an eternal and beautiful Paradise, in which God Himself is glad to dwell. A pious prince or lord who supports or protects such a pastor can have a part in all this. Indeed, this whole work and all the fruits of it are his, as though he had done it all himself, because without his protection and support the pastor could not abide.[8]

In this encomium to the pastoral office, Luther (like CA XIV) cuts the Gordian knot of the "democratic" or "hierarchical" construal of pastoral authority. What gives the pastoral offices authority lies precisely in God's intention to create a new world through preaching, baptizing, presiding at the Lord's Supper, forgiving sin, and teaching. The authority of the pastoral office does not stem from the ways that the Christian assembly places a person in the office but in the divinely sanctioned office itself and its proper exercise. Questions of the essential or functional nature of that office's authority finally miss the point of this glorious calling.

---

8. LW 13:52–53.

15

"ORDER IN THE CHURCH!"

The story is told of an isolated Scottish Presbyterian congregation, where the new minister noticed that when the churchgoers filed out of their medieval building, they would first bow slightly in the direction of a whitewashed wall before greeting him at the door. Only when renovations removed centuries of whitewash, did the surprised congregants and their pastor discover underneath the blank wall remnants of a fifteenth-century fresco depicting Mary and the baby Jesus. Old traditions die hard! But, despite vociferous (Protestant) denials, which imagine a return to the purity of a tradition-less, first-century Christianity, traditions are part and parcel of the Christian church's life.

In fact, as much as Word and sacraments may define the assembly of all believers and saints and their true unity, the church consists of many more things. Each congregation, to say nothing of each larger church body, develops traditions for worship, for special celebrations, and for organizing its life. Indeed, CA VII had already mentioned such matters, but did not go very far in defining them. The CA's ecclesiology thus encompasses three articles: VII, VIII, *and* XV. In placing this article here, the CA encloses its discussion of sacraments (including ordination) within its description of the church. This spells out the Lutheran definition of church in distinction to both the Reformed and the Roman Catholic traditions. Missing are any direct references to the bishop of Rome and that church's so-called "universal" traditions, something the *Confutation* immediately notes. Missing also are any claims of universal *biblical* traditions, such as church discipline, as one may find in the confessions of some Reformed churches.[1] Instead, the CA defines anything outside of the Word and sacraments (CA I–XIV) in terms of human traditions. But rather than sanction those traditions by invoking a single authoritative source (the pope or the Bible), the CA judges human traditions on the basis of their service to the church and their concomitant support of its message: justification by grace through faith on account of Christ (CA IV).

CA XV

[German]

Concerning church regulations made by human beings, it is taught to keep those that may be kept without sin and that serve to maintain peace and good order in the church, such as specific celebrations, festivals, etc. However, people are also instructed not to burden consciences with them as if such things were necessary for salvation. Moreover, it is taught that all rules and traditions made by human beings for the purpose of appeasing God and of earning grace are contrary to the gospel and the teaching concerning faith in Christ. That is why monastic vows and other traditions concerning distinctions of foods, days and the like, through which people imagine they can earn grace and make satisfaction for sin, are good for nothing and contrary to the gospel.

[Latin]

Concerning church rites they teach that those rites should be observed that can be observed without sin and that contribute to peace and good order in the church, for example, certain holy days, festivals, and the like.

However, people are reminded not to burden consciences, as if such worship were necessary for salvation.

They are also reminded that human traditions that are instituted to win God's favor, merit grace, and make satisfaction for sins are opposed to the gospel and the teaching of faith. That is why vows and traditions concerning foods and days, etc., instituted to merit grace and make satisfaction for sins, are useless and contrary to the gospel.

Reflections

"Concerning church regulations made by human beings . . ." Differences between the German and Latin shed light on two matters. First, by adding the phrase "made by human beings" this article explicitly excludes those

---

1. For example, the Belgic Confession of 1561 includes church discipline among the marks of the church. See Philip Schaff, ed., *Creeds of Christendom*, vol. 3: *The Evangelical Protestant Creeds*, 4th ed. (Reprint: Grand Rapids: Baker, 1977), 419.

divine regulations discussed above, namely the Word, sacraments, and public ministry (CA I–XIV). This point aroused the suspicion of their Roman opponents in Augsburg, who in the *Confutation* distinguished universal from particular rites, where the latter arose from the God-given order of the Roman church. Second, the German regulations (*Ordnungen*) is translated in the Latin with *ritibus* (here: rites) and serves as another indication that the phrase in CA XIV (*rite vocatus*) has to do with good order and not with particular religious rituals.

"... [I]t is taught to keep those that may be kept without sin and that serve to maintain peace and good order in the church, such as specific celebrations, festivals, etc." Here the drafters offer a single, clear criterion by which to measure all church regulations: their effect in the assembly of believers. That effect has three aspects. The first aspect asks whether a regulation fosters sin. Here the German translation of the Apology by Justus Jonas helps clarify what Melanchthon meant. At the end of Ap XV, Melanchthon refers to these ordinances with the Greek term *adiaphora*, which Jonas translates paraphrastically as "customs that can be kept without sin or burden to the conscience."[2] This implies that the phrase "kept without sin" refers precisely to *adiaphora*, what in Latin are called *indifferentia*, undifferentiated matters that are neither right nor wrong on their face. These Latin and Greek terms from Stoic philosophy often appear in the ethical discussions of the Reformers. Their insistence that such a category of human rules exists contrasted with such thinkers as Thomas Aquinas, who, while admitting the existence of the category of *thought*, argued that *in reality* there were no such actual cases, since the church itself by its decrees determined right and wrong. Already in the *Invocavit Sermons* delivered in March 1522, Luther insisted upon judging a broad area of church life not simply by right or wrong but by love for the neighbor and by the need for peace in the Christian assembly. Although Luther never uses the Greek term (*adiaphora*), he does occasionally use the Latin (*indifferentia*) and the German equivalent (*Mitteldinge*), although in some cases later clashes over *adiaphora* after Luther's death may have influenced how the *Table Talk* recorded Luther's statements.[3] In any case, the point here is to underscore that the discussion is about human ordinances that are not a matter of life or death, good or evil.

The other two aspects about such regulations concern peace and good order. These specifically encompass what one might call an ecclesiastical "first

---

2. Ap XV.52, n. 405 (BC, 230).
3. For a discussion of this, see Timothy J. Wengert, *A Formula for Parish Practice: Using the Formula of Concord in Congregations* (Minneapolis: Fortress Press, 2017), chapter 10. The Latin *indifferentia* is often mistakenly translated "indifferent," which in modern English means "things that do not matter," whereas the Latin means instead non- (*in-*) differentiated (*differentia*): serious matters where one cannot determine whether they are right or wrong.

use" of the law.[4] All three aspects of a regulation's effect are not ideals (i.e., *perfect* peace and *the very best* order). Instead they are practical, down-to-earth measures that any Christian community can apply easily to their current situation. Here, in matters regarding human regulations, human reason is called upon to determine what the best action may be. First, is this a matter that does not directly violate God's will? Does it maintain or establish peace? Does it help the community order its life in a good way? These simple questions avoid some of the worst excuses to break the church's unity rampant among Christians today: "Because I lost the vote . . ." or "Because my feelings were hurt . . ." or "Because I did not get what I wanted. . . ." Regulations will always be less than perfect, and less-than-perfect human beings with flawed human reason will always administer them. But these simple goals help keep things in perspective and serve the Christian community.

The examples of such ceremonies given here barely scratch the surface. In fact, this article sets up the lengthier arguments in CA XXVI and XXVII regarding fasting and monastic vows, as the conclusion of this article already hints at. Clearly the language in the first part of this sentence is far broader than simply the celebration of certain festivals in the church, but at this stage the CA is defining its arguments as narrowly as possible. Not surprisingly, the *Confutation* more or less accepts this part of CA XV.

"However, people are also instructed not to burden consciences with them as if such things were necessary for salvation." Having begun with a positive assessment of regulations, CA XV can now concentrate on two limits to such regulations, both of which arise directly out of CA IV and justification by grace through faith on account of Christ. Indeed, this discussion shows how closely the central articles on justification (CA II–VI, especially IV–V) inform all of the other articles in the CA. The "burdening of consciences" is directly related to the proper effect of justification, namely (Rom 5:1), "peace with God." To burden the conscience is the very opposite of the gospel of forgiveness, life, and salvation as the Reformers experienced it. Of course, their opponents at this point possessed long lists of things necessary for salvation, as Melanchthon points out in the Apology.

Imagining that this stricture only applies to late-medieval abuses sells it short. This problem goes deep into human creature's lack of fear of and faith in God (CA II) and its resultant destruction of justification by faith (alone!) with the human desire to "obtain righteousness" through its works. The result of such bad preaching and teaching (the "people" who "are instructed" are specifically Evangelical teachers)—in any corner of the Christian church—results in the worst possible result: the burdening of consciences. Here there is

---

4. Lutherans defined the so-called *usus civilis* or first [civil] use of the law as the way God works in this world to maintain order and restrain evil. A *usus ecclesiasticus* would have the same effect in the church.

no compromise possible, no mixing of faith and works in determining one's standing before God, because such confusion *always* burdens the weak (and makes the strong proud of their accomplishments).

"Moreover, it is taught that all rules and traditions made by human beings for the purpose of appeasing God and of earning grace are contrary to the gospel and the teaching concerning faith in Christ." The second limitation has to do with the intention of "*all* rules and traditions." The Reformers judged late-medieval piety in terms of its intent. Indeed, a better translation of "for the purpose of" would be "with the intention of." Given Melanchthon's reaction to the *Confutation's* rejection of this section, it would appear that the drafters had not expected that their opponents would actually justify *any* human regulations on the basis of "appeasing God and earning grace."[5] Indeed, the drafters tie this directly to CA III and IV: "contrary to the gospel and the teaching concerning faith in Christ." This further explains why the true unity of the church, described in CA VII, cannot rely on human regulations: that would defy the very heart of the gospel itself. The trouble again rests with the Old Creature, which continues to create special, *human* rules to smuggle into our relationship with God. Sometimes, it is even a matter of a "rule" that eliminates or reduces human regulations—under the pretense that this is the true intent of Christ and the gospel. In *all* cases, however, what is at stake for the Evangelical party in Augsburg is the gospel and faith in Christ. Thus, this article, when combined with CA XII, hearkens back to the very origins of the Reformation and the *causa Lutheri* (Luther's legal case with Rome) and to Luther's initial rejection of the practice of indulgences and (somewhat later) of monastic vows and other traditions.

"That is why monastic vows and other traditions concerning distinctions of foods, days and the like, through which people imagine they can earn grace and make satisfaction for sin, are good for nothing and contrary to the gospel." Here the Latin gives a slightly different entry point into these specific traditions. By using the word "instituted," the Latin blames those church leaders who have made this false connection between such traditions and grace or satisfaction for sin. The German, by contrast, focuses upon the effect on the practitioners ("people imagine"). Already in his letter to Archbishop Albrecht, written on 31 October 1517, Luther attacked both the preachers' claims and the people's false understanding.[6] This sentence, especially in combination with the previous two, demonstrates a sharp edge unlike any of the previous articles. In the first half of the CA, only article twenty employs

---

5. Ap XV.3 (BC, 223): "Although we expected our opponents to defend human traditions for other reasons, we never dreamt that they would actually condemn the proposition that we do not merit the forgiveness of sins or grace by observing human traditions."
6. See *Martin Luther's 95 Theses: With Introduction, Commentary, and Study Guide*, ed. Timothy J. Wengert (Minneapolis: Fortress Press, 2015), 32–36.

such acerbic language (although CA XVI will also place certain aspects of monasticism in question).

Did scholastic theologians teach such a thing regarding monastic vows? In Thomas Aquinas we find the argument that taking vows as a monk or friar was the equivalent of a second baptism, eliminating all the guilt and punishment of the sins committed up to that time.[7] For the Reformers such claims undermined completely God's grace and transformed a human undertaking into a salvific act. In this light, it is not surprising that the *Confutation* completely rejected this article.

We Teach and Confess

As a senior in college I became involved with a Christian community. We regularly prayed for the Holy Spirit to work among us and celebrated the gifts that the Spirit gave. We also were very serious about living in community, so that we were and could be the Word of God to those around us. The "household" to which I was assigned prayed together morning and night, ate meals together purchased out of a very meager weekly contribution from each of its ten members, and attended regular meetings with the entire community at least two or three times a week.

There was initially a certain joy and excitement in being a part of group that took seriously the call to live an increasingly apostolic lifestyle in secular Ann Arbor, Michigan. But that quickly became a burden for me and for others, as (despite our best efforts at prayer, fasting, and obedience) the goal of becoming truly Christian slipped further and further from our grasp. In fact, the more I worked at living a Christian life, the more frantic my life seemed to become. When I expressed the desire to enter a Lutheran seminary, one of the group's leaders cautioned that I had not yet progressed to the point where I was truly fit to go. That rather odd advice did not sway me, and yet only after I had left that community did I begin to realize (with the help of my late wife, Barbara) just how completely I had become convinced that the very human rules (called a covenant), which bound that group together, were in fact an invitation to trust my own efforts to get right or at least stay right with God. I doubt that the leaders realized what they were doing to their followers, but the danger of burdening the conscience and confusing human rules with divine grace remains a real one—not only for ephemeral groups spawned in part by the Jesus Movement of the 1970s but also for all Christian communities.

---

7. Thomas Aquinas, *Summa Theologica* II/II, q. 88, 186–89.

CA XV underscores the danger. *That* the assembly of believers and saints should and must employ human regulations and rules is no sin but rather an important way of maintaining peace and good order. But as soon as these rules become burdens to consciences or are proposed as ways to obtain, maintain, or improve one's relation to God, then even the very best regulations become demonic, undermining the very heart of the Christian assembly itself: the gospel and faith in Christ.

16

"DAILY LIFE *Is* THE
CHRISTIAN LIFE," PART 1

H e was just coming out of back surgery, so I suppose one could blame the anesthetic. But Tom, a repair shop manager at the local John Deere dealership, insisted on talking about a sermon that I had preached a few months earlier, on Labor Day. Given the traditionally low attendance, I decided to talk about work, using as my text Ephesians 6:5–9 and the discussion of servants and masters or, as I translated (following Luther's translation/paraphrase in the Small Catechism)[1] with twentieth-century social relationships in mind, workers and bosses. "I have been working at John Deere for twenty years," he began. "And until you said that God is really pleased with our daily work, I always thought that my Christian life had nothing to do with my workday. That has really made a difference for me."

One of the least well-known and most often misunderstood parts of Lutheran teaching has to do with the Christian life. Other Christians may separate day-to-day tasks from truly "Christian" works (like prayer, fasting, and almsgiving), or they may make efforts to separate themselves from the world entirely—through communal living, retreats, or even certain types of prayer. Others, while eager to talk about *Christian* callings, reduce them to actions leading or supporting the Christian community or to one's spiritual, baptismal calling (which, as will become clear in CA XXVIII, is a matter of God's *right* hand, not the left). Lutherans, to the puzzlement of some and

---

1. Small Catechism, "The Household Chart," 10–11 (BC, 366–67). This was the only time in over forty years of ministry that I did not preach on the appointed texts of the Common Lectionary.

to the consternation of others, claim that one's daily life *is* one's Christian life—anywhere the neighbor is served in love and the Old Creature is driven to minister to the poor and needy in the world instead of fulfilling its self-serving ways.

Luther and Melanchthon, not reticent to use philosophy in understanding *this* world and humanity's place in it, borrow from Aristotle via the medieval tradition and identify three orders or arenas in which we operate: *oikonomia, politia,* and *ecclesia*: household (both home and workplace), government (including all interactions within society), and the church (consisting of the concrete positions within the visible structures of church life). Within each of these three spheres, various offices exist—each of which arises from God's concrete calling (German: *Beruf*; Latin: *vocatio*).[2] Of course, all people, not just Christians, are engaged in these various tasks. The only difference between Christians and everyone else lies in faith (*not* the works themselves), because Christians, as believers, can truly trust God's promise that these daily, menial tasks for serving others and creation as God's creature are *God's* calling.[3] The exclusion of boasting in Paul's rendition of justification (Rom 3:27; 1 Cor 1:29, 31; 2 Cor 12:9; Eph 2:9) and Jesus's insistence that believers are either split-brain patients (not knowing left from right [Matt 6:3]) or sheep who think they're goats (Matt 25:37–39) connect Christian activities in this world to faith (not works). Even St. Bernard, as Luther once recounted, viewed the Christian life as lost as soon as one began measuring one's progress.[4] Faith alone hears God's call to serve the neighbor with "a free and merry spirit."[5]

CA XVI

[German]

Concerning public order and secular government it is taught that all political authority, orderly government, laws, and good order in the world are created and instituted by God and that Christians may without sin exercise political authority; be princes and judges; pass sentences and administer justice

[Latin]

Concerning civic affairs they teach that lawful civil ordinances are good works of God and that Christians are permitted to hold civil office, to work in law courts, to decide matters by imperial and other existing laws, to impose just punishments, to wage just war, to serve as soldiers, to make legal

---

2. Luther redefined the German word *Beruf* in line with his insight into human callings (Latin: *vocatio*) from God in daily life.
3. For a fine explanation of this point, see Michael Bennethum, *Listen! God Is Calling!* (Minneapolis: Fortress, 2003).
4. See LW 10:53, citing Bernard of Clairvaux, *Epistola XCI.3*, in *Opera Genuina*, vol. 1: *Epistola CCCCXLIV, et VII Opuscula* (Lyon and Paris: Perisse Frères, 1854), 84.
5. SD VI.17 (BC, 590).

according to imperial and other existing laws; punish evil-doers with the sword; wage just wars; serve as soldiers; buy and sell; take required oaths; possess property; be married, etc.

Condemned here are the Anabaptists who teach that none of the things indicated above is Christian.

Also condemned are those who teach that Christian perfection means physically leaving house and home, spouse and child, and refraining from the above-mentioned activities. In fact, the only true perfection is true fear of God and true faith in God. For the gospel teaches an internal, eternal reality and righteousness of the heart, not an external, temporal one. The gospel does not overthrow secular government, public order, and marriage but instead intends that a person keep all this as a true order of God and demonstrate in these walks of life Christian love and true good works according to each person's calling. Christians, therefore, are obliged to be subject to political authority and to obey its commands and laws in all that may be done without sin. But if a command of the political authority cannot be followed without sin, one must obey God rather than any human beings (Acts 5 [:29]).

contracts, to hold property, to take an oath when required by magistrates, to take a wife, to be given in marriage.

They condemn the Anabaptists who prohibit Christians from assuming such civil responsibilities.

Because the gospel transmits an eternal righteousness of the heart, they also condemn those who locate evangelical perfection not in the fear of God and in faith but in abandoning civil responsibilities. In the meantime the gospel does not undermine government or family but completely requires both their preservation as ordinances of God and the exercise of love in these ordinances. Consequently, Christians owe obedience to their magistrates and laws except when commanded to sin. For then they owe greater obedience to God than to human beings (Acts 5 [:29]).

Reflections

"Concerning public order and secular government . . ." At first glance, this article seems to concern itself only with the *ordo politicus*. First in the middle sections do we discover its broader context. Two incentives shape this article. On the one hand, the drafters want to underscore their rejection of what they label Anabaptist positions. A year earlier in Speyer the imperial diet had renewed ancient imperial rescripts banning rebaptism. In his tract *Against the Rebaptizers* Melanchthon had emphasized the Anabaptists' crimes against the political order and urged their strict punishment. On the other hand, the authors also wanted to build their own defense *for* civil disobedience. The Evangelicals, too, were viewed by some in the empire as little more than anarchists, intent upon destroying imperial power. Thus, the CA had to demonstrate the princes' law-abiding nature while at the same time explaining why they could not follow certain imperial laws (including the non-enforcement of the 1521 Edict of Worms that banned Luther's teaching).

"**. . . [I]t is taught that all political authority, orderly government, laws, and good order in the world are created and instituted by God . . .**" The Latin addresses an overstatement in the German by including a single adjective ("lawful") for all manner of civil authority. This clarifies the "all" in the German text and makes some exceptions to the rule possible. Yet the statement "all political authority" is dependent upon the equally broad statement about the "powers that be" in Romans 13:1–7 and implies that the drafters could not imagine a society in which there was not some form of government, from which came orderly government, laws, and good order—no more than one could imagine a world without gravity. "Political authority" is descriptive; "orderly government" and "good order" are prescriptive, setting up the criteria by which to judge how well any authority in this world functions. All of these things are creations of God for this world and its well-being. Already here Melanchthon may well have had in mind not simply Anabaptists but other classical authors, who had argued that governments were little more than robber bands (see below). In the same way today, many assume that politics and government are evil on the face of it, thereby undermining the very God-given, social structures that keep the peace.

"**. . . [A]nd that Christians may without sin exercise political authority; be princes and judges; pass sentences and administer justice according to imperial and other existing laws; punish evil-doers with the sword; wage just wars; serve as soldiers; buy and sell; take required oaths; possess property; be married, etc.**" Although Anabaptist teaching may seem to provide the counterpoint for this list, there may also be another adversary underneath: political philosophy. Augustine, basing arguments on Cicero, insisted that without justice, governments were little more than robber bands.[6] Quite to the contrary, CA XVI lists the normal activities of government and rather than beginning with some idealized criticism of "politics" and "government" asserts instead that Christians may perform these activities "without sin."

The first phrase, "**exercise political authority**" (literally, simply "to be in government") may function as the overarching theme of the specific activities that follow. Of course here one must reckon with the particular contours of governmental rule at the time. In the principalities that made up the empire,

---

6. See Augustine, *City of God* IV.4, using a fragment from Cicero, *On the Republic*, III.14.24.

the prince exercised the ultimate legislative, judicial, and executive powers. At the same time, there were also those who functioned as judges or soldiers (whose tasks included what we today consider policing). Princes and judges, then, had responsibility to administer justice. The early sixteenth-century was seeing a shift from local codes of law (similar in some ways to English Common Law, called in one version the *Sachsenspiegel* [Saxon "mirror"]) to imperial, Roman law (which continues to serve as the underlying basis of the law codes in Europe today). For this reason, CA XVI mentions both law codes.

The phrase, **"punish evildoers with the sword,"** refers not only to capital punishment but actually includes any coercive punishment at all: imprisonment, fines, confiscation of property, and the like, as the Latin makes clear (**"to impose just punishments"**). That CA XVI sanctions such governmental activity indicates that the Reformers have a different take on Jesus's command to "turn the other cheek" than some who were labeled Anabaptists. Instead of seeing this and other biblical texts as commands to withdraw from the rough-and-tumble of social life, thus separating the Christian from the surrounding society, Luther and his compatriots combine the believer's life into two spheres, working in this world under the law and living by faith in the world to come. This means that Christ's prohibition of all forms of personal vengeance does not exclude rulers and judges from keeping order—but always for society's sake and not for personal gain or revenge. Luther even argues that the prince can best intervene in matters as "ein fremder Freund" (a foreign or alien friend), one who has no dog in the fight, so to speak.

Some may view **"waging just war and serving as soldiers"** as an anachronism, given the possibility for annihilation in war and for the devastation that modern soldiery may inflict. For one thing, soldiers were at the same time the police authority. For another, "just war" theory actually provided important checks on political behavior. Unlike churches that declare all wars unjust and thus remove themselves from any conversation about a particular governmental policy, churches that allow for the possibility of just war must on a case-by-case basis determine whether a war is just or not, thereby forcing the government to justify its actions.[7] Of course, to be a just war the conflict must meet several criteria: the exercise of lawful authority, appropriate intention, and a legitimate cause.[8] To these, Luther

---

7. The result of this for Lutherans in the United States is that a truly Lutheran position, which allows particular wars to be unjust, has been deemed unconstitutional for a soldier seeking "conscientious objector" status. Thus, in the Vietnam War, Lutherans could be and were jailed for refusing to serve. Moreover, the armed services do not allow for individual soldiers to question their superior's commands on the ground of conscience, something crucial to Luther's own advice to soldiers. See his *Whether Soldiers, Too, May Be Saved* (LW 46:87–143).

8. For a summary of this complicated theory, see Bernd Wannenwetsch, "Just War," in *The Cambridge Dictionary of Christian Theology*, ed. Ian A. McFarland et al. (Cambridge: Cambridge University Press, 2011), 255–57.

adds that only truly defensive wars could be just and that rebellion, in which a lesser authority resists a higher one, was always unjust. Only when lawyers convinced Luther and Melanchthon in 1531 that the emperor was the first among equals with the other electors, would he accede to his prince, Elector John, forming a defensive alliance against Emperor Charles V. As with capital punishment, when Lutherans argue about just wars, they do not make their case based upon "Christian ideals" but based upon pragmatic arguments. Given the human penchant for judging, we may always want to make universal claims about "justice," "rights," or "God's will," but practical arguments, on the contrary, limit themselves to the harm done directly by a specific policy or course of action. For example, the arguments against capital punishment will involve the specific injustice and uncertainty of the legal system and not the higher moral claims of divine righteousness. In the same way, arguing about specific wars forces the Christian to articulate precisely how this particular war harms the citizenry. Of course, all such arguments are only approximations and are all subject to error and miscalculation. But this also limits such arguments and eliminates global claims of a higher level of Christian rightness and forces Christians to live squarely in the world rather than to escape from it. For Lutherans the ethical question is never simply "How does some universal truth apply here?" but rather "How best do I love my neighbors in this situation?"

The final list (**"buy and sell; take required oaths; possess property; be married, etc.,"** where the Latin adds **"to make legal contracts"**) leaves the realm of government per se and summarizes Christian life in this world. To be sure, all of these things do not properly exist outside of society and government (*politia*), but they also describe life in the household (*oikonomia*). Moreover, this part of the list also takes aim at late-medieval monasticism, which in some instances insisted that monks not even touch money let alone have worldly possessions or be married. The taking of oaths also refers to specific Anabaptist groups that refused to take oaths of fealty (on the grounds that Jesus had forbidden them in the Sermon on the Mount), and the possession of property refers to those sixteenth-century groups who held property in common (supposedly imitating the book of Acts). Marriage, too, then seen as a lower form of Christian life compared to monastic celibacy, now regains in CA XVI its place as an arena in which one can fully lead a Christian life.[9]

This entire list implies that for the Evangelical party in Augsburg daily life *is* the Christian life. The mundane things in life—buying and selling, possessing a driver's license and voting, owning things and being in a household—are

---

9. The Latin "to take a wife, to be given in marriage" simply reflects that in that language and culture the male was said to "take a wife" and the female "to be given in marriage" by her father. This inequality is avoided not only in the German version but also in Luther's statements about the nature of marriage in Large Catechism, "Ten Commandments," 217–19 (BC, 415).

good things in God's eyes. Of course, all of these things are also fraught with dangers, since exchanging goods and services, swearing to tell the truth or to uphold a nation's constitution, owning things, and being married all can be distorted and lead to sin—sins covered in the fifth through eighth commandments, especially the way Luther reads them in his Small Catechism.[10] But if someone teaches that Christians must forego these things—as either a monk or an Anabaptist—it does not according to CA XVI make better Christians, living on a higher moral plane (what medieval theologians called in the case of monks a state of perfection).

"**Condemned here are the Anabaptists who teach that none of the things indicated above is Christian.**" This exaggerated, blanket condemnation of Anabaptist teaching (which, for example, held marriage in high esteem) is more accurately stated in the Latin: "They condemn the Anabaptists who prohibit Christians from assuming such civil responsibilities." Yet the condemnation goes far beyond a few sixteenth-century Christian groups, since Christians today may also show a real disdain for daily life and its ambiguities. An idealized view of the "Christian life" leaves a person searching for ways to escape this life and find a pure place to practice true religiosity.

"**Also condemned are those who teach that Christian perfection means physically leaving house and home, spouse and child, and refraining from the above-mentioned activities. In fact, the only true perfection is true fear of God and true faith in God.**" As we saw in CA V, when the drafters want to condemn a teaching of their opponents, they do it without naming names. Thus, the *Confutation* accepts this article without exception and even provides a Bible passage to back it up (Rom 13:1–7). But, as was hinted at above, this condemnation aims directly at late-medieval monastic practices. According to scholastic theology, a person existed in any one of three states: a state of sin, a state of grace, or a state of perfection. A person who died while in a state of (mortal) sin went to hell; a person in a state of grace could perform truly good, meritorious works and, having undergone sufficient purgation after death, entered heaven; a person in a state of perfection was not by any means perfect but was, by virtue of their lifelong monastic vows, in a higher spiritual state where sins were less damaging and good works even more powerful. To a lesser extent, vowing to undertake a pilgrimage (and thus also leaving "house and home") also was seen as such a work of supererogation.

By contrast, the Reformers reclaimed daily life, with its tasks and disappointments, its sorrows and joys, as the true arena for the Christian life, where one no longer need talk of the merit or perfection of works but only faith in the God who created and preserves all things. Thus, true perfection is no longer a work at all but rather fear of and faith in God. This transformation

---

10. Small Catechism, "Ten Commandments," 9–16 (BC, 352–53).

of perfection, explained in much greater detail in CA XXVII, shows how the CA connects the Christian life to justification by faith. No longer are our good works conditions for perfection but instead fearing and trusting God both give the very perfection we cannot ever attain through our works and reorient our life toward faith.

"For the gospel teaches an internal, eternal reality and righteousness of the heart, not an external, temporal one." Unlike the previous articles, CA XVI provides far more detail concerning the Evangelical position, relying here on what Melanchthon elsewhere calls the twofold righteousness. We may better understand what the Reformers mean (what some label the doctrine of the two kingdoms or two modes of governing) by distinguishing between God's two hands. With the right God is bringing in the world to come proclaimed in the gospel ("an internal, eternal reality and righteousness of the heart"—that is, the believer's standing *coram Deo* [in God's presence]); with the left God creates and preserves this world, establishing and maintaining good order and restraining evil ("an external, temporal" reality, *coram mundo* [in this world]).

"The gospel does not overthrow secular government, public order, and marriage but instead intends that a person keep all this as a true order of God and demonstrate in these walks of life Christian love and true good works according to each person's calling." Over fifty years ago, Robert Handy, a professor of American church history, wrote a book entitled *A Christian America*, recounting the many efforts (mostly Reformed) Christians and their churches have undertaken to impose a Christian ethic upon the United States. Such eagerness to make America Christian again stands in stark contrast to CA XVI, which confesses that God is at work in every land and nation through government, public order, and family life. The gospel neither takes a person out of daily life nor insists that daily life need conform to some special, "Christian" ethic. For the first time in the CA we encounter the German word, *Stand* (plural: *Stände*). It is related to the legal term in English of having "standing" in a court of law. While older translations used the term "estate" (as in the "estate of marriage"), the word really has a far richer meaning as the arenas or "walks of life" in which a Christian operates. Moreover, CA XVI also introduces the word "calling" (German: *Beruf*). This revolutionizes Christian good works by taking them out of the world of hyper-piety and placing them squarely in this world. Thus, for example, Luther finds good works in a father changing diapers (in faith), a pious hired hand hauling manure to the field, in a servant girl making the beds, and the like.[11] It means that one's Christian life is simply overflowing with opportunities for good works—ones that take

---

11. LW 45:39–40 (a father changing diapers); LW 21:266 (a hired hand hauling manure); LC, "Ten Commandments," 145–46 (BC, 406; a servant girl making beds).

place any time our behavior helps a neighbor in need and even include safe driving or paying taxes!

"Christians, therefore, are obliged to be subject to political authority and to obey its commands and laws in all that may be done without sin. But if a command of the political authority cannot be followed without sin, one must obey God rather than any human beings (Acts 5 [:29])." Now comes the surprise ending of this article. As we stated in the introduction, the CA has two concurrent (but not competitive) goals: to confess the faith and to prove that the signers are not rebels. While the preface, written by the Saxon electoral chancellor, Gregor Brück, underscores the princes' desire to obey to Emperor Charles V, CA XVI defends these same princes' civil disobedience. Far from being an afterthought, these two sentences throw down the gauntlet before the imperial diet: the issue is *not* willful disobedience by rogue princes but a matter of conscience. They will follow imperial law "in all that may be done without sin." Suddenly, the Evangelical party has established the central criterion for judging their own behavior: obedience to God rather than to any civil authority. The arguments in the disputed articles (CA XXII–XXVIII) follow directly from this assertion of conscience. There is a limit to obedience to civil authorities, and it is found in the first commandment and Peter's rendition of that commandment in Acts 5. No wonder that Luther, too, in introducing the fourth commandment in the Large Catechism insists upon the same limit for obedience to parents, teachers, and governing officials: "If God's Word and will are placed first and are observed, nothing ought to be considered more important than the will and word of our parents, provided that these, too, are subordinated to God and are not set in opposition to the preceding commandments."[12]

There are two places where the two "kingdoms" (German: *Reiche*) or "governments" (German: *Regimente*) come together. First of all, God's two hands are, after all, *God's* hands. What God wants for this world and the creation (namely, life) and for the world to come (namely, eternal life) come from God's heart, that is, from God's mercy. But, second, they also meet in the believer. Here the "without sin" of CA XVI points relentlessly to the cross that Christians bear in the world, that is, to the struggle to discern how best to act in a particular situation. "What is God's Word and will in this case?" "How best does one obey God?" "Will this harm my neighbor in this concrete situation?" Such questions require an investigation of Scripture, a knowledge of how Christians in other similar situations have acted, a use of rigorous logic to determine the consequences of one's behavior and deep humility, so that

---

12. LC, Ten Commandments, 116 (BC, 402).

believers never can claim to provide the ultimate answer but only tentative ones (cf. Acts 15:28, "It seemed good to the Holy Spirit and to us . . .").[13]

We Teach and Confess

Given their monastic experience, Martin Luther and many of his compatriots had experienced a very different approach to the Christian life. Much of this article, as we have seen, is as much aimed at their criticisms of that experience as at any rumors they may have heard about Anabaptists. While the vast majority of Protestants have no experience (positive or negative) with monks, nuns, or friars, they still are tempted to divide the Christian life into different strata. One of the most egregious forms is what I call "congregational monasticism." A member of my Wisconsin congregation told me about how her parents and younger sister moved to Texas where they got caught up in this trap. The mother "volunteered" forty hours a week in the congregation's office; the father, a salesman often on the road, would not head home on Fridays but go straight to the church where he worked on a variety of projects the entire weekend before heading off again on Monday. And the neglected daughter? Her sister recounted how, in order to get some attention from her parents, she threatened suicide—an action that finally brought them back down to earth and to the divine callings they had been neglecting.

We might term another oft-repeated mistake as "salvation by turning pro." I would often get a laugh out of first year seminarians when asking them if, upon going home for Thanksgiving, their family asked them (sometimes for the very first time) to pray over the meal. But a far more poignant example came when a very conservative mother in our congregation in North Carolina had a sick infant in the hospital, and my late wife and I went to pray with her at home while the pastor headed off to the hospital, where her husband was keeping watch. (The baby recovered quite well, by the way.) After my (rather non-descript) prayer, she burst out, "I wish my husband had become a pastor or a missionary!" Under duress, people say confusing things, of course, but I couldn't help but ponder how this mother (too conservative to imagine *she* might become a pastor) somehow assumed that in order to be truly leading a *Christian* life her husband, in training to be a hospital administrator, should really have given everything up and turned "pro."

The teaching about the two hands of God (or Two Kingdoms) underlies the Lutherans' insistence in CA XVI on the goodness of daily life. One helpful way to view this teaching is to contrast this very down-to-earth approach to

---

13. The long-time parish pastor, Franklin Drews Fry, summarized this approach to Lutheran ethics as "RBG," that is, "reverent, best guess," insisting that for the Christian "there is nothing absolute but the absolution."

humanity's penchant for (or addiction to) ideals.[14] In English the word "ideal" can simply mean good goals or even aims that accord to God's will. Ideals, however, when let loose on society, household, or church quickly become destructive. We know this well from politics where seemingly good ideals ("Make the world safe for democracy" or "This is the war to end all wars" or "From each according to their ability; to each according to their need" or [not so much a slogan as a religion] laissez-faire capitalism or "Get the government off our back" or "Make our nation great again" or . . .), suddenly spell death to the neighbor in countless ways.[15] By contrast, the facts both that God is ruling two worlds (this one and the one to come) and that God forbids idolatry and commands love of the neighbor in need mean that we must measure everything not according to the rightness of our ideas but by the good or harm done to actual neighbors.

Perhaps no modern theologian expressed Luther's insight into vocation better than Dr. Martin Luther King, Jr. In 1966, he addressed students at a local Philadelphia, Pennsylvania high school and said the following.[16]

> And when you discover what you will be in life, set out to do it as if God Almighty called you at this particular moment in history to do it. If it falls your lot to be a street sweeper, sweep streets like Michelangelo painted pictures. Sweep streets like Beethoven composed music. Sweep streets like Leontyne Price sings before the Metropolitan Opera. Sweep streets like Shakespeare wrote poetry. Sweep streets so well that all the hosts of heaven and earth will have to pause and say, "Here lived a great street sweeper who swept his job well."

---

14. This was first suggested to me in Gerhard Forde, *Where God Meets Man: Luther's Down-to-Earth Approach to the Gospel* (Minneapolis: Augsburg, 1972), 89–115.

15. The same thing happens in the church when ideals such as moral purity, inclusivity, equality, or racial or gender superiority overpower the gospel and force the entire church into a desperate search for perfection.

16. Reprinted on the fortieth anniversary of the speech in the *Philadelphia Inquirer*, 8 January 2006.

17

"WHO'S IN CHARGE HERE?"

Since the mid-nineteenth century in America, every generation seems eager to spawn a new set of speculators about when the end of the world with its last judgment will occur. The Millerites chose 1843 or 1844. The Jehovah's Witnesses first fixated on 1914. In the 1970s Hal Lindsey dominated the religious book market with *The Late, Great Planet Earth.* More recently, an entire series of novels, the "Left Behind" series, based its characters and events upon the prognostications of Tim LaHaye. There seems to be a lot of money to be made and many folks to be (mis)led in the apocalyptic marketplace.

Already in the sixteenth century, people were speculating about the end of the world.[1] In the case that directly affected CA XVII, a former Anabaptist, Augustine Bader (before 1500–1530), predicted that the thousand-year reign of Christ would commence on Easter Sunday, 1530, beginning with punishment and transformation on earth.[2] Although Bader, a weaver and citizen of Augsburg, had been in early 1528 a leader of an Anabaptist community there, differences with them led him to leave that community, sell his house, and embark on his own apocalyptic path. In part under the influence of Hans Hut, who had predicted the end for 31 May 1528 (the day of Pentecost), and of other Anabaptists (Oswald Leber and Ulrich Trechsel from Strasbourg),

---

1. An early case in the Middle Ages involved the Franciscan Joachim of Fiore and his followers. Others followed suit.
2. The most recent work on Bader, upon which this section is based, is by Anselm Schubert, *Täufertum und Kabbalah: Augustin Bader und die Grenzen der Radikalen Reformation* (Gütersloh: Gütersloher Verlagshaus, 2008), 33–201.

Bader began to style himself a special prophet from God. Especially from Leber, Bader became aware of certain cabbalistic views in Jewish writings and their interpretations by rabbis in Worms, who entertained speculation about the approaching arrival of the Messiah. He also knew of the widely circulated story (from Jewish tradition via Pseudo-Methodius) about the ten lost tribes of Israel being shut up in a mountain and released upon the world as the "Red Jews," which in the sixteenth century had become associated with the Turks, who in 1529 had reached the gates of Vienna.[3] Bader believed that he and his infant son would be the ruler over the imminent thousand-year kingdom and even had royal regalia made for the occasion.

Bader holed up with his family and followers in a variety of places near Ulm and Blaubeuron, but the last of them placed him directly in the jurisdiction of Outer Austria (which controlled Württemberg at the time) and its ruler, Archduke Ferdinand (brother of Charles V and later Emperor Ferdinand I). With Bader's arrest, torture and execution, he was cited as a horrid example of the dangerous excesses of Lutheranism in the Holy Roman Empire. Beginning already in 1527 in his territories, Ferdinand had not only viewed Anabaptists as heretics (to be punished under the Edict of Worms from 1521 and later under decisions reached at the Diet of Speyer in 1529) but even more as anti-governmental rebels. Shortly before 20 January 1530, Bader was arrested and held prisoner in Stuttgart, where he was interrogated several times. From various official sources, it is clear that his connection to other Anabaptists was not nearly as important to the authorities as the political threat that they thought he represented. As a result, what even the investigators labeled "fantasies" became a case that also placed the Evangelical imperial princes under suspicion.

Officials at the courts of Ferdinand and his brother, Charles V, feared that this represented an attempt by the deposed duke of Württemberg, Ulrich, to regain his lands. (He later succeeded with the help of the Landgrave Philip of Hesse in 1534.) The imperial brothers imagined that the Evangelical party wanted to start a peasants' uprising in south German lands in order to prevent the Diet of Augsburg from taking place. An official in Stuttgart even thought that the actions of Bader were merely a camouflage for far worse actions from the Evangelical princes. Duke George of Saxony, one of Luther's most vociferous opponents, even met with his cousin Elector John of Saxony on 15 February 1530 to confront him with these charges. But this case also had direct consequences for other Anabaptists, so that Duke George of Saxony redoubled his efforts to rid his territories of these "rebels." (He also believed that the Jews, and not so much the Lutheran princes, were to blame for Bader's

---

3. See Andrew Gow, *"The" Red Jews: Antisemitism in the Apocalyptic Age 1200–1600* (Leiden: Brill, 1995).

beliefs.) The Margrave of Brandenburg-Ansbach suspected (rightly) that the imperial court was unfairly using Bader's case against the Evangelical princes. Elector John of Saxony, by contrast, sent a delegation to Ferdinand petitioning the Archduke to drop any such accusation against the elector. When the electoral Saxon delegation presented their confession of faith (the Schwabach Articles) to Charles V in Innsbruck in May 1530, the case of Bader still hovered over conversations between the emperor and the papal legate, Cardinal Campeggio. The latter sent to Rome not only a Latin translation of the articles but also a report labeled, "The Fruit of the Lutheran Gospel among the [Ana–] Baptists in Germany." No wonder Campeggio wrote to Rome that the only way to get rid of the Lutherans in Germany was "with fire [for the heretics] and the sword [for their princely protectors]."[4] No wonder also that the Saxon delegation established in June 1530 a back channel through Philip Melanchthon to convince the cardinal otherwise.

When the case was put before representatives of the Swabian Circle (or District), which met in Augsburg in late February and March 1530, the representatives dismissed the Austrian claim of rebellion and judged Bader's beliefs to be crazy foolishness (German: *Buberei*). They urged that his capital punishment be carried out before Easter (17 April), just to prove that the authorities placed no stock in his prophecies. Instead, the Circle focused its suspicion on the Jews, who were suspected of spying for the Turks, a charge reflected in Josel von Rosheim's memoires.[5] Protocols of Bader's interrogation were published in Augsburg and included reports dated 12 and 16 March 1530. Bader was executed with his own sword on 29 March 1530.

Throughout the sixteenth century, Luther and the Lutherans were *more* apocalyptic in their worldview than the two other major branches of Western Christianity (Roman Catholic and Reformed). This became especially evident in Philip Melanchthon's early work on Daniel and in Luther's 1530 rewritten preface to Revelation, in which Gog and Magog were identified with the "Red Jews" and, thus, the Turks.[6] Thus, as with Bader, the siege of Vienna also influenced the Wittenberg Reformers. But, for the most part, they refrained from speculating about a precise date for the end of the world. For example, Philip Melanchthon accepted a saying in the Jewish kabbalah (attributed to a Rabbi Elijah whom he mistakenly thought was the biblical prophet Elijah) that the history of the world would be divided into three ages: of the patriarchs (4000 BC to 2000 BC), of the law (2000 BC to 1 BC) and the age of the messiah (AD 1 to AD 2000). Because Jesus promised the

---

4. Schubert, *Täufertum*, 181, n. 804, notes that Johannes Fabri's attack against the Evangelicals from July 1530 used parts of Campeggio's report.
5. He represented Jewish interests at the imperial court.
6. See WA Bi 7:471, where in a gloss to Rev 20:8 Luther states, "'Gog': that is the Turks, who come from Tartar and are called the red Jews."

final age would be shortened for the sake of the elect, Melanchthon thought the end would arrive early in the last five hundred years of this third age. But neither he nor Luther ever started speculating about particular times and places. Indeed, for them it was far more important to realize that all Christians are living in "these last days" (Heb 1:2) than to obsess over the "day and hour." Moreover, baptism, by joining believers to the death and resurrection of Jesus already ushers each Christian into the final judgment and eternal life.

CA XVII

[German]

It is also taught that our Lord Jesus Christ will return on the last day to judge, to raise all the dead, to give eternal life and eternal joy to those who believe and are elect, but to condemn the ungodly and the devils to hell and eternal punishment.

Rejected, therefore, are the Anabaptists who teach that the devils and condemned human beings will not suffer eternal torture and torment.

Likewise rejected are some Jewish teachings, which have also appeared in the present, that before the resurrection of the dead saints and righteous people alone will possess a secular kingdom and will annihilate all the ungodly.

[Latin]

They also teach that at the consummation of the world Christ will appear for judgment and will bring to life all the dead. He will give eternal life and endless joy to the righteous and elect, but he will condemn the ungodly and the devils to endless torment.

They condemn the Anabaptists who think that there will be an end to the punishments of condemned human beings and devils.

They also condemn others who are now spreading Jewish opinions, that before the resurrection of the dead the godly will take possession of the kingdom of the world, while the ungodly are suppressed everywhere.

Reflections

"It is also taught that our Lord Jesus Christ will return on the last day to judge, to raise all the dead, to give eternal life and eternal joy to those who believe and are elect, but to condemn the ungodly and the devils to hell and eternal punishment." This statement startles some Lutherans today, who cannot imagine that judgment has anything to do with God. The confessors in Augsburg, however, did not doubt the biblical witness or the ecumenical creeds that all point to such judgment. There are two sides to this article: first, that Christ will return; second, that he comes with a purpose (to judge, resurrect, give life, and condemn). The first part echoes the most ancient of Christian prayers: Maranatha! Come, Lord Jesus! There is a brokenness and unresolved nature to this world that drives us to cry out to God not just for rescue or help in the moment but, more fully, for salvation in the end. This longing is common to the church of every age, even when not as clearly expressed in some times as in others. Perhaps in times of uncertainty, when facing the destruction of war, disease, economic collapse, and death (the four horsemen of the Apocalypse), Christians once again discover that they are not in control of their own future but that their lives and the life of the whole world and creation itself rest in God's hands, not ours.

But Christ's coming is not a passive mystical experience of some vague ontological union with the divine but an active work—one more proof of the centrality of God's mercy. Christ is coming to judge the living and the dead, as the creeds say. And that judgment involves resurrection, the gift of eternal life for the elect and condemnation of all evil. Those who are so sure of their own righteousness need fear such a judgment, but believers—that is, precisely those elect in whom God the Holy Spirit works faith (CA V)—will find at the judgment the same merciful-to-sinners God who encountered them in life (CA III–IV). Far from supporting the judgmental attitude found among some Christians, who use the last judgment as a club with which to bash either their perceived enemies or at least their hapless hearers, this rather low-keyed description in CA XVII makes clear that in the end (and at the End) everything rests in God's hands, not ours. And we know those hands to bear the marks of the nails. Even in condemnation, this promise reigns: God will, one day, eliminate all death and all evil.

"Rejected, therefore, are the Anabaptists who teach that the devils and condemned human beings will not suffer eternal torture and torment." Here the CA rejects a truly miniscule number of folks (including Hans Denck and Melchior Rinck) who, unlike any others who practiced believers' baptism (and thus rejected the validity of infant baptism), were convinced that all would finally be saved. This was, of course, a very ancient Christian teaching going back to Origen of Alexandria, who taught the return of all souls to the One (*apokatastasis*). This and the following condemnation were not part of the Schwabach Articles, demonstrating that it was first in Augsburg that the Evangelical party felt constrained to stress their rejection of any and all "Anabaptist" teaching. Why they mention this particular teaching is not stated. Perhaps they worried that such a teaching again undermined external morality so that by condemning it they once again proved themselves to be upstanding citizens of the empire. They underscored this connection by including this article directly after the article on secular authority, a connection made more urgent through the case of Augustin Bader.

"Likewise rejected are some Jewish teachings, which have also appeared in the present, that before the resurrection of the dead saints and righteous

people alone will possess a secular kingdom and will annihilate all the ungodly." The Latin version is frankly clearer, in that they are condemning those spreading this particular "Jewish opinion" about the reign of the "godly" (or, at least, Augustin Bader and his infant son). It would appear that Melanchthon and the other drafters had read the published report of Bader's interrogation and crafted this section accordingly. As we will also see in CA XX, this sentence proves the historically conditioned nature of the CA. However, rather than such contextualization undermining the authority of the CA as a confession of faith, it shows instead how concerned the drafters were to respond to actual charges and set the (political) record straight.

They also clearly distinguished this teaching from other criticisms of Anabaptists. The political pressure on the Evangelical princes and theologians must have been tremendous, as they searched for ways to express their Christian orthodoxy while not undermining the central teaching of the Reformation. Here especially we hear strains of what some have called "an ecumenical proposal for the church catholic," although it might be better to call it also at the same time an Evangelical confession for the church catholic.

We Teach and Confess

On a few occasions over the last five hundred years, Lutherans have taken stabs at calculating the precise end of the world, but CA XVII has in some ways acted as an inoculation against such rigorous speculation for the most part. Instead, this article has underscored God's complete control of the future. Far from being a frightening prospect, the confession that Christ will return contains perhaps some of the most comforting, good news of all. There is a-coming, a "great, gettin'-up morning," as the spiritual puts it. In the meantime, we may leave the final judgment where it belongs: in the wounded hands of the savior of the world.

Given all of the twisted interpretations of Revelation, the Lutheran bishop, Hanns Lilje's commentary, *The Last Book of the Bible*,[7] stands apart. It was written in the stark light of World War II by a member of the Confessing Church in Germany, whose later career as a Lutheran bishop of Hannover and an ecumenist mark him as an important figure in post-war German Lutheranism. Living and working in a situation of such awful social, political, and military devastation, Lilje proves that perhaps the only people who should tackle that book are those who are composing at the same writing desk that John the Revelator used: in the midst of true persecution, where the only thing on which the believer may rely both in the present misery and for the future is God's mercy. Suddenly, Revelation 5 (where *only* the Lamb

---

7. Philadelphia: Muhlenberg Press, 1957.

who was slain can break the seals and open the scroll containing the history of the future) takes center stage and provides the window through which to interpret that entire, technicolor book. Then the book itself is washed in the Lamb's blood, so to speak, so that speculation ends, and trust in God and God's future may finally begin. Then the voices of Augustin Bader and all other prognosticators and prophets fade away and Christians may join in singing, "This is the feast of victory for our God, for the Lamb who was slain has begun his reign."

18

THE CAPTIVE WILL

It is simply everywhere—this claim that human beings have a "free will." We see it in movies and television shows; we read it in a wide variety of philosophers; and it dominates many Christians' self-understanding, not only in this country but also around the world. Even one Lutheran theologian recently argued that because young people whom he had encountered wanted to feel like they are participating in their religious future, one must accede to their wishes and grant them free will. So, given all of this, it *must* be true, right? Human beings may be sinful and weak but *surely* they have the freedom to choose Jesus. Have *you* decided for Jesus?

Against this overwhelming convergence, Lutherans in Augsburg answered a resounding no! We are bound to sin; we are so addicted to ourselves that any and all claims to be able to choose our religious future are merely signs of that addiction. Indeed, the picture of addiction actually helps clarify the situation. Alcoholics in denial about their disease almost invariably claim that they can stop drinking any time they want, that they have free choice in the matter, even though they do not. The human addiction to the self, however, is at least as devious, since it is not just that we cannot choose but that the very claim to choose *is* a symptom of the disease.

Part of the astounding power of this addiction to free choice comes in the human ability to twist the biblical witness to serve our selfish ends. Take Peter's confession in Matthew 16. In response to Jesus's question ("Who am I?"), Peter blurts out, "You are the Messiah, the Son of the living God." How does Jesus respond? Does he say, "Great choice, Peter; I knew you had it in you"? No! Instead he says, "Flesh and blood have *not* revealed this to you but my Father in heaven." Yet the addicted-to-the-self self cannot believe it. The prologue to the fourth Gospel (John 1:12–13) also discusses the nature of faith (especially powerfully put in the New International Version): "Yet to all who did receive him, to those who believed in his name, he gave the right [NRSV: power] to become children of God—children born not of natural descent, nor of human decision or a husband's will, but born of God." As already discussed in chapter 5, when in John 3 Jesus insists on being born from above (*anothen*), Nicodemus, the quintessential theologian of free choice, thinks this is all about being born a second time ("again," which is the other meaning of *anothen*) by crawling back into his mother's womb. Instead, Jesus makes "water and Spirit" and *not* "human free choice" the means of this divine birth. What, after all, is more passive than birth? St. Paul in Romans 9:16 (a section aptly labeled by the New International Version as "God's Sovereign Choice") insists: "It does not, therefore, depend on human desire [literally: will] or effort, but on God's mercy."

Worse yet, the "proof texts" for choice depend upon a very narrow reading of the Bible. True, Joshua 24:15 says, "Choose this day." But the entire verse reads (NIV): "But if serving the Lord seems undesirable to you, then choose for yourselves this day whom you will serve, whether the gods your ancestors served beyond the Euphrates, or the gods of the Amorites." We do have a choice of idols; that is for sure! The addicted-to-choosing self, even when "choosing" God is still first choosing the self, since the theological sentence is still conditional and still has the "I" as its subject: "If *I* choose God, then God will save me." Even if one invokes some help from the Holy Spirit, such theology cannot *by definition* be centered in God's unconditional, merciful promise (John 15:16): "You did not choose me, but I chose you."

Another favorite verse, often depicted in art, comes from Revelation 3:20 ("Here I am! I stand at the door and knock. If anyone hears my voice and opens the door, I will come in and eat with that person, and they with me"). The words are addressed to a specific situation in Laodicea where Christians who are already believers are judged to be lukewarm. Why not instead cite Jesus's word to the church in Philadelphia? Revelation 3:8 reads "See, I have placed before you an open door that no one can shut."

But our defense of "free choice" not only distorts the biblical witness, it also rests upon a human delusion: that we can actually make such decisions and keep them. As with claims to fulfill the law, the boast that we can decide is unmasked with a single question: "How are you doing?" Then human fickleness, inability, and unwillingness are revealed, and we can only cry out with the leper in Mark 1:40: "Lord, if *you* choose, you can make me clean."

Historically speaking, where does this Christian addiction to choice come from? On the one hand, it is truly the religion of the Old Creature obeying the voice of the tempter ("You will not die; you will be like gods, deciding what's right and what's wrong"). Thus, our challenges to God's grace will never disappear. On the other, certain Western philosophical strains, especially when medieval theologians combined Plato and Aristotle, resulted in the defense of free choice. The human soul, scholastic theologians believed, was divided into two parts: intellect (*intellectus*) and will (*voluntas*). While theologians such as Thomas Aquinas championed the intellect over the will (the former collected knowledge and then presented it to the will for action), others, notably in the late Middle Ages Gabriel Biel, insisted that the will controlled the intellect. Some argued that the intellect possessed a faculty called the *synteresis* (from the Greek word for conscience) that possessed the right knowledge of moral actions even after humanity fell into sin. Within the will was another faculty, a spark of free choice (*liberum arbitrium*), also unsullied by the fall. Thus, when Biel argued that "to those who do what is in them God will not deny grace," he meant that God rewards those who exercise this God-given faculty of free choice.[1]

Already six months after distributing the *95 Theses*, Luther prepared a set of theses for debate before his Augustinian colleagues' meeting in Heidelberg. They included a frontal assault on the "free choice," which Luther labeled a "thing in name only." This claim to exercise such freedom over against God was the very heart of sin. "The person who believes that one can obtain grace 'by doing what is in oneself' adds sin to sin and thus becomes doubly guilty," he argued.[2] When in 1521 these statements were included in the papal bull [i.e., bulletin] threatening excommunication (*Exsurge, Domini*), Luther penned assertions against the bull, arguing that any claim that the free choice played a role in salvation undermined God's grace.[3] The leading Greek scholar of Luther's day, Erasmus of Rotterdam, viewed these assertions as undermining healthy religious discourse. Thus, in 1524 when he finally entered the lists against Luther in his *Discussion of Free Choice*, Erasmus chose to discuss the pros and cons of free choice, and he criticized Luther's assertiveness as unbecoming of a true Christian theologian.

Luther's 1525 reply, *On the Bound Choice*, countered that Erasmus's (feigned) neutrality actually determined from the outset the outcome of his discussion of Scripture passages about free will. In this debate, however, Luther also admits that human beings *do* have free choice when it comes to "things below," that is, with the actions that affect this life (*coram mundo* [in the world] or *coram hominibus* [among human beings]). It is only *coram Deo*

---

1. Heiko A. Oberman, *The Harvest of Medieval Theology: Gabriel Biel and Late Medieval Nominalism*, 3rd ed. (Durham, NC: Labyrinth, 1983), 120–34.
2. Thesis 16 of the *Heidelberg Disputation* (TAL 1:83). See also thesis 13 (TAL 1:82): "Free will, after [the fall into] sin, exists in name only, and when 'it does what is within it,' it commits a mortal sin."
3. WA 7:142–49.

(in God's presence) that free choice is excluded. At one point, Erasmus, the moral philosopher, exclaims that if human beings do not have free choice they will not do good. Luther responds: "None can!" Precisely the myth of human ability clouds any "neutral" discussion of this topic.

Of course, Wittenberg's theology was always constructed upon two pillars: defining a theological topic and considering its effects. When the Erasmuses of this world insist upon free choice, Lutherans insist upon the bound choice as a way of killing the Old Creature's dreams and schemes. But in the 1530s a new kind of pastoral problem arose among those who had convinced themselves that God had not chosen them and, thus, that God's promises could not apply to them. To these people Luther insisted that God's promise outweighed even predestination. If he were to discover at the last judgment that he was not among the predestined, Luther said, he would simply insist that he was baptized and therefore God had no choice but to let him into heaven! Melanchthon addressed the same problem by emphasizing Ezekiel 33:11: "I take no pleasure in the death of the wicked but that they turn from their ways and live." God's deepest will is not sovereignty or justice but mercy and love.

Among Reformed Christians, matters took a somewhat different turn. When John Calvin answered the attacks of the Roman Catholic theologian Albertus Pighius with a strict view of predestination, Melanchthon nicknamed him "our Zeno" (after the founder of the deterministic philosophy of the Stoics).[4] This may have been unfair to Calvin, but his successor in Geneva, Theodore Beza, explicated a doctrine of "double predestinarian superlapsarianism," arguing that God elected some to salvation and others to damnation already before the fall (Latin: *super lapsum*). He did this to protect God's sovereign grace and eliminate all human merit. In the Netherlands, Jakob Arminius objected to this approach and insisted on the will's freedom enabled by the Holy Spirit. Reformed opponents of his followers, meeting in Dort for a synod in 1618, condemned this point of view and insisted upon humanity's total depravity and upon God's unconditional election of and preservation of the saints through God's irresistible grace. This position, especially espoused by some Puritan theologians in England, came under renewed attack by John Wesley, the guiding light of the Methodist movement in England. He agreed that human beings were totally depraved but, to avoid any hint of what many viewed as determinism, he insisted that the Holy Spirit preveniently acted upon sinners to bestow upon them once again their lost ability to turn to God. As Methodism along with some forms of Baptist theology spread throughout the United States, the sophistication of Wesley's argument was lost and the freedom of the will became increasingly

---

4. John Calvin, *The Bondage and Liberation of the Will: A Defence of the Orthodox Doctrine of Human Choice against Pighius*, ed. A. N. S. Lane, trans. G. I. Davies (Grand Rapids: Baker, 1996).

the single-most-important presupposition for the camp meetings, revivals, and weekly worship among Christians. It also spread in the mission fields, as American Christianity, with its insistence on human freedom, influenced more and more parts of the world. For all those convinced that they must make a decision before God will save them, CA XVIII comes as a breath of fresh air, saving them from impossible choices through God's gracious, merciful choice: "You are mine; I choose you."

CA XVIII

[German]

[Latin]

Concerning free will it is taught that a human being has some measure of free will, so as to live an externally honorable life and to choose among the things reason comprehends. However, without the grace, help and operation of the Holy Spirit a human being cannot become pleasing to God, fear or believe in God with the whole heart, or expel innate evil lusts from the heart. Instead, this happens through the Holy Spirit who is given through the Word of God. For Paul says (1 Cor 2 [:14]): "Those who are natural do not receive the gifts of God's Spirit."

In order that it may be recognized that nothing new is taught here, these are the clear words of Augustine concerning free will, quoted here from the third book of the *Hypognosticon*: "We confess that there is a free will in all human beings. For all have a natural, innate mind and reason—not that they can act in matters pertaining to God, such as loving or fearing God with their whole heart—but they do have the freedom to choose good or evil only in the external works of this life. By 'good' I mean what can be done by nature: whether to work in the field or not, whether to eat and drink, whether

Concerning free will they teach that the human will has some freedom for producing civil righteousness and for choosing things subject to reason. However, it does not have the power to produce the righteousness of God or spiritual righteousness without the Holy Spirit, because "those who are natural do not receive the gifts of God's Holy Spirit" [1 Cor 2:14]. But this righteousness is worked in the heart when the Holy Spirit is received through the word. In Book III of *Hypognosticon* Augustine says this in just so many words: "We confess that all human beings have a free will that possesses the judgment of reason. It does not enable them, without God, to begin—much less complete—anything that pertains to God, but only to perform the good or evil deeds of this life. By 'good deeds' I mean those that arise from the good in nature, that is, the will to labor in the field, to eat and drink, to have a friend, to wear clothes, to build a house, to marry, to raise cattle, to learn various useful skills, or to do whatever good pertains to this life. None of these exists without divine direction; indeed, from him and through him they have come to visit a friend or not, to dress or undress, to build a home, to marry, to engage in a trade, and to do whatever may be useful and good. To be sure, all of this neither exists nor endures without God, but everything is from him and through him. On the other hand, a human being can by personal choice do evil, such as to kneel before an idol, commit murder and the like."

Rejected here are those who teach that we can keep the commandments of God without grace and the Holy Spirit. For although we are by nature able to do the external works of the commandments, yet we cannot do the supreme commandments in the heart, namely, truly fear, love and believe in God.

into being and exist. However, by 'evil deeds' I mean the will to worship an idol, to commit murder, etc."

They condemn the Pelagians and others who teach that without the Holy Spirit by the powers of nature alone, we are able to love God above all things and can also keep the commandments of God "according to the substance of the acts." Although nature can in some measure produce external works—for it can keep the hands from committing theft or murder—nevertheless it cannot produce internal movements, such as fear of God, trust in God, patience, etc.

Reflections

"Concerning free will it is taught that a human being has some measure of free will, so as to live an externally honorable life and to choose among the things reason comprehends." Philip Melanchthon begins this article much in line with his own arguments against Erasmus.[5] He takes Luther's small admission in the *Bondage of the Will* and makes sure that people do not imagine the Evangelicals are determinists (often nicknamed "Manichaeans" after the fourth-century sect that held only those with a spark of the divine Logos could ascend through the heavens back to the One). We have choice precisely where free choice belongs: in deciding about matters of this life. Even here, however, our weak flesh and the devil often hinder even these choices.[6] Nevertheless, when it comes to daily life, in matters subject to our reason, we can exercise free choice. We cannot blame our bad choices on fate or God.

"However, without the grace, help and operation of the Holy Spirit a human being cannot become pleasing to God, fear or believe in God with the whole heart, or expel innate evil lusts from the heart." This spells out the human dilemma: "Without the grace, help, and operation of the Holy Spirit" we are helpless. This echoes CA V, where the Holy Spirit uses means to

---

5. See Timothy J. Wengert, *Human Freedom, Christian Righteousness: Philip Melanchthon's Exegetical Dispute with Erasmus of Rotterdam* (New York: Oxford University Press, 1998).
6. Ap XVIII.5 (BC, 234).

make and keep believers. The Latin is even blunter: "It [the will] has no power [Latin: *vim*]." This "power" of the will is precisely the "free choice" (*liberum arbitrium*) or, rather, it would be except that regarding God there is no such power at all. CA XVIII describes the four things that we cannot do echoing the language of original sin (CA II: "lack of fear of God and faith in God"; "innate evil lusts") and justification (CA IV: "pleasing to God"). Human beings cannot fix the core problem in their relation to God, namely, that we do not fear or believe in God. Instead we trust ourselves (and our ability to choose). The only medicine to fix this sickness unto death is the Holy Spirit.

This emphasis on the Holy Spirit here and in CA V may come as a surprise to Lutherans who often seem to neglect the role of the Holy Spirit in their teaching. Other, so-called "Holy Spirit" churches may talk a lot about the "Spirit" but they rarely if ever claim that the Holy Spirit creates faith in them through God's Word. Instead, they argue, this is the work human beings do to "earn" (or at least receive) the Holy Spirit. Moreover, such churches often concentrate on the gifts of the Holy Spirit (especially "tongues," "healing," and "prophecy"), which Paul describes later in 1 Corinthians 12, but do not give attention to the one gift that no Christian can live without: true trust in God (1 Cor 12:3: "No one can say, 'Jesus is Lord' but by the Holy Spirit"). Because Lutherans confess that without the Holy Spirit they cannot even believe in God, they can lay a remarkable claim to being the "Holy Spirit church." As Luther wrote in 1529 in his Small Catechism: "I believe . . . that I cannot believe . . . , but that the Holy Spirit has called me through the gospel."[7] Without the Holy Spirit, we are nothing!

"Instead, this happens through the Holy Spirit who is given through the Word of God." This paraphrase of CA V reminds us that CA XVIII is using earlier articles to make its case. Starting with CA XVI, the drafters began to discuss a series of theological articles derived from specific controversies: obedience to the emperor (CA XVI); the Augustin Bader affair (CA XVII); the debate with Erasmus and others (CA XVIII and XIX); the relation of faith and works raised by Eck's *404 Articles* (CA XX), and prayers to saints (CA XXI). These debates are not merely differences in practice (as in CA XXII–XXVIII) but involve applying the basics of the gospel (CA I–XV) to specific theological problems. The Latin version ("But this righteousness is worked in the heart when the Holy Spirit is received through the word") is not quite as clear about the action of the Holy Spirit, but the end result is the same. Human beings cannot choose God; God chooses them. But because Lutherans tie this choice to the work of the Spirit *through the Word*, they never face the same anxieties about predestination as their Reformed cousins. Our election takes place

---

7. SC, "Creed," 6 (BC, 355).

precisely through the means of grace—that is, the Word of God audible and visible—and not merely in some divine backroom that faith cannot penetrate. **"For Paul says (1 Cor 2 [:14]): 'Those who are natural do not receive the gifts of God's Spirit.'"** The use of this Bible verse is interesting for several reasons. For one thing, probably unbeknownst to the Reformers, Thomas Aquinas also often cited this text to distinguish natural knowledge and powers from faith and "supernatural" knowledge. For another, already in his 1522 annotations on this verse, Melanchthon insists that the phrase "those who are natural" does not refer simply to corporal lusts but to those "using reason, the kind of people that Socrates, Zeno, or Paul—before his conversion—were."[8] Thus, despite the way some scholastic theologians used this text, Paul excludes the highest parts of the human being from a relation to God. In 1522, Melanchthon was contrasting human reason to the work of the Holy Spirit.

"In order that it may be recognized that nothing new is taught here, these are the clear words of Augustine concerning free will, quoted here from the third book of the *Hypognosticon* . . ." The *Hypognosticon* (more accurately: *Hypomnesticon*) was a product of the ancient church attributed to Augustine in the medieval manuscript tradition (although even then Augustine's authorship was questioned). In the seventeenth century and continuing through the twentieth a range of authors and dates were proposed for the document. More recently John Edward Chisholm[9] has argued that Prosper of Aquitaine wrote the work, although his thesis has not met with universal acceptance. Despite objections by Alexander Y. Hwang[10] among others, Chisholm's proposal certainly places the work squarely in the orbit of Prosper and his circle of supporters. This introduction to the longest citation in the CA reveals the drafters' intention in quoting sources from the ancient church. First, they want to underscore that they are squarely within the catholic (i.e., universal) tradition of the church. What they have to say is not new. Second, the charge of heresy always involves suspicion of novelty. While today's theologians, mirroring the society in which we live, may seem addicted to the "newest" trends, the Reformers and their opponents were highly suspicious of novelty. New does not mean better, and it certainly does not mean being faithful. Third, they imply that their opponents (especially Erasmus of Rotterdam in his famous debate with Luther over freedom of choice) are the

---

8. Philip Melanchthon, *Annotations on First Corinthians*, trans. John Patrick Donnelly (Milwaukee: Marquette University Press, 1995), 53.

9. John Edward Chisholm, *The Pseudo-Augustinian Hypomnesticon against the Pelagians and Celestians: Introduction* (Fribourg: University Press, 1967).

10. Alexander Y. Hwang, *Intrepid Lover of Perfect Grace: The Life and Thought of Prosper of Aquitaine* (Washington, DC: Catholic University of America Press, 2009), 22–25.

innovators and thus likely to be entertaining heterodox ideas.[11] Even though this text is most likely Prosper's, the conclusion remains: this way of talking about human choice is not new and need not be rejected out of hand. No wonder the *Confutation* accepted this article!

The Latin version of the CA quotes the *Hypognosticon* word for word, but by comparing the German to it, we learn in two instances just how the Reformers were interpreting it. Where the Latin original has "the judgment of reason," the German expands it to "a natural, innate mind [or intellect] and reason." The succinct Latin phrase, "It does not enable them, without God, to begin—much less complete—anything that pertains to God," is purposely expanded to include "such as loving or fearing God with their whole heart," which clearly comes from the Reformers' own view of original sin in CA II and explains what they understand the *Hypognosticon* to be talking about. Most importantly, this lengthy citation confirms what Melanchthon especially gleaned from Luther: the clear distinction between the free choice of good or evil actions in our life with others (Latin: *coram hominibus*) and the impossibility of doing anything vis-à-vis God (*coram Deo*). For Melanchthon and his fellow drafters, this protected the Christian message on two sides. The Evangelicals were neither Pelagian nor Manichaean; that is, they eliminated all works from the relation to God but allowed freedom (and, thus, rejected Stoic or Manichaean determinism) in the actions pertaining to this life. To this same end, Melanchthon most often distinguished between a civil righteousness (*iustitia civilis*) and a righteousness of faith or divine righteousness (*iustitia fidei* or *divina*).

Latin: *"They condemn the Pelagians and others who teach that without the Holy Spirit by the powers of nature alone, we are able to love God above all things and can also keep the commandments of God 'according to the substance of the acts.' Although nature can in some measure produce external works—for it can keep the hands from committing theft or murder—nevertheless it cannot produce internal movements, such as fear of God, trust in God, patience, etc."* This addition in the *editio princeps* of 1531 reveals the continuation of an attack on Gabriel Biel and other late-medieval teachers that had already begun in September 1517 with Luther's theses on scholastic theology.[12] Biel had reduced the "grace given freely" (*gratia gratis data*) to humanity's natural powers and God's giving of the commandments. This meant that when human creatures "do what is in them" (*facere quod in se est*) they are able to love God above all things but only "according to the substance

---

11. It is an open question to what degree Luther was familiar with this text, although he may have gotten the image of the human being ridden either by the devil or by God from it (MPL 45:1632). See LW 33:65–66 (*On the Bondage of the Will*); WA 59:325 and WA 41:451 (cf. WA 41:141; a sermon from 1535).

12. LW 31:9–16.

of the acts" (*quoad substantiam actuum*). This restriction helped Biel avoid the notion that human beings had all they needed without any contribution from God. Even though the acts themselves represented complete fulfillment of the law, Biel argued, believers also need another kind of grace, the grace that makes acceptable (*gratia gratum faciens*) infused into the soul as a disposition to love (*habitus charitatis*). Then they could fulfill the law "according to the intention of the lawgiver" (*quoad intentionem legislatoris*), who intended that human beings must first possess the grace that makes them acceptable. Against these scholastic notions, this addition to CA XVIII argues that natural human beings can produce some externally good works, but in their hearts they are still (without God) ruled by sin and, as CA II predicts, cannot fear or trust in God.

The astounding thing about Biel's position is its reappearance in Christian theology and practice. The appeal to human free choice over against God results in the law systematically destroying grace by reducing it to things received in creation and thereby forces people back onto their own powers and devices. Then theologians have to find some place for God's mercy to act in such a way that it does not break the law. When we encounter either Christian leaders who insist that people "decide for Jesus" or people who have been duped by this message, we can help them most by clearly defining grace as God's mercy in Christ and by eliminating works from faith (and, hence, from our relation to God). Those who "do what is in them" sin! Absent the Holy Spirit, our actions are always twisted by our addiction to ourselves.

We hear, "No one can choose God," so we respond, "But at least we can reject, can't we?" Yes, except that's all we do on our own, and, in any case, why would you want to do that? To this we splutter, "Oh, I don't want to do this. I was just asking theoretically." And with that the Old Creature and its desperate schemes to stay in charge are laid bare. So then it tries another tack. "If faith is a gift, I'll just wait until God gives it to me"—as if faith were something you could carry around in your pocket! Faith is relationship arising from the hearing of God's promise; it is falling in love (or, as I recently learned from Taiwanese Lutherans, "falling in Love River"). "Waiting around" is just another word for unbelief. "Well, what about all those who have never heard the gospel in (fill-in-the-blank)?" Again, a theoretical question based upon the Old Creature's logic, to which one can only answer: "They are in God's hands. What's keeping you from telling them the good news of God's merciful choice?"

When all the Old Creature's theories run out, we may finally ask a far more serious, personal question: "Why doesn't my loved one believe?" Then our questions are no longer hypothetical but concrete and heartfelt. Then we are left (with the disciples of every age) simply sowing the good seed of God's promise among them and taking a nap (Mark 4:26–29) or, as Luther paraphrased this text, drinking beer with our friends.[13] Then we are left praying to God for our loved ones and leaving them in Christ's wounded hands—far better responses than blaming them for their captivity (and imagining that we are not in the same boat with them). Then we can even, in moments of desperation, throw the keys at God's door (to use a sixteenth-century German saying for it) and ask God "Why?" God can withstand our questioning far better than our neighbors can take our pestering them to do the one thing we are *all* incapable of doing: deciding on our own for Jesus.

We Teach and Confess

The pictures we use to discuss this topic help to some degree to draw us closer to the truth. For example, one way to understand Luther's skepticism concerning humanity's ability to "discuss" free choice is to compare it to what happens when a spouse makes a unilateral decision (say, to buy an expensive computer or some other bauble) and his or her partner objects vehemently. The perpetrator feigns neutrality by saying, "Don't get so angry, dear. Let's talk about this like reasonable, balanced adults." Except that it is too late! The die is cast and the computer-buyer is anything but neutral, having already taken matters into his or her own hands. Discussion only covers up the one-sided choice already undertaken.

One objection to the bound choice has to do with predestination—something found throughout Scripture and yet denied by many who so vociferously proclaim their allegiance to the Bible (but more strenuously their allegiance to free choice). Other sixteenth-century theologians treated predestination from the point of view of strict logic and thereby, at least according to Lutherans, undermined the effectiveness and comfort of God's promises by always adding an "if" to them: "*If* you are among the elect, this promise is for you." Then the very uncertainty to which Luther had objected in arguments with late-medieval scholastic theologians (who insisted that persons could never know for certain whether the absolution applied to them), came in through the back door. Instead, as Robert Kolb has brilliantly argued, Lutherans maintain a "broken," anti-logical view of predestination, applying it only to salvation but insisting that our condemnation is our own fault.[14]

---

13. LW 51:77.
14. Robert Kolb, *Bound Choice, Election, and Wittenberg Theological Method: From Martin Luther to the Formula of Concord* (Grand Rapids: Eerdmans, 2005), 260. For a fierce theological defense of the bondage of the will, see Steven D. Paulson, *Luther's Outlaw God*, vol. 1: *Hiddenness, Evil, and Predestination* (Minneapolis: Fortress, 2018).

This illogic, however, arises from the language of love, not logic, where lovers often talk about their relationship in predestinarian terms: "It just *had* to be"; "Our marriage was made in heaven"; or "What would have happened if we had not bumped into each other coming off the elevator at that hotel?" Paul employs this language of love, not logic, in Ephesians 1:3–6 (NIV):

> Praise be to the God and Father of our Lord Jesus Christ, who has blessed us in the heavenly realms with every spiritual blessing in Christ. For he chose us in him before the creation of the world to be holy and blameless in his sight. In love he predestined us for adoption [as a full heir] through Jesus Christ, in accordance with his pleasure and will—to the praise of his glorious grace, which he has freely given us in the One he loves.

Any time we use predestination to frighten souls or to make them uncertain of their standing before God, we destroy God's own loving intention and the faith of our uncertain neighbors.

What do we do, then, if a neighbor or loved one does not believe? This was Paul's initial, personal question in Romans 9. When one hears that our relation to God is unconditional, one often asks this question—so much so that when it would come up in class discussion I would tell students that they had asked "Question 9."[15] That is, they were following in the footsteps of St. Paul, who also proclaimed God's unconditional mercy and therefore came invariably to this question. In fact, only the proclamation of God's unconditional love and grace will lead us to ask "Question 9" and shows us that we are finally on the right, Pauline track. Moreover, in the end we can only fall back upon God's grace and cry with Paul at the end of Romans 11:33: "O the depth of the riches and wisdom of the knowledge of God! How unsearchable his judgments!"

When I was a youth pastor in the 1970s, my pastoral advice to worried parents when their children seemed to have abandoned the faith was not to stop sharing God's good news with them but more importantly to pray the first two petitions of the Lord's Prayer specifically for that child in light of Luther's explanations from the Small Catechism. "Hallowed be your name for my child!" (That is, may the Word of God be taught in its truth and purity for them.) "Your kingdom come for my child!" (That is, may God send the Holy Spirit so that they come to trust that very Word.) Our lives are in God's hands.

---

15. They also asked another question, based upon Romans 6, that I labeled "Question 6." See above.

19

"The Devil Made Me Do It—Not!"

F lip Wilson, that brilliant comedian of the 1960s and '70s, used several outrageous characters in his television show, including Geraldine, something of a floozy, whose favorite line often ended up on the lips of Wilson's fans: "The devil made me do it!" One misapplication of the preceding article demanded its own article in the CA, and this was the accusation that the Reformers taught a form of determinism and thus, in essence, blamed God for evil. The response was univocal: we have no one to blame but ourselves. My teacher David Steinmetz, to describe the human responsibility for sin, used a twisted paraphrase of a gospel hymn, "We are falling deep in sin—whoopee!" Human beings are not only responsible for sin, they downright enjoy it.

CA XIX

[German]

Concerning the cause of sin it is taught among us that although almighty God has created and preserves all of nature, nevertheless the perverted will causes sin in all those who are evil and despise God. This, then, is the will of the devil and of all the ungodly. As soon as God withdrew his hand, it turned from God to malice, as Christ says (John 8 [:44]): "When [the devil] lies, he speaks according to his own nature."

[Latin]

Concerning the cause of sin they teach that although God creates and preserves nature, nevertheless the cause of sin is the will of those who are evil, that is, of the devil and the ungodly. Since it was not assisted by God, their will turned away from God, as Christ says in John 8 [:44], "When [the devil] lies, he speaks according to his own nature."

Reflections

"Concerning the cause of sin it is taught among us that although almighty God has created and preserves all of nature . . ." This article starts off in a very different direction, affirming that God is indeed sovereign creator. There is not some second, malevolent force of equal power drumming up evil in the world. In arguing against Erasmus, Melanchthon had also emphasized God's general power over all things.[1] Often those who want most to protect God from evil take a different tack, invoking fate, luck, or the forces in creation as the cause of evil and thus eliminating God's responsibility. Such speculation about God's role in evil (called theodicy) does little real good and only withdraws God from the messiness of this world. In *Bondage of the Will* Luther observes the following. From humanity's perspective, God *does* often seem to be the source of evil (or at least its enabler). But this notion actually drives a person away from speculation or rationalization and toward faith that, despite appearances, God is good. Most of our own attempts to exonerate God, on the contrary, undermine faith in God and cause us to put our trust in our reason's ability to figure out these matters.

". . . [N]evertheless the perverted will causes sin in all those who are evil and despise God. This, then, is the will of the devil and of all the ungodly." Why do theological assertions like this one make us so nervous? This is not a proof, the carefully crafted conclusion of a theological argument. It is simply an assertion—or, more accurately, a confession of sin. "'Twas I, Lord Jesus, I it was denied Thee; I crucified Thee." For those looking for answers and proof, such assertions will always disappoint. "The perverted will causes sin"—the very will that cannot fear, love, or trust in God above all things. *Our* will! Melanchthon knows only too well the kind of attacks being leveled at the Reformers because of their emphasis on the bound choice and God's sovereign grace. All he can do is assert against these claims what he views as true: humanity must take full responsibility for its sin.

"As soon as God withdrew his hand, it turned from God to malice . . ." God who is preserving creation withdrew his hand and humanity jumped straight into sin, without anyone pushing them. It is no different than leaving two teenagers in heat in a dark room unattended. No matter how many times one may teach abstinence or morality of one kind or another and appeal to their reason to consider the consequence of their actions, once the lights are out and the cat is away . . . No matter how unavoidable it may appear, sinning is second nature to us—"Whoopee!"

". . . [A]s Christ says (John 8 [:44]): 'When [the devil] lies, he speaks according to his own nature.'" This biblical text may seem somewhat out

---

1. Timothy J. Wengert, *Human Freedom, Christian Righteousness: Philip Melanchthon's Exegetical Dispute with Erasmus of Rotterdam* (New York: Oxford University Press, 1998), 80–109.

of place. However, in his annotations on John from 1523, Melanchthon connects this text with free choice. "Such are all who are not in Christ. It is easy to discern the nature of human wisdom and righteousness so that you can easily judge what free choice is capable of. This is what Scripture attacks in the wisdom of the world."[2] Free choice is naturally capable of sin—whether the devil's choice or ours—it simply loves to sin. "Whoopee!"

We Teach and Confess

Theodicy—attempts to exonerate divine providence, goodness, and power in the face of evil—is a term invented by the Lutheran philosopher Gottfried Leibniz (1646–1716). It tried to answer a philosophical problem, posed in the early stages of the Enlightenment, one that arises when one limits the ability of human choice and wants to attribute power to a sovereign God. It also arises quite naturally from human experience, when one asks why a loved one died or why a random natural disaster occurred. It is curious that before the Enlightenment there was no direct and thorough discussion of this issue, and some today even question whether theodicy is a helpful category for theology. The glib answers to the experience of evil are clearly not always very helpful. "God needed another angel" may comfort a distraught mother for whom the assurance that God has not somehow blinked and that the death of her child was not random, but it may not help another mother at all and cause her to rage, "If God is that cruel, I want nothing to do with that kind of God." The seemingly helpful exoneration of God ("God did not cause this evil but let it happen") caused one widower to write to the local newspaper, "That's like someone standing at the edge of a swimming pool while watching someone drown in it!"

CA XIX does not attempt to answer this problem, perhaps because in the sixteenth century believers understood far better than we do that they had no answer to it except to assert two things: God creates and preserves; evil is our own fault. More than that, we cannot answer but can only cry with Paul, "O the depth of God's wisdom!" and, with the whole church, cry "Maranatha!" (Come, Lord Jesus!). Anything more forces us to abandon God's promises for the safety of our own reason. Thus, in his Small Catechism Martin Luther called "Deliver us from evil" the sum of all the petitions of the Lord's Prayer. Here we pray that God "would take us from this valley of tears to himself in heaven." In the face of evil, that prayer is all we have.

---

2. CR 14:1126.

20

CONSOLING FAITH *AND* GOOD WORKS

W hen the Evangelical teachers arrived in Augsburg with their princely retinues, a new book was coming off the presses in Ingolstadt, only fifty miles from Augsburg, written by their chief opponent, Johannes Eck. The *404 Articles*[1] contained 386 heretical statements culled from the writings of Luther and his circle, of Ulrich Zwingli and his collaborators, and even of some Anabaptists. One of the most serious charges was that the Reformers forbade good works. Of course, this was not just a theological complaint; it also had political ramifications. After all, Emperor Charles V's "favorite" good work for his subjects was obedience to the emperor. Thus, Eck was accusing the Reformers of being anarchists. CA XX, the longest of the doctrinal articles, is their response.

It happened almost every time I taught justification by faith alone—"Up and Down Religion" (what my students once labeled "Chutes and Ladders," after the children's board game). Someone would ask, "This sounds too good to be true. Why don't we just sin to get more grace?" As I mentioned earlier, this is Question 6—Paul's anticipation of his opponents' objection to God's unconditional mercy in Christ (Romans 6): "Shall we sin the more, that grace

---

1. Johann Eck, *Four Hundred Four Articles for the Imperial Diet at Augsburg* (1530), no. 198 [199] – 205 [206], in *Sources and Contexts of the Book of Concord*, ed. Robert Kolb and James A. Nestingen (Minneapolis: Fortress, 2001), 31–82. The questions dealt with in CA XX cover nos. 198–205 [199–206], in *Sources and Contexts*, 56–57.

may more abound?" When people ask this question seriously (and not just to set a trap for the teacher), then we can assure them that they really are caught up in Pauline logic, because they are asking Paul's question. Undermine the unconditional nature of God's mercy, and Paul's question in Romans 6 (and the question about predestination in Romans 9) would disappear. But the challenge remains: How can we teach God's no-strings-attached mercy without turning Christians into spiritual anarchists?[2]

Martin Luther, too, dealt directly with this charge in his tract from 1520, *Freedom of a Christian*. As mentioned above, although at first glance this work appears to be divided into two equal parts (the Christian as "Free Lord of All" and the Christian as "Servant of All"), when Luther finally arrived at the second section he makes two things very clear. First, the entire second part answers the mean-spirited taunts of his opponents, who say that if they follow Luther's position they will simply abandon any and all good works. Of course, they do not believe this but only want to show how absurd Luther's position is, to which Luther responds, "Not so, you wicked people, not so!"[3] Thus, at every turn, Luther returns repeatedly in this second section to his discussion of faith from the first section.

Second, good works can *never* be separated from justification by faith; truly good works follow inevitably and spontaneously from justification by faith alone. This means that the later Protestant addiction to dividing justification from sanctification is not just wrong but wicked, in reality always undermining God's mercy and selling the Holy Spirit short. No! We are justified, sanctified [which really just means "made holy"], and even glorified by faith alone and not by our works. To live the sanctified life is no different than leading the justified life; it happens by faith alone in the merciful promise of our savior. Preachers' (and others') incessant worry about good works simply shows their unbelief, and ours!

---

2. I have sometimes heard Lutheran theologians, who should know better, speak of this charge as one of the weaknesses of Lutheranism: that Lutherans are uncertain about the role of good works in the Christian life. This simply means that they reject the Lutheran solution to this problem and prefer to smuggle good works into justification, thereby destroying the merciful message of the gospel and replacing it with more law. This may be a proper Reformed solution to the problem, but it has nothing to do with the Lutheran witness to the gospel.

3. TAL 1:510. Luther follows the ancient rules of rhetoric here, so that this entire second section is actually conceived and written as the *confutatio*, the refutation of anticipated objections from one's opponents.

CA XX

[German]

CONCERNING FAITH AND GOOD WORKS

Our people are falsely accused of prohibiting good works. But their writings concerning the Decalogue and other writings demonstrate that they have given good and useful account and admonition concerning proper Christian walks of life and works, about which little had been taught before our time. Instead, for the most part childish, unnecessary works—such as rosaries, the cult of the saints, joining religious orders, pilgrimages, appointed fasts, holy days, brotherhoods and the like—were emphasized in all sermons. Our opponents also no longer praise such unnecessary works as highly as they once did. Moreover, they have also learned to speak now of faith, about which they did not preach at all in former times. Rather, they now teach that we do not become righteous before God by works alone, but they add faith in Christ, saying that faith and works make us righteous before God. Such talk may offer a little more comfort than the teaching that one should rely on works alone.

Because at present the teaching concerning faith, which is the principal part of the Christian life, has not been emphasized for such a long time, as all must admit, but only a doctrine of works was preached everywhere, our people have taught as follows:

In the first place, our works cannot reconcile us with God or obtain

[Latin]

CONCERNING FAITH AND GOOD WORKS

Our people are falsely accused of prohibiting good works. For their writings on the Decalogue and others on similar subjects bear witness that they have given useful instruction concerning all kinds and walks of life: what manner of life and which activities in every calling please God. In former times preachers taught too little about such things. Instead, they urged childish and needless works, such as particular holy days and fasts, brotherhoods, pilgrimages, the cult of the saints, rosaries, monasticism and the like. Since our adversaries have been reminded about these things, they are now unlearning them and do not preach about such useless works as much as in former times. They are also beginning to mention faith, about which there once was an astonishing silence. They teach that we are not justified by works alone, but they combine faith and works, saying that we are justified by both. This teaching is more tolerable than the previous one and can offer more consolation than their old teaching.

Therefore, because the teaching concerning faith, which ought to be the principal one in the church, has languished so long in obscurity—everyone must grant that there has been a profound silence concerning the righteousness of faith in preaching while only the teaching of works has been grace. Instead, this happens through faith alone when a person believes that our sins are forgiven for Christ's sake, who alone is the mediator to reconcile the Father. Now all who imagine they can accomplish this by works and can merit grace, despise Christ and seek their own way to God contrary to the gospel.

This teaching about faith is publicly and clearly treated in Paul at many places, especially in Eph 2 [:8-9]: "For by grace you have been saved through faith, and this is not your own doing; it is the gift of God—not the result of works, so that no one may boast...."

That no new interpretation is introduced here can be demonstrated from Augustine who diligently deals with this matter and also teaches that we obtain grace and become righteous before God through faith in Christ, and not through works. His whole book *On the Spirit and the Letter* proves it.

Now although untested people despise this teaching is completely, it is nevertheless the case that it is very comforting and beneficial for timid and terrified consciences. For the conscience cannot find rest and peace through works but by faith alone, when it concludes on its own with certainty that it has a gracious God for Christ's sake, as Paul says (Rom 5 [:1]): "Therefore, since we are justified by faith, we have peace with God."

In former times people did not emphasize this comfort but instead drove the poor consciences to their own works. As a result, all sorts of works were undertaken. For the conscience forced some into monasteries, in the

promoted in the church—our people have instructed the churches about faith in the following way:

To begin with, they remind the churches that our works cannot reconcile God or merit grace and forgiveness of sins, but we obtain this only by faith when we believe that we are received into grace on account of Christ, who alone has been appointed mediator and atoning sacrifice through whom the Father is reconciled. Therefore, all who trust that they merit grace by works despise the merit and grace of Christ and seek a way to God without Christ through human powers, since Christ has said about himself [John 14:8a]: "I am the way, and the truth, and the life."

This teaching concerning faith is treated in Paul everywhere. Eph 2 [:8-9]: "For by grace you have been saved through faith, and this is . . . not the result of works...."

So that no one may quibble that we have contrived a new interpretation of Paul, this entire approach is supported by the testimonies of the Fathers. In many writings Augustine defends grace and the righteousness of faith against the merit of works. Ambrose teaches similar things in *Concerning the Calling of the Gentiles* and elsewhere. For in *Concerning the Calling of the Gentiles* he says: "Redemption by the blood of Christ would become worthless and the preference for human works would not give way to the mercy of God if justification, which takes place by grace, were due to antecedent merits. For then it would be the worker's wage rather than the donor's gift."

hope of obtaining grace there through the monastic life. Some devised other works as a way of earning grace and making satisfaction for sins. Many of them discovered that a person could not obtain peace by such means. That is why it became necessary to preach this teaching concerning faith in Christ and diligently to emphasize it, so that each person may know that God's grace is grasped by faith alone, without merit.

We must also explain that we are not talking here about the faith possessed by the devil and the ungodly, who also believe the story that Christ suffered and was raised from the dead. But we are talking about true faith, which believes that we obtain grace and forgiveness of sin through Christ.

All who know that in Christ they have a gracious God call upon him and are not, like the heathen, without God. For the devil and the ungodly do not believe this article about the forgiveness of sin. That is why they are enemies of God, cannot call upon him, and cannot hope for anything good from him. Moreover, as has now been indicated, Scripture talks about faith but does not label it knowledge such as the devil and the ungodly have. For Heb 11 [:1] teaches that faith is not only a matter of historical knowledge, but of having confidence in God to receive his promise. Augustine also reminds us that we should understand the word "faith" in Scripture to mean confidence in God—that God is gracious to us—and not merely such knowledge of these stories as the devils also have.

Further, it is taught that good works should and must be done, not

Moreover, although this teaching is despised by those without experience, nevertheless devout and anxious consciences find by experience that it offers the greatest consolation. For consciences cannot be calmed by any work but only by faith when they are certain that they have a God who has been reconciled on account of Christ. As Paul teaches in Rom 5 [:1]: "Therefore, since we are justified by faith we have peace with God." This whole teaching must be referred to that struggle of the terrified conscience, and it cannot be understood apart from that struggle. That is why those who are wicked and without experience judge it badly. For they imagine that Christian righteousness is nothing but civil and philosophical righteousness.

In former times, consciences were vexed by the doctrine of works; they did not hear consolation from the gospel. Conscience drove some into the desert, into monasteries, where they hoped to merit grace through the monastic life. Some contrived other works to merit grace and make satisfaction for sins. Consequently, it was essential to pass on and restore this teaching about faith in Christ so that anxious consciences should not be deprived of consolation but know that grace and forgiveness of sins are apprehended by faith in Christ.

People are also reminded that the term "faith" here does not signify only historical knowledge—the kind of faith that the ungodly and the devil have—but that it signifies faith which believes not only the history but also the effect of that a person relies on them to earn grace, but for God's sake and to God's praise. Faith alone always takes hold of grace and forgiveness of sin. Because the Holy Spirit is given through faith, the heart is also moved to do good works. For before, because it lacks the Holy Spirit, the heart is too weak. Moreover, it is in the power of the devil who drives our poor human nature to many sins, as we observe in the philosophers who tried to live honestly and blamelessly, but then failed to do so and fell into many great, public sins. That is what happens to human beings when they are separated from true faith, are without the Holy Spirit, and govern themselves through their own human strength alone.

That is why this teaching concerning faith is not to be censured for prohibiting good works. On the contrary, it should be praised for teaching the performance of good works and for offering help as to how they may be done. For without faith and without Christ human nature and human power are much too weak to do good works: such as to call on God, to have patience in suffering, to love the neighbor, to engage diligently in legitimate callings, to be obedient, to avoid evil lust, etc. Such lofty and genuine works cannot be done without the help of Christ, as he himself says in John 15 [:5]: "Apart from me you can do nothing."

the history, namely, this article of the forgiveness of sins, that is, that we have grace, righteousness, and forgiveness of sins through Christ.

Now all who know that they are reconciled to the Father through Christ truly know God, know that God cares for them, and call upon him. In short, they are not without God, as are the heathen. For the devils and the ungodly cannot believe this article of the forgiveness of sins. Hence they hate God as an enemy, do not call upon him, and expect nothing good from him. Augustine also reminds his readers in this way about the word "faith" and teaches that in the Scriptures the word "faith" is to be understood not as knowledge, such as the ungodly have, but as trust that consoles and encourages terrified minds.

Beyond this, our people teach that it is necessary to do good works, not that we should count on meriting grace through them but because it is the will of God. It is only by faith that forgiveness of sins and grace are apprehended. Moreover, because the Holy Spirit is received through faith, consequently hearts are renewed and endowed with new affections so as to be able to do good works. For Ambrose says: "Faith is the mother of the good will and the righteous action." For without the Holy Spirit human powers are full of ungodly affections and are too weak to do good works before God. Besides, they are under the power of the devil, who impels human beings to various sins, ungodly opinions and manifest crimes. This also may be seen in the philosophers, who, though they tried to live honestly, were still not able to do so but were defiled by many obvious crimes. Such is the weakness of human beings when they govern themselves by human powers alone without faith or the Holy Spirit.

Hence it is readily apparent that no one should accuse this teaching of prohibiting good works. On the contrary, it is rather to be commended for showing how we can do good works. For without faith human nature cannot possibly do the works of the First or Second Commandments. Without faith it does not call upon God, expect anything from God or bear the cross, but seeks and trusts in human help. Consequently, all kinds of urges and human designs rule in the heart when faith and trust in God are lacking. That is why Christ said (John 15 [:5]): "Apart from me you can do nothing." And the church sings: "Without your will divine / Naught is in humankind / All innocence is gone."

Reflections

"Concerning faith and good works." This is the first time that the original versions of the CA bear a heading—captions for the first twenty-one articles first appear in much later printings of the work. Already this shows how important the drafters considered this subject. The very fact that most of this article concentrates on faith ought again warn us not to imagine that we can separate the two things and assume that they are simply different topics of theological conversation. If when speaking of works you leave out faith, there is no chance of understanding good works properly.

"Our people are falsely accused of prohibiting good works." This is such a startlingly different beginning to an article that even the *Confutation* derides it as more a defense of the Evangelicals' preachers rather than an article of faith. But true theology and confession never occur in a vacuum and always address the real challenges of the day. The Reformers had read Eck's *404 Articles* and knew how dangerous a charge this was, both theologically and politically. Moreover, beginning in this way indicates that this article, the one that most reflects Melanchthon's own theology and language, takes on certain aspects of classical rhetoric, as indicated in the historical introduction above.[4] This sentence reflects the *status controversiae*, the main point of controversy and introduces the Reformers' proof that this statement is false.

"But their writings concerning the Decalogue and other writings demonstrate that they have given good and useful account and admonition concerning proper Christian walks of life and works, about which little had been taught before our time. This is the positive side of the preceding sentence. It shows the sophistication of Melanchthon's arguments. First, he refers directly to the Decalogue, because he knows that the opposition defines good works very differently and because Luther's catechisms had just appeared in print. Second, he immediately connects such works to "walks of life" (German: *Stände*), a term first introduced in CA XVI. Christian walks of life do not divide clergy from laity or those under a vow from those who are not. Christian life is precisely the everyday lives of believers, filled with diaper changes, manure hauling, and other societal responsibilities. The Latin underscores this when it states, "concerning all kinds and walks of life[5]: what manner of life and which activities in every calling please God." The "in every calling" immediately makes all Christian activity equal and God-pleasing. Third, he turns the tables and begins a sustained criticism of past preaching. The importance of his focus on preaching will become clear in the next sentence.

"Instead, for the most part childish, unnecessary works—such as rosaries, the cult of the saints, joining religious orders, pilgrimages, appointed fasts, holy days, brotherhoods and the like—were emphasized in all sermons. Here Melanchthon throws down the gauntlet and dismisses typical late-medieval preaching and piety in a single stroke. We know from the preaching manuals produced before the Reformation just how prevalent such sermons were.[6] To call these things listed here "childish, unnecessary works," represents a frontal attack on late-medieval piety. Melanchthon's focus on preaching echoes Luther's concerns already expressed in the *95 Theses* and in *Freedom of a Christian*. Wittenberg's reform aimed at transforming the proclamation of the gospel.

---

4. See Timothy J. Wengert, "Philip Melanchthon's Last Word to Cardinal Lorenzo Campeggio, Papal Legate at the 1530 Diet of Augsburg," in *Dona Melanchthoniana: Festgabe für Heinz Scheible zum 70. Geburtstag*, ed. Johanna Loehr (Stuttgart-Bad Cannstatt: Frommann-Holzboog, 2001), 457–83; and Charles Arand, "Melanchthon's Rhetorical Argument for *Sola Fide* in the Apology," *Lutheran Quarterly* 14 (2000): 281–308.
5. Here the Latin, *"genera vitae"* (kinds or walks of life), affirms the English circumlocution of the German *Stand*, since there is also no direct equivalent in Latin.
6. John W. O'Malley, "Luther the Preacher," in *The Martin Luther Quincentennial*, ed. Gerhard Dünnhaupt (Detroit: Wayne State University Press, 1985), 3–16.

"Our opponents also no longer praise such unnecessary works as highly as they once did. Moreover, they have also learned to speak now of faith, about which they did not preach at all in former times. Rather, they now teach that we do not become righteous before God by works alone, but they add faith in Christ, saying that faith and works make us righteous before God. Such talk may offer a little more comfort than the teaching that one should rely on works alone." It is hard to determine the degree to which Melanchthon is employing irony bordering on sarcasm here, or whether he is truly complimenting the change among his opponents. Martin Luther once joked in a Table Talk that Melanchthon's criticism of his enemies was often so subtle that they did not even know they were being attacked![7] He *is* certainly dismissing their earlier preaching as simply "justification by works alone."

The issue of "faith and works" continues to dog Lutheran/Roman Catholic discussions to this day, as reflected in the *Joint Declaration on the Doctrine of Justification*. This document, however, addresses the issue far more helpfully when it states: "But whatever in the justified precedes or follows the free gift of faith is neither the basis of justification nor merits it."[8] But if Melanchthon is being ironic, then he is pointing out the underlying fallacy of mixing faith and works: "It may offer a little more comfort," but not enough to console the terrified conscience. This mention of "comfort" also puts the reader on alert that comfort, like preaching, is going to be central to Melanchthon's exposition of faith and works in CA XX.

Latin: "Therefore, because the teaching concerning faith, which ought to be the principal one in the church, has languished so long in obscurity—everyone must grant that there has been a profound silence concerning the righteousness of faith in preaching while only the teaching of works has been promoted in the church—our people have instructed the churches about faith in the following way." What follows is the proof of the main proposition. Throughout this article, the Latin often gives a fuller, more dramatic account—typical of Melanchthon's remarkable Latin style. The teaching of faith "has languished so long in obscurity" about which "there has been a profound silence" in that "only the teaching of works has been promoted." This emotive Latin style is designed to move the reader to the evangelical side of the argument. It is designed to ingratiate the reader (especially, of course, the emperor) into listening to the Reformers' view. It also allows Melanchthon the chance to restate once again the central arguments of CA IV and VI, now using far more pointed language. This makes CA XX, I believe, the central article of the entire Augsburg Confession, a good place for teachers to begin

---

7. WA TR 1:140 (no. 348) and 4:637 (no. 5054). See also Timothy J. Wengert "Luther and Melanchthon—Melanchthon and Luther," *Luther-Jahrbuch* 66 (1999): 55–88.
8. *The Joint Declaration on the Doctrine of Justification* (Grand Rapids: Eerdmans, 2000), 19 (par. 25).

in explaining the heart of the Lutheran "proposal" (or, better, "confession") to the church catholic.

"In the first place, our works cannot reconcile us with God or obtain grace. Instead, this happens through faith alone when a person believes that our sins are forgiven for Christ's sake, who alone is the mediator to reconcile the Father." The first thing these confessors always say about faith is that it is the opposite of works. "Our works cannot reconcile us" rejects any and all mixing of faith and works in our standing before God. Thus, the "a little more comfort" (above) should probably be taken as sarcasm and not a genuine approval of such a position. Here, for the first time, the CA confesses that justification occurs "through faith *alone.*" They had, of course, introduced this language in CA VI but then not as their own formulation but rather as that of "Ambrose" (i.e., pseudo-Ambrose normally called Ambrosiaster). As in many other instances, however, "faith alone" is not a freestanding concept but rather the summary of all of those exclusive phrases (what Melanchthon will later call *particulae exclusivae*) in Paul that eliminate works. Moreover, Melanchthon connects "faith alone" to "Christ alone." One should not take the Latin addition, "and atoning sacrifice," as approval of the Anselmian theory of the atonement but rather as a reference to Romans 3:25 and the elimination of *all* human works of satisfaction, which was one way that Melanchthon's opponents viewed good works. Through his death Christ satisfied all punishment for sin and removed all guilt by reconciling humankind to the Father.

Latin: "Therefore, all who trust that they merit grace by works despise the merit and grace of Christ and seek a way to God without Christ through human powers, since Christ has said about himself [John 14:8a]: 'I am the way, and the truth, and the life.'" When Christians abandon justification by faith alone, there are two consequences. First, they despise Christ's merit and mercy. This is not just an old-fashioned problem of Melanchthon's opponents but it still dogs the church today, where preachers and teachers rush to abandon God's grace in order to talk about the "really important" matters of this or that (politically liberal or conservative) work. Some, when challenged on this point, reveal that they simply assume that "everyone knows that it is about Christ's grace," which is scant comfort, given that the Old Creature can know many things without believing or experiencing them.

The second consequence results from "seeking one's own way to God without Christ through human powers." This "seeking" metaphor mirrors the picture of "Up Religion" used earlier in this book. Either it is Christ and faith *alone* or it is all a matter of human works where Christ finally is not savior but merely another example or lawgiver. The fuller Latin version provides an important Scripture passage, often misconstrued by those who want to mix faith and works today. As Melanchthon sees it, Christ as "way, truth and life" excludes any and all works (not just those done by adherents to other religions). Instead of using this passage to look down our noses at other religions, we must use it on ourselves: "Christ is the way, not your works." Then the narrow-minded exclusivity for which some use this text is replaced by the truly good news that Christ saves us, not we ourselves.

"This teaching about faith is publicly and clearly treated in Paul at many places, especially in Eph 2 [:8–9]: 'For by grace you have been saved through faith, and this is not your own doing; it is the gift of God—not the result of works, so that no one may boast. . . .'" Melanchthon now provides a three-fold proof of the Evangelicals' claim, based upon the three authorities to which all Christians may appeal: Scripture, the witness of the ancient church, and experience. He begins with Scripture. Having already referred to Romans 3–4 in CA IV, he uses another remarkable text from Ephesians. Not only are all works eliminated here but also another reason for not importing works into one's relation to God becomes clear: boasting (even boasting about how sorry we are). Augustus Toplady, a Calvinist opponent of John Wesley, penned a hymn (beloved by Methodists!) that makes this very point: "Not the labors of my hands can fulfill Thy law's demands; could my zeal no respite know, could my tears forever flow, all for sin could not atone; Thou must save, and Thou alone."[9]

German: "That no new interpretation is introduced here can be demonstrated from Augustine who diligently deals with this matter and also teaches that we obtain grace and become righteous before God through faith in Christ, and not through works. His whole book *On the Spirit and the Letter* proves it. The second authority for Lutherans comes from the ancient (and medieval) church, what the Latin version of the CA calls "the testimonies of the Fathers." Like John the Baptist in John 1, the Fathers point to the Lamb of God who takes away the sin of the world. As with CA XVIII, these references aim to prove that the CA does not present any heretical novelty. The German references *On the Spirit and the Letter*, Augustine's explication of the book of Romans, a very important document for Lutherans at this time. Already in 1515–1516 Martin Luther had relied heavily upon this book in his early lectures on Romans.[10] In the 1530s Melanchthon revised the statutes of the theology faculty in Wittenberg to include mandatory lectures on this tract, and we know that only a few years later the tract was printed in Wittenberg (with a preface by Martin Luther) and lectured upon in 1545 by

---

9. Augustus M. Toplady, "Rock of Ages," *Evangelical Lutheran Worship* (Minneapolis: Augsburg Fortress, 2006), no. 623, v. 2.

10. See Leif Grane, *Modus loquendi theologicus: Luthers Kampf um die Erneuerung der Theologie (1515–1518)* (Leiden: Brill, 1975).

Johannes Bugenhagen, Wittenberg's chief pastor and a member of the theology faculty.[11]

Latin: **"In many writings Augustine defends grace and the righteousness of faith against the merit of works. Ambrose teaches similar things in** *Concerning the Calling of the Gentiles* **and elsewhere. For in** *Concerning the Calling of the Gentiles* **he says: 'Redemption by the blood of Christ would become worthless and the preference for human works would not give way to the mercy of God if justification, which takes place by grace, were due to antecedent merits. For then it would be the worker's wage rather than the donor's gift.'"** This Latin version of the same section in CA XX, while referring to Augustine more generally as a defender of "grace and the righteousness of faith" against meritorious works, calls upon another church father, Ambrose, for support. At this point, no one knew that Prosper of Aquitaine wrote *Concerning the Calling of the Gentiles*. We have already encountered him in CA XVIII as the probable author of the *Hypognosticon*. He was a follower of Augustine and a fierce critic of the Pelagians, so it is not surprising that his writings witness to the same exclusion of works that the Reformers' did. The most striking line is the last, "For then it would be the worker's wage rather than the donor's gift." Earning, meriting, and reward all imply a far different relation to God than grace, mercy, and gift. This insight is not just some oddball invention of Martin Luther's introspective conscience or a product of his existential anxiety. Such explanations are projections invented by biographers of Luther since the dawn of Pietism in the late seventeenth century down to this very day. The Reformers call upon Augustine, Ambrose, and Prosper, among others, and demonstrate that this message stands at the very heart of Christianity. "Faith alone" does not represent some sort of psychological defect, nor is it the product of a peculiar early-modern culture. It simply casts the human creature back onto the never-ending, all-encompassing grace and mercy of God in Christ. Otherwise, Christ might as well have stayed in heaven, sitting on a satin cushion and drinking lotus tea. Prosper (and the Reformers) were right: it is not merit but gift—thanks be to God!

Latin: **"Moreover, although this teaching is despised by those without experience, nevertheless devout and anxious consciences find by experience that it offers the greatest consolation. For consciences cannot be calmed by any work but only by faith when they are certain that they have a God who has been reconciled on account of Christ. As Paul teaches in Rom 5 [:1]: 'Therefore, since we are justified by faith we have peace with God.' This whole teaching must be referred to that struggle of the terrified conscience, and it cannot be understood apart from that struggle. That is why those who are wicked and without experience judge it badly. For they**

---

11. WA Br 12:386–88, dated 1533 or later.

imagine that Christian righteousness is nothing but civil and philosophical righteousness." The third authority in Lutheran theology is experience—not experience in general or in theory but the practical experience of actual justification. Already in 1520, in the opening paragraphs to the Latin version of *Freedom of a Christian*, Martin Luther makes this clear.[12] Here the Latin, Melanchthon's favorite language for accurately presenting Reformation theology, gives an expanded version of the role of experience. He underscores several crucial points about justification by faith.

First, Melanchthon emphasizes that those without experience will always despise this teaching. The Old Creature simply cannot imagine, let alone tolerate, God's gracious mercy in Christ to be the center of Christian proclamation. At the end of this paragraph Melanchthon returns to such false judges, calling them wicked and adding that "they imagine that Christian righteousness is nothing but civil and philosophical righteousness." This summarizes a lengthy refutation of Erasmus's view of the freedom of choice from Melanchthon's 1528 commentary on Colossians.[13] But it also calls to mind Luther's distinction between the inner and outer human being from *Freedom of a Christian*. Human beings cannot help but judge matters according to the appearance of righteousness rather than the righteousness bestowed upon Christians gratis and received by faith alone.

Second, references to the anxious, terrified conscience call to mind the distinction already made in CA XII and defined in the Apology XII as the work of the law. This is matched by the consoling effect of faith in God's promise—also introduced in CA XII. The German stresses the movement from law to gospel even more strongly when it states that "it is very comforting and beneficial for timid and terrified consciences." Thus, experience really arises from the effect of justification by faith—a crucial part of all Reformation teaching. As the Latin states, "This whole teaching must be referred to that struggle of the terrified conscience, and it cannot be understood apart from that struggle." Terror is not some introspective malady but a true experience of the entire person standing before God and accused by the law. Indeed, reducing this to spiritual affections or emotions simply gives the Old Creature another way to gain control: "If I am just sad enough or miserable enough, then God will love me."

---

12. Martin Luther, *Freedom of a Christian* (1520), in TAL 1:487–88: "Many people view Christian faith as something easy, and quite a few people even count it as if it were related to the virtues. They do this because they have not judged faith in light of any experience, nor have they ever tasted its great power. This is because a person who has not tasted its spirit in the midst of trials and misfortune cannot possibly write well about faith or understand what has been written about it. But one who has had even a small taste of faith can never write, speak, reflect, or hear enough about it. As Christ says in John 4[:14], it is a 'spring of water welling up to eternal life.'"
13. Timothy J. Wengert, *Human Freedom, Christian Righteousness: Philip Melanchthon's Exegetical Dispute with Erasmus of Rotterdam* (New York: Oxford University Press, 1998), 96–106.

Finally, Melanchthon offers proof for this from Scripture, citing Romans 5:1. We learn what he means not only from his 1532 *Commentary on Romans* but also in his *Disposition of Romans* from 1529/30. There he remarks that Paul, after describing the nature of justification by faith in Romans 3–4 (cf. CA IV!), now turns to its effect in Romans 5:1: "peace with God." "First [in Rom 5:1] the proposition [of Romans] is repeated. Then [the proposition] is explained from the effects of faith. For faith brings about a tranquility of the conscience, and it arises in the midst of all kinds of struggles and afflictions. Third, consolation is added."[14] This meticulous analysis of the letter's rhetorical structure, Melanchthon's unique contribution to the interpretation of this book, lies behind CA XX's simple reference. For Melanchthon this gets to the very heart of Paul's argument and the argument of CA XX, already foreshadowed by the earlier references to comfort. "We have peace with God!"

"In former times people did not emphasize this comfort but instead drove the poor consciences to their own works. As a result, all sorts of works were undertaken. For the conscience forced some into monasteries, in the hope of obtaining grace there through the monastic life. Some devised other works as a way of earning grace and making satisfaction for sins. Many of them discovered that a person could not obtain peace by such means. That is why it became necessary to preach this teaching concerning faith in Christ and diligently to emphasize it, so that each person may know that God's grace is grasped by faith alone, without merit." This passage connects faith to preaching, mentioned in passing above. In the Latin "they *did not hear* consolation from the gospel" matches with the concluding comment in the German "it became *necessary to preach* this teaching." Justification is not simply a "right doctrine" to be drummed into people (so that justification by faith alone turns into justification by right answer alone). It is a matter of preaching and hearing, as Paul makes clear in Romans 10:6–17. Moreover, this offers a far more detailed criticism of the regnant piety, monasticism, and other works designed to earn grace. In our own day, the list may vary (for example, to forbid drinking, dancing, and smoking), but the end result remains the same. The Latin then connects this teaching to the introduction: "so that anxious consciences should not be deprived of consolation but know that grace and forgiveness of sins are apprehended by faith in Christ." Again Melanchthon binds the effect of justification ("anxious consciences" [law] and "consolation" [gospel]) to faith in God's unconditional promises.

"We must also explain that we are not talking here about the faith possessed by the devil and the ungodly, who also believe the story that Christ

---

14. CR 15:456–57.

suffered and was raised from the dead. But we are talking about true faith, which believes that we obtain grace and forgiveness of sin through Christ. All who know that in Christ they have a gracious God call upon him and are not, like the heathen, without God. For the devil and the ungodly do not believe this article about the forgiveness of sin. That is why they are enemies of God, cannot call upon him, and cannot hope for anything good from him. Moreover, as has now been indicated, Scripture talks about faith but does not label it knowledge such as the devil and the ungodly have. For Heb 11 [:1] teaches that faith is not only a matter of historical knowledge, but of having confidence in God to receive his promise. Augustine also reminds us that we should understand the word "faith" in Scripture to mean confidence in God—that God is gracious to us—and not merely such knowledge of these stories as the devils also have."

After defining justification by faith alone and its effects, Melanchthon turns to a second topic, which remained an important divide between late-medieval Christians and the Reformers, the nature of faith. Because scholastic theologians often viewed faith as assent to the truth of the church's teaching and thus argued that someone in a state of sin also possessed faith, they could not imagine how "faith alone" could save. Melanchthon refers indirectly to a phrase in the Epistle of James (2:19) about the devils also believing in order to distinguish historical faith from true faith. In this way, he offers a reinterpretation of that passage by not contrasting faith to works, as James does, but historical faith to "true faith" (as opposed to a dead faith). True faith actually believes it is forgiven and thus offers consolation to the sinner—something the devil cannot do (let alone the person addicted to their own righteousness). Already in his *Loci communes* of 1521, Melanchthon had distinguished between historical knowledge and confidence or trust.

Melanchthon is always looking to connect teaching to its effects. In this case, as he does consistently throughout his later career, he talks about the immediate fruits of faith. Consolation itself is the first fruit. But with that comes other things: prayer and hope for blessings. On the contrary, the ungodly "are enemies of God, cannot call upon him, and cannot hope for anything good from him." Calling upon God on the basis of works means not actually calling upon God at all but trusting in one's own deeds. Hoping for good from God also disappears when connected to one's religious actions (Luke 18:9–14: "I thank you God that I am not like others"). Only justification by faith alone bears immediate, spontaneous fruit in a Christian's life: comfort, prayer, and hope (cf. Rom 5:1–5).

To support his argument here, Melanchthon provides two authorities. The first, Hebrews 11:1, was already translated by Luther in his 1522 New Testament as *Zuvorsicht* (confidence). In lectures on Hebrews from 1517–1518, Luther had already criticized an ontological interpretation of the phrase "*substance* of things hoped for" and instead understood it (like Chyrsostom) as the thing upon which a person stood (the *sub-stantia*).[15] And in his *Annotations on the New Testament* from 1516 Erasmus had also suggested that the Greek be translated as "certitude" and ridiculed scholastic attempts to understand the passage. The second refers to either Augustine or pseudo-Augustine.[16] Here especially the Latin returns to the effects of law and gospel, when it states that faith is not to be defined as knowledge "but as trust that consoles and encourages terrified minds."

"Further, it is taught that good works should and must be done, not that a person relies on them to earn grace, but for God's sake and to God's praise." Finally after all this, Melanchthon arrives at a third topic: good works. This alone should encourage those who question whether Lutherans today emphasize faith too much to ask themselves why they ask that question. Perhaps they have not noticed the flood of legalistic preaching pouring from Christian pulpits the world over or the constant harping on Christians to earn or at least to deserve God's blessings. Melanchthon's earlier warning ("there has been a profound silence concerning the righteousness of faith in preaching") still obtains today. Like Luther in *Freedom of a Christian*, Melanchthon concentrates all of his energy on faith, so that no one can boast of his or her works (let alone preach in such a way as to rob folks of the comfort of the gospel). Even in the first sentence under the topic "good works," Melanchthon hardly gets halfway through before returning to faith and grace.

"Good works should and must be done . . . for God's sake and for God's praise." Everyone agrees with this, but the proper question to ask is "Why do them?" Here the German version explains the more general Latin term ("will of God") with the more specific: "for God's sake and for God's praise." By viewing faith in Christ as a relationship based upon merciful love (rather than on law and works), these phrases make perfect sense. The one in love always wants to know and follow the beloved's wishes and does things purely

---

15. LW 29:229–31.

16. In his sermons on 1 John 5 (Tractate X.2; MPG 35:2055), Augustine states: "Now a person who believes in Christ but hates Christ possesses a confession of faith out of a fear of punishment not out of love for the crown, for the demons also fear being punished." In Pseudo-Augustine [=Honorius of Autun], *Concerning the Knowledge of the True Life*, 37 (MPL 40:1025) we read: "What is the difference between believing God and believing in God (true faith)? Is there some difference? . . . The teacher [answers]: 'There is a great difference. Demons and pagans also believe God but do not believe *in* God. For they believe that there is a God who created all things and has power over all things. But only those reach out to him with love toward him believe *in* God. . . . This faith exists as the life of the soul and through it the righteous live [Rom 1:17]. This faith is nurtured with faith just as the body is renewed by food. It is enlivened by love just as the body is made alive by the soul.'" Both sources connect faith to love (cf. Gal 5:6), but Melanchthon connects it instead to confidence and trust, as did Erasmus in his *Annotationes in Novum Testamentum* (Basel: Froben, 1527), 656.

for the sake and honor of the beloved, as Peter blurts out in John 6:68: "Lord, to whom can we go? You have the words of eternal life." At the same time, any boasting or earning favor falls away (*"not . . .* to earn grace") in the face of God's unconditional declaration: "You are mine; you are forgiven."

"**Faith alone always takes hold of grace and forgiveness of sin.**" For a second time in this last section, Melanchthon underscores the difference between faith and works, as though it cannot be emphasized enough. Of course, the Old Creature, always chafing under God's sovereign mercy, will try to turn the "takes hold" into a work. But imagining that Melanchthon is describing a human work here is as foolish as people rescued from drowning who pat themselves on the back for holding on to the rescuer or life preserver. Faith is a clinging, but only in the way that an infant clings to a mother's finger—"Lord, to whom shall we go?"

"**Because the Holy Spirit is given through faith, the heart is also moved to do good works. For before, because it lacks the Holy Spirit, the heart is too weak.**" Here the Latin provides a more complete picture and reflects Melanchthon's understanding of what might be called the psychology of faith. "**Moreover, because the Holy Spirit is received through faith, consequently hearts are renewed and endowed with new affections so as to be able to do good works. For Ambrose says: 'Faith is the mother of the good will and the righteous action.'**"[17] Faith receives the Holy Spirit; it does not earn it. The heart's movement or renewal includes being endowed with new "affections," Melanchthon's term for the very deepest human inclinations.[18] These affections, bestowed by the Holy Spirit, then move the believer to good works. Of course, to some modern scholars Melanchthon's use of such terms for the functions of the soul or heart betrays Luther's theology. Far more it underscores his deep commitment to define faith as genuine relationship and not in terms of merit and reward. By adding a brief reference to Ambrose [i.e., Prosper of Aquitaine], Melanchthon continues to emphasize that the Reformers have not invented new doctrine but rather are returning to the church's oldest and best theology.

Latin: "**For without the Holy Spirit human powers are full of ungodly affections and are too weak to do good works before God. Besides, they are under the power of the devil, who impels human beings to various sins, ungodly opinions and manifest crimes. This also may be seen in the philosophers, who, though they tried to live honestly, were still not able to do so but were defiled by many obvious crimes. Such is the weakness of human beings when they govern themselves by human powers alone without faith or the Holy Spirit.**" The basic ideas for Melanchthon's statements come

---

17. Citing Prosper of Aquitaine, *De vocatione omnium gentium*, I, 25 (MPL 51:676).
18. This occurs not only his 1521 *Loci communes* but also his *Scholia on Colossians* of 1528. See Wengert, *Human Freedom, Christian Righteousness*, 53, 68, and 106.

almost word for word from his 1528 commentary on Colossians, where his opponent was Erasmus. The Dutch humanist was precisely that "philosopher" who tries to live honestly but fails miserably. Even when admitting to free choice in this life, Melanchthon always remembers humanity's weakness and the devil's power. He emphasizes the centrality of the Holy Spirit's actions in salvation, an oft-overlooked aspect of Melanchthon's theology. Without faith and the Holy Spirit human beings can do nothing.

Latin: "Hence it is readily apparent that no one should accuse this teaching of prohibiting good works. On the contrary, it is rather to be commended for showing how we can do good works." Here Melanchthon brings his argument to a surprising conclusion, turning the tables on accusers like Eck (or Erasmus). Precisely *because* the Evangelicals emphasize faith, they end up teaching rightly about good works. Without faith and the Holy Spirit, good works are impossible. This implies, of course, that because their opponents neglect faith their works-happy approach cannot possibly bring people to do truly good works. By connecting the possibility of good works to both the bondage of the will (CA XVIII) and original sin (CA II), Melanchthon turns attention back to the Holy Spirit's work and faith (CA IV–V).

Latin: "For without faith human nature cannot possibly do the works of the First or Second Commandments. Without faith it does not call upon God, expect anything from God or bear the cross, but seeks and trusts in human help. Consequently, all kinds of urges and human designs rule in the heart when faith and trust in God are lacking." The Latin here echoes the claim of CA II that the human being is "without fear of God or faith in God" by emphasizing the works of the first two commandments, which, as Luther had demonstrated in the 1520 *Treatise on Good Works* and his 1529 Large Catechism, rest exclusively on trust. Again Melanchthon contrasts the fruits of faith (prayer, hope, patience) with trust in human help. The German also adds examples from the second table of the law: "to love the neighbor, to engage diligently in legitimate callings, to be obedient, to avoid evil lust." There follows a small exposition of the first commandment similar to Luther's in the Large Catechism. Outside of true faith the human being trusts itself, is subject to a far different set of affections (here: "urges"), and has only its own welfare at heart.

Latin: "That is why Christ said (John 15 [:5]): "Apart from me you can do nothing." And the church sings: 'Without your will divine, Naught is in humankind; All innocence is gone.'" The use of the fourth Gospel as a kind of peroration highlights the way Melanchthon is arguing. The point in talking about faith and works is not to crush souls with the law (where is the comfort in that?) but rather to drive them back to reliance on Christ alone. One may talk all one wants about the importance of good works, but without Christ they will never truly happen. Here Melanchthon adds a familiar

Latin sequence used during the week of Pentecost and addressed to the Holy Spirit (so that the "your" would have readily been understood as referring to the Holy Spirit).[19] One wonders, given these remarkable testimonies of Scripture and the church's ancient prayer, why any preacher would approach good works outside of faith, the work of Christ and the will of the Holy Spirit. And yet misleading preaching on good works gushes from pulpits (Protestant and Catholic alike), as if faith were simply a prolegomenon or even an enemy of good works.

We Teach and Confess

This way of talking about good works serves as a warning to those who worry that Lutherans talk too much about faith. If Philip Melanchthon could not help himself, but had to preface the entire article with a lengthy discussion of faith and then, even in the midst of his discussion of good works, had to return repeatedly to God's action and faith, what gives preachers today leave to imply that only works really matter? In fact, yelling at good trees to bear good fruit has no effect; instead, plant good trees, that is, announce Jesus's unmerited, unconditional grace and mercy to them: "Without me, you can do nothing." All too often Christian preaching devolves into yelling at good plants and seeds to grow, thereby undermining Christ's love and the Holy Spirit's power. The following vignettes may help in comprehending CA XX's approach.

In addition to the *Frog and Toad* story by Arnold Lobel, called "The Garden" and described in comments on CA VI, there are two other snapshots that may help. First, Jesus offers a parallel in his parable of the sleeping sower, who simply plants the seed and takes a nap. Mark 4:26–29: "The seed sprouts and grows; he knows not how." Or, second, in the words of Luther's 1522 sermon delivered immediately after his return to Wittenberg from protective custody in the Wartburg Castle: "And while I slept, or drank Wittenberg beer with my friends Philip [Melanchthon] and [Nicholas von] Amsdorf . . . The Word did everything."[20] That is, dear souls, preach the blessed gospel!

---

19. From the sixth verse of the medieval hymn "Come Holy Spirit" (*Veni Sancte Spiritus*), which was the sequence used during the Octave of Pentecost that in 1530 ran from 5 to 12 June (i.e., after the Evangelicals had arrived in Augsburg). A literal translation reads: "Without your divine sway, nothing is in humanity, nothing that is not harmful."
20. LW 51:77.

21

Honor Saints; Praise Christ

We may thank Google for the ease with which a person can locate just the proper saint for any number of problems. One of the most popular saints, it would appear, is St. Jude, who is there to help in financial crises and other lost causes. Most websites on the subject remind visitors that these saints are *not* being worshiped but rather are being called upon to intercede with God, much the way Christians on earth may also pray for one another. But a few imply a more direct connection between the saint and petitions—not surprising give the rough and jumbled world of fact and fiction in cyberspace.

In the sixteenth century the distinction between intercession by and worship of saints was perhaps even more confused for common folk. In his Large Catechism, Luther described matters this way.

> Again, look at what we used to do in our blindness under the papacy. Anyone who had a toothache fasted and called on St. Apollonia; those who worried about their house burning down appealed to St. Laurence as their patron; if they were afraid of the plague, they made a vow to St. Sebastian or Roch. There were countless other such abominations, and everyone selected his own saint and worshipped him and invoked his help in time of need. In this category also belong those who go so far as to make a pact with the devil so that he may give them plenty of money, help them in love affairs, protect their cattle, recover lost property, etc., as magicians and sorcerers do. All of them place their heart and trust

elsewhere than in the true God, from whom they neither expect nor seek any good thing.[1]

Luther expresses his concern, shared with the drafters of CA XXI, in the last sentence: "place their heart and trust elsewhere than in the true God." By calling into question praying to saints, the Reformers upended overnight a major aspect of late-medieval piety. The role of the saints and especially Mary as mediators between sinners and a righteous God dominated many practices of the time. Even the purchase of indulgence letters were designed to transfer the merits of Christ, Mary, and the saints to the purchaser. For example, Mary was often depicted spreading her outer robe around a multitude of believers who took refuge with her, shielding them from the wrath of her returning Son.

But was this a change of practice or a matter of doctrine? Such an article was missing from the Schwabach Articles and appeared first in the Torgau memoranda, which defended changes in practice among Evangelicals. At some point while composing the CA, this article took its place—albeit the last place—among the doctrinal articles. It rounds out the miscellaneous articles beginning with CA XVI. However, as the *Confutation* proclaims, CA XXI is one of the most vulnerable to criticism—a reflection of the fact that Luther and Melanchthon (in the Apology) do not deny that the saints *may* pray for believers. Nevertheless, they also insist that there is no scriptural authorization for the invocation of saints.

No wonder that the *Confutation* responded so sharply to this article! Johann Eck and his coauthors clearly thought that they had the Evangelicals dead to rights here. They were astounded that the princes and cities would have allow such completely damnable errors, given that St. Jerome had defeated the heretic Vigilantius eleven hundred years earlier on this issue. After providing a list of heretics (Albigensians, Waldensians, and others) who had over the centuries held the same view as CA XXI, they, in agreement with the entire orthodox Christian church, rejected this article completely, listing the consensus of a host of church fathers (Augustine, Bernard, Jerome, Cyprian, Chrysostom, and Basil). They then mustered several Bible passages from the Old Testament (Zechariah 1 and Job 33), the New Testament (John 12, Revelation 5), and the Apocrypha (Baruch 3 and 2 Macc 15). They also described Cyprian's letter to Pope Cornelius before attacking the CA's use of Scripture (1 Tim 2 and 1 John 4). There is one mediator of redemption but many mediators of intercession,

---

1. LC, "Ten Commandments, 11–12 (BC, 387). Apollonia was martyred on 9 February 248 or 249. Because the executioners pulled her teeth out, she was regarded as helping against toothache. Laurence, a Roman deacon, was reputed to have been martyred by being roasted on a gridiron on 10 August 258. Sebastian, a Roman martyr, was executed on 20 January, early in the fourth century (?), reputedly by being shot with arrows. Roch, reportedly a Franciscan monk from Montpelier, devoted himself to caring for victims of the plague in Italy. His feast day is 16 August.

including Moses (Deuteronomy 5, Exodus 17 and 30), Paul (Acts 27, Romans 15, 2 Cor 1, and Colossians 4), and Peter (Acts 12). "Therefore Christ is our primary and, indeed, greatest advocate, but, because the saints are members of Christ (1 Cor 12 and Ephesians 5) and conform their wills to Christ's, and they gaze upon their head, Christ, it cannot be doubted that they pray for us."[2] Augustine states, "The Christian people celebrate the memories of the martyrs with religious solemnity to stimulate imitation of them, to participate in their merits, and to be helped through their prayers."[3] This refutation, however, only underscores how far apart the two sides were.

CA XXI

[German]

Concerning the cult of the saints our people teach that the saints are to be remembered so that we may strengthen our faith when we see how they experienced grace and how they were helped by faith. Moreover, it is taught that each person, according to his or her calling, should take the saints' good works as an example. For instance, His Imperial Majesty, in a salutary and righteous fashion, may follow the example of David in waging war against the Turk. For both hold a royal office that demands defense and protection of their subjects. However, it cannot be demonstrated from Scripture that a person should call upon the saints or seek help from them. "For there is only one single reconciler and mediator set up between God and humanity, Jesus Christ" (1 Tim 2 [:5]). He is the only savior, the only high priest, the mercy seat, and intercessor before God (Rom 8 [:34]). He alone has promised to hear our prayers.

[Latin]

Concerning the cult of the saints they teach that saints may be remembered in order that we imitate their faith and good works, according to our calling. Thus, the emperor can imitate the example of David in waging war to drive the Turks from our native land. For both of them are kings. However, Scripture does not teach calling on the saints or pleading for help from them. For it sets before us Christ alone as mediator, atoning sacrifice, high priest, and intercessor. He is to be called upon, and he has promised that our prayers will be heard. Furthermore, he strongly approves this worship most of all, namely, that he be called upon in all afflictions. 1 John 2 [:1]: "But if anyone does sin, we have an advocate with the Father."

---

2. CR 27:128, author's translation (cf. *The Confutation of the Augsburg Confession*, art. 21, in *Sources and Contexts of the Book of Concord* [Minneapolis: Fortress, 2001], 120).

3. Augustine, *Against Faustus*, bk. 20, ch. 21.

According to Scripture, in all our needs
and concerns it is the highest worship
to seek and call upon this same Jesus
Christ with our whole heart. "But if
anyone does sin, we have an advocate
with the Father, Jesus Christ, the righteous." [1 John 2:1]

Reflections

"Concerning the cult of the saints our people teach that the saints are to
be remembered so that we may strengthen our faith when we see how they
experienced grace and how they were helped by faith." The Reformers here
state an obvious truth held by both sides in Augsburg. The lives of the saints
clearly strengthen believers' faith, since they provide great examples of how
we live by faith and grace alone. This single-minded focus on faith and grace
again echoes CA III–VI and underscores the central premise of the CA that
all believers (past and present) stand before God as equally in need of mercy.

"Moreover, it is taught that each person, according to his or her calling, should take the saints' good works as an example." Besides the common grounding of all believers' life in God's grace, the saints also provide
examples. Luther had already alluded to this in the 95 Theses, where he noted
that the merits of Christ and the saints work death for the Old Creature and
encouragement for believers.[4] The Confutation takes this and the previous
sentence to be relatively minor points of agreement, but for CA XXI faith and
Christian callings are central. Here the language of CA XVI and XX converge.
The Christian lives on earth not in fear of God's judgment or uncertain about
one's standing before God (and therefore in need of the intervention of the
saints) but certain of God's grace in Christ and freed to serve the neighbor
according to their callings.

"For instance, His Imperial Majesty, in a salutary and righteous fashion, may follow the example of David in waging war against the Turk. For
both hold a royal office that demands defense and protection of their subjects." This example shows the political acuity of the drafters. What better
example of following the saints could they come up with than the emperor's
own calling to protect and defend his subjects—a great reminder that he
needed the Protestants' support to do so. It is worth noting that the drafters
curtail the emperor's powers to defensive war for the sake of one's subjects and

---

4. Thesis 58: "Nor are they [the treasures of the church] the merits of Christ and the saints,
because, even without the pope, these merits always work grace for the inner person and cross,
death and hell for the outer person." See TAL 1:42.

make no mention of imperial designs on France or the Papal States and the recently concluded war against them.

"However, it cannot be demonstrated from Scripture that a person should call upon the saints or seek help from them. 'For there is only one single reconciler and mediator set up between God and humanity, Jesus Christ' (1 Tim 2 [:5]). He is the only savior, the only high priest, the mercy seat, and intercessor before God (Rom 8 [:34]). He alone has promised to hear our prayers. According to Scripture, in all our needs and concerns it is the highest worship to seek and call upon this same Jesus Christ with our whole heart. 'But if anyone does sin, we have an advocate with the Father, Jesus Christ, the righteous' [1 John 2:1]." This objection to prayers to saints, when compared to the *Confutation*'s response, demonstrates just how far apart the two sides are and how they are clearly speaking past one another. The Evangelical teachers' chief concern is the undermining of Christ's unique mediatorial role between God and humanity. The *Confutation* distinguishes between his exclusive redemptive role and the intercessory role of Christ and the saints within the one body of Christ. But, practically speaking, CA XXI sees little difference between redemption and intercession. Indeed, as Melanchthon had already argued in CA XX, the fruits of faith include hope in God and prayers to God.

Here, as in the previous article, the drafters relentlessly worry about undermining true worship of God by faith alone ("to seek and call upon this same Jesus Christ *with our whole heart*"). They recognize that Christian practice in their day did not actually distinguish between redemption and intercession but instead was simply undermining Christ's work and believers' worship of him. The phrases "one mediator" (1 Tim 2:5), "only Savior" (that is, high priest, mercy seat, and intercessor; Rom 8:34), and "advocate" (1 John 2:1) exclude anything that would undermine that unique office. "*Solus Christus*" [Christ alone] is not simply a theoretical doctrine or a pious slogan; it had practical consequences for the Reformers. Neat theoretical distinctions (in this case between redemption and intercession) miss the point that believers cast themselves upon God's mercy in Christ alone. There could be no other "way, truth and life." However much one might excuse the early church's honoring of the saints, in late-medieval Christianity the practice appeared to the Evangelicals to block access to Christ and his grace, replacing it with human attempts to mollify God's wrath and judgment. Thus, this article applied in practical ways the *solus Christus* to the daily life of a Christian.

This practicality, also part of CA XX, and the emphasis upon experience mark the deepest divide between the confessors in Augsburg and their opponents.[5] The differences lie not simply in doctrine but in the way that

---

5. For a thorough examination of the role of the saints in early Lutheranism, see Robert Kolb, *For All the Saints: Changing Perceptions of Martyrdom and Sainthood in the Lutheran Reformation*, 2nd ed. (Eugene, OR: Wipf & Stock, 2018).

such teaching affects believers. Thus, there can be little doubt that the saints and angels pray continually before God's throne for all believers, as Lutherans today may confess in the proper preface for Easter: "With Mary Magdalene and Peter and all the witness of the resurrection, with cherubim and seraphim and all the company of angels." This even may imply that they do not simply pray with us but also for us. And yet even that possibility dare not undermine that far more important fact of Christian life: that we are saved on account of Christ alone and that anything undermining that central proclamation of the Christian faith—even if it is correct—must be set aside in favor of Christ's mercy. The whole company of heaven may well be praying for us, joining the chorus of our own voices in begging God for mercy ("Sovereign Lord . . . how long?" [Rev 6:10]), but that act dare not obscure the far more important fact that all of our prayers—for ourselves or our neighbors—occur *in Christo* (in Christ). Without him, we are nothing. This is perhaps the most powerful witness to justification by faith alone: that the Evangelicals in Augsburg refuse to let anything detract from God's mercy in Christ, who alone is savior, advocate, and mediator.

We Teach and Confess

The year 2001 marked the first time my congregation celebrated All Saints' Sunday after the death of my first wife. I was miles away, driving toward a teaching "gig" in eastern Pennsylvania. But I knew the exact moment when, along with other members of that congregation who had died in the past year, her name would be read out to the ringing of the church bell. And, riding down the highway, I burst into tears. My sainted wife had died, and I was bereft.

During the Reformation, "All Saints' Day" did not often make the cut among acceptable saints' days that continued to be celebrated in Evangelical churches. Indeed, the list was, for the most part, reduced to biblical saints: Paul, Peter, Mary, and the rest. All Saints' Day had been set up by medieval Christians to include precisely those saints whose names no one knew or had forgotten but who were still part of the "cloud of witnesses" of which Hebrews 12:1 speaks. With the renewal of worship among American Lutherans, which started in the mid- to late nineteenth century, All Saints' Day was reintroduced—but with one remarkable difference to its medieval predecessor. The "saints" quickly became not simply unknown saints that no one wanted to offend. Suddenly the word "saint" took on its original, broader meaning (as first used by Paul) of referring to *all* believers. With no more concern about extended stays in Purgatory after death, Lutherans saw All Saints' Day (and, later, All Saints' Sunday) as an opportunity to remember "those who had died in the Lord," including my dear Barbara. In medieval practice, November 2, "All Souls' Day," made a nod toward all souls (saved or not) and allowed believers to pray for them. But by the twentieth century Lutherans amalgamated the two days into one, assuring that we would never forget all the "blessed departed" but also insisting that, by virtue of their baptisms into Christ, all are saints. In that worship and, indeed, in all worship, we are surrounded by that very cloud of worshipers who remind us of faith in God's grace and exemplify living by faith alone and who may well be praying for us. We are, indeed, all part of the same body of Christ, offering our prayers and praise to *his* glory and *his* praise.

Interlude

PRACTICING THEOLOGY

What is theology for? The answer to this question has eluded many a theologian, to say nothing of ordinary churchgoers. For example, it may appear that the job of the church historian is simply to recount history—in a winsome way, one hopes—but still the accent must be on the content, the facts: the dates and times and people that comprise the story. Yet the greatest compliment such a person can receive occurs when a believer approaches the podium after a talk and thanks the presenter not just for information but also for a renewed orientation in the present. "Thanks, Professor! I really needed to hear that." It's true that accurate facts still carry weight and that fair-mindedness must never be neglected, but the purpose cannot stop there but must include the person's life and faith. Theology is neither a theoretical science nor simply information; it is an applied science. In 1990 the Lutheran theologian Gerhard Forde wrote what might be considered his systematic treatment of the subject but titled it *Theology Is for Proclamation*, rejecting all forms of speculation and insisting that if Christian theology did not serve the proclamation of the gospel it was not really theology at all.[1]

This interlude between the two sections of the CA defines Evangelical theology and grounds itself in the real world of believers in several different ways. First, it insists that its account of teaching serves faith and becomes dangerous if it does not. Second, it argues that such theology arises out of the shared experience of Christians throughout time. Finally, it insists that faithful practice flows from such teaching and seeks to ameliorate any abuses. Good teaching (which is what theology is) is for the entire life of the faithful.

---

1. Gerhard O. Forde, *Theology Is for Proclamation* (Minneapolis: Fortress, 1990).

Conclusion to the First Part and Introduction to the Second Part

[German]

This is nearly a complete summary of what is preached and taught in our churches for proper Christian instruction and the comfort of consciences, as well as for the improvement of believers. For we certainly wish neither to expose our own souls and consciences to grave danger before God by misusing the divine name or Word nor to pass on or bequeath to our children and descendants any other teaching than that which accords with the pure Word of God and Christian truth. Since, then, this teaching is clearly grounded in Holy Scripture and is, moreover, neither against nor contrary to the universal Christian church—or even the Roman church—so far as can be observed in the writings of the Fathers, we think that our opponents cannot disagree with us in the articles set forth above. That is why those who undertake to isolate, reject, and avoid our people as heretics, without having themselves any solid basis in divine command or Scripture, act in a very unfriendly and hasty manner, contrary to all Christian unity and love. For the dissension and quarrel are chiefly over some traditions and abuses. Since, then, there is nothing unfounded or deficient in the principal articles and since this our confession is godly and Christian, the bishops should in all fairness act more leniently even if there were a deficiency in regard to tradition—although we hope to offer solid grounds and reasons why some traditions and abuses have been changed among us.

[Latin]

This is nearly a complete summary of the teaching among us. As can be seen, there is nothing here that departs from the Scriptures or the catholic church, or from the Roman church, in so far as we can tell from its writers. Because this is so, those who claim that our people are to be regarded as heretics judge too harshly. The entire dissension concerns a few specific abuses, which have crept into the churches without any proper authority. Even if there were some difference in these matters, the bishops should have been so lenient as to bear with us on account of the confession we have now recounted. For even the canons are not so severe as to demand that rites should be the same everywhere, nor have the rites of all churches ever been the same. Nevertheless, the ancient rites are, for the most part, diligently observed among us. For the accusation is false that all ceremonies and ancient ordinances are abolished in our churches. Truth is, there has been a public outcry that certain abuses have become fused to the common rites. Because such abuses could not be approved with a good conscience, they have been corrected to some extent.

...

Articles in Which an Account Is Given of the Abuses That Have Been Corrected

Since the churches among us do not dissent from the catholic church in any article of faith but only set aside a few abuses that are new and were

206

...

Disputed Articles, Listing the Abuses Which Have Been Corrected

Nothing contrary to Holy Scripture or to the universal, Christian church is taught in our churches concerning articles of faith. Rather, only some abuses have been corrected which in part have crept in over the years and in part have been introduced by force. Necessity demands that we list them and indicate reasons why correction is permissible in these matters so that Your Imperial Majesty may recognize that we have not acted in an unchristian or sacrilegious manner. On the contrary, we have been compelled by God's command (which is rightly to be esteemed higher than all custom) to permit such corrections.

accepted because of corruption over time contrary to the intention of the canons, we pray that Your Imperial Majesty will graciously hear about the changes and our reasons for them, so that the people may not be compelled to observe these abuses against their conscience. Your Imperial Majesty should not believe those who disseminate shocking false accusations among the people to inflame the hatred of others against our people. First they gave occasion for this disagreement by embittering the minds of good folk. Now they are trying to increase the discord by the same method. For Your Imperial Majesty will undoubtedly discover that the form of teaching and ceremonies among us is more tolerable than what these perverse and malicious people describe. Indeed, the truth cannot be gathered from the rumors of the crowd or the curses of our enemies. However, it can easily be judged that nothing contributes more to preserving the dignity of ceremonies and cultivating reverence and piety among the people than conducting ceremonies properly in the churches.

Reflections

"This is nearly a complete summary[2] of what is preached and taught in our churches for proper Christian instruction and the comfort of consciences, as well as for the improvement of believers." The German text reveals that Evangelical theology only makes sense when it connects right doctrine to its

---

2. German: *fast die Summa*. Although in modern new High German "*fast*" means almost or nearly, in the sixteenth century it more often meant complete or full (as in "this is for all intents and purposes a complete summary"). This avoids the (mistaken) notion held by some modern interpreters that CA I–XXI is somehow lacking in some areas.

purpose: instruction, comfort, and improvement. Otherwise, even "correct" doctrine may fail to reach its God-given goal: to make believers. Good theology is never an academic exercise; it must always serve the assembly of believers in concrete ways with proper instruction, comfort, and improvement. Were these criteria applied to present-day works, how many would survive? Yet, as we have seen throughout the first twenty-one articles, the question of a teaching's effect is not an add-on to its definition but squarely part and parcel of its meaning. Especially the number of times the CA refers to comfort indicates just how seriously it takes such application. This way of presenting these articles is not accidental but intentional, because otherwise the teaching itself could not be true: Christian theology is for instruction, comfort, and improvement—or else it is not Christian theology at all.

"For we certainly wish neither to expose our own souls and consciences to grave danger before God by misusing the divine name or Word nor to pass on or bequeath to our children and descendants any other teaching than that which accords with the pure Word of God and Christian truth." In the eyes of the CA's drafters the danger of bad teaching is enormous. It immediately breaks the second and third commandments and, thus, the first table of the Decalogue. In the Large Catechism Luther had said as much in his exposition of the second commandment.[3] Bad teaching also betrays one's own offspring, and thus it has terrible consequences for one's own conscience and for one's descendants in the faith. But, as CA XX reminds us, the experience of moving from terror to comfort brings with it through the Holy Spirit its own motivation for spreading the same comfort for others. Thus, the act of confessing in Augsburg also serves as the purest form of evangelism, "one beggar telling another where to get some bread."[4] "According with the pure Word of God and Christian truth" is not an empty phrase of hyper-orthodoxy, where justification by faith quickly becomes justification by right answer, but it appeals to the same effect of God's Word, namely, to comfort the terrified, to forgive the sinner, and to raise the dead. Here "purity" and "truth" slake the hunger and thirst of starving and parched wanderers in the desert.

"Since, then, this teaching is clearly grounded in Holy Scripture and is, moreover, neither against nor contrary to the universal Christian church— or even the Roman church—so far as can be observed in the writings of the Fathers, we think that our opponents cannot disagree with us in the articles set forth above." The measure for good theology is not simply its effect but its faithfulness to authorities outside itself. This implies submitting

---

3. LC, "Ten Commandments," par. 54 (BC, 393): "The greatest abuse, however, is in spiritual matters, which affect the conscience, when false preachers arise and present their lying nonsense as God's Word."

4. See Dandapati Samuel Satyaranjan, *The Preaching of Daniel Thambirajah (D. T.) Niles: Homiletical Criticism* (Delhi: ISPCK, 2009), 270.

the theologian's interests to others in the church—a concept quite foreign to modern theology where the individual's untrammeled reason and opinion hold sway. Already in the *97 Theses* of September 1517 and then again in the *Heidelberg Disputation* of March 1518, Luther attacked the regnant theology of his day and its dependence not on the church fathers or Scripture but on the theologians' ability to use Aristotle to support their positions, especially on the matter of free choice (*liberum arbitrium*). Against this addiction to human wisdom (whether one's own or that of some philosopher), the CA places two authorities—the very ones used especially in CA XX but also elsewhere in the document. The first, Scripture, provides "grounding" and reflects the Reformers' commitment to God's Word as the *primum et verum*, the first and true authority for all teaching. Given how relatively seldom the CA quotes Scripture, this claim may seem rather weak. But, as we have seen, where they cite Scripture they are actually providing more than simply "proof texts" but are often calling upon a decade or more of serious dedication to interpreting the biblical witness. Grounding theology upon Scripture is never simply a matter of finding a few favorite verses to twist (as many in the sixteenth century loved to say) like a nose of wax.

The second level of authorization comes from the "universal Christian church," which Melanchthon renders in the Latin as the *ecclesia catholica* (universal [catholic] church). Already before the Reformation, the Apostles' Creed's "*catholica*" had been rendered "Christian" in German translations. Here, to underscore the intent, the CA even adds to the German the word "universal." This refers especially to the Apostles' and Nicene Creeds (cited in CA I and III), and it indirectly calls into question the exclusive claims of the Roman church to be church, since the CA then adds "or to the Roman church" as a separate entity. Again, the CA in the German emphasizes not the papal decrees or canon law but the Fathers, especially Ambrose and Augustine.[5] Nevertheless, later the Latin mentions the canons of the church (that is, canon law) positively, and the disputed articles will cite both papal decrees and canon law.

The drafters of the CA never saw themselves breaking away from the church to form a new, "reformed" church (despite some later Protestant claims). Continuity in teaching was important not simply to prove that the Evangelicals were not heretics but also to demonstrate that God had never abandoned the church or its gospel. At the same time, the CA defines a different degree of authority for this second level by insisting upon noncontradiction of their theology with that of the past. This echoes Melanchthon's

---

5. As we have seen, some of these quotes arise from what was later designated Ambrosiaster, pseudo-Ambrose, and pseudo-Augustine, especially writings now attributed to Prosper of Aquitaine. Ambrose and Augustine were two of the four Latin "doctors of the church" (along with Pope Gregory I and Jerome).

definition of patristic authority as he calls it in the Latin of CA XX, the *testimonia patrum* (CA XX.12 [BC, 55]; testimonies of the Fathers), but it also allows for a certain distance from some comments that the Reformers reject or only partially accept.[6]

"That is why those who undertake to isolate, reject, and avoid our people as heretics, without having themselves any solid basis in divine command or Scripture, act in a very unfriendly and hasty manner, contrary to all Christian unity and love." Here, in an attempt to put their opponents on the defensive, the drafters level several charges against them. The opposition has not only acted too hastily and wrongly separated themselves from the Evangelical party, but they have also judged the case without proper justification from Scripture. Here the primary authority, Scripture, forms the basis of the CA's criticism. But there is a third side to the Evangelicals' complaint: that this behavior is contrary to Christian unity and love. After enduring charges of breaking the unity of the church for at least twelve years, the drafters turn the tables and accuse their opponents of this very crime. In the Apology Melanchthon even names names, blaming in Ap XIV the bishops and, more specifically in Ap XII.125–30, the papal legate Cardinal Campeggio.

This view of the Reformers, hardly universally acknowledged among Roman Catholics (and even some Lutherans) today, should give all Christians pause, as we consider the dangers of dividing the church. Who, indeed, is most to blame for division in churches and congregations? When have Christians been shown the door (or given the cold shoulder) without any reasonable grounds from Scripture? How often have unity and love played second fiddle to our own ambitions and claims to purity of doctrine or practice? Above all others, church leaders need to answer these questions and take responsibility for disunity in Christ's church, as the following statements in this transitional section make clear.

"For the dissension and quarrel are chiefly over some traditions and abuses. Since, then, there is nothing unfounded or deficient in the principal articles and since this our confession is godly and Christian, the bishops should in all fairness act more leniently even if there were a deficiency in regard to tradition—although we hope to offer solid grounds and reasons why some traditions and abuses have been changed among us." Here the drafters begin to look forward to the next section and insist that the changes in traditions and abuses are secondary to the clear catholicity of the preceding articles of doctrine. This alone, they argue, should have caused the bishops (represented at the imperial diet in Augsburg) to deal more leniently with the Evangelicals. In June, on behalf of the Saxon court Melanchthon made several

---

6. This becomes clearer in the second edition of the Apology, which contains implicit criticism of Augustine's sanative view of justification.

approaches to Roman prelates, including Archbishop Albrecht of Mainz and Cardinal Campeggio, but to no avail, so that the rebuke here is based upon lived experience. Moreover, in some dioceses, bishops had actively sought to banish or arrest Evangelically minded preachers, priests, and other religious.

But is it possible to separate traditions from confession of faith? The CA insists here that it is, not so much by separating the two but by joining them so that the one is the basis for the other. Given that the confession of faith is not deficient or unfounded but godly and Christian, there is no reason to quarrel over changes in tradition or, worse yet, condemn such changes as heretical. But already in 1518 this became the center of the case against Luther, when the papal court theologian, Sylvester Prierias, dismissed Luther's objections to the practice of indulgence sales by arguing that the church could not err in practices sanctioned by the pope.[7]

Latin: "For even the canons are not so severe as to demand that rites should be the same everywhere, nor have the rites of all churches ever been the same. Nevertheless, the ancient rites are, for the most part, diligently observed among us. For the accusation is false that all ceremonies and ancient ordinances are abolished in our churches." Here in the Latin version, the canons of the church are, for the first time, invoked. But this claim of variety in worship and practices was particularly irritating for the diehard defenders of papal authority, who saw this as undermining the pope's ability properly to shepherd the church. But the second half of this statement brings up an interesting aspect of Lutheran practice. Unlike other Reformed or Anabaptist communities, Lutherans went to great lengths to preserve existing patterns of worship and church life, such as the shape of the Mass, the liturgical calendar and lectionary, the various church offices, and the like. Rather than see this as a "conservative" or "incomplete" Reformation (often the charge of other groups), Lutherans defined these things as *adiaphora* (undifferentiated matters) and thus worth keeping, as long as they served the common good of the Christian assembly. Such an attitude stems from Luther's own reaction to the changes wrought by the reform party in Wittenberg during his sojourn in the Wartburg Castle (1521–1522). Upon his return in March 1522, Luther rejected the hasty attempts by his own collaborators (who had the backing of Wittenberg's city council) to usher in reforms in liturgy and other practices as failing to take into account the weak. Patience and love rather than right theology rule in the Christian assembly. The notion that there was a single, right way to do things (called into question by the biblical witness itself), undermined the Christian assembly and set people down the path of finding some (mythical) unique form of Christian worship and practice.

---

7. See Scott Hendrix, *Luther and the Papacy: Stages in a Reformation Conflict* (Philadelphia: Fortress, 1981), 46–52.

Latin: "Truth is, there has been a public outcry that certain abuses have become fused to the common rites. Because such abuses could not be approved with a good conscience, they have been corrected to some extent." Already in Theses 81–91 of the *95 Theses*, Luther assembled a list of objections to indulgences that he gleaned from a variety of contemporary sources and put in the mouth of a "sharp layperson."[8] In 1530, the Latin version of the CA also appeals to public opinion—a relatively new phenomenon related to the beginnings of the Reformation and Luther's publication of his *Sermon on Indulgences and Grace*, which made him the first living, best-selling author in a vernacular language the world had ever seen. But the moral justification for correcting such abuses comes not so much from public opinion but from a good conscience. Luther had already appealed to his own conscience before Cardinal Cajetan in 1518 and, more famously, before Emperor Charles V in Worms in 1521.[9] This argument, important already in medieval moral theology, puts a unique burden on the respondents, who have to prove not only that a particular act is against the law but also that the grounds for such an act do not violate the perpetrator's conscience. This plea for toleration—not always heeded by the Evangelicals themselves in situations where they were in control—forms a crucial measure for many church disputes (including in the articles that follow), and it forces church leaders to care for bound consciences when it comes to the church's policies and practices.

"Disputed Articles, Listing the Abuses Which Have Been Corrected. Nothing contrary to Holy Scripture or to the universal, Christian church is taught in our churches concerning articles of faith. Rather, only some abuses have been corrected which in part have crept in over the years and in part have been introduced by force." This introduction to the second part of the CA carries on some of the same themes found in the conclusion of the first part. The drafters invoke the authority of Scripture and the church catholic. They stress the elimination of abuses and provide a history of sorts for how such abuses got into the church in the first place ("crept in" or "introduced by force" [especially in the case of celibate priests]). The Latin text, by describing the abuses as "corruption over time contrary to the intention of the canons," lays claim to legal grounds for changes based upon canon law, which will be an important part of the argument for several of the following articles. Already in the *95 Theses* Luther had claimed that abuses regarding indulgences were introduced "while the bishops were sleeping."[10]

Latin: ". . . [W]e pray that Your Imperial Majesty will graciously hear about the changes and our reasons for them, so that the people may not be

---

8. TAL 1:44–45.
9. LW 31:112–13; TAL 1:146–47.
10. TAL 1:36, thesis 11.

compelled to observe these abuses against their conscience." The Latin text appeals directly to Charles V at this point (the German text does so a bit later) but reveals the two aspects of the Evangelicals' arguments. On the one hand, the CA will defend the reasons for the changes (from Scripture and tradition). On the other, the Reformers made these changes for the sake of conscience. This is a crucial aspect of the argument and shows one connection between the central doctrine of the CA (justification by grace through faith on account of Christ) and changes in practice: for the sake of the bound conscience.

Latin: "Your Imperial Majesty should not believe those who disseminate shocking false accusations among the people to inflame the hatred of others against our people. First they gave occasion for this disagreement by embittering the minds of good folk. Now they are trying to increase the discord by the same method." In the Latin (as opposed to the briefer German) we learn the machinations of the enemy: making false accusations, unfairly stirring up the hatred of people, and increasing discord. Thus, the CA provides a summary of the history of the dispute from 1517 to the present. It began with false accusations (against Luther) that riled up others or poisoned his reputation with otherwise fair-minded people (through the papal and imperial condemnations of 1521). Now people (such as Johannes Eck with his *404 Articles* and Cardinal Campeggio) are doing the same thing with their accusations of heresy at Augsburg. The only recourse for the Evangelicals is a direct appeal to the emperor himself.

"Necessity demands that we list them and indicate reasons why correction is permissible in these matters so that Your Imperial Majesty may recognize that we have not acted in an unchristian or sacrilegious manner. On the contrary, we have been compelled by God's command (which is rightly to be esteemed higher than all custom) to permit such corrections." Here the arguments of the German and Latin diverge, almost as if there were different drafters of this material. The German is far more theological and argues first that the Evangelicals' behavior is above reproach (neither unchristian nor sacrilegious). Then it hearkens back to the arguments of CA XV by contrasting God's command to custom and, by implication, it invokes CA XVI, where one must obey God rather than (in this case) human custom—which in the empire had the force of law.

Latin: "For Your Imperial Majesty will undoubtedly discover that the form of teaching and ceremonies among us is more tolerable than what these perverse and malicious people describe. Indeed, the truth cannot be gathered from the rumors of the crowd or the curses of our enemies. However, it can easily be judged that nothing contributes more to preserving the dignity of ceremonies and cultivating reverence and piety among the people than conducting ceremonies properly in the churches." The Latin focuses on the malice of the enemies, who have perversely twisted the nature of the changes. It begs the emperor (in the Latin text for a third time) to ignore such rumors and judge the case more fairly. Then it adds another kind of argument altogether: that the (proper) way the Evangelicals behave actually preserves the ceremonies better and (what had to be important to any emperor) increases the people's piety. This argument goes a long way in clarifying the Evangelical party's view of themselves in relation to the fifteen-hundred-year history of the church. Far from assuming that any medieval practice was false (so that the goal would have been to create a re-formed church), the Evangelicals argued that by removing from present ceremonies any aspects that contradicted both Scripture and the original intent of these rites they could enhance their claim to continuity with the church catholic and actually increase the piety of the people.

We Teach and Confess

A recent brochure came in the mail, advertising a convocation about how to "rethink" Sunday morning. It boasted: "better questions, bolder experiments." It insisted one ask, "To what more faithful future are Christian communities now being called?" By signing up, one could "ask some fresh questions and engage them more boldly." To be sure, many observers sense that the church in North America in general and Lutheranism in particular are struggling. The advertisement, however, offers a typically Americanized solution of "God helps those who help themselves," and it assumes that new is always better. This way of doing theology and shaping practice now dominates church thinking worldwide.

Over against such captivation to religious novelty stands the CA, pleading for a theology grounded in Scripture and respectful of tradition. It encourages measuring theology by its *consolatory* effect, not simply by its content and certainly not by its novelty, and it insists that the conscience ought to find comfort in the teachings and actions of the Christian assembly. The CA champions unity and love, not division and rejection of those whose practices differ from one's own. At the same time, it cares about abuses in the church and what such abuses do now to the weak and what they may do in future generations.

PART TWO

PRACTICING THE FAITH
(THE DISPUTED ARTICLES)

The following chapters (22–28) are based on what the Augsburg Confession calls the "Disputed Articles." Because of the length of these articles, they are included in the "Appendix, Articles 22–28," starting on p. 300 of this volume. The format of the articles matches the pagination style used in *The Book of Concord: The Confessions of the Evangelical Lutheran Church*, Robert Kolb and Timothy J. Wengert, eds. (Minneapolis: Fortress Press, 2000), 60–103. The German text will run on the left and the Latin on the right on each two-page spread.

22

B<small>READ</small> *AND* W<small>INE</small>

D rink of it, all of you!" Jesus's commandment seems so obvious, and
yet in 1415 at the Council of Constance the bishops, gathered in solemn assembly and reacting to the protests of Jan Hus and other so-called
Utraquists ("both-kind-ists"), mandated taking the cup away from the laity.[1]
They thereby confirmed a practice that had developed within the medieval
Western church. They argued that the entire Christ was offered in each ele-
ment and implied what Gabriel Biel later argued explicitly: that there was a
difference between the laity and the clergy. Only the latter were required to
receive both kinds on behalf of the entire community. (In supporting this
practice, the *Confutation* insisted that because only apostles were in the upper
room, the words "all of you" applied only to the ordained.) Looking back at
this change in practice today, it would seem that the Reformers were simply
440 years ahead of their time, especially since the Vatican II council reversed
their predecessors and allowed (but did not mandate) reception in both kinds
by all Christians.

The Lord's Supper is a remarkable gift to the church from Christ. In all
expressions of Christianity, this sacrament "moves the heart" (to use Melanchthon's apt phrase in Ap XXIV.70 [BC 271]). Changes in practice wrought
by Evangelical communities during the early Reformation marked a fundamental, visible shift for all participants. Beginning tentatively in September
1521 and in a more orderly fashion in 1526, Wittenberg clerics instituted
Communion in bread *and* wine for all communicants. When the Saxon

---

1. In Luther's interview with the archbishop of Trier at the Diet held in Worms (1521), the question of the authority of councils came down to Constance, in large part because of its handling
of Hus and the Utraquists.

visitors (especially Philip Melanchthon) encountered some, who (for reasons of conscience) would not receive the cup, they made allowances in the *Instruction by the Visitors* of 1528—a policy that remained in place until 1538.[2] This so-called conservatism represented on the contrary an insistence that the church should never coerce individual consciences for whom enforcing even a biblical, ancient practice might harm their conscience.

This article provides insights into several aspects of Evangelical theology. First, it shows the drafters using all three authorities (Scripture, the Fathers, and experience [cf. CA XX]) to defend their deviation from medieval practice. Second, the article's very use of Scripture and tradition demonstrates *in concreto* aspects of the Reformation interpretation of the Bible and handling of the tradition. Third, it hints at a general approach to similar matters of practice for today's church.

For the text of Article 22, see pp. 300–03.

Reflections

"**Among us both kinds of the sacrament are given to the laity for the following reason. There is a clear order and command of Christ in Matt 26 [:27]: 'Drink from it, all of you.' Concerning the cup Christ here commands with clear words that they all should drink from it.**" The modern argument about whether this is truly the *ipsissima verba Christi* was unthinkable and, frankly, remains inconsequential for the Christian assembly gathered around Word and sacrament. The CA uses "all of you" *not* to criticize their opponents' practice of withholding the cup from the laity but rather to justify their own change in practice. The "clear command" and "clear words" from Christ's lips (according to Matthew) suffice to justify the practice. But these words also help elucidate what the Reformers meant by the *claritas Scripturae* (clarity of Scripture). This is not some sort of narrow fundamentalism but instead a commonsense approach to the meaning of an actual text. That is, Matthew 26:27 really does say, "all of you." Any gloss excepting the laity is simply that: a gloss, which functions more to obscure the meaning of the words rather than to clarify them.

"**So that no one can contest and interpret these words as if they only applied to priests, Paul indicates in 1 Cor 11 [:21] that the whole assembly of the Corinthian church used both kinds.**" The description of the Lord's Supper in 1 Corinthians was especially important for Melanchthon, who would insist in the argument against the Zwinglians that the phrase *koinonia tou somatos Christou* (participation in the body of Christ; 1 Cor 10:16) helped explain what Christ meant by "This is my body" and proved that the *cum pane*

---

2. LW 40:288–93.

(Christ's real presence "with the bread") had biblical warrant. Here, however, CA XXII shows what the Reformers mean by *Scriptura sui interpres* (Scripture as its own interpreter). The text "all of you" receives its best interpretation from Paul's description of the Corinthian congregation's practice. When Jesus said "All of you," Paul knew it meant "everyone" (and not just all priests).

"Moreover, this usage remained in the church for a long time, as can be demonstrated from the historical accounts and from the writings of the Fathers. Cyprian mentions in many places that the cup was given to the laity in his time. St. Jerome says that the priests who administer the sacrament distribute the blood of Christ to the people. Pope Gelasius himself ordered that the sacrament should not be divided (dist. 2, chap. *Concerning Consecration*). Not a single canon with the order to receive only one kind can be found." The way the drafters use patristic sources and canon law (including a citation from a pope) demonstrates a marked difference in how they, as opposed to their opponents, employ this second type of authority. Whereas the opponents understand the consensus of the church to constitute the sum of all witnesses (so that, in this case, the Council of Constance must be given equal or more weight to the ancient church's witness), the Reformers insisted, from the very beginning of the Reformation, that one must go *ad fontes* (to the [oldest and purest] sources) to help determine good theology and practice in the church. In this way, the Reformers viewed themselves as being far more "conservative" (i.e., conservation-minded), whereas their opponents were guilty of innovation, in this case initiating a practice that contradicted Christ and the early church.

The Latin version makes this even clearer when it states: "Only a quite recent custom holds otherwise. However, it is evident that a custom, introduced contrary to the commands of God, must not be approved, as the canons testify (dist. 8, ch. '*Veritate*,' and the subsequent chapters)." Here the drafters are referring to rules of interpretation for church law found within canon law itself! This is, perhaps, one of the most delightful ironies in this article's mode of argumentation. No wonder that the *Confutation* employs in part rather convoluted arguments to prove their point (since they must admit that lay Communion in both kinds was practiced) and insists instead that the Evangelical position demonstrates both an abuse and disobedience.[3]

"Nobody knows when or through whom this custom of receiving only one kind was introduced, although Cardinal Cusanus mentions when this custom was approved." The reference to the fifteenth-century theologian, Nicholas Cusanus, indicates at the very least that the Evangelical party, which otherwise ignores the good cardinal's teaching, had done their homework.

---

3. See the *Confutation*, art. 22, in: *Sources and Contexts of the Book of Concord*, ed. Robert Kolb and James A. Nestingen (Minneapolis: Fortress, 2001), 120–23. In Ap XXII.6–8 in BC 245–46, Melanchthon remarks on the weakness of their argument.

Although the Council of Constance had approved the practice, it clearly had older roots in the Western church's practice although no direct sanction until relatively late in the church's life. This very lack of support indirectly confirms CA XXII's skepticism about the practice.

"**Now it is obvious that this custom, introduced contrary to God's command and to the ancient canons, is not right. Accordingly, it was not proper to burden the consciences of those who desired to use the sacrament according to Christ's institution and to compel them to act contrary to the order of our Lord Christ.**" First after summarizing the argument from Scripture and tradition do the drafters introduce their third authority, namely experience. The "experience" here is the burdening of consciences that desire to act according to Christ's institution and not contrary to his command (as opposed, of course, to the command of the church). In light of this argument from conscience, it is easier to understand the Saxon flexibility about allowing those conscience-bound believers who could not (yet) bring themselves to receiving the cup. In any case, the two defining factors here are Christ's word and the conscience.

"**Furthermore, because dividing the sacrament contradicts Christ's institution, the customary procession with the sacrament has also been discontinued.**" This final line is somewhat disingenuous. The more substantive reason for eliminating processions with the host has to do with the point of the Supper (namely, the eating and drinking) and the Reformers' changing views about the duration of Christ's presence (although this first becomes an expressed issue in the 1540s).[4] Its mention here, however, relates directly to the first public display of Evangelical rejection of traditional practice. On 16 June 1530, Corpus Christi Day, the emperor required the attendance of all members of the imperial diet at the traditional procession of the consecrated host. Landgrave Philip of Hesse refused to bow or take off his hat as the host passed by, making quite clear that he no longer would have anything to do with this practice. He hardly did it simply because the sacrament was "divided," but clearly the drafters thought that this mild explanation of his behavior sufficed to defend it. These extra-curricular uses continue to distinguish Lutheran and Roman Catholic practice today.

We Teach and Confess

"Here I am for you!" This paraphrase of Christ's two-fold promise in the Lord's Supper defines what is central to the Supper and, by extension, what is not. At the Supper individuals receive not merely memorial tokens of bread

---

4. See Timothy J. Wengert, "Luther and Melanchthon on Consecrated Communion Wine (Eisleben 1542–43)," *Lutheran Quarterly* 15 (2001): 24–42.

and wine for Christian unity but Christ's very presence for their forgiveness, life, and salvation. Undermining this institution seems unnecessary and perhaps even dangerous for believers gathered together in assembly around the table. So, Christians are encouraged to bring the staff of life and a festal drink to the table, distributing them freely among believers for the strengthening of their baptismal faith.[5] Christ has not abandoned us in this life but offers himself to us and for us in this meal. Here there are neither Jew nor Greek, slave nor free, male and female, or even lay and ordained but one body of baptized believers fed with Christ's body and blood in the bread and wine. What could better unite us than this heavenly food and drink? What now more sadly divides Christians than our inability or unwillingness to celebrate that presence and those gifts around a single table? Philip Melanchthon's stirring words in the Apology XXII still hold true today: "The sacrament was instituted for consolation and encouragement of terrified hearts, when they believe that the flesh of Christ, given for the life of the world, is their food, and when they believe that they are made alive by being joined to Christ."[6] Who of us would want to deny Christians access to this meal in its entirety?

---

5. For the connection to baptism, see LC, "Lord's Supper," par. 23–27 in BC 469. For the designations of bread and wine, I am grateful to Gordon Lathrop.
6. Ap XXII.10 in BC 246.

23

Happy Conscience, Happy Life

And then there is sexuality! How can this God-given force of nature, which most mammals seem to have figured out without much anxiety, cause so much apprehension among human creatures? The Christian preference for celibacy among clergy and among men and women under vows has a variety of causes: a deep-seated worry about the desires and urges of the "flesh" derived from regnant philosophies of the ancient world; biblical sanctioning of the single life (Matt 19:10–12 and 1 Cor 7); the desire to define Christianity and its view of the Christian life as a pilgrimage toward the world to come over against classical conceptions of a worldly good life; self-denial as a sign for others trapped in a world of family responsibilities.

Modern Christianity is filled with examples of sexual strictures gone awry. Although scandals involving Roman Catholic priests may have far more to do with an insensitive hierarchy than with the effects of celibacy per se, there are plenty of Protestant problems as well. Many teens encouraged to sign vows (!) of abstinence but not given proper (around-the-clock?) supervision are (not surprisingly) unable to keep their promises. Politicians and movie moguls seem to imagine that standard measures of decency do not apply to them. Even common folk may find themselves unable to withstand the pull of an over-sexed society. What's a Christian to do? How may Christian churches find their way through this minefield?

From nearly the beginning of the Reformation, Luther was skeptical of what human beings could promise God. Already in 1519, he viewed perpetual monastic vows of poverty, chastity, and obedience as undercutting the baptismal vow.[1] In 1520 he expanded on that argument in *The Babylonian Captivity of the Church*.[2] By 1521 several in Wittenberg were calling into question the enforced celibacy of clergy. And in the same year Luther wrote from the Wartburg his *Judgment of Martin Luther on Monastic Vows*, which was especially hard on the vow of celibacy.[3] By 1523, with the wholesale marriages of priests, monks, and nuns underway, he wrote a tract, *The Estate of Marriage*,[4] in which he praised this estate above all others. Although he remained essentially an Augustinian friar until June 1525, when he married Katharina von Bora, Luther realized the difficulties raised by the requirement of celibacy for priests. Many of his statements about sex (including comments in the Large Catechism)[5] were quite down-to-earth. He was convinced that one could no more command the person lacking the gift of celibacy not to desire sexual intimacy than to put fire and cloth together and command them not to burn. It is important to realize that Luther was not against celibacy per se. Indeed, one of his closest colleagues, Nicholas von Amsdorf, never married, and Prince Georg von Anhalt, whom Luther later ordained to be bishop of Merseburg, was also single.

But in Augsburg, and already in the Torgau memoranda, the Reformers took up the issue about required celibacy of priests not just as a religious practice but as a political necessity, a law of the empire. On this issue, the Evangelicals needed to defend both their changes in practice and their claim to be obedient citizens. No wonder that the German version even includes a direct address to the emperor! Indeed, much of what they wrote in CA XXIII has far more to do with the political realities than anything else. Nevertheless, the mode of argumentation again gives insight into how the drafters of the CA constructed their practical theology of "justification by grace through faith on account of Christ." It also tells us just how much authority they bestowed on early Christian practice.

This defense of married clergy is by far the weakest in the CA. It is one thing to show that God supports marriage, that the early church had married clergy, and that scandal arises from forcing celibacy on those who do not have the gift of continence. But it is a great leap to conclude that therefore priests *should* be married. The drafters of the CA, however, did not believe they needed to meet such a high standard for defending their change of practice. Utilitarian arguments were designed to move government officials. As far as theological arguments over practice go, they will always fall short. The one thing the drafters of CA XXIII could not do was prove the necessity of

---

1. Martin Luther, *The Holy and Blessed Sacrament of Baptism* (1519) in TAL 1:220–22.

2. Martin Luther, *The Babylonian Captivity of the Church* (1520) in TAL 3:77–84.

3. LW 44:243–400.

4. LW 45:11–49.

5. LC, Ten Commandments, 199–221 (BC, 413–16).

married clergy directly. They could only argue by analogy, holding to their assumption that what the ancient church did was purer, the standard against which present practice must be measured. Although this article may seem rather unfocused and repetitive, nevertheless, the fact that so many of the Evangelical priests and pastors were married caused Charles V, in his 1548 decree giving an interim solution to the religious division in the empire and nicknamed the Augsburg Interim, to allow married priests and Communion in both kinds to the Evangelicals.

For the text of Article 23, see pp. 302–08.

Reflections

"From everyone, both of high and low degree, a mighty, loud complaint has been heard throughout the world about the flagrant immorality and dissolute life of priests who were not able to remain chaste; their vices reached the height of abomination." Unlike the doctrinal articles, the drafters of the CA include here a new "authority," namely, public opinion. In some ways, one could say that Luther "invented" public opinion, as his 1518 *Sermon on Indulgences and Grace* became the first "best-seller" in a vernacular language by a living author that the world had ever seen. But already in the late fifteenth century imperial diets had drawn up lists of grievances (*Gravamina*) against the Roman church and its practices. Of course, the CA exaggerates the problem, since its drafters knew well that there were also chaste priests adhering to the promises of celibacy. As mentioned above, some leaders of the Reformation remained single. But there was little doubt that many priests had found the promise of celibacy too burdensome to keep.

"In order to avoid so much terrible offense, adultery and other immorality, some priests among us have entered the married state. They give as their reason that they are compelled and moved to do so by the great distress of their consciences, especially since Scripture clearly proclaims that the married state was instituted by God to avoid sexual immorality, as Paul says that to avoid immorality, 'Each man should have his own wife' [1 Cor 7:2] and again, 'For it is better to marry than to be aflame with passion' [1 Cor 7:9b]. When Christ says, in Matt 19[:11], 'Not everyone can accept this teaching,' he shows that he knew human nature quite well, namely, that few people have the gift to live a celibate life. For 'God created humankind . . . male and female,' (Gen 1 [:27]). Experience has made it all too clear whether human power and ability can improve or change the creation of God, the supreme Majesty, through their own intentions or vows without a special gift or grace of God." With the word "some," the CA understates the number of priests who had married. Their grounds for marrying included not only avoiding offense and adultery but also a distress of consciences bound to certain clear passages of Scripture. But the passages cited outlined three reasons for priests to marry: the avoidance of immorality (1 Cor 7), the limited number of people who had received the gift of celibacy, and the creation of God. Only God's intervening gift could change God's created order. This connection broadened the reasons for married priests beyond the typical pleas to end immorality to a far deeper theological basis: God's creation and God's extraordinary gifts.

"What good, honorable, chaste life, what Christian, honest or upright existence has resulted for many? For it is clear—as many have confessed about their own lives—how much abominable, terrifying disturbance and torment of conscience they experienced at the time of their death. Therefore, because God's Word and command cannot be changed by any human vow or law, priests and other clergy have taken wives for themselves for these and other reasons and causes." In contrast to these biblical reasons for marriage, the CA places the "abominable, terrifying disturbance and torment of conscience." Of course, the appeal to conscience may explain why a priest might have to marry, but it does not explain why he would remain a priest. That explanation comes next.

"It can also be demonstrated from the historical accounts and from the writings of the Fathers that it was customary in the Christian church of ancient times for priests and deacons to have wives. This is why Paul says in 1 Tim 3 [:2]: 'Now a bishop must be above reproach, the husband of one wife.'" The CA now lays out an argument for married priests, beginning with a vague reference to the church Fathers and a specific reference to St. Paul.

"It was only four hundred years ago that priests in Germany were compelled by force to leave the married state and take the vows of celibacy. But they all offered so much serious and strong resistance that an archbishop of Mainz, who had promulgated the new papal decree, was nearly crushed to death during an uprising of the entire clergy. In the beginning, this same prohibition was so hastily and ineptly enforced that the pope at the time prohibited not only future marriages of priests but also broke up existing marriages of long standing. Of course, this was not only contrary to all divine, natural, and civil laws but also was totally opposed and contrary to the canons that the popes themselves had made and to the most renowned councils." The drafters now proffer an argument about the forced celibacy of German priests and the resistance of the entire clergy. They highlight the depravity of this action by describing the breaking up of existing marriages. This violation of every kind of law possible is made worse by the fact that it even violated canon law. This kind of argumentation highlights a profound difference between the two sides. The drafters insist on the humanist return to the oldest sources (*ad fontes*) to determine the best practices in the church. A later decision by council or pope cannot overturn the earlier consensus of the church, particularly, as in this case, when the later decision wrought such strong resistance and disorder. Their opponents, on the contrary, view the church's tradition more organically, where later decisions clarify God's will and the church's practice and, thus, can change earlier practice.

"**Many godly and intelligent people of high standing have also often expressed similar opinions and misgivings that such enforced celibacy and prohibition of marriage (which God himself instituted and left open for individuals to enter) never introduced any good but rather many great and evil vices and much scandal. Moreover, as his biography indicates, one of the popes himself, Pius II, often said and had these words recorded: there may well have been some reason why the clergy was prohibited from marrying; but there were many better, greater and more important reasons why they should again be free to marry. Undoubtedly, Pope Pius, as an intelligent and wise man, made this statement because of grave misgivings.**" The drafters must have realized that simply an appeal to past practice was not enough to defend their case. Thus, they added this paragraph. They refer in general to the opinions of "godly and intelligent people" who support marriage over *enforced* celibacy. This coercion has caused the scandal referred to in the opening sentences of CA XXIII. But then (unlike the Latin, which had referred to Pope Pius II earlier), they describe the account by his biographer, Bartholomeo Platina (1421–1481). The citation of Platina is no accident. Here was a Renaissance thinker who had served the humanist pope, Pius II, before being imprisoned by his (anti-humanist) successor, Pope Paul II, and then released and made the Vatican librarian by Pope Sixtus IV. It was at that point in his career that Platina wrote *Concerning the Lives and Customs of the Popes*, published in Venice in 1518, in which (not surprisingly) Paul II is vilified and Pius II praised.[6]

"**Therefore, in loyalty to Your Imperial Majesty we are confident that, as a most praiseworthy Christian emperor, Your Majesty will graciously take to heart the fact that now in these last times and days of which Scripture speaks, the world is becoming more wicked and human beings more frail and infirm.**" In appealing directly to Emperor Charles V, the drafters signal an end to one form of argument and the beginning of another. It is unprecedented in the CA: using an argument about the end of the world. The *senex mundi* (the old age of the world in the Latin version) is transformed into the

---

6. Bartholomeo Platina, *De vitis ac gestis pontificum historia* (Venice: Pinzi, 1511), 157v, refers to Pius II's opinion about married priests in the midst of a longer encomium to his attempts to improve church life. "To enrich the virtues of the clerics [and] to make their vices poorer, it seemed [to him] a great reason for needing to restore allowing marriage for the majority of priests." ("Virtutes clerum ditasse uitia pauperem facere: Sacerdotibus magna ratione sublatas nuptias maiori restituendas uideri.")

"Last Days" in the German. This overall pessimism about the world should not to lead to despair but to gracious action by Charles. This kind of appeal, however, may in part show how dissatisfied the drafters were with their arguments, since they needed to show compelling reasons for priests to marry.

"Therefore it is most necessary, useful, and Christian to give this situation thorough inspection, so that the prohibition of marriage may not cause worse and more shameful immorality and vices to gain ground in German lands. For no one will ever be able to change or arrange these matters better or more wisely than God himself who instituted marriage to help human frailty and to prevent sexual immorality. The old canons also state that sometimes severity and rigor must be alleviated and relaxed for the sake of human weakness and to prevent and avoid greater scandal. Now that certainly would be Christian and highly necessary in this case. How can the marriage of priests and clergy, especially of the pastors and others who are to serve the church, be disadvantageous to the Christian church as a whole? There may well be a shortage of priests and pastors in the future if this harsh prohibition of marriage should last much longer." In addressing the emperor directly, the drafters now go over some of their previous arguments: the need to prevent greater immorality and God's assistance for human frailty through instituting marriage. A new wrinkle comes with the reference to canon law, which allows the relaxation of certain rules on the same grounds (human weakness and avoiding scandal). They then present a utilitarian argument by asking how married clergy harms the church and pointing out that if things stay as they are there will soon be a shortage of pastors.

"Thus, that priests and clergy may marry is based on the divine Word and command. Moreover, the historical accounts demonstrate that priests were married and that the vow of celibacy has caused so much awful, unchristian offense, so much adultery, such terrible, unprecedented immorality and abominable vice that even some of the sincere cathedral clergy and also some courtiers in Rome have often confessed and complained how such abominable and overwhelming vice in the clergy would arouse the wrath of God. It is, therefore, quite deplorable that Christian marriage has not only been prohibited but also most swiftly punished in many places, as if it were a great crime." The drafters continue to summarize their earlier arguments based upon Scripture, historical precedent, and the avoidance of scandal. They then introduce vague references to others (presumably allied with the opposition) among the cathedral canons and members of the papal court who worry about God's wrath upon such a scandal-producing rule as mandatory celibacy. The conclusion points in a new direction, namely, the deplorable punishment of clergy who defied the church's rigid rule of celibacy—as if it were a great crime. Indeed, all the arguments up to this point have been trying to demonstrate that married clergy cannot be considered a great crime under any circumstances. Thus, the princes allied with Rome have no business punishing such priests.

"**And yet, God commanded in Holy Scripture to hold marriage in high esteem. Moreover, the marital state is also highly praised in imperial laws and in all monarchies—wherever there has been law and justice. Only in this day and age are people beginning to be tortured without cause, simply because they are married—especially priests who above all should be spared. This is done not only contrary to divine law but also to the canons. In 1 Tim 4[:1, 3] the apostle Paul calls the teaching that prohibits marriage a teaching of the devil. Christ himself says in John 8[:44] that the devil is a murderer from the beginning. These two statements fit well together. For it certainly must be a teaching of the devil to prohibit marriage and then dare to maintain such a teaching with the shedding of blood.**" The continual repetition shows the drafters' own struggles to present a cogent argument. God's Word, secular decrees, and canon law prove the goodness of marriage and (by extension) "prove" that no one should be punished for being married—least of all priests. But then comes a very different, new argument: Paul calls the prohibition of marriage demonic (1 Tim 4), the devil is a murderer (John 8), therefore murdering married priests is of the devil. Indeed, Luther himself had already brought 1 Timothy 4 into the discussion in *The Address to Christian Nobility*.[7] This argument about the devil's murderous intent allows the drafters to apply Paul's warning to the present situation, where some were meting out draconian punishment on married priests.

"**However, just as no human law can abolish or change God's command, neither can any vow change God's command. That is why St. Cyprian advised that women who do not keep the vow of chastity should get married. He says in Epistle 11: "But if they are unwilling or unable to keep their vows of chastity it is better for them to marry than to fall into the fire through their lusts, and they should see to it that they cause no offense to their brothers and sisters." In addition, all the canons show great lenience and fairness toward those who have made vows in their youth, as is the case with large numbers of priests and monks who entered their vocations out of ignorance when they were young.**"Here CA XXIII moves its argument from married priests (who were not under a vow) to monks and nuns, who sometimes took vows when they were young, despite restrictions in canon law. But it is not at all clear how this corresponds directly to the problem of married priests, except to the extent that many monks and friars were later ordained.

---

7. Martin Luther, *Address to Christian Nobility* (1520), in TAL 1:425.

Latin: "But the command of God still exists, the custom of the church is well known, and impure celibacy produces many scandals, adulteries, and other crimes deserving punishment by good magistrates. Despite all that, it is astonishing that such ferocious opposition to the marriage of priests still exists." The Latin text succinctly summarizes the heart of the drafters' proof: God's command, the custom of the church, and scandal. Yet this is hardly logical proof of why the church should allow married priests. Indeed, the final sentence begs the question and shows just how tentative this argument remains. Their problem lies in the self-imposed restrictions on their arguments, which prevents them from directly invoking criticisms of the papacy. Thus, except for the reference to the archbishop of Mainz, they are unwilling to blame corrupt papal theology for unjustly imposing celibacy on priests.

We Teach and Confess

"Your Majesty will graciously take to heart . . ." In certain practical matters of the Christian church, arguments are finally not about right and wrong but an appeal to the leader's conscience. This kind of approach may seem particularly weak when the opposition is demanding logical, legal justification for such changes, but it finally mirrors Paul's own arguments in Romans 14–15. For the sake of the weak *all* practical, moral issues cannot simply appeal to right rules and regulations. And perhaps in matters of sexuality this is most important. Here we are dealing not just with vague commands regarding the right thing to do but deep-seated urges and drives that defy being easily harnessed by laws. Here, scandal really does have its own logic and prevents a simplistic appeal to human decrees. When it comes to such decisions, it is crucial *not* to make edicts but rather to consider the effects of such rulings on individual consciences. As soon as such ideals like celibacy become fixed, unbreakable laws, the weak are inevitably crushed. Then the church and its leaders need graciously to take such matters to heart and practice mercy and love, not strictness.

24

"Once for All"

In the clandestine seminary of Finkenwalde, where Dietrich Bonhoeffer taught from 1935 to 1937, the altar in the chapel bore a single Greek word: *eph-hapax* (once for all). In the face of Nazi propaganda calling for sacrifices to the *Vaterland*, the radical Confessing Church insisted that Christ eliminated all such sacrifices, "once for all" (Rom 6:10; Heb 7:27; 9:12; 10:10). The centrality of Christ's sacrifice for sin for the life of the world becomes nowhere more vivid than in the Lord's Supper, where the results of that act are distributed to the communicants.

The Lord's Supper both unites and divides Christians. It unites us with Christ and, thus, with one another as he draws us closer to himself. But our varying interpretations divide us in at least two ways. When Christ takes the bread and promises, "Here I am," some view this as a symbolic presence and others as a real presence (cf. CA X). When Christ promises, "Here I am *for you*," some emphasize the sacrament's effect by the (mere) performance of the rite, while others insist that the words "for you" invite and, hence, require faith to be true. CA XXIV takes aim at this second division, the specific rift between Lutherans and Roman Catholics.

For the text of Article 24, see pp. 308–12.

231

Reflections

Latin[1]: "Our churches are falsely accused of abolishing the mass. In fact, the mass is retained among us and is celebrated with the greatest reverence. Almost all the customary ceremonies are also retained, except that German hymns, added for the instruction of the people, are interspersed here and there among the Latin ones. For ceremonies are especially needed in order to teach those who are ignorant. Paul advised [1 Cor 14:2, 9] that in church a language that is understood by the people should be used." Many of the CA's opponents viewed the Mass as a sacrifice performed by the priest, offering to God an unbloodied sacrifice of Christ's body and blood to the Father for the sins of those present or of those for whom the Mass had been purchased. Thus, when the Evangelicals removed all references to any propitiatory sacrifice, they effectively stopped celebrating the Mass completely in the eyes of their opponents. So the first thing that Melanchthon and the other drafters do in the Latin version (which functioned as a kind of rhetorical narration of the facts) is to confirm that the liturgy itself had not changed. Indeed, even in the *Deutsche Messe* (German Mass), published in 1526, Luther kept the basic *ordo* of the Latin Mass. When Reformers from Augsburg, who in 1536 participated in negotiations leading to the Wittenberg Concord on the Lord's Supper between Wittenberg and such cities as Strasbourg and Augsburg, experienced Wittenberg's liturgy, they were shocked at how traditional it remained. CA XXIV justifies liturgy in the vernacular, which the Vatican II council finally allowed for in the 1960s, on the basis of the need for instruction and the suggestion of St. Paul.

Latin: "The people have grown accustomed to receiving the sacrament together—all who are fit to do so. This also increases reverence and respect for public ceremonies. For people are admitted only if they first had an opportunity to be examined and heard." Second, continuing this same argument, the first sentence of this paragraph points indirectly to the actual bone of contention here: private Masses recited at side altars without any congregants. Instead, the Wittenberg congregation (and others in Evangelical cities and principalities) had become accustom to a common celebration on Sundays and certain feast days. According to CA XXIV, the results were reverence and increased instruction about the meaning of the meal.

Latin: "The people are also reminded about the dignity and use of the sacrament—how it offers great consolation to anxious consciences—so that they may learn to believe in God and expect and ask for all that is good from God. Such worship pleases God, and such use of the sacrament

---

1. The Latin version, which is somewhat fuller than the German, will be used primarily in this commentary section.

cultivates piety towards God. So it does not appear that the mass is held with greater devotion among our adversaries than among us." Third, this part of the description of the sacrament goes directly to the heart of the CA: justification by faith ("so that they may learn to believe . . .") and the effect of the gospel ("it offers great consolation to anxious consciences"). The Lord's Supper is not a work that satisfies God's justice; it is not simply a sign of Christian fellowship; it is not a way of demonstrating our commitment to God. It provides comfort to anxious consciences. Then, and only then, does God delight in our worship and do we grow into true godliness. For these three reasons then (using the vernacular for instruction; involving the entire congregation; emphasizing the comfort of the gospel), the Reformers could claim a higher level of devotion than among their adversaries. With this the die is cast!

Latin: **"However, for a long time there has been a serious public outcry by good people that masses were being shamefully profaned and devoted to profit. It is public knowledge how widely this abuse extends in all places of worship, what kind of people celebrate masses only for a revenue or stipend, and how many celebrate contrary the canons' prohibitions. But Paul severely threatens those who treat the Eucharist unworthily, when he says [1 Cor 11:27]: 'Whoever, therefore, eats the bread and drinks the cup of the Lord in an unworthy manner will be answerable for the body and blood of the Lord.' Accordingly, when the priests among us were instructed concerning this sin, private masses were discontinued among us, since there were hardly any private masses held except for the sake of profit."** Here the practical complaint about Roman practice becomes the basis of the drafters' criticism and forms the main rhetorical proposition of this article: private Masses were indeed "for sale." This practice, unheard of in Eastern Orthodoxy, turned the Lord's Supper into one of the chief ways that priests earned their livings, drawing upon gifts from the living to say Masses in perpetuity for the souls of their departed ancestors. In 1518 at the Castle Church in Wittenberg, we know that six thousand such Masses were recited for the souls of electors and electresses buried there. Many priests were ordained exclusively for this purpose, earning from Luther and others the nickname "Mass priests." All of these Masses were daily recited by a single priest standing before one of the Castle Church's many altars. For the Reformers *this* (and not simply sinfulness, as later Lutheran Pietists imagined) constituted an unworthy reception of the sacrament. Breaking the connection between the Supper and profit became an important aspect of the revolution in practice emanating from Wittenberg and other centers of the Reformation.

Latin: **"Nor were bishops ignorant of these abuses. If they had corrected them in time there would be less dissension now. By their negligence many vices have been allowed to creep into the church. Now, when** it is too late, they are beginning to complain about the calamities in the church, although this tumult was occasioned by those same abuses which had become so obvious they could no longer be tolerated. Great dissensions have arisen concerning the mass, concerning the sacrament: perhaps the world is being punished for such an enduring profanation of masses as has been tolerated in the church for many centuries by the very people who could and should have corrected them. For it is written in the Decalog [Exod 20:7]: 'The Lord will not acquit anyone who misuses his name.' Since the beginning of the world no divine matter seems ever to have been so devoted to profit as the mass." Accusing bishops of not fulfilling their office is a new wrinkle in CA's arguments found only in the Latin version, but it goes back to the *95 Theses*, where Luther suspected that bad teaching about indulgences had snuck into the church "while the bishops slept." Indirectly, the drafters seem to imply that the "great dissensions" (between Wittenberg and the Swiss) were also the fault of bishops—punishment for the "profanation of masses" they tolerated. Selling Masses was a terrible misuse of God's name, which God would surely punish.

Latin: "The following view increased private masses without end: Christ had by his passion made satisfaction for original sin and had instituted the mass in which an offering might be made for daily sins, mortal and venial. From this came the common opinion that the mass is a work which *ex opere operato* blots out the sins of the living and the dead. Here began a debate on whether one mass said for many is worth as much as special masses for individuals. That debate produced this endless multitude of masses." This view, rejected by the *Confutation* as a distortion of Eucharistic theology, was nevertheless popular in late-medieval piety. Christ's death took care of original sin (the grace of which was distributed in baptism) but the unbloodied sacrifice of Christ's body and blood could now atone for daily sins. On top of this, the Mass was thought to be effective *ex opere operato* (by the [mere] performance of the rite). (See CA XIII for a reference to this doctrine.) What Augustine intended by the phrase, namely, that the New Testament sacraments do not depend for their efficacy upon the virtue of celebrant or of recipient but upon the work of God, became the basis for a practice in which the Mass confected a quantity of grace, which could be distributed to designated persons (living or dead). Added to this, the Mass for a single person was understood to be worth more than the Mass celebrated on Sunday morning for many. The German addition underscores the Reformers' concern, namely, the way human beings undermine faith by focusing on human works: "and with this work people wanted to obtain from God everything they needed. Meanwhile, faith in Christ and true worship of God were forgotten." With this addition, one discovers again that justification by faith lurks underneath the drafters' concerns.

Latin: "Our people have warned that these opinions do not agree with the Holy Scriptures but instead undermine the glory of Christ's passion. For the passion of Christ was an offering and satisfaction not only for original guilt but for all other remaining sins, as is written in Heb [10:10, 14]: 'We have been sanctified through the offering of the body of Jesus Christ once and for all,' and 'By a single offering he has perfected for all time those who are sanctified.'" CA XXIV, in a kind of rhetorical confirmation, now proffers three arguments (numbered only in the German) against private Masses and their sale. It relies on one of the CA's fundamental arguments: the centrality of Christ alone for salvation. (See especially CA XX.) The *eph–hapax* of Hebrews 10 has direct consequences for the centrality of Christ alone in all aspects of Christian life. The German version labels this teaching of the Mass as a sacrifice a novelty (to which surprisingly the *Confutation* agrees): "It is an unprecedented novelty in church doctrine that Christ's death should have made satisfaction only for original sin and not for other sins as well. Consequently, we hope everyone understands that such error is not unjustly rebuked."

German: "In the second place, St. Paul teaches that we obtain grace before God through faith and not through works. Clearly contrary to this is the misuse of the mass where people imagine that they may obtain grace through performing this work. For everyone knows that the mass is used for removing sin and obtaining grace and all benefits from God—not only for the priest himself but also for the whole world and for others, living or dead. *And this takes place through performing the work,* ex opere operato, *without faith.*" When one "undermines the glory of Christ's passion," it simultaneously destroys justification by grace through faith on account of Christ. The German is a fuller exposition of this second argument and, in the 1531 *editio princeps*, relying on the Latin original, even refers to the performance of the Mass *ex opere operato*, that is, without needing faith. This gets to the heart of the dispute. The Evangelicals will not permit the performance of any practice to insinuate itself into one's relation to Christ and thus to destroy trust in his promises. Of course, today other practices, which could even be labeled magical, continue to undermine the sacraments. The point of the sacrament of baptism, the return to baptism in the sacrament of absolution, the sacrament of the altar—to say nothing of ordination or even confirmation— is always to create and strengthen faith through the application of God's promise directly to the participants. Here all human works melt in the warm sun of God's grace. And yet, the Old Creature continually searches for ways to make the sacraments into works that we perform or to make faith into a commitment we undertake. Either way, human actions swallow God's mercy and Christ's love.

Latin: "But Christ commands that it be done in memory of him. The mass, therefore, was instituted so that the faith of those who use the sacrament should recall what benefits are received through Christ and should encourage and console the anxious conscience. For to remember Christ is to remember his benefits and realize that they are truly offered to us. It is not enough to remember the history, because the Jews and the ungodly can also remember that. The mass is to be used for the purpose of offering the sacrament to those who need consolation, just as Ambrose says: 'Because I always sin, I ought always to take the medicine.'" The Latin version derives this third point (in the German version's counting) from the Words of Institution themselves, giving a new twist to the anamnesis. The "memory" is not recalling the event of Christ's death on the cross (as Zwingli had argued); that can be done by anyone (Jas 2:19; cf. CA XX's definition of faith). Instead, faith itself is reminded of the gospel (Christ's benefits; CA III), which "should encourage and console the anxious conscience" (cf. CA XIII and XX). Here the Latin is far more direct than the German, where the language seems to objectify the effect of the sacrament.[2] Ambrose of Milan, whose tract on the sacraments was very influential, tied the Supper to healing and to the life of the Christian sinner.[3] The sacrament is for those who need consolation: "Here is Christ *for you*." It is precisely the "for you" that undermines the late-medieval use of *ex opere operato* for understanding the Supper. The remembrance arising out of faith alone catches us up in Christ's saving act, creating and strengthening that very faith.

German: "Now since the mass is not a sacrifice for others, living or dead, to take away their sins but should be a Communion where the priest and others receive the sacrament for themselves, we celebrate it in this fashion. On holy days and at other times when communicants are present, mass is celebrated, and those who desire it receive the sacrament." Here the German version offers more detail than the Latin. First, rejecting the notion that the Mass is an expiatory sacrifice reveals an entirely different face of the Lord's Supper, namely, as a true Communion. Luther had already stressed this fellowship in his 1519 sermon on the sacrament. Celebrating the Mass privately contradicts the main purpose of the sacrament: to gather the faithful together around the meal to celebrate Christ's presence and to receive his gifts. The only reason *not* to celebrate the Mass weekly would be if there were no communicants, since the Evangelicals did not allow private Masses. The regular celebration of the Lord's Supper, common in all Lutheran churches of the time, slowly gave way to pious attempts to fence the sacrament in the late seventeenth century and to suspicions of ritualism among more Enlightened types of the late eighteenth century and beyond. Suddenly, what had

---

2. German (emphasis added): "The sacrament *makes them aware* that they are promised grace and forgiveness of sin by Christ. That is why this sacrament requires faith and without faith is used in vain."

3. Ambrose, *Concerning the Sacraments* (*De sacramentis*), V, 4, 25 (MPL 16:464; CSEL 73: 58, 12).

been a weekly occurrence in Wittenberg became a four-times-a-year event, as preaching and new definitions of "worthiness" choked out the fellowship of sinners around their savior. Only in the twentieth century have Lutheran churches once again slowly begun to enjoy more frequent Communion.[4]

Latin: **"Nor is this custom new in the church. For the ancient teachers before the time of Gregory do not mention private masses, but often speak of the common mass. Chrysostom says that the priest stands daily at the altar, inviting some to Communion and keeping others away. And it is apparent from the ancient canons that one person celebrated the mass, from whom the rest of the presbyters and deacons received the body of Christ. For the words of the Nicene canon read: 'Let the deacons receive Holy Communion in order after the presbyters from the bishop or from a presbyter.' Concerning Communion Paul also commands [1 Cor 11:33] that people should wait for one another so that there may be a common participation."** The careful reiteration of the church's early history reminds us once again of the authority the drafters of the CA placed upon the ancient church and its practices. The CA employs these particular examples to underscore the communal aspect of the Supper. Again, the drafters interpret "unworthy eating" in 1 Corinthians as a lack of fellowship and not some sort of defective theology or incomplete sorrow for sin, as would happen in later Lutheran practice. Private Masses (especially for the dead) undermined the very purpose for which Christ instituted the meal in the first place: the strengthening of faith *and* community.

Latin: **"Since, therefore, the mass as we conduct it has on its side the example of the church, from Scripture and the Fathers, we are confident that it cannot be disapproved, especially since the customary public ceremonies are for the most part retained. Only the number of masses is different, and on account of the great and manifest abuses it would certainly be good to limit them. For in former times mass was not celebrated every day, even in churches most frequented, as the *Tripartite History*, Book IX, testifies: 'But again, in Alexandria, on Wednesday and Friday Scriptures are read and the teachers interpret them, and everything is done except the solemn practice of the Offering.'"** In a kind of peroration, the drafters never stray far from the underlying point of these seven final articles: no change actually deviates from Scripture or the ancient church's practice. Therefore, there is no need to break the unity of the church over these variations. The argument that only the number of Masses had been altered also appeared in Melanchthon's letter to Archbishop Albrecht of Mainz from July 1530.[5] Here the drafters coupled this mild appeal with a mention of "abuses." Their final

---

4. A congregation of which I was a member began celebrating the Eucharist weekly. When a sixth grader I was teaching learned that his sins were completely forgiven in the Supper, he burst out, "Boy, it's lucky we get this every week!" Lucky indeed!

5. See MBW *Texte* 4/1:476-85 (no. 1002).

proof text from the highly regarded *Tripartite History* simply indicates that daily Mass (the norm in most churches and often a requirement for priests) was not always celebrated everywhere.

We Teach and Confess

He burst into tears as I said the familiar words, "This is my body, given for you," in the Minneapolis hospital room, and the bed upon which he was sitting shook. This 450-pound man, who was about to undergo an at-the-time dangerous surgery to help him reduce his weight to healthy levels, was receiving a different kind of health food altogether. As St. Ambrose once remarked, when it comes to any other food we turn it into us, but here at the Table the true body of Christ turns us into it, as a true "medicine of immortality." This indescribable benefit came into that room that day not because of who I was or as if I were making an offering to God nor because of how repentant he felt, but through the promise and New Testament initiated by Christ alone, who extends the grace and mercy of his death and resurrection in this meal— a truly moving experience of true fellowship with Christ and his body, the church, an experience that moves us from death to life.

25

The Only Absolute

Ralph stared at me with his one good eye—his other having succumbed to the melanoma that was slowly eating away at his body. Between us in the sunroom of his house was a TV table with bread and wine from my communion "kit." We began this Lord's Supper liturgy (his last) with the confession and forgiveness—what the Reformers loved to call the sacrament of absolution. We recited: "We confess that we are in bondage to sin and cannot free ourselves." Then I looked at him from less than four feet away and announced, "God our heavenly Father has had mercy upon us and has given his only Son to die for us, and for his sake forgives us all our sin. As a called and ordained minister of the church of Christ and by his authority, I announced to you the entire forgiveness of all your sins, in the name of the Father, and of the Son and of the Holy Spirit. Amen." Except that Ralph didn't say "Amen." Instead he looked at me, his face etched with astonishment: "That's really something, Pastor." Yes, it is—not just for Ralph, but for everyone who avails themselves of the absolution in public or in private.

CA XXV argues its case for changing the way people use private confession on two fronts. First and foremost, this rite offers comfort to the conscience under attack from sin, death, and the devil. Second, by not requiring the scrupulous enumeration of all sins, it rescues the sacrament from a pernicious legalism in which precisely those who need forgiveness the most (terrified consciences) find their way blocked by feelings of inadequacy vis-à-vis their work of confessing.

For the text of Article 25, see pp. 312–15.

Reflections

"Confession has not been abolished by the preachers on our side. For the custom has been retained among us of not administering the sacrament to those who have not previously been examined and absolved." Going to a modern Lutheran congregation today, one would hardly know that this is still true. Instead, many congregation members know nothing about private confession and assume instead that only Roman Catholics practice it. Moreover, with the exception of some congregations that require members to register ahead of time for Holy Communion, seldom if ever do congregations any longer require private conversations with the pastor before receiving the Supper. And yet, in many North American Lutheran congregations, public confession and absolution remain a central opening part of the liturgy. CA XXV labels a going to confession before the Lord's Supper a "custom," and it is true, as Luther admitted, that forgiveness of sins is also offered in the Lord's Supper (so that occasionally he would go to the Supper without prior confession). But why should we not avail ourselves of this remarkable, physical gift of forgiveness, as often as possible and in as many ways as possible?

"At the same time, the people are diligently instructed how comforting the word of absolution is and how highly and dearly absolution is to be esteemed. For it is not the voice or word of the person speaking it, but it is the Word of God, who forgives sin. For it is spoken in God's stead and by God's command." As Pastor Franklin Drews Fry once said (cf. chapter 11), "There is nothing absolute in life except the Absolution." This is the point of both private and public confession: to receive absolution. Here, as in the other sacraments, the one who speaks the absolution is transparent: it is *God's* Word, spoken in *God's* stead, by *God's* command. This is why pastors should think twice (or more times) before jettisoning the standard absolution for something they imagine is more up-to-date. "As a called and ordained servant of Christ and by his authority, I announce to you the entire forgiveness of all your sins." To this, pastors might want to add from time to time: "If it were up to me, given how you treated me at the last congregational meeting, I wouldn't forgive a single one of you. But this didn't grow in my garden, so only 'by Christ's authority' do I do it." The true irony, however, comes from the fact that many churches boasting of prophecies and special revelations from God have no clue about the one thing that God really wants to say, namely, "Son, your sins are forgiven" (Mark 2:5). So the true prophets in the church are neither those who boast special revelations nor those who are concerned for social justice—as important as those things may be—but precisely those who announce the most unbelievable news of all: "You are forgiven; you belong to Christ; your dead will rise again."

"Great diligence is used to teach about this command and power of the keys, and how comforting and necessary it is for terrified consciences. It is also taught how God requires us to believe this absolution as much as if it were God's voice resounding from heaven and that we should joyfully find comfort in the absolution, knowing that through such faith we obtain forgiveness of sin." Comfort for terrified consciences! Again and again the CA returns to the central experience of justification by faith (CA IV–V, XX): consolation for the disconsolate. Yet CA XXV will not rest with what some might imagine is a magical word smeared on the ears of those who confess, like some sort of fake salve peddled by the hawkers of patent medicine in the Old West. The "requirement" (if you want to call it that) is not works of contrition or satisfaction, as in the old practice of penance, but faith. The absolution is "God's voice sounding from heaven." It is a wonder that more people in Lutheran congregations don't faint or swoon when, in the service of public confession, the pastor announces the forgiveness of sin. Is it that we cannot quite believe that almighty God would speak such a remarkable word directly to us? Still, the two always go together: God's unconditional promise and faith that is both created by and receives that very promise.

"In former times, the preachers, while teaching much about confession—never mentioned a single word about these necessary matters but instead only tormented consciences with long enumerations of sins, with satisfactions, with indulgences, with pilgrimages, and the like." As with the other articles in this section, CA XXV also describes the bad practice that precipitated the Evangelicals' changes. Instead of comfort, the consciences only found torment: both in the requirement to confess *all* mortal sins and in the "satisfactions" of temporal punishment that the confessor then required of the penitent after declaring the absolution. The Latin text, echoing CA XX, goes so far as to accuse the late-medieval church of silence: "The people are also most diligently taught concerning faith in the word of absolution, about which there was a great silence before now." "Faith in . . . absolution!" Now there's a concept for you!

"Moreover, many of our opponents themselves confess that our side has written about and dealt with true Christian repentance more appropriately than had been done in a long time." It is not clear whom the drafters had in mind here. This argument, which Melanchthon made about other teachings of Luther as well,[1] effectively used the opposition's words as endorsing the Reformers' alteration of practice. In fact, the Lutherans maintained private and public confession and absolution almost without exception. Other groups, such as the Reformed and Anabaptists eliminated such rites as "papistical" and "non-biblical accretions." To be sure, the medieval church developed the sacrament of penance in ways that hardly had direct biblical precedent. But Lutherans have a completely different approach to the church's

---

1. See, for example, Ap XII.4 (BC, 188).

tradition. They are not biblicistic, nor do they insist that the church must be purified from "anti-Christian" practices. Their single criterion for judging *all* practices is to ask how a particular practice strengthens faith and comforts the believer. It is never enough to say, "The Bible says . . ." Nor does it ever suffice to claim to return to the Scripture and the primitive church's practice! Such a return to first-century practice is impossible and results in the worst possible kind of legalism, where the disconsolate are denied consolation in the name of biblical norms—real or imagined.

"Concerning confession, it is taught that no one should be compelled to enumerate sins in detail. For this is impossible, as the Ps [19:12] says: 'But who can detect their errors?' And Jer [17:9] says: 'The human heart is so devious that no one can understand it.'" This marked a substantial difference in practice between the late-medieval church and the Evangelicals. The directive to confess all sins was aimed at the devious Old Creature, who would just as soon not "'fess up" to its transgressions. But in the course of time it became a burden to sensitive consciences, who wracked their memories in an attempt to ferret out every last sin of thought, word, and deed. To combat this problem, called scrupulosity, medieval penitential manuals encouraged confessors to try several pastoral techniques designed to comfort such souls. We know that early in his time in the monastery, Luther's novice master, Johann Greffenstein, reminded him of the article in the Creed: "I believe . . . in the forgiveness of sins."[2] But in general, medieval confession of sin demanded confession of *all* known mortal sins, something that CA XXV asserts is impossible.

"Miserable human nature is so mired in sins that it cannot see or know them all. If we were absolved only from those sins that we can enumerate, we would be helped but little. That is why it is not necessary to compel people to enumerate sins in detail." After concentrating on the comfort of absolution (CA IV), the drafters move on to focus on the human condition itself (CA II). Thus, the impossibility is rooted so deeply in the sinner that nothing he or she does can possibly help to comprehend the depth of the problem. In addition, if forgiveness were only offered for those sins that we remember, the

---

2. This according to Philip Melanchthon's June 1546 account of Luther's life, published as the preface to the second volume of Luther's Latin works. See Franz Posset, *The Real Luther: A Friar at Erfurt & Wittenberg: Exploring Luther's Life with Melanchthon as Guide* (St. Louis: Concordia, 2011). Greffenstein and Johann von Staupitz also used other techniques. The widely circulated claim that Luther suffered from scruples is exaggerated and ignores the fact that in comments from the *Table Talk* Luther insists that von Staupitz's comments were not always helpful (LW 54:94–95 [no. 518]). To cite a different oral tradition, Stephen Ozment was said to have observed that the majority of sixteenth-century Christians were worried about whether they were sheep or goats (e.g., in a state of sin or grace; saved or damned; elect to heaven or condemned to hell); Luther worried whether God was carnivorous or herbivorous—something that has nothing to do with scruples.

underlying "root sin" (i.e., the inherited sinful nature often called original sin) goes unnoticed.[3] The curved-in-upon-itself nature of humanity (*incurvatus in se*) prevents us from seeing how deeply flawed we are—rather like the alcoholic convinced of still having the ability to stop drinking. In the end, enumeration of sins in confession works against the law by making us imagine we can rightly examine ourselves and against the gospel by limiting its effects to what we do in confession. The Latin version contrasts this enumeration to the comfort of the gospel when it states "consciences could never find peace, because many sins cannot be seen or remembered."

"This was also the view of the Fathers, as one finds it in dist. I of *Concerning Confession* where these words of Chrysostom are quoted: 'I do not say that you should offer yourself up in public, or accuse yourself, or plead guilty before another person. Instead obey the prophet who says, "Reveal your way to the Lord" [Ps 37:5; Vulgate]. Therefore confess to the Lord God, the true judge, in your prayer. Do not speak your sin with the tongue, but in your conscience.' Here one can clearly see that Chrysostom does not force anyone to enumerate sins in detail. The marginal note in the *Decretum, Concerning Confession*, dist. 5 also teaches that confession is not commanded in Scripture but was instituted by the church."** The articles defending changes in practice among the Evangelicals take great pains to include not only biblical authorities for support but also the Fathers and, especially in CA XXV, canon law itself. The drafters have done their homework and know how to use the complex web of citations and cases in canon law to their advantage.

"Nevertheless, the preachers on our side diligently teach that confession is to be retained because of absolution (which is confession's principal and foremost part) for the comfort of terrified consciences and because of other reasons." Not only the Reformers but already Thomas Aquinas could call this the sacrament of absolution.[4] As a conclusion, the drafters circle back to their first and most important point: The absolution provides comfort. As explained above, this also explains why Evangelicals could retain something that has only indirect authorization in Scripture. The ambiguous phrase in the German, "and because of other reasons" is more clearly explicated in the Latin version, where we read: "Nevertheless, confession is retained among us both because of the great benefit of absolution and because of other advantages for consciences." This is still such a surprising way to do theology: focusing not just on what a topic is or where it is authorized but rather on its effect.

---

3. This same argument appears in the Formula of Concord, where the Epitome II.9 (BC 489) reads: "The damage [caused by sin] is so indescribable that it cannot be recognized by our own reason but only from God's Word. The damage is such that only God alone can separate human nature and the corruption of this nature from each other."

4. Thomas Aquinas, *Summa Theologica* III, q. lxxxiv, a. 3, ad 5.

No wonder that in 1531, when Luther added a section on Confession to his Small Catechism, he included these instructions: "A confessor, by using additional passages of Scripture, will in fact be able to comfort and encourage to faith those whose consciences are heavily burdened or who are distressed and under attack."[5] The very practice that so vexed Luther in the monastery had become a chief means of battling distress and attack (*Anfechtung*).

We Teach and Confess

She confessed some awful things that she had done—bad enough that the courts had taken away her children from her. But, as we sat in her living room, she told her sad story with a dry eye, almost as if she were talking about someone else. What was a young pastor to say when her terrible litany came to an end? "You know, Mary, God forgives you all your sin." Then, upon hearing God's judgment in the matter, she burst into tears. And *that* is why the absolution is the only absolute thing in a Christian's life. It alone is comfort for the lost and terrified conscience—enough to make us burst into tears or shouts of Alleluia.

---

5. SC, Confession, 29 (BC, 362).

26

APPLYING JUSTIFICATION BY FAITH TO DAILY LIFE

"What about your Lenten discipline?" a new member inquired. As a young pastor, I was somewhat surprised, although I certainly understood why a former Roman Catholic might ask that question. Later, as a professor, I ran into students and pastors who seemed to think that making sure they and their congregations "gave something up for Lent," was central to Lutheran identity. To the new member, I answered by referring to Christian freedom. "You don't have to give up anything, but if you wish to and feel more at peace doing so, then please do." To future leaders of the church, however, I tended to begin by describing the behavior of my sister and me growing up: we always gave up eating whale meat.

"What Am I required to do?" That cry bedevils all manner of religion in our day and age, especially people looking for a "special" or "better" or "more authentic" way to live the Christian life. Add to this the adage, "He or she is a creature of habits"—except that the true bugbear of human existence is not so much "habits" as "rules and regulations." Many religions have such rules, especially dietary restrictions, designed at least originally to demarcate their group from others, to appease the divine, or to impose discipline on wayward souls. Somehow in the course of time the rules become ends in themselves, and what we eat or drink, what we wear, or whether we marry become the distinguishing marks of a religion. In that regard, Christianity often plays the "odd man out," given that Jesus broke the Sabbath (one of the Ten Commandments), his disciples picked grain on the Sabbath, and Paul struggled with those who insisted upon circumcision or the avoidance of foods sacrificed to idols (in an attempt to keep the First Commandment). Of course, growing up in a conservative Lutheran environment, the forbidden fruits were drinking, card playing, and dancing—but the results were the same: worried consciences who had to lie to themselves and others about their standing before God.

This article, while ostensibly about food regulations, expands quickly to include all kinds of human regulating of religious life. But, in their defense, the drafters immediately gravitate to the very center of the CA in a stunning example of how to apply justification "by grace, through faith on account of Christ" to daily life. In that connection, this article may be one of the most helpful of all for shaping Christian life in the present. Once again, we learn that the Christian life is daily life (cf. CA XVI and XX) and that all attempts to confuse faith in Christ with external works and disciplines have no place in the believer's life. The *Confutation* answers this radical appeal to Christianity's roots with a rather weak argument, namely, from Romans 13 and the requirement to obey ecclesiastical authorities, especially bishops, in order to coerce the flesh. Furthermore, the *Confutation* distinguishes universal rites, which must be obeyed, from "provincial" ones. In no sense, however, do they address the Evangelicals' underlying challenge. Here, more than in any other article, do we discover just how far apart the theological presuppositions of the two groups actually were and how easy it is to replace God's grace with a mess of legalistic pottage.

For the text of Article 26, see pp. 314–21.

Reflections

Latin: **"It has been a general conviction, not only of the people but also of those who teach in the churches, that distinction of foods and similar human traditions are useful works for meriting grace and making satisfaction for sins. That the world thought so is evident from the fact that daily new ceremonies, new ordinances, new holy days, and new fasts were instituted and that the teachers in places of worship exacted these works as necessary worship for meriting grace and viciously terrified consciences if people omitted any of them. Much misfortune has ensued in the church from this conviction concerning traditions."** The opening paragraph, especially in the Latin, outlines precisely how the CA will argue its case. The problem is not regulations in and of themselves but the way in which regulations get mixed into one's relation to God, with the resulting "viciously terrified consciences." During the Reformation, this confusion arose from the demand in penance to make satisfaction for the temporal punishment for sin—part of the original complaint in the *95 Theses* (cf. CA XII). This insistence against smuggling works into our relation to God once again demonstrates that theology can *never* simply be about providing "right answers" to doctrinal or practical questions. Instead, church leaders must *always* measure those answers by the effect on the weak. Making a practice "necessary for salvation" simply results in all manner of mischief in the Christian church. Of course, today Christians impose rules without referring to "salvation" directly, and yet by implication this is still the case. As soon as one set of practices is labeled "better" than others, the devil is on the loose and terror reigns supreme.

Latin: "**In the first place, it has obscured the teaching concerning grace and the righteousness of faith, which is the chief part of the gospel and which ought to be present and prominent in the church so that the merit of Christ is well known and that faith, which believes in the forgiveness of sins on account of Christ, may be exalted far above works and other acts of worship. That is why Paul puts the greatest weight on this article and removes the law and human traditions to show that Christian righteousness is something other than works of this kind. Christian righteousness is faith that believes we are received into grace on account of Christ. This teaching of Paul has been almost completely smothered by traditions, which have given rise to the opinion that grace and righteousness are supposed to be merited through distinctions of food and similar acts of worship. No mention of faith was made in the practice of repentance; only these works of satisfaction were proposed. The whole of repentance was thought to consist of them.**" CA XXVI gives three separate arguments for why Evangelical churches no longer enforce such regulations. The first and most important arise from our relation to God—based upon Christ's work, not ours. The language is right out of CA IV: Christ, grace, and faith all come together to provide a completely different approach to God. Here again, as in CA III and IV, the invocation of Christ's "satisfaction" for sin is not proof of some sort of theory of the atonement but rather a way to eliminate all human satisfaction. Everything depends upon grace and mercy in Christ and, thus, upon faith (alone!). The drafters call especially upon Paul at this point and thereby dismiss any and all theories about Paul (old or new) that imagine he was only interested in removing a few "human traditions" from Christian practice. Were it only a matter of such practices, then truly an "introspective consciousness" might be to blame, but in fact Paul is out to eliminate *all* law from our relation to God: "Christian righteousness is faith that believes we are received into grace on account of Christ." Can anything be clearer than that? All works, no matter how moral, and all practices, no matter how upright, are now excluded.

Here a slight correction of the Latin is in order, so that it should read: "No mention of faith was made in the practice of *Penance*; only these works of satisfaction were proposed. The whole of *[the Sacrament of] Penance* was thought to consist of them." This again demonstrates that the original struggle over indulgences and penance continued to play a role in how the Evangelicals constructed their arguments.

German: "In the second place, such traditions have also obscured God's commands. For these traditions are placed far above God's commands. This alone was considered the Christian life: whoever observed festivals this way, prayed in this way, fasted in this way, and was dressed in this way was said to live a spiritual, Christian life. On the other hand, other necessary good works were considered secular, unspiritual ways of life: that each person is obliged to act according to his or her calling—for example, that the father of a family works to support his wife and children and raises them in the fear of God; that the mother of a family bears children and looks after them; that a prince or rulers govern a country, etc. Such works, commanded by God, had to be a "secular and imperfect" way of life, while the traditions had to have impressive names, so that only they were called "holy and perfect" works. That is why there was no end or limit in the making of such traditions." The second argument contrasts God's law to human regulations. This insistence on special clothes, food, and worship practices continues with various religious groups today. Some insist on *not* praying the Lord's Prayer; others insist on speaking in tongues (or *not* speaking in tongues); still others claim that only their way of baptizing is Christian. But the list goes on and on! Here, however, CA XXVI is not contrasting human laws to the Ten Commandments so much as to the daily life of the vast majority of Christians (then and now). By radically eliminating a "special Christian life" or a "Christian morality," based upon some separate set of biblical regulations, the CA introduces a completely different way to view the Christian life. The myth (still popular today) of separating "carnal Christians" from "true believers" simply wrenches people away from life in this world and attempts to create another, "better," "holier" set of people. For CA XXVI, of course, this anticipates the arguments against the monastic claims to perfection in the next article. In this context, however, it reflects just how much of Christian life in the late Middle Ages derived from monasticism and its practices: clerical celibacy; praying the hours; self-denial to the harm of one's family. The same quest for spiritual perfection continues to plague Christians of all stripes today.

Latin: "In the third place, traditions brought great dangers to consciences because it was impossible to keep them all, and yet people judged these observances to be necessary acts of worship. Gerson writes that many fell into despair, and some even took their own lives because they felt that they could not keep the traditions. Meanwhile, they never heard the consolation that comes from the righteousness of faith and from grace. We see that the summists and theologians collected the traditions, looking for a fair and gentle solution for consciences. They did not altogether succeed;

instead, in the process they entangled consciences even more. Schools and sermons were so busy gathering traditions that they had no time even to mention Scripture or to look for more useful teachings concerning faith, the cross, hope, the dignity of civil affairs, and the consolation of consciences in adverse temptations. Hence Gerson and certain other theologians bitterly complained that they were so bogged down by these quarrels over traditions that they could not turn their attention to a better kind of teaching. Augustine also forbids burdening consciences with such observances and prudently reminds Januarius that these things must be observed as an indifferent matter; that is what he said." The third argument turns to the Christian's experience and the problem of the terrified conscience. It is easy to imagine that such consciences do not exist today in a world where, presumably, "anything goes," but in fact people still struggle with doing the right thing and pleasing some divine or human parent. More to the point: endangering consciences is precisely what much of what passes as Christianity is still doing to people. The CA points to a different approach to consciences altogether: Christianity is not about rules and regulations; it is about forgiveness, resurrection, and the defeat of evil. That is, it is all about Christ crucified and risen.

As in the other articles of this section (CA XXII–XXVIII), the CA wants to show that it is not saying anything new. So it appeals first to Jean Gerson, a Parisian scholastic theologian who showed remarkable sensitivity toward pastoral matters. Then it makes general comments about "summists," scholastically trained theologians who commented on church laws and wrote instruction manuals for priests to use in the confessional. It begins with praise for their efforts to relieve consciences, but then points out that they misdiagnosed the problem. The solution was not simply finding "kinder, gentler" rules but eliminating any notion that rule keeping determines one's relation to God. Moreover, the search for nice rules simply distracts people from what really matters, namely, the central message of Scripture itself and its application to the Christian. The Latin version here gives a lengthier list than the German, one that corresponds to Philip Melanchthon's own lists of topics in his basic theological textbook, the *Loci communes*: "faith, cross, hope, dignity of civil affairs." This is where Christians actually live and work: in this world (cf. CA XVI). The goal of preaching and teaching is not to remove people from their daily lives or protect them from it, but to equip them in those very walks of life with faith, cross, and hope: faith in trusting God for mercy; cross in seeing through the sufferings of this "valley of tears" to the Savior; hope in God's promise of a new world in which sin, death, and evil will be vanquished for good. Gerson's criticism of teaching in his day could easily apply to today, when remarkably bright, talented teachers and preachers become so wrapped up in academic squabbles that the gospel and its effect on believers lose their voice. Augustine's admonition abides: do not confuse undifferentiated matters [*adiaphora*], which are neither right nor wrong, with the comfort of the gospel.

Latin: "**Our people, therefore, must not be viewed as having taken up this cause by chance or because they hate bishops, as some wrongly suspect. There was great need to warn the churches of those errors that had grown out of a misunderstanding of traditions. For the gospel compels us to insist in the church on the teaching concerning grace and the righteousness of faith, which can never be understood if human beings think that they merit grace by observances of their own choice. So they teach that we cannot merit grace or make satisfaction for sins through the observance of human traditions. Hence observances of this kind are not to be thought of as necessary acts of worship.**" The appeal to Augustine in the previous paragraph in the Latin actually poses a dilemma for the drafters of the CA. If these practices are *adiaphora*, then why not simply follow them? Moreover, given Romans 13 and its command to obey authorities, there is a divine command behind such obedience. It is necessary for the CA to set aside the charge that the Evangelicals were simply bishop haters who stumbled on this matter by chance. Of course, in Zurich under Ulrich Zwingli's direction the rejection of bishops was far more central to that reform, one that did not see these regulations as undifferentiated matters, neither right nor wrong, but rather rejected such practices as anti-biblical. Wittenberg's theologians and their allies argued very differently. It was not that the church could not keep certain traditions—a church without traditions is impossible—but rather that such traditions as the medieval church preserved had become misunderstood. The issue always returns to CA IV–VI (XX) and justification by grace through faith on account of Christ. "The gospel compels us to insist in the church on the teaching concerning grace and the righteousness of faith, which can never be understood if human beings think that they merit grace by observances of their own choice." It is not keeping certain traditions that is the problem but imagining that such things earn something from God. The CA witnesses to a gospel centered in God's unconditional promise of mercy in Christ. Here there can be no reciprocity, no quid pro quo, no earning anything before God. Instead, the Christian life rests upon faith *alone* in God's grace *alone* through Christ *alone*. Nothing else in the Christian life can claim any such necessity.

Latin: "**They add testimonies from Scripture. In Matt 15 [:1–20] Christ defends the apostles for not observing a customary tradition, despite the fact that it was considered a neutral matter and to have a connection with the purifications of the law. However, he says [Matt 15:9]: 'In vain do they worship me' with human precepts. So he does not require a useless act of worship. Shortly thereafter he says [Matt 15:11]: 'It is not what goes into the mouth that defiles a person.' Again, Rom 14 [:17]: 'For the kingdom of God** is not food and drink.' Col 2 [:16]: 'Therefore do not let anyone condemn you in matters of food and drink or of observing festivals . . . or sabbaths.' *Again [Col 2:20–21]: 'If with Christ you died to the elemental spirits of the universe, why do you live as if you still belonged to the world? Why do you submit to regulations, "Do not handle, Do not taste, Do not touch"?'* Peter says in Acts 15 [:10–11]: 'Now therefore why are you putting God to the test by placing on the neck of the disciples a yoke that neither our ancestors nor we have been able to bear? On the contrary, we believe that we will be saved through the grace of the Lord Jesus, just as they will.' Here Peter prohibits the burdening of consciences with additional rites, whether of Moses or others. And 1 Tim 4 [:1–3] calls the prohibition of food teachings of demons because it conflicts with the gospel to institute or perform such works for the purpose of meriting grace through them or to think that Christian righteousness might not be able to exist without such acts of worship." CA XXVI is one of the articles that evinces a far higher rhetorical structure than most of the others. It begins with a statement of the problem of bad preaching regarding traditions, followed by three separate facets of the problem (God's promise, law, conscience). Then, it summarizes the Evangelical teaching over against this bad instruction. What follows now is the *confirmatio* [proof] of this teaching, using a raft of biblical passages—the most found in any article. The stakes are high, of course. Not following the required fasts and other traditions was not simply a quaint church rule, it was the law of the land. If the Evangelicals' opponents could demonstrate such blatant disrespect for ecclesiastical and imperial law, they could prove the Evangelicals were simply outlaws, who deserved punishment "by fire and sword."

The CA's response comes right out of Philip Melanchthon's theological playbook. In calling his theological masterwork the *Loci communes* [commonplaces], he was employing a strategy of reading Scripture that grouped together various texts under their proper category or commonplace. Jesus, Paul, and Peter all condemn confusing human traditions with God's mercy. These proofs were so important that for the CA's *editio princeps* Melanchthon even adds another section of Colossians 2 [here in italics], in line with his commentaries on Colossians from 1527 and 1528.[1] By citing these texts, all of which concern dietary rules, the CA places the harshest criticism of its opponents on the lips of the church's highest authority, Paul, especially in 1 Timothy 4:1–3, where he calls it demonic. Given what modern scholars say about the origin of these various biblical sources, one can marvel at the fact

---

1. See Timothy J. Wengert, *Law and Gospel: Philip Melanchthon's Debate with John Agricola of Eisleben over "Poenitentia"* (Grand Rapids: Baker, 1997), and Timothy J. Wengert, *Human Freedom, Christian Righteousness: Philip Melanchthon's Exegetical Dispute with Erasmus of Rotterdam* (New York: Oxford University Press, 1998).

that Christians throughout the first century of the church's existence worried about confusing regulations with God's mercy.

Latin: "Here our adversaries charge that our people, like Jovinian, prohibit discipline and the mortification of the flesh. But something quite different may be detected in the writings of our people. For concerning the cross they have always taught that Christians should endure afflictions. To be disciplined by various afflictions and crucified with Christ is a true and serious, not a simulated, mortification." Continuing to follow standard rhetorical form, CA XXVI then inserts an *confutatio*, that is, a reply anticipating specific charges of the opponents. The mention of Jovinian is scarcely random. Indeed, Martin Luther's opponents had early suspected that his appeal to freedom and salvation for all outside the works of the law mirrored Jovinian, a fourth-century monk who attacked celibacy and the ascetic life. He was condemned by Pope Siricius in 390 and 391, by Ambrose, and by Jerome, whose lengthy tract, *Adversus Iovinianum* [against Jovinian], proposed a strict reading of 1 Corinthians 7 and derived much of its argument from pagan literature critical of women.[2] This tract was so important to Luther that he produced his own separate commentary on 1 Corinthians 7, attacking Jerome's interpretation throughout.[3] In rejecting the charge that the Evangelicals were Jovinians, CA XXVI reframes the original charges, so that the issue here is no longer celibacy but rather any discipline of the flesh. The point is that such discipline is always law, that is, always aimed at restraining and putting to death the Old Creature. Without saying so, it implies that no one dare confuse this discipline and cross with the gospel. Thus, both Jovinian and the CA's critics receive criticism here: Jovinian for wanting to eliminate all discipline of the flesh; the critics for confusing such human, external discipline with the gospel and salvation.

But is the Christian life really all about the cross? Inhabitants in today's prosperous societies and their prosperity gospel gurus eagerly ignore and blithely misconstrue this statement. To use Luther's categories from the 1518 *Heidelberg Disputation*, the alternative to the cross is always a theology of glory. Either one falls off on the side of Jovinian and proclaims a "gospel" that avoids all suffering and insists that "true" believers will always receive material and physical blessings from God. (To which Jesus would say, "They have their reward.") Or one insists on a glory in human works of self(ish) denial, where we get to choose our discipline and "cross" (the more balsa wood the better). To this the CA says no! Crosses are not self-chosen ("simulated") nor can they be avoided (a la Jovinian). Instead they are laid upon us because of

---

2. See Angelo di Berardino, ed., *Patrology*, vol. 4: *The Golden Age of Latin Patristic Literature from the Council of Nicea to the Council of Chalcedon*, trans. Placid Solari (Westminster, MD: Christian Classics, 1986), 239.
3. LW 28:1–56.

the weakness of our very humanity. All believers and only believers suffer attacks on their faith, that is, on God's promise of help. In fact, avoiding the crosses, suffering, and attacks in this life is as impossible as avoiding sin or death. No wonder that the final three petitions of the Lord's prayer force us daily to beg for forgiveness, rescue from trials, and deliverance from death and evil.[4]

Latin: "In addition, they teach that all Christians should so train and restrain themselves with bodily discipline, or bodily exercises and labors, that neither overexertion nor idleness may lure them to sin. But they do not teach that we merit forgiveness of sins or make satisfaction for them through such exercises. Such bodily discipline should always be encouraged, not only on a few prescribed days. As Christ commands [Luke 21:34]: 'Be on guard so that your hearts are not weighed down with dissipation.' Again [Mark 9:29]: 'This kind [of demon] can come out only through prayer and fasting.' And Paul says: 'I punish my body and enslave it.' Here he clearly shows that he punished his body not to merit forgiveness of sins through such discipline but to keep the body under control and fit for spiritual things and to carry out his responsibilities according to his calling. Therefore, fasting itself is not condemned, but traditions that prescribe, with peril to conscience, certain days and foods, as if works of this kind were necessary acts of worship." The CA tries hard to limit the debate to one question: the necessity of such discipline. *That* Christians practice discipline to restrain their worst urges is true, but as a kind of via media, so that neither laxity nor overzealousness destroys the body. Still, justification by faith alone looms large, and the drafters can hardly write a sentence about the goodness of discipline without insisting that it does not earn anything with God. It is "peril to conscience" not allergy to discipline that shapes the Evangelicals' teaching on this matter.

Latin: "Nevertheless, many traditions are kept among us, such as the order of readings in the mass, holy days, etc., which are conducive to maintaining good order in the church. But at the same time, people are warned that such acts of worship do not justify before God and that no punishable sin is committed if they are omitted without offense. Such freedom in human rites was not unknown to the Fathers. For in the East Easter was kept at a different time than in Rome, and when the Romans accused the East of schism because of this difference, they were admonished by others that such customs need not be alike everywhere. Irenaeus says: 'Disagreement about fasting does not dissolve the unity in faith,' and Pope Gregory indicates (dist. 12) that such diversity does not damage the unity of the church. In the *Tripartite History*, Book IX, many examples of dissimilar

---

4. See SC, "Lord's Prayer," par. 15–20 (BC, 358).

rites are collected, and this statement is made: 'It was not the intention of the apostles to make decrees about festivals but to preach good conduct among people and godliness.'" Here the drafters introduce another aspect of Evangelical theology: the distinction between the law in the church (understood as maintaining order) and gospel. For the sake of good order (cf. CA XV, XVI, and XXVIII), Christians have always had rules—otherwise, how would one know when to come to worship, what hymn or song to sing, what text of Scripture to read? And these rules will always mean that other behavior is excluded. If a congregation worships at 10 am or reads three lessons or sings five hymns, it is not worshiping at 8 am, reading only one lesson or singing no hymns. Leaders can then decide, in their situation, what rule best serves the good order of that place and enhances the proclamation of the gospel and the unity of Christians in every place. But, like a broken record, the CA reminds the readers that differences in such matters are not church dividing and must not be linked to salvation.

Saving the best for last in confirming their position, the drafters introduce patristic evidence. The fight over Easter is particularly poignant, since it represents an example where other churches upbraided the Church of Rome—which is just what the drafters of the CA want the emperor to imagine in this case. The citation of Irenaeus will take on new meaning fifty years later, when Lutherans use the same citation in the Formula of Concord in an effort to solve their internal disputes over *adiaphora*.[5] The reference to Pope Gregory is to the *Decretals*, a collection of canon law ascribed to Pope Gregory IX. Finally, the German summarizes the precise quote in the popular *Tripartite History* of the church: "It was not the intention of the apostles to institute festivals but to teach faith and love." By referring to preferred preaching on faith and love the drafters are echoing the argument made in CA XX and throughout the CA.

We Teach and Confess

Why this addiction to having the right rules and assuming that by following them the doer will earn something religiously significant? It goes back to the snake's temptation in the garden: "You will be like gods, deciding what's right and what's wrong." As soon as people "get religion," they start imposing their rules on others and promising enormous spiritual (and sometimes even physical) rewards. Even when people throw in the caveat ("Of course, you cannot earn salvation"), the activities become so central that they overwhelm trust in God's mercy, and justification by grace through faith on account of

5. See article ten of the Formula of Concord (BC, 515–16, 635–40), and Timothy J. Wengert, *A Formula for Parish Practice: Using the Formula of Concord in Congregations* (Minneapolis: Fortress Press, 2017), 165–79.

Christ becomes justification by working sincerely and hard. Moreover, as will also become clear in the next article, a person's calling in the world becomes undermined by a desperate search for religiosity.

Of course, any attempt to escape rules in the church altogether only leads to chaos and uncertainty. There is a place for helpful rules and good order in every Christian congregation. Otherwise no one would know when to show up, what parts of the Bible in which translation to read, and the like. The problem lies not in the regulations but in the kind of authority we ascribe to them. Church regulations serve the good order of our communities and thereby have no intrinsic religious value. For Lutherans, the measuring stick for everything in the church is only and always justification by grace alone without the works of the law. This serves the community of believers by strengthening faith in Christ's mercy—alone!

27

DAILY LIFE *IS* THE
CHRISTIAN LIFE, PART 2

W hatever the weaknesses in monasticism of the late Middle Ages, it was
still a thriving institution in Europe during the early sixteenth century.
Orders, notably the Franciscan and Augustinian friars, were in the process of
renewal in Spain and Germany. While some monasteries were undermanned,
others were attracting new adherents, as the case of Martin Luther, who
became an Augustinian friar in 1505, indicates. There were, of course, legends
criticizing "fat monks" for living off the largess of others and lustful ones for
acting out sexually, but there were also plenty of pious Christians whose decision to join the ranks of the *perfecti* by taking a vow of poverty, chastity, and
obedience was religiously motivated. For monks, nuns, and friars, entering a
monastery or friary put them in a special spiritual state of perfection—not
that they were morally perfect but rather that, because they were under a vow,
their good works achieved more merit before God and their sins were less
harmful. Thomas Aquinas had even equated the monastic vow with the grace
received in baptism, whereby all of the guilt and punishment of a person's
previous sins were removed.

Other criticisms of the monastic life came from the ranks of human-
ists, who rebuked monasticism and scholastic theologians (who were often
friars) for moral lapses and intellectual nitpicking—to say nothing of poor
Latin. But with Martin Luther and the Reformation, a completely new kind
of objection arose, based both upon the superiority and continued work of a
believer's baptismal vow and upon the distinction between law and gospel as
related to Christian freedom. In other words, the Reformers' main criticism

focused on the ways that monastic vows and practice undercut justification by grace through faith on account of Christ, made people rely on their own works for salvation, and undermined their true Christian callings in the world. These criticisms are reflected in the CA XXVII, which functions as another great example of how the drafters applied CA IV and CA XVI to the daily life of a Christian.

It might be easy to ignore this article, simply because nowadays Lutherans rarely encounter monks, nuns, or friars—despite the fact that such houses continued in many Lutheran areas during and after the Reformation, since the Reformers were bent on correcting abuses, not necessarily eliminating such a lifestyle. Despite being exempted from his vows in 1520, even Luther remained an Augustinian friar until 1524, three years *after* having published his attack on monastic vows—albeit living as "Daniel among the lions."[1] But sin is lurking today among well-intentioned folks who are still searching for a separate, Christian lifestyle superior to that of other, carnal people. They search for a "Christian ethic" apart from the mundane tasks of daily life and, in the process, stumble into spiritual pride while robbing others of the certainty that their daily life *is* their Christian life.

As we already noted in CA XVI, on the one hand many who are not clergy or "rostered leaders" think that the Christian life is only truly lived when one is spending all one's time inside a church building—as a kind of congregational monasticism. On the other, these same people may think that only those whose full-time calling is serving the church as a pastor, teacher, missionary, or other leader demonstrate the truly Christian life. But Lutherans, with their foolish notion that *daily* life is the Christian life, point to absolutely mundane, sixteenth-century things: fathers caring for their household (and not being "absentee"); mothers caring for their children (thus, not laboring under the "curse of Eve"); rulers, whose authority derives not from robber bands but from God's ordinance, governing well (as opposed to selfishly). These examples only scratch the surface. Nevertheless, they still lead some to imagine that Lutherans were preaching a kind of spiritual anarchy.[2] Lutherans are nothing if not secular and unspiritual in their approach to ethics. What foolish weakness!

For the text of Article 27, see pp. 320–31.

---

1. Heiko Oberman, "Martin Luther Contra Medieval Monasticism: A Friar in the Lion's Den," in *Ad fontes Lutheri: Toward the Recovery of the Real Luther: Essays in Honor of Kenneth Hagen's Sixty-Fifth Birthday*, ed. Timothy Maschke et al. (Milwaukee: Marquette University Press, 2001), 183–213.

2. See CA XX.1–2 (BC 52–53). For more on Luther's understanding of vocation, see Michael Bennethum, *Listen! God Is Calling!* (Minneapolis: Augsburg Fortress, 2003).

Reflections

In speaking of monastic vows, it is necessary, first of all, to consider how they were viewed earlier, what kind of life there was in the monasteries, and how much happened in them daily that was contrary not only to God's word but also to papal canons. For at the time of St. Augustine monastic vocations were voluntary. Later, when proper discipline and teaching became corrupted, monastic vows were contrived. With them, as in a prison of their own devising, people wanted to restore discipline. "A prison of their own devising," marks the CA's attempt to place monasticism of its day into its proper historical context. Everyone knew that monasticism had arisen in the ancient church, where Greek Christians like Anthony and later Basil of Caesarea and Latin Christians like Augustine and Benedict of Nursia had established solitary living in community focused on prayer and work as a Christian ideal. Here they put their finger on the central problem: monastic vows in the ancient church were voluntary; vows in sixteenth-century Europe were permanent—according to church law and secular law. To smuggle a nun out of her cloister (as did a herring salesman for Katharina von Bora [Luther's later wife] and others), was a capital crime—witness the execution of another such smuggler in ducal Saxony at the same time. But underneath this criticism lurks an important aspect of Christian life from the Lutherans' point of view: Christian freedom. Good works cannot be extorted from a person but arise, as a later Lutheran will put it, out of "a free and merry spirit."[3]

In addition to monastic vows many other things were introduced, and a great number of bonds and burdens were laid on many even before they had attained an appropriate age. Many persons also entered monastic life in ignorance. Although they were not too young, they nevertheless did not sufficiently estimate and understand their capabilities. All of those who were entangled and ensnared in this way were forced and compelled to remain in such bondage, in spite of the fact that even papal canons would have set many of them free. It was more difficult in nunneries than in monasteries, even though it would have been seemly to spare the women as the weaker gender. Such rigor and severity also displeased many devout people in former times. For they certainly noticed that both boys and girls had been stuck away in monasteries for the sake of keeping them alive. They certainly also noticed how badly this arrangement turned out and what offense and burdening of consciences it caused. Many people complained that the canons were not respected at all. In addition, monastic vows have such a reputation that even many monks with little understanding were clearly displeased. These criticisms did not arise in the Reformation but had been part of continuing complaints during the late Middle Ages. Young

---

3. Martin Treu, *Katharina von Bora* (Wittenberg: Drei Kastinien, 1995), 13–21.

people were left in the care of monasteries, often for financial reasons; others who may have voluntarily entered a monastery had no idea what they were getting into. "Entangled and ensnared," described a good number of those under vows, who had little recourse to leave—despite the fact that church law allowed for exceptions to monastic vows. Melanchthon adds that there should have been even more leniency shown to nuns, "as the weaker gender." This patriarchal approach, echoing biblical language (cf. 1 Pet 3:7), would, in the drafters' eyes, strengthen their overall argument. How could the straight jacket of perpetual vows not take into account those whom the society generally considered needing extra protection—the young, the ignorant, and women? The drafters always have the basic legal argument of these seven articles in the back of their minds. Thus, they not only list the moral complaints of their contemporaries but also appeal to church law ("the canons") itself. The Evangelical princes and cities have changed things in their territories to conform more closely to church law than their opponents. Of course, their opponents will reject this argument, but it is important to realize why such an appeal shows up in this article.[4]

It was pretended that monastic vows would be equal to baptism, and that through monastic life one could earn forgiveness of sin and justification before God. Indeed, they added that one earns through monastic life not only righteousness and innocence, but also that through it one keeps the commands and counsels written in the gospel. In this way monastic vows were praised more highly than baptism. It was also said that one could obtain more merit through the monastic life than through all other walks of life, which had been ordered by God, such as the office of pastor or preacher, the office of ruler, prince, lord, and the like. (These all serve in their vocations according to God's command, Word, and mandate without any contrived spiritual status.) None of these things can be denied, for one can find them in their own books. The confessors in Augsburg do not condemn the monastic life per se but insist instead that the original goals of the monastic life had been terribly distorted in the course of time. Here they list their theological complaints, all of which derive from justification by faith alone. People were being taught: monastic vows as equal to baptism; the earning of righteousness before God; the distinction between commands and counsels (and the monastic ability to fulfill both); the disparity between the monastic life and common "walks of life" (German: *Stände*) in this world; and the notion that one walk of life could be more spiritual than another. As we have already seen, earlier articles (especially CA VI, XVI, and XX) form the basis of these criticisms.

---

4. The final objection is somewhat obscure, although the Latin ("To make matters worse, vows had such a reputation that it clearly would have displeased the monks of former times, if they had been a little wiser") seems to indicate the general problem that the original intentions of monasticism's founders were contradicted by later practice.

When we encounter the courageous, committed Christians who now inhabit monastic and mendicant orders today (Roman Catholic or Protestant), we dare not condemn them out of hand using this article. We must first inquire after their motivations and whether their teachings still undermine the good news that we are saved by grace through faith on account of Christ alone. Take the notion of a vow representing a second baptism. In today's churches rarely would a Franciscan or Jesuit or Benedictine make such a claim. Yet there are many other Christian communities that undermine God's promise in holy baptism and claim a second "baptism in the Holy Spirit" and other later steps toward an "abundant" Christian life. This human hankering after a higher, more spiritual life truly undermines God's mercy in Christ. We seem incapable of believing that baptism and the promises it holds suffice as the basis of our relation to God. Surely we can improve on things by becoming more serious, more committed, more "spiritual."

Then there is the myth of commands and counsels. This division of God's commands for all people (as in the Decalogue) from Christ's counsels (especially poverty, chastity, and obedience) violates Scripture's purpose in two ways. On the one hand, it imagines that the commandments of God do not include Christ's statements (especially in the Sermon on the Mount) about judging others, seeking revenge, using money (Matt 5:21–48; 7:1–5), and the like, when in fact these statements serve simply to drive his hearers to the realization that they are outside of God's favor and need that very grace (alone) to live. That is, the notion of such "counsels" reduces the law's power. On the other hand, the idea that taking a vow grants believers the ability to fulfill both commands and counsels undermines the grace of God and, thus, the gospel's power. Again, today it is not so much Benedictines and others in Roman Catholic orders who make this false distinction but rather self-proclaimed "evangelical" Christians who distinguish "carnal" Christians from "spiritual" ones or who make a special set of (often nonbiblical) rules to differentiate truly committed Christians from the hoi polloi.

This leads to the most serious challenge of all: the undermining of daily life as true "walks of life" for Christians. Whether we invent a kind of "congregational monasticism" or insist that clerical "pros" make better Christians, the result remains the same: everyday life takes a backseat to spiritual "stars." Instead, the common pastor in his or her pulpit and the hearers, the government official fulfilling his or her office and the citizens, or even (cf. CA XVI) the father or mother, the head of a household or business, and the child or the employee serve in equally "spiritual" callings. This remarkable reordering of the Christian life goes back to Luther's criticisms of monasticism from 1521 (*The Judgment of Martin Luther on Monastic Vows*)[5] and even back to his

---

5. LW 44:243–400.

Address to Christian Nobility from the previous year.[6] In these works Luther insists that there are not two Christian "walks of life" (*Stände*) but only one Christian walk of life (*Stand*)—that of believer. Within this one arena there are many different callings: pastor and congregant; governing authority and the governed; parent and child; employer and employee. No Christian can invent higher, more spiritual callings from the God-given callings in household, workplace, society (government), and church. This radical heart of Lutheran ethics has still to penetrate Lutheran pulpits or classrooms—let alone Lutheran hearts. What a remarkable piece of good news: daily life *is* the Christian life!

Furthermore, whoever was so ensnared and ended up in the monastery learned little about Christ. At one time there were schools of Holy Scripture and other disciplines useful for the Christian church in the monasteries, so that pastors and bishops were taken from the monasteries. But now the picture is quite different. In former times, people adopted the monastic life in order to study Scripture. Now they pretend that the monastic life is of such a nature that through it a person may earn God's grace and righteousness before God—indeed that it is a state of perfection, far above all other walks of life instituted by God. All this is mentioned, without any disrespect intended, in order that everyone may better grasp and understand what and how our people teach and preach. One of the most famous complete manuscripts of the New Testament was found in the Greek monastery of Sinai in the nineteenth century. "*Sinaiticus*," as it was named, helped scholars to establish the correct text of the Greek New Testament, but it also points to one truth about these early monks. While the drafters of the CA do not mention all of the motivations for the formation of monasteries and friaries, clearly preserving and passing on the Christian message played a special role throughout the centuries and down to today. But monks also played other important roles in the early church's life. Situated in the wilderness, they (like Jesus during his forty days in the desert) lived in such wastelands not to escape daily life but to provide a first line of attack against the devil. Thus, they supported all those Christians in the Roman Empire's cities through their prayer and work. Contrast this symbiotic relationship with the situation in the late Middle Ages, where those under a vow were labeled "*perfecti*," people in a state of perfection—not that they were perfect but rather that they were on a special, fast track toward holiness and perfection. Their sins were not as harmful, and their good works (including the monastic life itself) were more meritorious than other walks of life.

---

6. TAL 1:421–24.

Despite the views of the Reformation typical in the nineteenth and twentieth centuries (namely, that democratic freedoms emerged from the Reformation), in no way should one draw a direct connection between Luther's teaching and our present democratic societies. In one way, however, Luther and these early Lutherans actually taught a far more radical form of equality than any democratic institution may boast of today. Equality in all walks of life completely undermines American worship of affluence, where "the rich get richer [and deserve it] and the poor get poorer." All such distinctions disappear when we stand before God wholly dependent upon God's mercy and not upon our works.

In the first place, it is taught among us concerning those who are inclined to marry, that all those who are not suited for celibacy have the power, authority, and right to marry. For vows cannot annul God's order and command. Now God's command reads (1 Cor 7 [:2]): "But because of cases of sexual immorality, each man should have his own wife and each woman her own husband." Not only God's command urges, compels, and insists upon this, but also God's creation and order direct all to the state of marriage who are not blessed with the gift of virginity by a special work of God, according to God's own word (Gen 2 [:18]): "It is not good that the man should be alone; I will make him a helper as his partner." After outlining their criticisms of the current state of monasticism, the drafters describe what the Evangelical territories have done to rectify the situation. This first point is aimed at church and imperial law that held it was illegal for a monk or nun to leave the monastery (and, hence, marry). Even myths that the anti-Christ would be born of the union of a monk and nun helped reinforce the danger of allowing those under a vow to break it. To support this argument, the CA does not restrict itself to worrying about sin and immorality (1 Cor 7) but also argues from creation itself. It takes a special gift of celibacy to overcome the laws of nature.

What objections can be raised against this? People may praise the vow and obligation as highly as they want, but they still cannot force the abrogation of God's command. The teachers say that vows made contrary to papal law are not even binding. How much less should they be binding or have legal standing when they are contrary to God's command! If there were no reasons for allowing the annulment of the binding vows, popes would also not have given dispensation and release from them. For no human being has the right to break an obligation derived from divine laws. That is why the popes were well aware that some balance should be used in regard to this obligation and have often given dispensation, as in the case of the king of Aragon and many others. If, then, dispensations were granted for the maintenance of temporal interests, how much more fairly should dispensations be granted for the sake of the souls' needs. The Reformers begin with

Scripture in order to overcome canon law's objections and then to use this very ecclesiastical law against itself. If vows that contradict a lesser code of law ("papal law") are invalid, then the greatest law of all ("God's command") cannot be contravened (even by canon law). But, of course, canon law itself contains exceptions to allow for annulment of binding vows.

While this argument may seem appropriate only to this particular case, it in fact contains within it a central premise of the Lutheran approach to ethical dilemmas. The German text refers to "some balance" (German: *relaxiren*) and the Latin to "treated with fairness" (Latin: *aequitas*). Both refer to the broader ethical category called in Greek *epieikeia* (reasonableness, equity, clemency). They used it so much that it actually found its way into theological German of the time. This speaks against the moralist's (or legalist's) way of proceeding ethically: define a moral norm and apply it strictly to all cases. On the contrary, *epieikeia* demands that the rule-enforcer show mercy, or clemency, and conform the law to the case rather than the other way around. The Reformers will use this not only for human laws but also for divine laws. Thus, for example, Luther knew that Jesus had not given the adulterous party in a marriage permission to remarry. But he thought that for the sake of such persons, who still had desires for companionship, they could flee to a distant country, where no one knew them, and get married there.[7] For another example, the person whose conscience did not allow them to receive the wine at communion (despite Jesus's clear command, "Drink of it all of you") was allowed communion in bread alone for at least ten years in Wittenberg, until it was clear that those who still resisted were more likely stubborn than conscience-bound.[8] To those who chant mindlessly, "The Bible says it, I believe it, that settles it," the Reformers would ask instead, "What is the effect of such rigidity upon the weak?" or, as they put it here, "the souls' needs"?

Next, why do our opponents insist so strongly that vows must be kept without first ascertaining whether a vow has integrity? For a vow should not be forced but voluntary in matters within human power. However, it is well known to what degree perpetual chastity lies within human power and ability. Moreover, there are few—men or women—who have taken monastic vows on their own, willingly and after due consideration. They were talked into taking monastic vows before they understood what was involved. At times, they were also forced and driven to do so. Accordingly, it is not right to argue so rashly and insistently about the obligation of vows, in view of the fact that everyone confesses it is against the nature and integrity of a vow to be taken by force, but rather it should be taken with good counsel and due consideration. Here the CA proposes a second argument for their

---

7. LW 45:32–33.
8. LW 40:288–93.

lifting the perpetuity of monastic vows. Vows, by their very nature, must be voluntary. Yet many had clearly entered monasteries or friaries not willingly but under one form of duress or another. Not only is it unclear whether someone can make such a lifelong vow, but it is also clear that many were talked into something they did not fully understand. Either way, the vow collapses of its own weight and loses legitimacy. These very technical, legal grounds—still very much in force today regarding contracts—show how open the Reformers were to using the law of nature and society to making their case regarding church practice.

Some canons and papal laws annul vows made under the age of fifteen years. For they take into consideration that before this age a person does not have sufficient understanding to decide how possibly to determine or arrange an entire life. Another canon concedes still more years to human frailty, for it forbids taking monastic vows before the eighteenth year. This provides an excuse and reason for a great many to leave the monasteries. For a majority entered the monastery in childhood before attaining such age. As with the first argument, here again the CA employs canon law against itself (or, rather, against its opponents). This line of argument is very important for the drafters, since it allowed them (and their rulers) to insist that, far from breaking church and imperial law, they were instead following in the spirit of existing law. While they may have exaggerated the effect of their arguments ("a great many" and "a majority"), still we must not forget that some of the early Reformers were friars (Martin Luther and Martin Bucer) and that many knew the problems of monks, nuns, and friars unable to leave their cloisters.

Finally, even if the breaking of monastic vows might be censured, it could not be concluded from this that the marriage of those who broke them should be dissolved. For St. Augustine, cited in "Marriage Matters" (q. 27, chap. 1), says that such a marriage should not be dissolved. Now St. Augustine certainly does not have a low reputation in the Christian church, even though some have subsequently differed from him. Now comes a third argument. One specific complaint had to do not simply with leaving the monasteries but with the subsequent marriage of such people (including, of course, Martin Luther and Katharina von Bora). Here the drafters, for the sake of argument, are willing to concede the main argument to their opponents. Even if monastic vows should not have been broken, this would not give the authorities grounds for breaking up marriages—something that had indeed occurred on occasion. The cleverness of this argument should not be overlooked. It is not simply that the drafters are relying upon Augustine, but rather upon Augustine as quoted in canon law itself! Here again, the authority (canon law) often used against the Reformers was being used to buttress their own arguments.

Although God's command concerning marriage frees and releases many from monastic vows, our people offer still more reasons why monastic vows are null and void. For all service of God instituted and chosen by human beings without God's command and authority to obtain righteousness and God's grace is contrary to God, the holy gospel, and God's decree, as Christ himself says (Matt 15 [:9]): "In vain do they worship me, teaching human precepts as doctrine." St. Paul also teaches everywhere that righteousness is not to be sought in our precepts and services of God contrived by human beings, but that righteousness and innocence before God come from faith and trust, when we believe that God receives us in grace for the sake of Christ, his only Son. At this point Melanchthon and his fellow drafters switch gears from legal arguments to the gospel itself. Here, finally, CA IV, XV, and XX take center stage, and we get a vivid demonstration of how these early Lutherans derive church life and theological judgment from justification "by grace through faith on account of Christ" or, as they put it here: "righteousness . . . before God . . . from faith and trust, when we believe that God receives us in grace for the sake of Christ, his only Son." The CA does not hereby eliminate human commands and precepts as important tools for maintaining order in church life but rather forbids all such matters from making any contribution to our relation to God. All human works are eliminated, and a Christian is thrust once again upon God's mercy alone.

Now it is quite evident the monks have taught and preached that their contrived spiritual status makes satisfaction for sin and obtains God's grace and righteousness. What is this but to diminish the glory and praise of the grace of Christ and to deny the righteousness of faith? It follows from this that the customary vows have been improper and false services of God. That is why they are also not binding. For a godless vow, made contrary to God's command, is null and void, just as the canons also teach that an oath should not bind a person to sin. If one reduces the Reformers' arguments to complaints about monasticism, then they have little importance today. But when one views their complaints as models for a far more pervasive human attitude, then suddenly the contrast between the CA's teaching and much that passes as Christianity today stands in sharp relief. The question to ask today is this: When has a "contrived spiritual status" that claims special privileges before God made inroads into our view of the Christian faith and life? How often do the boasts of Christian superheroes not deflect attention from Christ to themselves, thereby undermining faith, grace, and Christ? So much of what passes for Christianity today simply undermines God's command and replaces God's grace with human selfishness and sin.

St. Paul says in Gal 5 [:4]: "You who want to be justified by the law have cut yourselves off from Christ; you have fallen away from grace." Therefore, those who want to be justified by vows are also cut off from Christ and

fall away from the grace of God. For they rob Christ, who alone justifies, of his honor and give such honor to their vows and monastic life. In the early church, Jerome and Augustine disagreed about whether the reference to "law" in Paul meant simply ceremonial law (circumcision) or all law. In the sixteenth century, a similar debate arose between Erasmus on the one side and Luther and Melanchthon on the other. The notion has been revived (often with attacks on Luther) by those who claim to offer "new perspectives" on Paul. But even if Paul's letters may have been prompted by specific struggles over Jewish rites, his point was far broader, as this line from Galatians shows. At stake here is not a fight over ceremonies but a struggle against those whose teachings undermine Christ and grace. Puritanical moralists of Luther's day and ours are forever on the lookout for special, hyper-spiritual actions that pave our way to God's special blessings. At stake is not some esoteric "doctrine of justification" but Christ's honor and God's mercy. This is not about what laws matter in relation to God but that that relation is based upon no laws or works of ours but only upon God's unconditional love and favor.

No one can deny that the monks also taught and preached that they become righteous and earn forgiveness of sins through their vows and monastic life. In fact, they have contrived an even more useless and absurd claim, saying that they imparted their good works to others. Now if someone wanted to take all this to an extreme and bring accusation against them, how many items could be assembled that the monks themselves are now ashamed of and wish had never occurred! Besides all this, they persuaded the people that these humanly contrived spiritual orders were states of Christian perfection. Surely this means to praise works as the means of becoming righteous. Now it is no small offense in the Christian church to present to the people a service of God, which human beings have contrived without God's command, teaching that such service of God makes people innocent and righteous before God. For righteousness of faith, which ought to be emphasized most, is obscured when people are bedazzled with this strange angelic spirituality and false pretense of poverty, humility, and chastity. Of course for the Reformers, CA XXVII offers here a specific example of works righteousness run amok. While it knows that many good Christians were monks, nuns, and friars, it also knew how many (including some of the drafters) had had negative experiences of monasticism and the dangers it posed to the faith of simple Christians. This very way of life not only boasted of its works before God but also offered these works to others not under a vow, who by supporting these various foundations could participate in monastic blessings. How does this differ from those charlatans who offer prayer towels in the mail, or who make a great deal of the power of their personal prayers, or who claim a higher status before God and in the Christian community? People are easily fooled by promises of a higher, "angelic spirituality."[9] The very term *perfecti*, the perfect ones, with their chief vows of poverty, chastity, and obedience (here called humility) implied a kind of glory in human works—even if that were not its intent. But this bedazzling occurs on many levels today—even in as simple a way as when preachers boast of their own spiritual achievements from the pulpit, telling stories and narratives to impress the people with how God has used them and worked with them. Even St. Paul realizes the inherent evil in such self-congratulation and turns instead in 2 Corinthians to boast of his weaknesses!

In addition, the commands of God and proper, true service of God are obscured when people hear that only monks must be in the state of perfection. For Christian perfection is to fear God earnestly with the whole heart and yet also to have a sincere confidence, faith, and trust that we have a gracious, merciful God because of Christ; that we may and should pray for and request from God whatever we need and confidently expect help from him in all affliction, according to each person's vocation and walk of life; and that meanwhile we should diligently do external good works and attend to our calling. This is true perfection and true service of God—not being a mendicant or wearing a black or gray cowl, etc. However, the common people form many harmful opinions from false praise of the monastic life, such as when they hear the state of celibacy praised above all measure. For it follows that their consciences are troubled because they are married. Over against the claim that, in addition to being in either a state of sin or a state of grace, one by means of vows entered a state of perfection (not that the person was perfect but rather that their works and life were tending toward perfection), the CA defines perfection in a decidedly different way. Instead of insisting on the equivalent of "Nobody's perfect," the CA simply redefines perfection within the category of justification by faith alone. The individual aspects of this definition delineate an entirely different way of approaching the issue.[10]

The CA combines its commitment to law and gospel (cf. CA V and XII) with its understanding that the Christian is *simul iustus et peccator* (at the same time righteous and sinner). First, the Christian lives between complete fear of God and confidence/trust in God and God's grace. From this relationship, second, arise prayer and reliance on God's assistance in all affliction

9. For the use of this term in medieval spirituality, see Steven Chase, ed., *Angelic Spirituality: Medieval Perspectives on the Ways of Angels* (Mahwah, NJ: Paulist, 2003).

10. The full communion agreement between the United Methodists and the Evangelical Lutheran Church in America employed this same definition to overcome differences on the topic of perfection among Methodists and Lutherans. See *Confessing Our Faith Together: A Proposal for Full Communion between the Evangelical Lutheran Church in American and the United Methodist Church* (Chicago: Evangelical Lutheran Church in America, 2009), 7.

whatever one's station in life. Third, with one's relation to God completely dependent upon God's mercy in Christ, one goes to work for one's neighbor in all of one's callings from God. This "true service and perfection" contrast sharply to the monastic life with its habit and peculiar lifestyle—things that do not simply lead to spiritual pride but also undermine the common people's faith. Especially by concentrating on celibacy, monasticism inevitably questions the value of married life for Christians.

This marks the most important aspect of CA XXVII's argument for today: *not* that Evangelicals hated monks, nuns, and friars per se, but that any direct or indirect claim to a higher, more Christian way of life undercuts the faith of others. Thus, today, when some well-intentioned but misled folks ask a simple, baptized Christian whether he or she has been "born again" or "decided for Jesus" (already a misuse of John 3), it is not simply the particular claims of such "evangelists" for themselves that may deserve condemnation, but how such an approach to Christianity may undermine another person's trust in God's baptismal promises. Thus, for example, when the "Four Spiritual Laws" of "Campus Crusade for Christ," popular in the 1970s, labeled some Christians "spiritual" and others "carnal," it was falling into the same trap against which CA XXVII warns.

When the common people hear that only mendicants may be perfect, they cannot know that they may keep possessions and transact business without sin. When the people hear that it is only a "counsel" [of the gospel] not to take revenge, some will conclude that it is not sinful to take revenge outside their office. Still others think that revenge is not right for Christians at all, even on the part of political authority. Many examples are recorded of people leaving wife and child—even their civil office—and putting themselves into a monastery. This, they said, is fleeing from the world and seeking a life that is more pleasing to God than the other life. They were unable to realize that one should serve God by observing the commandments he has given and not through the commandments contrived by human beings. Now the life supported by God's command is certainly a good and perfect state, but the life not supported by God's command is a dangerous state. It has been necessary to keep people well informed about such matters. This appeal to the common folk, begun in the previous paragraph, continues here. Just as the monastic vow of chastity undermines those who are married, so the vow of poverty casts suspicion on those who handle money. Another complaint, clearly a *reductio ad absurdum*, has to do with the distinction, crucial for monastic spirituality, of commands and counsels. By making Christ's command not to take revenge a "counsel," one could (although no one ever did) imagine that those not under a vow could take revenge. Others (for example, certain strains of Anabaptism) went to the other extreme and imagined that the command not to seek revenge applied to every believer, thus making it impossible for governmental officials, whose office was to mete out justice in this world, ever to be Christians.

Underneath all of these matters lurked a far more vicious beast: human attempts to escape "this world" or "the flesh" for more spiritual ways of life, constructed by human beings. What invariably happens is that the human rules and regulations to build such utopian communities become ends in themselves—even to the point of obscuring God's commandments. In writing against monasticism, Luther especially contrasted rightful obedience to parents over against monastic insistence that their way of life lifted the burden of care for others outside the community.[11] God's law, summarized by St. Paul as, "Love your neighbor," gives any believer enough to do without ever having to run off on retreat or to a separate community or to a special status before God—all the worst kind of spiritual dangers.

In former times, Gerson also rebuked the errors of the monks about perfection. He showed that it was an innovation in his day to speak of monastic life as a state of perfection. There are so many ungodly notions and errors attached to monastic vows: that they justify and make righteous before God; that they must be Christian perfection; that through them a person may keep both the counsels of the gospel and the commandments; that they contain works of supererogation, beyond what is owed to God. Since, then, all of this is false, useless, and humanly contrived, monastic vows are null and void. Jean Gerson, an important medieval theologian from the University of Paris, provides a more recent "proof text" for the CA's strictures on the "state of perfection." With his words and a summary of the foregoing arguments, the drafters bring this article to a close with a bang: "Since, then, all of this is false, useless, and humanly contrived, monastic vows are null and void." Indeed, of all of the controversial articles in the CA, this contains one of the harshest conclusions, sure to arouse ire from the opponents.

We Teach and Confess

In 1529, in his Large Catechism, Martin Luther contrasted life in a German household (comprised of children, servants, and parents of the house) to what he viewed as the fabricated spirituality of the monastic life, which he himself had lived for nearly twenty years. By this time, the secret was out among these early Lutherans, who like Luther viewed daily life as the Christian life. Mundane tasks suddenly gained untold spiritual blessings, with a household maid joyfully dancing at the opportunity to make beds and thereby serve God and

---

11. See Luther's preface to his 1521 *Judgment of Martin Luther on Monastic Vows*, addressed to his own father. His point was not to reveal psychological problems in dealing with his father but rather to contrast monastic self-serving to love of neighbor (in this case, one's parents). See LW 48:329–36.

neighbor. The fourth commandment, "Honor your father and your mother," had been transformed from a burden and curse of those not able to live a monk's austere life into the highest blessing. Even so, Luther carefully distinguished between daily life that served others and faith that makes a person holy before God. Thus, here, too, faith and works are carefully differentiated to prevent the very distortion that so worried the drafters of the CA.

> What a child owes to father and mother, all members of the household owe them as well. Therefore menservants and maidservants should take care not just to obey their masters and mistresses, but also to honor them as their own fathers and mothers and to do everything that they know is expected of them, not reluctantly, because they are compelled to do so, but gladly and cheerfully. They should do it for the reason mentioned above, that it is God's commandment and is more pleasing to him than all other works. They should even be willing to pay for the privilege of serving and be glad to acquire masters and mistresses in order to have such joyful consciences and know how to do truly golden works. In the past these works were neglected and despised; therefore everyone ran in the devil's name into monasteries, on pilgrimages, and after indulgences, to their own harm and with a bad conscience.
>
> If this could be impressed on the poor people, a servant girl would dance for joy and praise and thank God; and with her careful work, for which she receives sustenance and wages, she would obtain a treasure such as those who are regarded as the greatest saints do not have. Is it not a tremendous honor to know this and to say, "If you do your daily household chores, that is better than the holiness and austere life of all the monks"? Moreover, you have the promise that whatever you do will prosper and fare well. How could you be more blessed or lead a holier life, as far as works are concerned? In God's sight it is actually faith that makes a person holy; it alone serves God, while our works serve people. Here you have every blessing, protection, and shelter under the Lord, and, what is more, a joyful conscience and a gracious God who will reward you a hundredfold.[12]

---

12. LC, "Ten Commandments," 143–46 (BC, 406–7).

28

WHY LUTHERANS LOVE(D) BISHOPS

The word *oversight* in English is an altogether strange word in that it has two different, almost opposite meanings. When we say, "That was an oversight on my part," we mean that we failed to see something we should have seen. But when we point to someone and state, "She has oversight for this project," we mean that this person is looking out for everything regarding a particular task. Already in the ancient Greek world, oversight (always understood in the second way) was expressed as *epi–skopé*: *epi* meaning "over" or "upon" and *skopé* meaning view or sight as in other Greek loan words like microscope and telescope. First-century Christians, beginning with St. Paul, used the related word, *episkopos* to designate those with oversight in the early churches (see Phil 1:1). Even though the Latin equivalent should have been *supervisor*, it appears that this word was not used until the Middle Ages and that, instead, the equivalent (at least according to Augustine, preaching on the Psalms to his congregation in Hippo) was *superintendens*. But Latin Christians did not translate the Greek but simply transliterated it, so that in their writings and in their translation of Paul's epistles they simply used the (Greek) word: *episcopos*, from which we derive words like "episcopal" or "episcopacy."

But Germanic, Scandinavian, and Anglo-Saxon Christians also borrowed the word as a designation for their church leaders, except that in the process they dropped that initial vowel along with the Greek ending (os) and heard a "sh" sound for the "sk." As a result, the term *bishop* lost all semblance of connection to either Latin or Greek, and the original meaning of the term was lost. (The same is true for the Greek term for elder, *presbyteros*, which by a similar process became the word *priest*.)

Besides the linguistic problems, in the medieval church (especially in the West) bishops also underwent a social and political transformation. In the Roman Empire, bishops in every major city or town oversaw the activities of Christians in their area (later designating their regions with the imperial word for a governor's territory, diocese). Thus, when the bishops living within a day's journey of Carthage assembled for a synod, over three hundred showed up! These small episcopal sees may still be found in parts of Italy. North of the Alps, however, towns were few and far between, so that the dioceses were much larger. Instead of dividing the sees as the population increased, the bishops continued to have oversight in these larger areas, assisted in their administration by coadjutor bishops, cathedral canons, and other priests connected to diocese.

Moreover, bishops assumed more and more political authority in addition to their religious duties. As feuds and political upheaval of the early Middle Ages gave way to parliaments and diets, bishops and abbots took their place alongside dukes, margraves, and other noblemen to rule their territories. In the Holy Roman Empire three especially important archbishops of the Roman garrison cities of Trier, Mainz, and Cologne were named "electors" and had, along with the Count of the Palatinate, the Duke of Saxony, the King of Bohemia, and the Margrave of Brandenburg, the authority to elect the emperor. Already Charlemagne had granted bishops large tracts of (largely uninhabited) land, which in the barter economy of early medieval Europe was the only way to ensure that bishops had the financial wherewithal to fulfill their duties as leaders of the church. But as forests were cleared and new towns and cities sprung up, these men became "prince-bishops," exercising as much secular power as religious authority. It is into this welter of competing religious and political claims that CA XXVIII enters the lists with remarkably positive things to say about the authority of bishops and pastors—especially remarkable in the light of later developments, especially in American Lutheranism.

For example, in 1970 some Lutherans in the United States began to call their leaders bishops. At a youth gathering in New Orleans in the mid-1970s, the Lutheran bishop of the area stood up and announced to the mystified young people, "I am neither a bishop nor the son of a bishop," using the prophet Amos's denial of being a prophet (Amos 7:14–15) to express his own uneasiness with the new title. Little did he seem to realize that early Lutherans not only welcomed oversight (*episkopé*) but also insisted upon it for their churches. What worried these Reformers was not the office of oversight but accretions to that office that had obscured its original function: to preach and teach the gospel to their people. Early attempts to rectify this problem resulted in several noteworthy shifts in understanding, many of which are reflected in CA XXVIII. For one thing, Luther reintroduced the ancient church's notion that each major town should have a bishop and sometimes called his friends who were pastors in such places "bishops." Because of the political implications of the word "bishop," it was confusing and constitutionally impossible to start dividing up bishoprics. Moreover, as long as most bishops in the empire remained faithful to Rome and sometimes even persecuted Evangelical pastors, preachers, and teachers, the Reformers quickly followed Augustine's lead and designated those with oversight *superintendentes* (still called superintendents in some Lutheran and Methodist churches).

Even in the United States when the first Lutheran synod was organized by Henry Melchior Muhlenberg in 1748, this "Pennsylvania Ministerium," first conceived as an association of pastors [ministers] and their congregations, included initially an office of superintendent, to be filled by the chief pastor at the Philadelphia church. Later on, Muhlenberg himself was designated the *praeses* (Latin for presider or superintendent). The Swedish church in the Delaware Valley also had enjoyed the services of a provost (empowered directly by the Swedish archbishop), who was chief pastor in the Wicaco congregation (later part of Philadelphia). Similarly, the Lutheran Church—Missouri Synod began its life in this country with a bishop, Martin Stephan, and only when his sexual indiscretions forced his removal from office did the leaders of this nascent church reject episcopal ministry in favor of an American, congregational polity. Some groups of Lutherans who arrived in the nineteenth century came because of persecution by church leaders in their homeland and thus were particularly opposed to bishops. In these cases, a better rule might have been "*abusus non tollit sed confirmat substantiam*" (abuse of something does not exclude but confirms the substance of the matter), as Luther points out in another context in the Large Catechism.[1]

But reasons for rejecting such oversight also stemmed from deeply held religious beliefs, namely, that the individual or, at least, the individual congregation and its pastor had near absolute control over its affairs. The irony is that such positions, when taken to their extreme, result in denigrating the pastoral office either by elevating pastors into congregational popes or by turning them into congregational hired hands. Either way, proper oversight languishes, and the preaching of the gospel suffers neglect.[2] Rather than throwing the episcopal baby out with the bathwater, CA XXVIII invites Lutherans to cherish proper evangelical oversight of the gospel, where true bishops may again embody Christ's saying in Luke ("Whoever hears you, hears me") and can strive with pastors and congregations to spread the gospel

---

1. LC, Baptism, par. 59 (BC, 464).
2. For more on this subject, see Timothy J. Wengert, *Priesthood, Pastors, Bishops: Public Ministry for the Reformation and Today* (Minneapolis: Fortress, 2008).

of Christ throughout the land, while at the same time calling Christians to account for this remarkable message of God's mercy.

The text of Article 28 can be found on pp. 330–43.

Reflections

"Many and various things have been written in former times concerning the power of bishops. Some have improperly mixed the power of bishops with the secular sword, and such careless mixture has caused many extensive wars, uprisings, and rebellions. For the bishops, under the guise of power given to them by Christ, have not only introduced new forms of worship and burdened consciences with reserved cases and with forcible use of the ban, but they also took it upon themselves to set up and depose emperors and kings according to their pleasure. Such outrage has long since been condemned by learned and devout people in Christendom. That is why our people have been compelled, for the sake of comforting consciences, to indicate the difference between spiritual and secular power, sword, and authority. They have taught that, for the sake of God's command, everyone should honor and esteem with all reverence both authorities and powers as the two highest gifts of God on earth." CA XXVIII has a similar structure to CA XX and other articles, in that it follows the rhetorical organization that includes a *narratio* [statement of agreed-upon facts], *status controversiae* [the main issue of controversy], *confirmatio* [proof], and *confutatio* [refutation of opponents' arguments]. This first paragraph forms an account regarding the facts of the case. Some in the past have confused political and episcopal power. On the contrary, the Evangelicals made sure to distinguish spiritual and secular authority. Indeed, the roots of this distinction first arose in 1519, with the publication of Luther's tract, *Two Kinds of Righteousness*, and from there passed into *Freedom of a Christian* (1520), *On Secular Authority* (1523), and *Whether Soldiers, Too, May Be Saved* (1526), as well as into Philip Melanchthon's *Loci communes* (1521/22) and commentary on Colossians (1527/28).[3] This distinction of a two-fold righteousness and thus of two separate ways God rules the world forms one of the most important bases of Lutheran thought. The reformers used it, on the one hand (as here), to restrain episcopal encroachment into the political realm, but in some instances, on the other (as in CA XVI), to prevent governmental meddling in the message of the gospel.

---

3. For Melanchthon, see Timothy J. Wengert, *Human Freedom, Christian Righteousness: Philip Melanchthon's Exegetical Dispute with Erasmus of Rotterdam* (New York: Oxford University Press, 1998) and Timothy J. Wengert, "Philip Melanchthon and a Christian *Politics,*" *Lutheran Quarterly*, 17 (2003): 29–62.

"Our people teach as follows. According to the gospel the power of the keys or of the bishops is a power and command of God to preach the gospel, to forgive or retain sin, and to administer and distribute the sacraments. For Christ sent out the apostles with this command (John 20 [:21–23]): 'As the Father has sent me, so I send you. . . . Receive the Holy Spirit. If you forgive the sins of any, they are forgiven them; if you retain the sins of any, they are retained.'" By defining the main issue [*status controversiae*] as the distinction between episcopal and political power, CA XXVIII first defines succinctly the office of bishop in terms of the gospel, basing its claim on John 20 and the forgiveness of sin. If the use of the word "comfort" in the first paragraph initially hints at the connection between this article and justification by faith, the echoes of CA V in this paragraph and the centrality of forgiveness make the point even more clearly. When bishops do not do their job, the gospel itself is at stake. By calling this "the power of the keys," of course, the reformers are granting their opponents' argument—enshrined in countless portraits of Peter and the bishops of Rome—that bishops hold the power of the keys in the church (cf. Matt 16:19).

"The same power of the keys or of the bishops is used and exercised only by teaching and preaching God's word and by administering the sacraments to many persons or to individuals, depending on one's calling. Not bodily but eternal things and benefits are given in this way, such as eternal righteousness, the Holy Spirit, and eternal life. These benefits cannot be obtained except through the office of preaching and through the administration of the holy sacraments. For St. Paul says [Rom 1:16]: 'The gospel is the power of God for salvation to everyone who has faith.' Now inasmuch as the power of the church or of the bishops bestows eternal benefits and is used and exercised only through the office of preaching, it does not interfere at all with public order and secular authority. For secular authority deals with matters altogether different from the gospel. Secular power does not protect the soul but, using the sword and physical penalties, it protects the body and goods against external violence." CA XXVIII now defines the office of bishop, using a definition already proposed in CA V on the "office of ministry" (Latin) or "office of preaching" (German). Although this coincidence could be used to argue against differences between pastors, ministers, and bishops, CA XXVIII is actually indicating what is central to Christian oversight and leadership in any church: the gospel of Jesus Christ. Moreover, this article insists upon the strict differentiation of episcopal and secular authority. To confuse these two offices means confusing law (which keeps order in the world and restrains wickedness) and gospel (which offers eternal things through the power of the Holy Spirit).

The Latin provides an even clearer picture of the difference, citing Psalm 119:50 ("Your promises gives me life") in addition to Romans 1:16. Moreover, the Latin provides an interesting analogy: "Therefore, since this power of the church gives eternal things and is exercised only through the ministry of the Word, it interferes with civil government as little as the art of singing interferes with it." Singing and civil government have next to nothing to do with one another but can easily be seen as two completely different realms. For the Reformers, the office of bishop is equally separate from civil government. One (preaching the gospel) has nothing really to do with the other (keeping order and restraining evil.)

"That is why one should not mix or confuse the two authorities, the spiritual and the secular. For spiritual power has its command to preach the gospel and to administer the sacraments. It should not invade an alien office. It should not set up and depose kings. It should not annul or disrupt secular law and obedience to political authority. It should not make or prescribe laws for the secular power concerning secular affairs. For Christ himself said [John 18:36]: 'My kingdom is not from this world.' And again [Luke 12:14]: 'Who set me to be a judge or arbitrator over you?' And St. Paul in Phil 3 [:20]: 'Our citizenship is in heaven.' And in 2 Cor 10 [:4–5]: 'For the weapons of our warfare are not merely human, but they have divine power to destroy strongholds ... arguments and every proud obstacle raised up against the knowledge of God.' In this way our people distinguish the offices of the two authorities and powers and direct that both be honored as the highest gifts of God on earth." The completely secularized Christian of the twenty-first century may read this and sniff, "Sounds like 'pie in the sky by and by.'" In the first place, one could respond with Gerhard Forde, "What's the matter? Don't you like pie?" That is, a certain bourgeois view of life makes this world the only one that matters, as if Christ were long dead and buried and would not return to judge the living and the dead. Then, as St. Paul notes (1 Cor 15:19), Christians, of all people, are most to be pitied. But while CA XXVIII did not anticipate that cruel response, it did realize perhaps an even worse situation: pastors and bishops ruling the world. The myth of a Christian America or a moral (Christian) majority running things in the United States stems from the same confusion of God's left and right hands. Invading alien offices, subverting laws, claiming divine power over secular authority, and controlling the administration of justice in this world are all modern symptoms of Christian addiction to political power.

Such things are simply not what God's right hand is all about. Moreover, the claim that Christians know better, have a higher ethic, or possess greater insight into government breaks the first commandment and sets Christians up over God and God's rule in creation. Christians have no more special power over government than over gravity, genetics, or the second law of thermodynamics. They can only pray God that these ordered things serve the good of the neighbor and themselves. Instead, church leaders have authority in a completely different but equally important realm of human existence: announcing in words—visible and aural—the coming rule of God in Christ, breaking in on this world in the weakness of the crucified.

The heaping up of Bible passages serves an important purpose here. It demonstrates the widespread conviction of the New Testament that Jesus embodies a very different kind of rule: *not* of this world and *not* involved in giving legal judgments, but rather in the heavenly places where the battle is joined against the forces of evil. The more human beings become addicted to this life and its blessings, the harder it is to imagine that the proclamation of the world to come is anything other than otherworldly and, thus, irrelevant. But because this in-breaking occurs by faith alone in God's merciful promises, this very gift of faith opens believers' eyes also to see this world and the neighbor as God's gift and to thank God for the good order around them.

"However, where bishops possess secular authority and the sword they possess them not as bishops by divine right but by human, imperial right, given by Roman emperors and kings for the secular administration of their lands. That has nothing at all to do with the office of the gospel." This innocuous paragraph contains an important application of the Lutheran understanding of vocation, namely, that a single individual may have different, sometimes even conflicting, callings from God. In this case, bishops of the Holy Roman Empire were also princes. Almost all of them came from noble families and possessed their sees as part of the dynastic politics of particular noble houses. Thus, for example, before Albrecht became Archbishop of Mainz, this important see was held by an ally of the electoral Saxon house of Wettin. When Albrecht became elector archbishop of Mainz, his brother ascended to the electoral Margraviate of Brandenburg, consolidating power for the Hohenzollern family. Moreover, each bishopric and abbacy controlled land, had subjects, passed judgments, raised armies, and collected taxes. For Lutherans this was no different than their pastors, such as Johannes Bugenhagen in Wittenberg, who at the same time proclaimed the gospel and exercised authority as a head of a Wittenberg household. In our own day, pastors can also raise children, pay taxes, and vote—or even run for elected office. Yet if pastors somehow claimed to have a special right to such things or even imagined that their way of exercising authority in these matters were higher and more righteous than others, or that they had a divine right in such mundane matters by virtue of their calling as ministers, then they would actually be undercutting any proper authority and setting themselves up as gods.

"So, when asking about the jurisdiction of bishops, one must distinguish political rule from the church's jurisdiction. Consequently, according to divine right it is the office of the bishop to preach the gospel, to forgive sin, to judge doctrine and reject doctrine that is contrary to the gospel, and to exclude from the Christian community the ungodly whose ungodly life

is manifest—not with human power but with God's Word alone. That is why parishioners and churches owe obedience to bishops, according to this saying of Christ (Luke 10 [:16]): 'Whoever listens to you listens to me.' But whenever they teach, institute or introduce something contrary to the gospel, we have God's command in such a case not to be obedient (Matt 7 [:15]): 'Beware of false prophets.' And St. Paul in Gal 1 [:8]: 'But even if we or an angel from heaven should proclaim to you a gospel contrary to what we proclaimed to you, let that one be accursed!' And in 2 Cor 13 [:8]: 'For we cannot do anything against the truth, but only for the truth.' And again [2 Cor 13:10]: 'Using the authority that the Lord has given me for building up and not for tearing down.' Canon Law also commands the same in Part II, Question 7 in the chapters entitled 'Priests' and 'Sheep.' And St. Augustine writes in the letter against Petilian that one should not obey bishops, even if they have been regularly elected, when they err or teach and command something contrary to the holy, divine Scripture. Having narrated the basic facts of the case, Melanchthon now reaches his conclusion: bishops must distinguish political power from the church's authority under the Word of God. By applying and expanding the argument in CA V, which defines the "office of ministry" (Latin) or "preaching office" (German), the true contours of episcopal leadership become clear: preaching the gospel, forgiving sin, judging right teaching, excommunicating the patently ungodly. All of these things, rightly understood, receive authority from service to the Word of God alone. To prove this from Scripture, Melanchthon then quotes one of the favorite verses of his opponents (Luke 10:16), turning it against them by narrowing the scope of episcopal authority on the one hand and citing other Scripture passages that limit the seemingly unlimited authority implied in the Lucan text.

Already the ancient church knew that certain passages in Scripture contradicted each other on their face. Even the New Testament points out certain tensions between Hebrew Scripture and Jesus's teachings (e.g., "You have heard it said . . . but I say . . ."). Origen used contradictions to unlock deeper spiritual meanings. Augustine often preferred to harmonize contradictions, especially when dealing with the chronology of Jesus's life. In the Middle Ages, the scholastic method posed *quaestiones* (technical questions) based upon such contradictions, resolving them with the use of Aristotelian logic. To interpret Luke 10 properly, Melanchthon constructs a new *quaestio*, placing restrictions on Christ's unrestricted promise using texts from Matthew and Paul. Now what had been an unconditional promise of apostolic (and, hence, episcopal) authority, suddenly must be subsumed under the truth of the gospel—a position also expressed and authorized by canon law and Augustine! Of course, Melanchthon is not interested in the circular argument suspected by his opponents ("Who then judges what is truth?"), although the final text (2 Cor 13:10) points out that the effect of teaching (i.e., experience) provides a sure criterion for the truth (cf. CA XX).

Some Lutherans today hanker after a reliable, clearly defined "*Magisterium*" that will bring clarity to the church's teaching and preaching. For the CA, however, this misses the point of the office of oversight, which exists not to guarantee the certainty of the gospel but rather to proclaim it to terrified consciences. Any uncertainty in the church's authorized (and, thus, authoritative) teachers—and there always is plenty—serves to drive hearers to the only faithful One, who invites all the heavy-laden to place the yoke of mercy upon their shoulders and to "learn from me."

"Whatever other power and jurisdiction bishops have in various matters, such as marriage or tithes, they have them by virtue of human right. However, when bishops neglect such duties, the princes are obligated— whether they like it or not—to administer justice to their subjects for the sake of peace, in order to prevent discord and great unrest in their lands." This innocuous paragraph contains one remarkable insight into one external difference between Lutherans and Roman Catholics that lasts down to this day. In Protestant lands, as a result of early arguments from Wittenberg and elsewhere, marriage law slowly migrated from ecclesiastical courts to special, separate family courts and thence back into secular law. To this day, few Protestants can understand why Roman Catholics also have church courts capable of annulling marriages. Not only is the term, annulment, rather off-putting (even for some Roman Catholics), but the notion that the church should regulate marriage is but a distant memory for these Protestants. The origin rests in CA XXVIII, where princes are invited to step into the breach where episcopal courts no longer functioned, both in marriage matters and in certain tax matters involving the church.

This paragraph rests upon the distinction first introduced in CA XVI: that one must differentiate between the righteousness and justice of this world and that of the next. In Luther's day, bishops were not merely leaders of the church but also princes. Where they failed in their princely duties (which in the view of CA XXVIII included marriage law and other matters of social order), other princes had to step in by virtue of their God-given office to keep order. By using words like "peace" and "prevent discord," the drafters of the CA are *not* giving princes authority over the gospel but rather over social order, thus maintaining the distinction between God's left and right hands.

"Furthermore, it is also debated whether bishops have the power to establish ceremonies in the church as well as regulations concerning food, festivals, and the different orders of the clergy. For those who grant bishops this power cite this saying of Christ (John 16 [:12–13]): 'I still have many things to say to you, but you cannot bear them now. When the Spirit of

truth comes, he will guide you into all the truth.' They also cite the example in Acts 15 [:20, 29], where the eating of blood and what is strangled was prohibited. They appeal as well to the transference of the Sabbath to Sunday—contrary to the Ten Commandments, as they view it. No other example is so strongly emphasized and quoted as the transference of the Sabbath. Thereby they want to maintain that the power of the church is great, because it has dispensed with and altered part of the Ten Commandments."

We find ourselves here in the midst of that part of a speech or writing that rhetoricians label the *confutatio*, where the speaker anticipates and refutes the opponents' objections. Clearly, the drafters know the specific arguments of the other side on this matter and try to describe them in a more or less balanced way, referring to individual passages of Scripture that argue for episcopal authority to make new doctrine. Jesus's statement in John 16 concerning the Spirit, the council of Jerusalem's decision to prohibit, among other things, the eating of *Blutwurst* (blood sausage), and the Christian practice of worshiping on Sunday provided the opponents' central scriptural arguments. In CA XXVIII, more strongly perhaps than anywhere else, the authors must engage each of these arguments in the following pages.[4]

"Concerning this question, our people teach that bishops do not have the power to institute or establish something contrary to the gospel, as is indicated above and as is taught by Canon Law throughout the ninth distinction. Now it is patently contrary to God's command and Word to make laws out of opinions or to require that by observing them a person makes satisfaction for sin and obtains grace. For the honor of Christ's merit is slandered when we take it upon ourselves to earn grace through such ordinances. It is also obvious that, because of this notion, human ordinances have multiplied beyond calculation while the teaching concerning faith and the righteousness of faith have been almost completely suppressed. Daily new festivals and new fasts have been commanded; new ceremonies and new venerations of the saints have been instituted in order that by such works grace and everything good might be earned from God."

The opening salvo of the Evangelicals' actual refutation dare not be overlooked. They cite Canon Law! All Christian witness derives from the notion that the church and its leaders serve under the gospel and not over it and that

---

4. On the question of the Sabbath, Martin Luther in the Large Catechism ("Ten Commandments," 87–97 [BC, 398–99]) took a different approach, arguing that the Word makes any day holy. Thus, he was not particularly worried about worship on a particular day of the week (Saturday or Sunday)—a position the shocked some nineteenth-century American Lutherans, who were determined to support "Blue Laws" (forbidding certain activities on Sunday) in the United States.

they thus cannot support anything contrary to the gospel![5] First, the Reformers object to basing "church law" on human opinion. This strips bishops of some sort of innate, supernatural power, as if their opinions superseded the human realm and channeled God's will directly. But it is not as if this claim has disappeared from Lutheran circles. Oftentimes, the arguments about church practice very quickly move from practical debates over what may serve the congregation best to heated arguments claiming the God-given nature of this or that practice. There are, of course, divine commands: baptize; preach; forgive sins; celebrate the Supper; set apart servants of the Word. But beyond this, how one orders our communal life is a matter of human judgment not divine command. Second, the most telling argument against confusing church order with God's will arises when Christians claim that following such regulations earns grace. This violates the central article of justification in two ways: it imagines that human activity merits something from God; this results in a diminution of God's grace in Christ. Here, too, the drafters' worry about a multiplication of practices finds parallels in many movements toward holiness today, where following certain human rules increases or assures a person's standing before God. Once again, the problem is not the existence of human rules—they are inevitable within the church for the sake of good order—but rather with the explicit or implicit claims to religious superiority made by following them.

"Moreover, those who institute human ordinances also act contrary to God's command when they attach sin to food, days, and similar things and burden Christendom with bondage to the law, as if in order to earn God's grace there had to be such service of God among Christians like the Levitical service, which God supposedly commanded the apostles and bishops to establish, as some have written. It is quite believable that some bishops have been deceived by the example of the law of Moses. This is how countless ordinances came into being: for example, that it is supposed to be a mortal sin to do manual labor on festivals, even when it offends no one else; that it is a mortal sin to omit the seven hours; that some foods defile the conscience; that fasting is a work that appeases God; that in a reserved case sin is not forgiven unless one first asks to be forgiven by the person for whom the case is reserved—despite the fact that canon laws do not speak of the reservation of guilt but only of the reservation of church penalties."

---

5. This point was also made at the Second Vatican Council, *Dei Verbum* 10 [Heinrich Denzinger, *Compendium of Creeds, Definitions, and Declarations on Matters of Faith and Morals* 43rd ed. (San Francisco: Ignatius, 2012), par. 4214, p. 922]: "This teaching office is not above the Word of God, but serves it, teaching only what has been handed on, listening to it devoutly, guarding it scrupulously, and explaining it faithfully in accord with a divine commission and with the help of the Holy Spirit."

Works righteousness, the main complaint of this section, comes in many forms. On the one hand, as the preceding paragraph argued, such works presume to make a claim on God's grace. On the other, they burden people whose performance falls short with guilt and sins. A great recent example of this same confusion arises with the nineteenth-century American attempts to preserve Sunday as a day of rest. When a Lutheran scholar pointed out that this contradicted everything Luther and the Augsburg Confession said about the issue, he faced numerous attacks.[6] The Pharisee in us wants to have certain and clear (God-ordained) rules to follow that will guarantee God's favor so that we can boast of spiritual accomplishments (Luke 18: "I thank you that I am not like others. . . . Look what I do!"). It would be easy to condemn the clueless, works-righteous folk of the sixteenth century without ever considering how often we fall into the same trap. ("I thank you, God, that I am not works righteous . . .")

"Where, then, did the bishops get the right and power to impose such ordinances on Christendom and to ensnare consciences? For in Acts 15 [:10] St. Peter prohibits placing the yoke on the necks of the disciples. And St. Paul tells the Corinthians [2 Cor 10:8] that they have been given authority for building up and not for tearing down. Why then do they increase sin with such ordinances?"

For all its rhetorical sophistication, this little paragraph might seem theologically unimportant, but that is furthest from the truth. The question is preeminently practical, because justification by faith—far from being simply a doctrine demanding assent—always includes its effect: comforting the terrified! Whereas Peter and Paul knew better, the bishops thought nothing, in the drafters' eyes, of crushing individuals and tearing them from God's grace. This, finally, is the criterion for judging all ordinances in congregations, synods, and the wider church. Does it burden people and crush them, tearing them down with laws rather than building them up with mercy?

"Indeed, clear sayings of divine Scripture prohibit the establishment of such ordinances for the purpose of earning God's grace or as if they were necessary for salvation. St. Paul says in Col 2 [:16–17]: 'Therefore do not let anyone condemn you in matters of food and drink or of observing festivals, new moons, or Sabbaths. These are only a shadow of what is to come, but the substance belongs to Christ.' Again [Col 2:20–23]: 'If with Christ you died to the elemental spirits of the universe, why do you live as if you still belonged to the world? Why do you submit to regulations, "Do not handle, Do not taste, Do not touch?" All these regulations refer to things that perish with use; they are simply human commands and teachings. These have

---

6. Henry Eyster Jacobs, "Sunday, Luth. View of," in: *The Lutheran Cyclopedia*, ed. Henry Eyster Jacobs and John A. W. Haas (New York: Scribner, 1899), 466–67.

indeed an appearance of wisdom.' Again, in Titus 1 [:14] St. Paul clearly prohibits paying attention to Jewish myths or human commandments, which obstruct the truth."

Colossians played an important part in Melanchthon's theological work of the 1520s, when he lectured on and produced two commentaries on the book.[7] For him, Paul's comments in Colossians 2:16–23 described precisely the situation in the late-medieval church, where all manner of human practices had overwhelmed the truth of God's mercy. Here the drafters of the CA focus this passage, more than any other, on the bishops' claims to enact practices necessary for salvation or earning God's favor. Paul was speaking directly to their situation, precisely because the heart of the "truth" is God's unmerited mercy in Christ—the very thing, the Reformers insist, that Paul was addressing. While some like Erasmus imagined that Romans and Galatians were talking about fights between Jewish and Greek Christians over circumcision, a practice long since irrelevant to the sixteenth century (to say nothing of the twenty-first), Colossians offers far broader warnings and addresses all Christian communities directly. Justification by grace through faith on account of Christ opens up new venues for hearing Paul directly address a different set of legalistic claims, rather than assigning his writings to the dust of history.[8]

"In Matt 15 [:14] Christ himself also speaks of those who drive the people to human commandments: 'Let them alone; they are blind guides of the blind.' And he rejects such service of God, saying [Matt 15:13]: 'Every plant that my heavenly Father has not planted will be uprooted.' If, then, bishops have the power to burden the churches with innumerable ordinances and to ensnare consciences, why does divine Scripture so frequently prohibit the making and keeping of human ordinances? Why does it call them teachings of the devil? Could the Holy Spirit possibly have warned against all this in vain?"

Lutheran arguments are not simply fixated on Paul. Here Christ himself becomes witness. CA XXVIII directly applies to the Reformers' own situation regarding Jesus's specific condemnations of those in his own day who drove people to keep human regulations and who claimed that such self-chosen works are divinely sanctioned. Such a use of Christ's words must have

---

7. Timothy J. Wengert, *Law and Gospel: Philip Melanchthon's Debate with John Agricola of Eisleben over "Poenitentia"* (Grand Rapids: Baker, 1997); Timothy J. Wengert, *Human Freedom, Christian Righteousness: Philip Melanchthon's Exegetical Dispute with Erasmus of Rotterdam* (New York: Oxford University Press, 1998).

8. For this reason, "new" perspectives on Paul are not "new" at all but rather are intent upon trapping Paul's proclamation in the past, so that the *only* way to assign his writings meaning in the present is by means of analogy. The direct address disappears into the distant past and Paul's admonitions appear to have little to do with the "real" world. See Erik Heen, "A Lutheran Response to the New Perspective on Paul," *Lutheran Quarterly* 24 (2010): 263–91.

astonished their opponents, who in the *Confutation* (as Melanchthon writes in the Apology) "make a great hue and cry" about the loss of priestly authority. Although Melanchthon claims that such authority is given through human institutions and was not the point of this article, the real cause of the opponents' upset rested in directing such texts against the Roman authorities.[9] The rhetorical plea ("burden," "ensnare") at the end of this section, coupled with a logical argument ("If then . . ."), clearly challenges those who refuse to apply these texts to the present context. Such a heaping up of human ordinances contradicts not only Paul and Jesus but also the Holy Spirit, the true author of Scripture who applies it to the human heart!

"Inasmuch as it is contrary to the gospel to establish such regulations as necessary to appease God and earn grace, it is not at all proper for the bishops to compel observation of such services of God. For in Christendom the teaching of Christian freedom must be preserved, namely, that bondage to the law is not necessary for justification, as Paul writes in Gal 5 [:1] : 'For freedom Christ has set us free. Stand firm, therefore, and do not submit again to the yoke of slavery.' For the chief article of the gospel must be maintained, that we obtain the grace of God through faith in Christ without our merit and do not earn it through service of God instituted by human beings."

Far more than Martin Luther, who often emphasized Christian freedom, Philip Melanchthon was worried by human license and thus stressed the law. Yet, every edition of his premier textbook on theology, the *Loci communes theologici* (best translated as "central theological themes") contained a section on Christian freedom. Melanchthon, who had read and praised Martin Luther's *Freedom of a Christian* (1520), realized that once human law-making runs amok, the grace of God is lost. Of course, it is not that there are no regulations in the church. The issue is rather the human penchant to earn God's mercy or deny it to others. While other writers treat theological topics by and large separately from one another, Melanchthon and the Lutherans insist upon relating every topic back to the very center of the gospel: "The chief article of the gospel must be maintained," that is, justification by grace, through faith, on account of Christ alone. This is not the result of narrowing one's point of view but rather focusing everything on the gospel, a method well summarized by Paul in Romans 14:8: "Whether we live or whether we die, we are the Lord's."

"How, then, should Sunday and other similar church ordinances and ceremonies be regarded? Our people reply that bishops or pastors may make regulations for the sake of good order in the church, but not thereby

---

9. See *The Confutation of the Augsburg Confession*, art. 28, in *Sources and Contexts of the Book of Concord*, ed. Robert Kolb and James A. Nestingen (Minneapolis: Fortress, 2001), 138.

to obtain God's grace, to make satisfaction for sin or to bind consciences, nor to regard such as a service of God or to consider it a sin when these rules are broken without giving offense. So St. Paul prescribed in Corinthians that women should cover their heads in the assembly [1 Cor 11:5], and that preachers in the assembly should not all speak at once, but in order, one after the other [1 Cor 14:30–33]. Such regulation belongs rightfully in the Christian assembly for the sake of love and peace, to be obedient to bishops and pastors in such cases, and to keep such order to the extent that no one offends another—so that there may not be disorder or unruly conduct in the church. However, consciences should not be burdened by holding that such things are necessary for salvation or by considering it a sin when they are violated without giving offense to others; just as no one would say that a woman commits a sin if, without offending people, she leaves the house with her head uncovered."

"For the sake of good order!" What one could call an ecclesiastical first use of the law: wearing hats (or not wearing them); speaking in order; following a certain rhythm in worship. The temptation—which faces *all* churches and not just late-medieval ones—is to turn human rules into divine commandments. Instead, Melanchthon spells out the underlying motivation for all order: "for the sake of love and peace" and "that there may not be disorder or unruly conduct." But as soon as consciences become burdened, all bets are off. This distinction marks the Christian gospel off from all other forms of religiosity, where such matters as head-coverings are not up for debate but (in some circles) are unbreakable, divine laws.

"The same applies to the regulation of Sunday, Easter, Pentecost, or similar festivals and customs. For those who think that the Sabbath had to be replaced by Sunday are very much mistaken. For Holy Scripture did away with the Sabbath, and it teaches that after the revelation of the gospel all ceremonies of the old law may be given up. Nevertheless, the Christian church instituted Sunday because it became necessary to set apart a specific day so that the people might know when to assemble; and the church was all the more pleased and inclined to do this so that the people might have an example of Christian freedom and so that everyone would know that neither the keeping of the Sabbath nor any other day is necessary." This paragraph, which deals with important rules of Christian ritual, condemns a kind of religiosity that reigned among American Protestants in the nineteenth and twentieth centuries.[10] Indeed, because of this caveat against confusing law and gospel, Lutherans in many corners of the world end up looking rather counter-cultural, if not anarchistic. We worship on Sunday so that people

---

10. Cf. the earlier discussion of Henry Eyster Jacobs about American Lutherans keeping the Sabbath.

know when to show up and to demonstrate our freedom (vis-à-vis worshiping on Saturday, the actual Sabbath) but not because of some God-given command mediated by bishops.

"There are many faulty debates about the transformation of the law, the ceremonies of the New Testament, and the change of the Sabbath. They have all arisen from the false and erroneous opinion that in Christianity one would have to have services of God that correspond to the Levitical or Jewish ones, and that Christ commanded the apostles and the bishops to invent new ceremonies that were necessary for salvation. Christianity has been permeated with these kinds of errors because the righteousness of faith was not taught or preached with purity and sincerity. Some argue that although Sunday cannot be kept on the basis of divine law, it must be kept almost as if it were divine law; and they prescribe the kind and amount of work that may be done on the day of rest. But what else are such debates except snares of conscience? For although they presume to moderate and mitigate human ordinances, there certainly cannot be any mitigation and moderation as long as the opinion remains and prevails that they are necessary. Now this opinion will persist as long as no one knows anything about the righteousness of faith and Christian freedom."

The teachers assembled in Augsburg were aware of various attempts to buttress priestly and episcopal authority by linking it to priesthood in the Old Testament. This continues to the present day when some insist that priests perform some sort of propitiatory sacrifice in the Mass effective *ex opere operato* [by the mere performance of the rite], so that this and other practices have saving significance. Again, according to the Reformers, the abandonment of justification by grace through faith (CA IV and V) resulted in these mistaken views of Christian authority finding their way into Christian teaching and practice.

Alongside this confusion arose the problem of necessity. As soon as something that is worthwhile in the community becomes worth something before God, Christian freedom is subverted by an almost divine "must," thereby destroying faith and freedom and ensnaring consciences. This single-minded method of viewing every teaching and practice from the vantage point of the justifying mercy and grace of God shapes the entire CA and demonstrates a very different way of doing theology from that of the sixteenth-century opposition and the twenty-first century equivalents. "Now this opinion will persist as long as no one knows anything about the righteousness of faith and Christian freedom."

"The apostles directed that one should abstain from blood and from what is strangled. But who observes this now? Yet those who do not observe it commit no sin. For the apostles themselves did not want to burden consciences with such bondage, but prohibited such eating for a time to avoid offense. For in this ordinance one must pay attention to the chief part of Christian doctrine, which is not abolished by this decree. Hardly any of the ancient canons are observed according to the letter. Many of their rules fall daily into complete disuse, even among those who observe such ordinances most diligently. Consciences can neither be counseled nor helped unless we keep this moderation in mind: that such ordinances are not to be considered necessary, and even disregarding them does no harm to consciences."

The drafters of the CA also approach the problem of ecclesiastical legalism and its confusion of divine and human (episcopal) authority by pointing out the transitory nature of even apostolic decrees, let alone other ancient canons. Here, too, they discover the gospel-centered nature of Christian community. Human decrees dare not abolish the heart of the gospel—the free forgiveness of sins in Christ—but exist to weave a path between Scylla of burdening consciences and the Charibdys of causing offense. This freedom with respect to church regulations, of course, must always aim at moderation, but in this context (given the danger of legalism to the conscience), leaders must always avoid harming consciences.

"Bishops could easily foster obedience if they did not insist on the observance of ordinances that cannot be observed without sin. However, now they engage in prohibiting both kinds of the holy sacrament or prohibiting marriage for the clergy; they admit no one to the ministry who refuses to swear an oath not to preach this doctrine, even though it is undoubtedly in accord with the holy gospel. Our churches do not desire that the bishops restore peace and unity at the expense of their honor and dignity (even though it is incumbent on the bishops to do this, too, in an emergency). They ask only that the bishops relax certain unreasonable burdens which did not exist in the church in former times and which were adopted contrary to the custom of the universal Christian church. Perhaps there were some reasons for introducing them, but they are not in tune with our times. Nor can it be denied that some ordinances were adopted without being understood. Accordingly, the bishops should be so gracious as to temper these ordinances, since such change does not harm the unity of the Christian church. For many ordinances devised by human beings have fallen into disuse with the passing of time and need not be observed, as papal law itself testifies. If, however, this is impossible and permission cannot be obtained from them to moderate and abrogate such human ordinances as cannot be observed without sin, then we must follow the apostolic rule, which commands us to obey God rather than any human beings [Acts 5:29]."

CA XXVIII now reaches the culmination not only of this article but also, it turns out, of the seven controverted articles (CA XXII–XXVIII) and, indeed, of the entire Confession. One of the chief complaints against the Evangelicals was the legal one. Disobedience to bishops (in theology and practice) always spelled breaking imperial law. At the end of their confession the drafters place this simple argument: If the bishops were more lenient about this one matter (the relation of church practice to the gospel), they would receive what they demand: obedience. But their legalism was not limited to minor matters but touched upon the very heart of the Saxon proposal for overcoming the division in the church: married priests, communion in bread and wine, and giving free course to the gospel. While begging the bishops to behave with gracious moderation (Greek: *epieikeia*), the drafters once again invoke Acts 5:29 [cf. CA XVI]. By casting the entire debate in terms of the gospel (CA IV and V), they never lose sight of what they consider the very heart of the gospel: that we are justified by grace, through faith, on account of Christ alone.

"St. Peter prohibits the bishops to rule as if they had the power to force the churches to do whatever they desired [1 Peter 5:2]. Now the question is not how to take power away from the bishops. Instead, we desire and ask that they would not force consciences into sin. But if they will not do so and despise this request, let them consider how they will have to answer to God, since by their obstinacy they cause division and schism, which they should rightly help to prevent."

This paragraph, along with the preceding one, form an epilogue or peroration for this article, not so much summarizing the entire argument but drawing out the one consequence that makes all the difference: not forcing consciences into sin. On this point, the Reformers now can point the finger at their opponents, the bishops, and accuse them (not the Evangelicals) of causing division through their own obstinacy. With this the die was truly cast, and the Evangelicals could now insist upon their own catholicity and openness and turn the tables on their opponents, putting on them the burden of destroying the church's unity with the only thing that truly does destroy it: any claims to legalistic authority.

We Teach and Confess

"Don't trust anyone over thirty!" "Get the government off our backs!" This and other equally misguided mantras shaped my generation in the 1960s, '70s, and '80s. Indeed, suspicion of authority runs deep in the American psyche and has easily spilled over into other cultures as well. Add to this American religious individualism, and it would seem that churches burdened with bishops are hopelessly out of date.

Yet the Latin saying, that abuse of something does not mitigate its proper use, is well worth remembering when it comes to ecclesiastical good order. Oversight for these confessors in Augsburg was not evil but welcomed—with this one caveat: that no human rule dare overstep its own bounds and encroach on the gospel itself. The bishop is the chief servant in the church, the one who (in the ancient church) eats last at the Supper, so that no one should go hungry at the feast.[11] His or her authority comes in the form of a foolish gospel—spoken, poured, and eaten—where good order serves the common good, prevents offense, and protects the conscience. This means that the bishop as overseer [*episkopos*] both overlooks those things that do not harm the gospel and oversees the preaching and teaching of the gospel, the false teaching of which is the one thing that can harm believers—throughout the church.

---

11. Gordon Lathrop, *The Pastor: A Spirituality* (Minneapolis: Fortress, 2006), 70.

Epilogue

WE CONFESS AND TEACH

They were caught in the act of confessing their faith:

- John, elector from the duchy of Saxony and his rather rotund son, John Frederick, who would succeed him 1532 and be stripped of his electoral title by 1548 in part over this very confession;
- Margrave Georg from the principality of Ansbach, nicknamed "the pious" for having introduced the Reformation into his lands;
- Ernst, duke of the small duchy of Lüneburg, nicknamed "the Confessor" for signing the document, along with his son, Francis;
- Philip, the dashing Landgrave of Hessen, whose later marital problems would nearly kill Philip Melanchthon and who, along with John Frederick, would end up imprisoned by the emperor in the wake of the Smalcald War;
- Wolfgang, Prince of Anhalt-Köthen, whose distant cousin, Georg von Anhalt-Dessau, would later be consecrated by Luther as bishop of Merseburg;
- And two imperial cities: Nuremberg, whose city councilmen included Jerome Baumgartner, a former student in Wittenberg, and whose chief teacher at the newly founded Aegidian Latin school, Joachim Camerarius, was Melanchthon's closest friend; and Reutlingen, whose Reformer and pastor, Matthäus Alber, fled in 1548 after the city was forced to capitulate to the imperial forces after the Evangelicals' defeat in the Smalcald War.

All caught in the act of confessing their faith—not because they had decided this action would champion Wittenberg's theology but because Emperor Charles V had forced their hand by demanding that they give an account of their faith and the changes they had made to practice in their principalities' and cities' congregations. Even more than the content of this Confession, this act of confessing shaped not just the document but also, more importantly, their witness within the church catholic down to the present day.

A pastor of the New York Ministerium in the 1950s told me that candidates to be ordained at the Ministerium's assembly were required to subscribe their names to the Augsburg Confession. In so doing they joined a long line of Lutherans caught in the act of confessing their faith—justified by grace through faith on account of Christ alone.

Perhaps, however, the most poignant example of such confessing appears in Martin Luther's funeral sermon for Elector John. When the elector died suddenly in 1532, Luther contrasted his physical death (which he nicknamed a *Kindersterben*, a child's death [pretending to die?]) with what had happened in Augsburg two years earlier.

> All [the elector's flaws] we shall pass over now and we shall stick to praising him, as St. Paul praises his Christians [in 1 Thess 1:13-14] saying that God will bring with him those who are in Christ, and we shall not look upon [the elector] according to his temporal death, but according to Christ's death and his spiritual death, which he died in accord with Christ.
>
> For you all know how, following Christ, he died two years ago in Augsburg and suffered the real death, not only for himself but for us all, when he was obliged to swallow all kinds of bitter broth and venom which the devil had poured out for him. This is the real, horrible death, when the devil wears a person down. There our beloved elector openly confessed Christ's death and resurrection before the whole world and he stuck to it, staking his land and people, indeed his own body and life upon it.[1]

---

1. LW 51:237, the first of two sermons delivered on 18 August 1532 at Elector John's funeral.

Conclusion to the Second Part

[German]

[Latin]

These are the chief articles that are regarded as controversial. For although many more abuses and errors could have been added, we listed only the principal ones in order to avoid prolixity and undue length. The others can easily be assessed in the light of these. In the past, there were many complaints about indulgences, pilgrimages, and the misuse of the ban. Moreover, pastors had endless quarrels with monks about hearing confession, funerals, sermons on special occasions, and countless other matters. All this we have passed over, being as considerate as we could, so that the chief points at issue may be better discerned. Moreover, it must not be thought that anything has been said or introduced out of hatred or effrontery. On the contrary, we have listed only matters that we thought needed to be brought up and reported on. We did this in order to make it quite clear that among us nothing in doctrine or ceremonies has been accepted that would contradict either Holy Scripture or the universal Christian church. For it is manifest and obvious that we have very diligently and with God's help (to speak without boasting) prevented any new and godless teaching from insinuating itself into our churches, spreading, and finally gaining the upper hand.

In keeping with the summons, we have desired to present the above articles as a declaration of our confession and the teaching of our people. Anyone who

We have recounted the chief articles that are regarded as controversial. For although more abuses could be mentioned, we have included only the principal ones to avoid prolixity. There have been grave complaints about indulgences, pilgrimages, and the misuse of excommunication. Parishes have been vexed by preachers who sell indulgences. There have been endless quarrels between pastors and monks concerning parochial rights, confessions, burials, and countless other matters. We have omitted matters of this sort so that the chief points, having been briefly set forth, can be more readily understood. Nothing has here been said or related to insult anyone. Only those things have been recounted which seemed to need saying. This was done in order that it may be understood that nothing has been accepted among us, in teaching or ceremonies, that is contrary to Scripture or the catholic church. For it is manifest that we have most diligently been on guard so that no new or ungodly doctrines creep into our churches.

In accord with the edict of Your Imperial Majesty, we have desired to present the above-mentioned articles. They exhibit our confession and contain a summary of the instruction by our teachers. If anything is found to be lacking in this confession, we are ready, God willing, to present more extensive information according to the Scriptures.

should find it defective shall willingly be furnished with an additional account based on divine Holy Scripture.

Your Imperial Majesty's most humble, obedient [servants]

John, Duke of Saxony; Elector
George, Margrave of Brandenburg[-Ansbach] Ernest, Duke of Lüneburg
Philip, Landgrave of Hesse
John Frederick, Duke of Saxony
Francis, Duke of Lüneburg
Wolfgang, Prince of Anhalt
The Mayor and Council of Nuremberg
The Mayor and Council of Reutlingen

Your Imperial Majesty's faithful and humble [subjects]

John, Duke of saxony, Elector
George, Margrave of Brandenburg
Ernest, With His Own Hand
Philip, Landgrave of Hesse, subscribes
John Frederick, Duke of Saxony
Francis, Duke of Lüneburg
Wolfgang, Prince of Anhalt
Senate and Mayor of Nuremberg
Senate of Reutlingen

Reflections

"These are the chief articles that are regarded as controversial. For although many more abuses and errors could have been added, we listed only the principal ones in order to avoid prolixity and undue length. The others can easily be assessed in the light of these." Some people think that this sentence implies there are other important articles omitted by the CA. But that is incorrect on two levels. For one thing, the drafters insist that they have listed the principal ones. That is, their single-minded concentration on justification by grace through faith on account of Christ is no obsession but rather gets to the very heart of the gospel and the church's life. For another, any and all omitted articles flow from this heart. This means that when facing "new" issues in today's church, the CA invites us to begin and end with justification by faith alone. In one way or another, everything relates back to and derives from this central message of the church.

"In the past, there were many complaints about indulgences, pilgrimages, and the misuse of the ban. Moreover, pastors had endless quarrels with monks about hearing confession, funerals, sermons on special occasions, and countless other matters. All this we have passed over, being as considerate as we could, so that the chief points at issue may be better discerned." We could make our own list of (frankly) foolish things over which the church agonizes in our day. Many of these fights obscure the gospel and make it hard not simply for theologians but for the faithful to figure out what matters. Some pastors and preachers may have such a hankering to be "relevant" that they forget what really matters to their sinful, dying hearers. Others, in a desire to foster pure teaching, may forget that these same hearers live in a broken world, where the pastor's calling is to tell the truth about the human condition and about God's mercy in Christ. Our calling is simply to discern "the chief points at issue."

"Moreover, it must not be thought that anything has been said or introduced out of hatred or effrontery. On the contrary, we have listed only matters that we thought needed to be brought up and reported on. We did this in order to make it quite clear that among us nothing in doctrine or ceremonies has been accepted that would contradict either Holy Scripture or the universal Christian church. For it is manifest and obvious that we have very diligently and with God's help (to speak without boasting) prevented any new and godless teaching from insinuating itself into our churches, spreading, and finally gaining the upper hand." One of the reasons that the CA has survived as a confession of faith down to this day arises from its irenic tone. Although, as has been noted, occasionally a barbed but veiled comment has subtly put the Evangelicals' opponents on notice that the CA's message condemns a particular practice or attitude. But the CA's spirit was not one of condemnation but of confession. The signers (see above) and their teachers are caught here in the act of confessing their faith.

Avoiding recriminations, however, comes from faithfulness: not just to the Bible but also to the confession of the universal, "catholic" church (Latin). Moreover, this faithfulness also prevents "new and godless teaching" from overwhelming Christ's flock. The present resurgence of interest in the Augsburg Confession, which started in the nineteenth century, demonstrates this second fruit of faithfulness. Lutheran churches around the globe continue to center their proclamation in the unmerited, free mercy of God in Christ for the life of the world as a function of this Confession of faith and its ongoing witness to justification by grace through faith on account of Christ alone. Every time a Lutheran church and its members stray from this unconditional gospel, the CA continues to call them back to the good news of salvation.

"In keeping with the summons, we have desired to present the above articles as a declaration of our confession and the teaching of our people. Anyone who should find it defective shall willingly be furnished with an additional account based on divine Holy Scripture." Confession and teaching are a matched set. When the church emphasizes only teaching, the CA easily becomes a club to keep wayward theologians in line, weeding out the heterodox and preserving the truth. But underneath lurks the worst kind of legalism, where justification by faith alone becomes justification by right answer alone, and knowledge and assent replace true faith in the order of salvation. Contrariwise, when the church emphasizes the act of confession alone, the gospel's content fades into the background and "taking a stand" (any stand!) becomes the sole mark of the church—as if Scripture and the confessions had no content at all. We actually have something to say to this broken, weary world and to the people who still drag themselves out of bed and crawl to church on a Sunday morning—and that cannot be reduced to "It doesn't matter what you believe, as long as you're sincere." As the Formula of Concord from 1576 will intone: "We believe, teach, and confess."

The CA also ends with a preview of coming attractions, especially (but not exclusively) the Apology (Defense) of the Augsburg Confession, on which Melanchthon will begin work in a few weeks. The fact that the CA is to a large extent devoid of biblical and historical references should not be taken as a weakness in argument but rather an insistence that this "creed for our time," as the Formula of Concord later calls it, single-mindedly confesses the faith in a simple, clear way. "Here is what we believe," it states. "For the 'why' please see the Apology." There Melanchthon pulls out all the rhetorical and dialectical stops, proving to his satisfaction that Lutherans did not simply make up their teachings but grounded them in the Scripture and the faith of the church. But analyzing that theological tour-de-force will have to await another Lutheran author.

"**Your Imperial Majesty's most humble, obedient [servants]: John, Duke of Saxony, Elector; George, Margrave of Brandenburg[-Ansbach]; Ernest, Duke of Lüneburg; Philip, Landgrave of Hesse; John Frederick, Duke of Saxony; Francis, Duke of Lüneburg; Wolfgang, Prince of Anhalt; The Mayor and Council of Nuremberg; The Mayor and Council of Reutlingen.**" Here, finally, are the confessors of this work. Unlike many of today's attempts at confession- and creed-writing, they did not produce this document while sitting by the fireplace in their castles or city halls. They were forced into this moment, caught in the act of confessing their faith. Moreover, as described in the introduction to this chapter, their signing this document was not without consequences.

We Teach and Confess

"We should diligently thank God for the blessing of having embraced our dear Elector [John] in Christ's death and having placed him in Christ's resurrection. For you know what kind of death he suffered at the imperial diet in Augsburg."[2] With these words delivered at Elector John's funeral in 1532, Martin Luther signaled how one should view the Augsburg Confession: not as a neat succession of disconnected doctrinal statements (to which unsuspecting future pastors and deacons must submit), but as a true confession: a moment of dying to self and rising in faith.

That "act of confessing" continued not only for those original princely and urban signers but also for others who subscribed, including a long list of

---

2. WA 36:244, 28–31.

reformers in 1537,[3] some of whom also had lost or would lose much because of their confessing. The same would be true for the 8,188 superintendents, pastors, preachers, and teachers who affixed their names to the *Book of Concord* in time for its publication in 1580. But even more! Subscribing this document today, especially when connected to ordination or consecration, is in fact a kind of dying—dying to one's former life; dying to one's self-chosen spiritualities (Col 2:23) and theologies—but also a form of rising: rising to a new calling within Christ's body; rising to be surrounded by a great cloud of witnesses (including the bishop and others participating in the rite) from St. Paul, St. Augustine, St. Bernard, Martin Luther, and Philip Melanchthon right down to one's own parents, spouse, children, or friends; and (most importantly) rising to renewed life and faith in Christ, so that we, too, are caught in the act of confessing our faith!

---

3. BC, 343–44.

Appendix
Articles XXII–XXVIII

The following text of Articles 22–28 is taken from *The Book of Concord: The Confessions of the Evangelical Church* (Minneapolis: Fortress Press), 60–103. They are used in conjunction with chapters 22–28 in this volume. The German version of the articles appear on the left pages and Latin versions on the right.

[XXII.] Concerning Both Kinds[123] of the Sacrament

1   Among us both kinds of the sacrament are given to the laity for the following reason. There is a clear order and command of Christ in Matthew 26[:27]:

2   "Drink from it, all of you." Concerning the cup Christ here commands with clear words that they all should drink from it.

3   So that no one can contest and interpret[124] these words as if they only applied to priests, Paul indicates in 1 Corinthians 11[:21] that the whole

4   assembly of the Corinthian church used both kinds. Moreover, this usage remained in the church for a long time, as can be demonstrated from the his-

5   torical accounts and from the writings of the Fathers.[125] Cyprian mentions in

6   many places that the cup was given to the laity in his time.[126] St. Jerome says that the priests who administer the sacrament distribute the blood of Christ to

7   the people.[127] Pope Gelasius himself ordered that the sacrament should not be

---

123. *Gestalt.* See above, n. 61.

124. *Glossieren,* from the Latin *glossa,* a marginal note, interlineation, or commentary on a text; a traditional medieval way of interpreting a text by adding short explanations to clarify difficult phrases.

125. Histories of the church show that the cup was generally given to the laity until the thirteenth century.

126. Cyprian, Epistle 57.2 (*CSEL* 3/2: 652, 7; *ANF* 5:337, where it is Epistle 53.2).

127. Jerome, *Commentary on Zephaniah,* c. 3 (*MPL* 25:1375).

[XXII.] Concerning Both Kinds[128]

Both kinds are given to the laity in the sacrament of the Lord's Supper because 1
this usage has the command of the Lord (Matt. 26[:27]), "Drink from it, all
of you." Christ here clearly instructs concerning the cup that all should drink. 2

So that no one would quibble that this pertains only to priests, Paul in 3
Corinthians [11:21] cites an example in which it appears that the entire church
was using both kinds. This usage continued in the church for a long time. It is 4
not known when or by which authority it was first changed, although Cardinal
Cusanus mentions when it was formally approved. Cyprian testifies in several 5
places that the blood was given to the people. Jerome testifies to the same thing, 6
saying: "The priests administer the Eucharist and distribute the blood of Christ
to the people." In fact, Pope Gelasius commands that the sacrament should not 7

---

128. *species,* literally "species," the technical term for the elements in the Lord's Supper.

8   divided (dist. 2, chap. *Concerning Consecration*).[129] Not a single canon with the order to receive only one kind can be found. Nobody knows when or through whom this custom of receiving only one kind was introduced, although

10   Cardinal Cusanus mentions when this custom was formally approved.[130] Now it is obvious that this custom, introduced contrary to God's command and to

11   the ancient canons, is not right. Accordingly, it was not proper to burden the consciences of those who desired to use the sacrament according to Christ's institution and to compel them to act contrary to the order of our Lord Christ.

12   Furthermore, because dividing the sacrament contradicts Christ's institution, the customary procession with the sacrament has also been discontinued.[131]

[XXIII.] Concerning the Marriage of Priests

1   From everyone, both of high and low degree, a mighty, loud complaint has been heard throughout the world about the flagrant immorality and dissolute life of priests who were not able to remain chaste; their vices reached the height

3   of abomination. In order to avoid so much terrible offense, adultery, and other immorality, some priests among us have entered the married state. They give as their reason that they are compelled and moved to do so by the great distress of their consciences, especially since Scripture clearly proclaims that the mar-

4   ried state was instituted by God to avoid sexual immorality, as Paul says that to avoid immorality, "Each man should have his own wife" [1 Cor. 7:2], and again,

5   "For it is better to marry than to be aflame with passion" [1 Cor. 7:9b]. When Christ says, in Matthew 19[:11], "Not everyone can accept this teaching," he shows that he knew human nature quite well, namely, that few people have the gift to live a celibate life. For "God created humankind . . . male and female"

6   (Gen. 1[:27]). Experience has made it all too clear whether human power and ability can improve or change the creation of God, the supreme Majesty, through their own intentions or vows without a special gift or grace of God. What good, honorable, chaste life, what Christian, honest, or upright existence has resulted for many? For it is clear—as many have confessed about their own lives—how much abominable, terrifying disturbance and torment of con-

8   science they experienced at the time of their death. Therefore, because God's

9   Word and command cannot be changed by any human vow or law, priests and other clergy have taken wives for themselves for these and other reasons and causes.

---

129. Gratian, *Decretum*, pt. III, *Concerning Consecration* (*de consecratione*), dist. 2, chap. 12. This collection of canon law was falsely ascribed to Pope Gelasius I. Gratian collected and edited church regulations, which since 1582 have been known as the *Code of Canon Law* (*Corpus Juris Canonici*).

130. Nicholas of Cusa, Epistle III to the Bohemians, shows that the Fourth Lateran Council in 1215 ordered the withdrawal of the cup from the laity.

131. A reference to the observance of the Corpus Christi festival on the Thursday following Trinity Sunday. Lutheran princes refused to participate in the Corpus Christi procession in Augsburg on 16 June 1530. Even "carrying the sacrament across the street" was later forbidden. However, see *LW* 54:407f. (WATR 5, no. 5314).

be divided (dist. 2, *Concerning Consecration*, chap., "We Discover"). Only a 8
quite recent custom holds otherwise. However, it is evident that a custom, 9
introduced contrary to the commands of God, must not be approved, as the
canons testify (dist. 8, chap., "Concerning the Truth,"[132] and the subsequent
chapters). In fact, this custom has been accepted not only in defiance of 10
Scripture but also in opposition to the ancient canons and the example of the
church. Accordingly, if persons preferred to use both kinds in the sacrament, 11
they should not have been compelled with offense to their conscience to do
otherwise. Because dividing the sacrament does not agree with the institution 12
of Christ, the procession, which has been customary up to now, is also omitted
among us.

[XXIII.] Concerning the Marriage of Priests

There has been a public outcry concerning the bad examples of priests who 1
have not been continent. On this account Pope Pius is reported to have said 2
that there were some reasons why marriage was taken away from the priests,
but that there are much weightier reasons why it should be given back to them.
For so writes Platina. Since, then, the priests among us wanted to avoid such 3
public scandals, they took wives and taught that it was lawful for them to marry
for the following reasons. In the first place, Paul says [1 Cor. 7:2, 9b]: "But 4
because of cases of sexual immorality, each man should have his own wife,"
and again: "For it is better to marry than to be aflame with passion." In the sec- 5
ond place, Christ says [Matt. 19:11], "Not everyone can accept this teaching,"
where he is teaching that not everyone is fit for celibacy, because God created
the human being for procreation (Gen. 1[:28]). It is not humanly possible to 6
change creation without a singular gift and work of God. Accordingly, those 7
who are not suited for celibacy should marry. For no human law or vow can 8
nullify a command and institution of God. For these reasons our priests teach 9
that it is lawful for them to have wives.

---

132. *De veritate,* in Gratian, *Decretum* I, dist. 8, chap. 4.

10   It can also be demonstrated from the historical accounts and from the writings of the Fathers that it was customary in the Christian church of ancient
11   times for priests and deacons to have wives. This is why Paul says in 1 Timothy
12   3[:2]: "Now a bishop must be above reproach, the husband of one wife."[133] It
was only four hundred years ago that priests in Germany were compelled by
force to leave the married state and take the vows of celibacy.[134] But they all
offered so much serious and strong resistance that an archbishop of Mainz,
who had promulgated the new papal decree, was nearly crushed to death dur-
13   ing an uprising of the entire clergy.[135] In the beginning, this same prohibition
was so hastily and ineptly enforced that the pope at the time prohibited not
only future marriages of priests but also broke up existing marriages of long
standing. Of course, this was not only contrary to all divine, natural, and civil
laws but also was totally opposed and contrary to the canons that the popes
themselves had made and to the most renowned councils.[136]

Many godly and intelligent people of high standing have also often
expressed similar opinions and misgivings that such enforced celibacy and
prohibition of marriage (which God himself instituted and left open for individuals to enter) never introduced any good but rather many great and evil
vices and much scandal. Moreover, as his biography indicates, one of the popes
himself, Pius II, often said and had these words recorded: there may well have
been some reason why the clergy was prohibited from marrying; but there were
many better, greater, and more important reasons why they should again be
free to marry.[137] Undoubtedly, Pope Pius, as an intelligent and wise man, made
this statement because of grave misgivings.

14   Therefore, in loyalty to Your Imperial Majesty we are confident that, as a
most praiseworthy Christian emperor, Your Majesty will graciously take to
heart the fact that now in these last times and days of which Scripture speaks,
the world is becoming more wicked and human beings more frail and infirm.

Therefore it is most necessary, useful, and Christian to give this situation
thorough inspection, so that the prohibition of marriage may not cause worse

---

133. Here citing the alternative reading in the NRSV, which corresponds to the German and
Latin texts.

134. Originally, priests were not permitted to marry a second time; then they could not marry
after their priestly vows; and since the fourth century they had to refrain from marital relations
altogether. However, it was not until the end of the eleventh century that the requirement of
celibacy was generally enforced by Pope Gregory VII. At that time most priests in Germany were
still married.

135. Siegfried of Mainz at synods in Erfurt and Mainz in 1075.

136. Gratian, *Decretum* I, dist. 82, chaps. 2–5; also dist. 84, chap. 4. The Council of Nicea
in 325 refused to require celibacy. See Socrates Scholasticus, *Ecclesiastical History* I, 11 (*MPG*
67:101–4; *NPNF*, ser. 2, 2:18).

137. Pope Pius II is reported to have said this, according to the Italian humanist historian
Bartholomeo Platina, *Concerning the Lives and Customs of the Popes* (*De vitis ac gestis pontificum*)
(Venice, 1518), 155b.

It is also evident that priests in the ancient church were married. For Paul 10–11
says [1 Tim. 3:2] that a married man should be chosen to be bishop. Not until 12
four hundred years ago were priests in Germany compelled to be celibate.
In fact, they were so opposed to it that the archbishop of Mainz was almost
crushed to death by angry priests in an uprising when he was about to publish
the edict of the Roman pontiff on this matter. The matter was handled in such 13
an uncivil manner that not only were future marriages prohibited but existing
marriages were also dissolved, even though this was contrary to all laws, divine
and human, and even to the canons made by popes and the most celebrated
councils.

Inasmuch as the world is growing old and human nature has become 14
weaker, it is fitting to exercise foresight so that no more vices creep into
Germany.

15
16
and more shameful immorality and vices to gain ground in German lands. For no one will ever be able to change or arrange these matters better or more wisely than God himself, who instituted marriage to help human frailty and to prevent sexual immorality. The old canons also state that sometimes severity and rigor must be alleviated and relaxed for the sake of human weakness and to prevent and avoid greater scandal.[138] Now that certainly would be Christian and highly necessary in this case. How can the marriage of priests and clergy, especially of the pastors and others who are to serve the church, be disadvan-

17
tageous to the Christian church as a whole? There may well be a shortage of priests and pastors in the future if this harsh prohibition of marriage should last much longer.

18
Thus, that priests and clergy may marry is based on the divine Word and command. Moreover, the historical accounts demonstrate that priests were married and that the vow of celibacy has caused so much awful, unchristian offense, so much adultery, such terrible, unprecedented immorality and abominable vice that even some of the sincere cathedral clergy and also some courtiers in Rome have often confessed and complained how such abominable and overwhelming vice in the clergy would arouse the wrath of God. It is, therefore, quite deplorable that Christian marriage has not only been prohibited but also most swiftly punished in many places, as if it were a great

19
20
21
crime. And yet, God commanded in Holy Scripture to hold marriage in high esteem.[139] Moreover, the marital state is also highly praised in imperial laws and in all monarchies—wherever there has been law and justice. Only in this day and age are people beginning to be tortured without cause, simply because they are married—especially priests who above all should be spared. This is

22
done not only contrary to divine law but also to the canons. In 1 Timothy 4[:1, 3] the apostle Paul calls the teaching that prohibits marriage a teaching of the devil. Christ himself says in John 8[:44] that the devil is a murderer from the

23
beginning. These two statements fit well together. For it certainly must be a teaching of the devil to prohibit marriage and then to dare to maintain such a teaching with the shedding of blood.

24
25
However, just as no human law can abolish or change God's command, neither can any vow change God's command. That is why St. Cyprian advised that women who do not keep the vow of chastity should get married. He says in Epistle 11: "But if they are unwilling or unable to keep their vows of chastity it is better for them to marry than to fall into the fire through their lusts, and they should see to it that they cause no offense to their brothers and sisters."[140]

---

138. Gratian, *Decretum* I, dist. 34, chap. 7; pt. II, chap. 1, q. 7, c. 5.

139. This sentence is lacking in the 1580 Book of Concord.

140. Cyprian, Epistle 62.2 (*ANF* 5:357, where it is numbered 61). The text uses the numbering of Cyprian's letters by the humanist Erasmus of Rotterdam. Other editions number it 4 (cf. *MPL* 4:366f. and *CSEL* 3/2: 474, 17–21).

Moreover, God instituted marriage to be a remedy against human infir- 15
mity. The canons themselves state that the old rigor should occasionally be 16
relaxed on account of human weakness—which is most desirable to have
happen in this case. It seems that the churches will soon be short of pastors if 17
marriage is forbidden for too long a time.

But the command of God still exists, the custom of the church is well 18
known, and impure celibacy produces many scandals, adulteries, and other
crimes deserving punishment by good magistrates. Despite all that, it is astonishing that such ferocious opposition to the marriage of priests still exists. God 19
has commanded that marriage be held in honor. The laws in all well-ordered 20
nations, even among the heathen, have adorned marriage with highest honors.
But now, contrary to the intention of the canons, capital punishment is cruelly 21
imposed—on priests no less!—for no other reason than marriage. Paul calls 22
the prohibition of marriage a teaching of demons (1 Tim. [4:1, 3]). This can 23
easily be understood, now that the prohibition of marriage is defended by such
punishments.

However, just as no human law can nullify a command of God, so no vow 24
can do so. Consequently, Cyprian advised that women who could not keep 25
the promise of chastity should marry. These are his words (Book I of Epistle
II): "But if they are unwilling or unable to persevere, it is better for them to
marry than to fall into the fire through their lusts; they certainly should not
give offense to their brothers and sisters."

The canons even exercise a measure of fairness toward those who made 26
vows before attaining the proper age, as has been customary to do until now.

26   In addition, all the canons show great lenience and fairness toward those who have made vows in their youth,[141] as is the case with large numbers of priests and monks who entered their vocations out of ignorance when they were young.

[XXIV.] Concerning the Mass

1, 9   Our people have been unjustly accused of having abolished the Mass.[142] But it is obvious, without boasting, that the Mass is celebrated among us with

7   greater devotion and earnestness than among our opponents. The people are instructed more regularly and with the greatest diligence concerning the holy sacrament, to what purpose it was instituted, and how it is to be used, namely, as a comfort to terrified consciences. In this way, the people are drawn to Communion and to the Mass. At the same time, they are also instructed about

2   other, false teaching concerning the sacrament.[143] Moreover, no noticeable changes have been made in the public celebration of the Mass, except that in certain places German hymns are sung alongside the Latin responses for the

3   instruction and exercise of the people. For after all, all ceremonies should serve the purpose of teaching the people what they need to know about Christ.

10   Now, because previously the Mass was misused in many ways (as has come to light) by turning it into a fair, by buying and selling it, and, for the most part, by celebrating it in all churches for money, such misuse was repeatedly

12   rebuked by learned and upright people—even before our time.[144] Now the preachers among us preached about this, and the priests were reminded of the terrible responsibility, which should properly concern every Christian, that whoever uses the sacrament unworthily is "answerable for the body and

13   blood" of Christ [1 Cor. 11:27]. Consequently, such mercenary Masses and private Masses,[145] which had up to now been celebrated under compulsion for the sake of money and stipends, were discontinued in our churches.

21   At the same time, an abominable error was also rebuked, namely, the teaching that our Lord Jesus Christ had made satisfaction by his death only for orig-

22   inal sin and had instituted the Mass as a sacrifice for other sins. Thus, the Mass was made into a sacrifice for the living and the dead for the purpose of taking

---

141. Gratian, *Decretum* II, chap. 20, q. 1, c. 5, 7, 9, 10, 14, 15.

142. For example, by John Eck, *404 Theses*, nos. 269–78. Luther retained the Mass, but without abuses. See, for example, *Concerning the Order of Public Worship* (1523) (WA 12:35–37; *LW* 53:11–14) and *The German Mass and Order of Service* (1526) (WA 19:72–113; *LW* 53:53–90).

143. As an example of such instruction, see the Large Catechism, "The Lord's Supper," based on sermons by Luther delivered during Holy Week, 1529.

144. By various critics, such as Nicholas of Cusa, the German Dominican mystic John Tauler, the French conciliarist John Gerson, and the influential German theologian Gabriel Biel.

145. Masses said for the special intentions of individuals, often called "votive Masses," which were celebrated in connection with a vow (*votum* in Latin). Compare Luther's *Exhortation to All Clergy Assembled at Augsburg* (1530) (WA 30/2: 293–309; *LW* 34:22–32).

[XXIV.] *Concerning the Mass*

Our churches are falsely accused of abolishing the Mass. In fact, the Mass 1
is retained among us and is celebrated with the greatest reverence. Almost 2
all the customary ceremonies are also retained, except that German hymns,
added for the instruction of the people, are interspersed here and there among
the Latin ones. For ceremonies are especially needed in order to teach those 3
who are ignorant. Paul advised [1 Cor. 14:2, 9] that in church a language that 4
is understood by the people should be used. The people have grown accus- 5
tomed to receiving the sacrament together—all who are fit to do so. This
also increases reverence and respect for public ceremonies. For people are 6
admitted only if they first had an opportunity to be examined and heard. The 7
people are also reminded about the dignity and use of the sacrament—how
it offers great consolation to anxious consciences—so that they may learn to
believe in God and expect and ask for all that is good from God. Such wor- 8
ship pleases God, and such use of the sacrament cultivates piety toward God. 9
So it does not appear that the Mass is held with greater devotion among our
adversaries than among us.

However, for a long time there has been a serious public outcry by good 10
people that Masses were being shamefully profaned and devoted to profit. It 11
is public knowledge how widely this abuse extends in all places of worship,
what kind of people celebrate Masses only for a revenue or stipend, and
how many celebrate contrary to the canons' prohibitions. But Paul severely 12
threatens those who treat the Eucharist unworthily, when he says [1 Cor.
11:27]: "Whoever, therefore, eats the bread or drinks the cup of the Lord in
an unworthy manner will be answerable for the body and blood of the Lord."
Accordingly, when the priests among us were instructed concerning this sin, 13
private Masses were discontinued among us, since there were hardly any private Masses held except for the sake of profit.

Nor were bishops ignorant of these abuses. If they had corrected them in 14
time there would be less dissension now. By their negligence many vices have 15
been allowed to creep into the church. Now, when it is too late, they are begin- 16
ning to complain about the calamities in the church, although this tumult was
occasioned by those same abuses which had become so obvious they could
no longer be tolerated. Great dissensions have arisen concerning the Mass, 17
concerning the sacrament: perhaps the world is being punished for such an 18
enduring profanation of Masses as has been tolerated in the church for many
centuries by the very people who could and should have corrected them. For it 19
is written in the Decalogue [Exod. 20:7]: "The Lord will not acquit anyone who
misuses his name." Since the beginning of the world no divine matter seems 20
ever to have been so devoted to profit as the Mass.

The following view increased private Masses without end: Christ had by his 21
passion made satisfaction for original sin and had instituted the Mass in which
an offering might be made for daily sins, mortal and venial. From this came the 22

23   away sin and appeasing God. Thereupon followed a debate as to whether one Mass celebrated for many people merited as much as a special Mass celebrated for an individual. This resulted in the countless multiplication of Masses, and with this work people wanted to obtain from God everything they needed. Meanwhile, faith in Christ and true worship of God were forgotten.

24   That is why instruction was given, clearly of necessity, so that everyone
25   would know how to use the sacrament properly. In the first place, Scripture demonstrates in many places that there is no other sacrifice for original sin or
26   any other sin than the one death of Christ. For it is written in Hebrews [9:28; 10:10, 14] that Christ offered himself once and thereby made satisfaction for all sins. It is an unprecedented novelty in church doctrine that Christ's death should have made satisfaction only for original sin and not for other sins as well. Consequently, we hope everyone understands that such error is not unjustly rebuked.[146]

28   In the second place, St. Paul teaches that we obtain grace before God
29   through faith and not through works. Clearly contrary to this is the misuse of the Mass where people imagine that they may obtain grace through performing this work. For everyone knows that the Mass is used for removing sin and obtaining grace and all benefits from God—not only for the priest himself but also for the whole world and for others, living or dead. *And this takes place through performing the work,* ex opere operato, *without faith.*[147]

30   In the third place, the holy sacrament was not instituted to provide a sacrifice for sin—for the sacrifice has already occurred—but to awaken our faith and comfort our consciences. The sacrament makes them aware that they are promised grace and forgiveness of sin by Christ. That is why this sacrament requires faith and without faith is used in vain.

34   Now since the Mass is not a sacrifice for others, living or dead, to take away their sins but should be a Communion where the priest and others receive the sacrament for themselves, we celebrate it in this fashion. On holy days and at other times when communicants are present, Mass is celebrated, and those
35   who desire it receive the sacrament. Thus, the Mass remains among us in its
39   proper use, as it was observed formerly in the church. This can be demonstrat-
36   ed from St. Paul (1 Cor. 11[:23-33]) and from many writings of the Fathers. For Chrysostom tells how the priest stands every day and invites some to
37   receive the sacrament, but forbids others to approach.[148] The ancient canons also indicate that one priest officiated and gave the sacrament to the other
38   priests and deacons. For the words of the Nicene canon read: "After the priests, the deacons shall receive the sacrament from the bishop or priest in order."[149]

---

146. "It is an . . . rebuked": lacking in the 1531 *editio princeps.*
147. The text in italics was first added to the 1531 *editio princeps.* For the phrase *ex opere operato,* see above, n. 75.
148. John Chrysostom, *Homilies on Ephesians,* Homily 3 (*MPG* 62:29; *NPNF,* ser. 1, 13:64).
149. Canon 18 of the Council of Nicea in 325.

common opinion that the Mass is a work which *ex opere operato*[150] blots out the sins of the living and the dead. Here began a debate on whether one Mass 23 said for many is worth as much as special Masses for individuals. That debate produced this endless multitude of Masses.

Our people have warned that these opinions do not agree with the Holy 24 Scriptures but instead undermine the glory of Christ's passion. For the passion 25 of Christ was an offering and satisfaction not only for original guilt but for all other remaining sins, as is written in Hebrews [10:10, 14]: "We have been 26 sanctified through the offering of the body of Jesus Christ once and for all," 27 and, "By a single offering he has perfected for all time those who are sanctified."

Likewise, Scripture teaches that we are justified before God through faith 28 in Christ. Now if the Mass blots out the sins of the living and the dead *ex opere* 29 *operato*,[151] justification comes from the work of the Mass, not from faith, which Scripture does not allow.

But Christ commands that it be done in memory of him.[152] The Mass, 30 therefore, was instituted so that the faith of those who use the sacrament should recall what benefits are received through Christ and should encourage and console the anxious conscience. For to remember Christ is to remember 31 his benefits and realize that they are truly offered to us.[153] It is not enough to 32 remember the history, because the Jews and the ungodly can also remember that. The Mass is to be used for the purpose of offering the sacrament to those 33 who need consolation, just as Ambrose says: "Because I always sin, I ought always to take the medicine."[154]

Since the Mass is such an imparting of the sacrament, among us one com- 34 mon Mass is held on every holy day, and it is also administered on other days if there are those who desire it. Nor is this custom new in the church. For the 35 ancient teachers before the time of Gregory[155] do not mention private Masses, but often speak of the common Mass. Chrysostom says that the priest stands 36 daily at the altar, inviting some to Communion and keeping others away. 37 And it is apparent from the ancient canons that one person celebrated the Mass, from whom the rest of the presbyters and deacons received the body of Christ. For the words of the Nicene canon read: "Let the deacons receive Holy 38 Communion in order after the presbyters from the bishop or from a presby- ter." Concerning Communion Paul also commands [1 Cor. 11:33] that people 39 should wait for one another so that there may be a common participation.

---

150. By the mere performance of an act. See *CA* XIII, n. 75.

151. By the mere performance of an act. See *CA* XIII, n. 75.

152. 1 Corinthians 11:25.

153. An oft-used concept of Melanchthon. See his *Loci* 1521, p. 21f.

154. Ambrose, *Concerning the Sacraments* (*De sacramentis*) V, 4, 25 (*MPL* 16:464; *CSEL* 73:58, 12).

155. Pope Gregory I.

40   No novelty has been introduced that did not exist in the church in days of old. No noticeable change has occurred in the public liturgy of the Mass, except that other, unnecessary Masses, which perhaps through misuse were celebrated besides the parish Mass, have been discontinued. Therefore this way of celebrating Mass should, in all fairness, not be condemned as heretical

41   or unchristian. For in former times, Mass was not celebrated every day in the large churches where there were many people, even on days the people assembled. As the *Tripartite History*, Book 9, indicates, in Alexandria Scripture was read and interpreted on Wednesday and Friday, and all these worship services were held without the Mass.[156]

[XXV.] Concerning Confession

1   Confession has not been abolished by the preachers on our side. For the custom has been retained among us of not administering the sacrament to those

2   who have not previously been examined and absolved. At the same time, the people are diligently instructed how comforting the word of absolution is and

3   how highly and dearly absolution is to be esteemed.[157] For it is not the voice or word of the person speaking it, but it is the Word of God, who forgives sin.

4   For it is spoken in God's stead and by God's command. Great diligence is used to teach about this command and power of the keys, and how comforting and necessary it is for terrified consciences. It is also taught how God requires us to believe this absolution as much as if it were God's voice resounding from heaven and that we should joyfully find comfort in the absolution, knowing that

5   through such faith we obtain forgiveness of sin. In former times, the preachers, while teaching much about confession, never mentioned a single word about these necessary matters but instead only tormented consciences with long enumerations of sins, with satisfactions, with indulgences, with pilgrimages, and

6   the like. Moreover, many of our opponents themselves confess that our side has written about and dealt with true Christian repentance more appropriately than had been done in a long time.

7   Concerning confession, it is taught that no one should be compelled to enumerate sins in detail. For this is impossible, as the psalm [19:12] says: "But

8   who can detect their errors?" And Jeremiah [17:9] says: "The human heart is so

9   devious that no one can understand it."[158] Miserable human nature is so mired in sins that it cannot see or know them all. If we were absolved only from those

---

156. *Historia tripartita*, written by the Roman monk Cassiodorus, was the principal book of church history used in the late Middle Ages, and it quotes here from Socrates Scholasticus, *Ecclesiastical History* V, 22 (*MPG* 67:635–40; *NPNF*, ser. 2, 2:132).

157. On requiring confession, see Luther, *An Order of Mass and Communion* (1523) (WA 12:215, 18–216, 19; *LW* 53:32f.), and *Instructions for the Visitors* (1528) (WA 26:220, 1–19; *LW* 40:296). On the comfort of absolution, see the Large Catechism, "A Brief Exhortation to Confession," 16–19.

158. A paraphrase based on the Latin Vulgate. For this argument see also *CA* XI.

Since, therefore, the Mass as we conduct it has on its side the example of 40
the church, from Scripture and the Fathers, we are confident that it cannot
be disapproved, especially since the customary public ceremonies are for the
most part retained. Only the number of Masses is different, and on account of
the great and manifest abuses it would certainly be good to limit them. For in 41
former times Mass was not celebrated every day, even in churches frequented
most, as the *Tripartite History,* Book IX, testifies: "But again, in Alexandria,
Scriptures are read on Wednesday and Friday and the teachers interpret them,
and everything is done except the solemn practice of the Offering."[159]

[XXV.] Concerning Confession

Confession has not been abolished in our churches. For it is not customary 1
to administer the body of Christ except to those who have been previously
examined and absolved. The people are also most diligently taught concerning 2
faith in the word of absolution, about which there was a great silence before
now. People are taught to make the most of absolution because it is the voice 3
of God and is pronounced following the command of God. The power of 4
the keys is praised and remembered for bringing such great consolation to
terrified consciences, both because God requires faith so that we believe such
absolution as God's own voice resounding from heaven and because this faith
truly obtains and receives the forgiveness of sins. In former times, satisfac- 5
tions were immoderately extolled; nothing was mentioned about faith, the
merits of Christ, or the righteousness of faith. On this point our churches can
scarcely be faulted. For even our adversaries are compelled to grant us that the 6
teaching concerning confession has been most carefully treated and brought
to light by our people.

What is more, they teach concerning confession that an enumeration of 7
faults is not necessary and that consciences should not be burdened with the
anxiety of having to enumerate all their faults. For it is impossible to recite
every misdeed, as the psalm [19:12] testifies: "Who can detect their errors?"
And Jeremiah [17:9]: "The heart is devious above all else; it is perverse." But 8–9
if no sins were forgiven except those which are recounted aloud, consciences

---

159. *oblatio.* Here used as a technical term for the Lord's Supper.

10
11
sins that we can enumerate, we would be helped but little. That is why it is not necessary to compel people to enumerate sins in detail. This was also the view of the Fathers, as one finds it in dist. 1 of *Concerning Confession*[160] where these words of Chrysostom are quoted: "I do not say that you should offer yourself up in public, or accuse yourself, or plead guilty before another person. Instead obey the prophet who says, 'Reveal your way to the Lord' [Ps. 37:5, Vulgate]. Therefore confess to the Lord God, the true judge, in your prayer. Do not speak your sin with the tongue, but in your conscience." Here one can clearly see

12
that Chrysostom does not force anyone to enumerate sins in detail. The marginal note in the *Decretum, Concerning Confession*, dist. 5,[161] also teaches that confession is not commanded in Scripture but was instituted by the church.

13
Nevertheless, the preachers on our side diligently teach that confession is to be retained because of absolution (which is confession's principal and foremost part) for the comfort of terrified consciences and because of other reasons.[162]

[XXVI.] Concerning the Distinction among Foods

1
In former times it was taught, preached, and written that distinction among foods and similar traditions instituted by human beings serve to earn grace

2
and make satisfaction for sin.[163] For this reason, new fasts, new ceremonies, new monastic orders, and the like were invented daily. They were fervently and strictly promoted, as if such things were a necessary service of God whereby people earned grace if they observed them or committed a great sin if they did

3
not. Many harmful errors in the church have resulted from this.

4
In the first place, the grace of Christ and the teaching concerning faith are thereby obscured. The gospel holds these things up to us with great earnestness and strongly insists that everyone regard the merit of Christ as sublime and precious and know that faith in Christ is to be esteemed far above all works.

5
For this reason, St. Paul fought vehemently against the Law of Moses and against human tradition so that we should learn that we do not become righteous before God by our works but that it is only through faith in Christ that

6
we obtain grace for Christ's sake. Such teaching has been almost completely extinguished by the instruction to earn grace with prescribed fasts, distinction among foods, dress, etc.

---

160. Gratian, *Decretum* II, chap. 33, q. 3 (*De poenitentia*, dist. 1, chap. 87, 4). The quotation is from Chrysostom, *Homilies on Hebrews,* Homily 31.6 (*MPG* 63:216; *NPNF,* ser. 1, 14:508).

161. A gloss to Gratian, *Decretum, De poenitentia* 5, 1. It reads: "It is better to say that it [confession] was instituted by some tradition of the universal church than from the authority of the Old or New Testament."

162. See, for example, the appreciation of private confession by Luther, *Confession concerning Christ's Supper* (1528) (*WA* 26:507, 17–27; *LW* 37:368–69).

163. For example, Thomas Aquinas, *Summa Theologiae* II, 2, q. 147, a. 1. "Fasting is practiced for three principal reasons: first, to restrain the concupiscence of the flesh . . . , second . . . , because through it the mind is more easily elevated to the contemplation of sublime things . . . , third, to make satisfaction for sin." (Thomas's *Summa* hereafter cited as *STh.*)

could never find peace, because many sins cannot be seen or remembered. 10
The ancient writers also testify that such enumeration is not necessary. For 11
Chrysostom is quoted in the canons as saying: "I do not say that you should
appear in public or should accuse yourself before others. But I want you to
obey the prophet who says [Ps. 37:5, Vulgate], 'Reveal your way before the
Lord.' Therefore, confess your sins to God, the true judge, with prayer. Declare
your sins not with the tongue but with the memory of your conscience." The 12
marginal note in *Concerning Confession* (dist. 5, chap., "Consider") admits
that confession is a matter of human law. Nevertheless, confession is retained 13
among us both because of the great benefit of absolution and because of other
advantages for consciences.

[XXVI.] Concerning the Distinction of Foods

It has been a general conviction, not only of the people but also of those who 1
teach in the churches, that distinction of foods and similar human traditions
are useful works for meriting grace and making satisfaction for sins. That the 2
world thought so is evident from the fact that daily new ceremonies, new ordinances, new holy days, and new fasts were instituted and that the teachers in
places of worship exacted these works as necessary worship for meriting grace
and viciously terrified consciences if people omitted any of them. Much mis- 3
fortune has ensued in the church from this conviction concerning traditions.

In the first place, it has obscured the teaching concerning grace and the 4
righteousness of faith, which is the chief part of the gospel and which ought
to be present and prominent in the church so that the merit of Christ is well-
known and that faith, which believes in the forgiveness of sins on account of
Christ, may be exalted far above works and other acts of worship. That is why 5
Paul puts the greatest weight on this article and removes the law and human
traditions to show that Christian righteousness is something other than works
of this kind. Christian righteousness is faith that believes we are received into
grace on account of Christ. This teaching of Paul has been almost complete- 6
ly smothered by traditions, which have given rise to the opinion that grace
and righteousness are supposed to be merited through distinctions of food
and similar acts of worship. No mention of faith was made in the practice of 7
repentance;[164] only these works of satisfaction were proposed. The whole of
repentance was thought to consist of them.

---

164. *poenitentia*. See *CA* XII, n. 65.

8   In the second place, such traditions have also obscured God's commands.
9   For these traditions are placed far above God's commands. This alone was
     considered the Christian life: whoever observed festivals this way, prayed in
     this way, fasted in this way, and was dressed in this way was said to live a
10   spiritual, Christian life. On the other hand, other necessary good works were
     considered secular, unspiritual ways of life: that each person is obliged to act
     according to his or her calling—for example, that the father of a family works
     to support his wife and children and raises them in the fear of God; that the
     mother of a family bears children and looks after them; that a prince or rulers
11   govern a country; etc. Such works, commanded by God, had to be a "secular
     and imperfect" way of life, while the traditions had to have impressive names,
     so that only they were called "holy and perfect" works.[165] That is why there was
     no end or limit in the making of such traditions.

12   In the third place, such traditions turned out to be a heavy burden to
     consciences. For it was not possible to keep all the traditions, and yet peo-
13   ple thought that keeping them was required for true service to God. Gerson
     writes[166] that many fell into despair doing this. Some even committed suicide
14   because they had heard nothing about the comfort of Christ's grace. For read-
     ing the summists[167] and theologians discloses how consciences became con-
     fused when these people tried to collate the traditions and sought fairness[168]
15   in order to help consciences. They were so occupied with such efforts that
     in the meantime they ignored all wholesome Christian teaching concerning
     more important matters, such as faith, comfort in spiritual trials,[169] and the
     like. Many upright and learned people before our time have also complained
     a lot about the fact that such traditions cause much quarreling in the church
     and thereby prevent devout people from coming to a right understanding of
16–17 Christ. Gerson and others complained bitterly about this. In fact, Augustine
     also was displeased that consciences were burdened with so many traditions.
     That is why in this connection he gives instruction that no one should regard
     them as necessary.[170]

18   Consequently, our people have not taught about these matters out of mal-
19   ice or contempt toward ecclesiastical authority. But dire need has necessitated
     instruction about the above-mentioned matters, which have arisen from a
20   misunderstanding of tradition. For the gospel demands that in the church one

---

165. Scholastic theologians argued that monks, friars, and bishops lived *in status perfectionis*. See, for example, Thomas Aquinas, *STh* II, 2, q. 184, a. 5.

166. John Gerson, *Concerning the Spiritual Life* (*De vita spirituali animae*), lectio 2.

167. Authors of collections of cases of conscience, written to instruct confessors, often entitled *Summa summarum*.

168. 1580 Book of Concord: *epieikeia*. Often left untranslated, this Stoic term was used by reformers to mean equity, balance, or mitigation, especially with laws or social norms.

169. *hohe Anfechtungen*.

170. Augustine, Epistle 54 to Januarius, II.2 (*CSEL* 34:160, 9ff.; *NPNF*, ser. 1, 1:300).

In the second place, these traditions obscured the precepts of God because 8
traditions were preferred far more than the precepts of God. All Christianity
was thought to consist of the observance of certain holy days, rites, fasts,
and vestments. These observances possessed the most distinguished titles 9
because they were the "spiritual life" and the "perfect life." Meanwhile the 10
commands of God pertaining to one's calling were not praised: that the head
of the household should rear the children, that a mother should bear them,
that a prince should govern his country. These were considered as "worldly"
and "imperfect" works, far inferior to those splendid observances. This error 11
greatly tormented pious consciences. They grieved that they were bound to an
imperfect kind of life: in marriage, in government, or in other civil functions.
They admired the monks and others like them and falsely imagined that the
observances of such people were more pleasing to God.

In the third place, traditions brought great dangers to consciences because 12
it was impossible to keep them all, and yet people judged these observances to
be necessary acts of worship. Gerson writes that many fell into despair, and 13
some even took their own lives because they felt that they could not keep the
traditions. Meanwhile, they never heard the consolation that comes from the
righteousness of faith and from grace. We see that the summists and theolo- 14
gians collected the traditions, looking for a fair and gentle solution[171] for consciences. They did not altogether succeed; instead, in the process they entangled consciences even more. Schools[172] and sermons were so busy gathering 15
traditions that they had no time even to mention Scripture or to look for more
useful teachings concerning faith, the cross, hope, the dignity of civil affairs,
and the consolation of consciences in adverse temptations. Hence Gerson and 16
certain other theologians bitterly complained that they were so bogged down
by these quarrels over traditions that they could not turn their attention to a
better kind of teaching. Augustine also forbids burdening consciences with 17
such observances and prudently reminds Januarius that these things must be
observed as an indifferent matter; that is what he said.

Our people, therefore, must not be viewed as having taken up this cause by 18
chance or because they hate bishops, as some wrongly suspect. There was great 19
need to warn the churches of those errors which had grown out of a misunderstanding of traditions. For the gospel compels us to insist in the church on 20
the teaching concerning grace and the righteousness of faith, which can never
be understood if human beings think that they merit grace by observances of
their own choice.

---

171. *epieikeia.*
172. *scholae*: universities.

should and must emphasize the teaching concerning faith. But this cannot be understood if people imagine that grace is earned through self-chosen works.

21   Concerning this the following is taught. No one can earn grace, become reconciled with God, or make satisfaction for sin by observing the aforesaid human traditions. That is why they should not be made into a necessary

22   service of God. Reasons for this are cited from Scripture. In Matthew 15[:9] Christ defends the apostles for not observing customary traditions, saying:

23   "In vain do they worship me, teaching human precepts as doctrines." Since he calls them "vain worship" they must not be necessary. Then soon thereafter he says: "It is not what goes into the mouth that defiles a person" [Matt. 15:11].

24   Likewise, Paul says in Romans 14[:17]: "For the kingdom of God is not food

25   and drink," and in Colossians 2[:16]: "Therefore do not let anyone condemn

27   you in matters of food and drink or of observing . . . sabbaths." Peter says in Acts 15[:10-11]: "Now therefore why are you putting God to the test by placing on the neck of the disciples a yoke that neither our ancestors nor we have been able to bear? On the contrary, we believe that we will be saved through

28   the grace of the Lord Jesus, just as they will." Here Peter forbids the burdening of consciences with additional external ceremonies, whether from Moses or

29   others. In 1 Timothy 4[:1-3] such prohibitions as forbidding food, marriage, and the like are called teachings of the devil. For it is directly opposed to the gospel to institute or perform such works for the purpose of earning forgiveness of sin through them or to suppose that no one may be a Christian without such service.

30   But the accusation that our people, like Jovinian,[173] prohibit mortification and discipline will not be found in their writings, which reveal something

31   quite different. For concerning the holy cross they have always taught that

32   Christians are obliged to suffer, and that this is proper and real, not contrived, mortification.

33   In addition, it is also taught that all are obliged to conduct themselves regarding bodily discipline, such as fasting and other work, in such a way as not

34   to give occasion to sin, but not as if they earned grace by such works.[174] Such bodily discipline should not be limited only to specific days but should be

35   maintained continually. Christ speaks about this in Luke 21[:34]: "Be on guard

36   so that your hearts are not weighed down with dissipation," and [Mark 9:29:]

37   "This kind [of demon] can come out only through prayer and fasting."[175] Paul

38   says that he punished his body and enslaved it [1 Cor. 9:27], indicating that

---

173. A Roman ascetic of the fourth century who opposed the monastic teaching about merits and the stages of ethical perfection. (In fact, he did not oppose "mortification and discipline," as Jerome had contended in slanderous writings against him.)

174. See, for example, Luther, *The Freedom of the Christian* (1520) (WA 7:59, 24–60, 29; *LW* 31:358–59). The original text is in the singular. For the word "grace" the 1531 *editio princeps* reads "forgiveness of sins or would be thereby pronounced righteous before God."

175. Cited here according to the alternative reading in the NRSV, which corresponds to the German and Latin texts.

So they teach that we cannot merit grace or make satisfaction for sins 21 through the observance of human traditions. Hence observances of this kind are not to be thought of as necessary acts of worship. They add testimonies 22 from Scripture. In Matthew 15[:1-20] Christ defends the apostles for not observing a customary tradition, despite the fact that it was considered a neutral matter[176] and to have a connection with the purifications of the law. However, he says [Matt. 15:9]: "In vain do they worship me" with human precepts. So he does not require a useless act of worship. Shortly thereafter he 23 says [Matt. 15:11]: "It is not what goes into the mouth that defiles a person." 24 Again, Romans 14[:17]: "For the kingdom of God is not food and drink." 25 Colossians 2[:16]: "Therefore do not let anyone condemn you in matters of food and drink or of observing festivals . . . or sabbaths." *Again [Col. 2:20-21]:* 26 *"If with Christ you died to the elemental spirits of the universe, why do you live as if you still belonged to the world? Why do you submit to regulations, 'Do not handle, Do not taste, Do not touch'?"*[177] Peter says in Acts 15[:10-11]: "Now 27 therefore why are you putting God to the test by placing on the neck of the disciples a yoke that neither our ancestors nor we have been able to bear? On the contrary, we believe that we will be saved through the grace of the Lord Jesus, just as they will." Here Peter prohibits the burdening of consciences 28 with additional rites, whether of Moses or others. And 1 Timothy 4[:1-3] calls 29 the prohibition of food teachings of demons because to institute or perform such works for the purpose of meriting grace through them or to think that Christian righteousness might not be able to exist without such acts of worship conflicts with the gospel.

Here our adversaries charge that our people, like Jovinian, prohibit dis- 30 cipline and the mortification of the flesh. But something quite different may be detected in the writings of our people. For concerning the cross they have 31 always taught that Christians should endure afflictions. To be disciplined by 32 various afflictions and crucified with Christ is a true and serious, not a simulated, mortification.

In addition, they teach that all Christians should so train and restrain 33 themselves with bodily discipline, or bodily exercises and labors, that neither overexertion nor idleness may lure them to sin. But they do not teach that we merit forgiveness of sins or make satisfaction for them through such exercises. Such bodily discipline should always be encouraged, not only on a few prescribed 34 days. As Christ commands [Luke 21:34]: "Be on guard so that your hearts are 35 not weighed down with dissipation." Again [Mark 9:29]: "This kind [of demon] 36 can come out only through prayer and fasting." And Paul says: "I punish my 37 body and enslave it" [1 Cor. 9:27]. Here he clearly shows that he punished his 38

---

176. *media res:* the Latin equivalent of adiaphora, things that can be done or omitted without harming the conscience.

177. The 1531 *editio princeps* and the 1580 and 1584 Latin versions of the Book of Concord add the words in italics.

39 mortification should not serve the purpose of earning grace but of keeping the body in a condition that does not prevent performing the duties required by one's calling. So fasting in itself is not rejected. Instead, we reject making it a required service with prescribed days and foods, for this confuses the consciences.

40 Our side also retains many ceremonies and traditions, such as the order of the Mass and other singing, festivals, and the like, which serve to preserve
41 order in the church. At the same time, however, the people are taught that such external worship of God does not make them righteous before God and that it is to be observed without burdening consciences, that is, no one sins
42 by omitting it without causing offense. The ancient Fathers also maintained
43 such liberty with respect to external ceremonies. For in the East the festival of Easter was celebrated at a date different from that in Rome.[178] When some wanted to divide the church over this difference, others admonished them
44 that there was no need to have uniformity in such customs. As Irenaeus says: "Diversity in fasting does not dissolve unity in faith."[179] Furthermore, concerning such diversity in human ordinances, dist. 12 also states that they are
45 not in conflict with the unity of Christendom.[180] The *Tripartite History*, Book 9, gathers many examples of diverse church customs and establishes a useful Christian saying: "It was not the intention of the apostles to institute festivals but to teach faith and love."[181]

[XXVII.] Concerning Monastic Vows

1 In speaking of monastic vows, it is necessary, first of all, to consider how they were viewed earlier, what kind of life there was in the monasteries, and how much happened in them daily that was contrary not only to God's Word but
2 also to papal canons. For at the time of St. Augustine monastic vocations were voluntary. Later, when proper discipline and teaching became corrupted, monastic vows were contrived. With them, as in a prison of their own devising, people wanted to restore discipline.[182]

---

178. In Asia Minor, Easter was observed on the day of the Jewish Passover (Nisan 14), the day of the full moon after the spring equinox. In the West, as in Palestine and Egypt, it was observed on the Sunday following.

179. In Eusebius of Caesarea, *Ecclesiastical History* V, 24, 13 (*MPG* 20:493–98; *NPNF*, ser. 2, 1:243).

180. Gratian, *Decretum* I, dist. 12, chap. 10.

181. Cassiodorus, *Tripartite Ecclesiastical History* IX, 38, quoting from Socrates Scholasticus, *Ecclesiastical History* V, 22 (*MPG* 67:628; *NPNF*, ser. 2, 2:130).

182. Until the Benedictine rule gained ascendancy in the West in about the eighth century, there were a variety of monastic rules. Withdrawal from monastic life was originally allowable.

body not to merit forgiveness of sins through such discipline but to keep the body under control and fit for spiritual things and to carry out his responsibilities according to his calling. Therefore, fasting itself is not condemned, but 39 traditions that prescribe, with peril to conscience, certain days and foods, as if works of this kind were necessary acts of worship.

Nevertheless, many traditions are kept among us, such as the order of 40 readings in the Mass, holy days, etc., which are conducive to maintaining good order in the church. But at the same time, people are warned that such acts 41 of worship do not justify before God and that no punishable sin is committed if they are omitted without offense. Such freedom in human rites was not 42 unknown to the Fathers. For in the East, Easter was kept at a different time 43 than in Rome, and when the Romans accused the East of schism because of this difference, they were admonished by others that such customs need not be alike everywhere. Irenaeus says, "Disagreement about fasting does not dissolve 44 the unity in faith," and Pope Gregory[183] indicates (dist. 12) that such diversity does not damage the unity of the church. In the *Tripartite History*, Book IX, 45 many examples of dissimilar rites are collected, and this statement is made: "It was not the intention of the apostles to make decrees about festivals but to preach good conduct among people and godliness."

[XXVII.] Concerning Monastic Vows

What is taught among us concerning monastic vows will be better understood 1 if it is remembered what the condition of the monasteries was and how much was done every day in these monasteries that was contrary to the canons. In 2 Augustine's time they were voluntary associations. Afterward, wherever discipline became corrupt, vows were added for the purpose of restoring discipline, as in a carefully planned prison.

---

183. Perhaps from Pope Gregory I, *Letters*, bk. 9, ep. 12 (*MPL* 77: 955–58; *NPNF* 13:8–9).

3–4   In addition to monastic vows many other things were introduced, and a great number of bonds and burdens were laid on many even before they had attained an appropriate age.[184]

5   Many persons also entered monastic life in ignorance. Although they were not too young, they nevertheless did not sufficiently estimate and understand

6   their capabilities. All of those who were entangled and ensnared in this way were forced and compelled to remain in such bondage, in spite of the fact that

7   even papal canons would have set many of them free.[185] It was more difficult in nunneries than in monasteries, even though it would have been seemly to

8   spare the women as the weaker gender. Such rigor and severity also displeased many devout people in former times. For they certainly noticed that both boys and girls had been stuck away in monasteries for the sake of keeping them alive. They certainly also noticed how badly this arrangement turned out and

9   what offense and burdening of consciences it caused. Many people complained

10   that the canons were not respected at all. In addition, monastic vows have such a reputation that even many monks with little understanding were clearly displeased.

11   It was pretended that monastic vows would be equal to baptism, and that through monastic life one could earn forgiveness of sin and justification before

12   God.[186] Indeed, they added that one earns through monastic life not only righteousness and innocence, but also that through it one keeps the commands

13   and counsels written in the gospel.[187] In this way monastic vows were praised more highly than baptism. It was also said that one could obtain more merit through the monastic life than through all other walks of life, which had been ordered by God, such as the office of pastor or preacher, the office of ruler, prince, lord, and the like. (These all serve in their vocations according to God's

14   command, Word, and mandate without any contrived spiritual status.) None of these things can be denied, for one can find them in their own books.

15   Furthermore, whoever was so ensnared and ended up in the monastery learned little about Christ. At one time there were schools of Holy Scripture and other disciplines useful for the Christian church in the monasteries, so

---

184. The dedication of children to monastic life by their parents was common in the Middle Ages and allowed by canon law.

185. See above, n. 182.

186. The comparison of monastic profession and baptism was common in the Middle Ages. See, for example, Thomas Aquinas, *STh* II, 2, q. 189, a. 3 ad 3. "It may reasonably be said that through entering a religious order a person attains remission of all sins . . . wherefore it is read in the *Lives of the Fathers* that those entering a religious order attained the same grace as the baptized."

187. Medieval theologians, following a development that can be traced back to Tertullian, distinguished between "precepts of the gospel," which must be observed for salvation, and "counsels of the gospel," which are not obligatory but enable one to attain salvation "better and more quickly." See, for example, Bonaventure, *Brief Speech* (*Breviloquium*) V, 9. Thomas Aquinas, *STh* II, 1, q. 108, a. 4, states: "This is the difference between a counsel and a precept, that a precept implies necessity, but a counsel is left up to the choice of the one to whom it is given."

Many other observances were gradually added to the existing vows. 3
Moreover, these chains were put on many, contrary to the canons, before 4
they had reached legal age. Many entered this kind of life mistakenly, for 5
even though they were old enough, they could not assess their own strengths.
Those who were thus entangled were compelled to remain, even though some 6
could have been freed by appealing to the canons. This was more the case in 7
the monasteries of women than in those of men, although the weaker gender
should have been the more spared. Such rigor displeased many good people 8
before our time. They saw girls and boys thrust into monasteries for the sake
of survival. They saw the unfortunate results of such an arrangement, what
scandals it created, and what snares were laid for consciences. They regretted 9
that in this most perilous matter the authority of the canons was completely
neglected and despised. To make matters worse, vows had such a reputation 10
that it clearly displeased those monks of former times who were a little wiser.

People said that vows were equal to baptism, and they taught that vows 11
merited forgiveness of sins and justification before God through this kind
of life. Indeed, they added that monastic life merited not only righteous- 12
ness before God but even more: that it kept not only precepts but also
Evangelical counsels. In this way they were convinced that the monastic pro- 13
fession was far better than baptism and that the monastic life was more meritorious than the life of magistrates, pastors, and the like, who are subject to
God's commands in their callings without artificial religious observance. None 14
of these things can be denied, for they appear in their books.

What happened later on in the monasteries? In former times they were 15
schools of Holy Scripture and of other subjects useful to the church; bishops and pastors were taken from there. Now everything is different, and it is

16 that pastors and bishops were taken from the monasteries. But now the picture is quite different. In former times, people adopted the monastic life in order to study Scripture. Now they pretend that the monastic life is of such a nature that through it a person may earn God's grace and righteousness before God—indeed that it is a state of perfection, far above all other walks of life

17 instituted by God.[188] All this is mentioned, without any disrespect intended, in order that everyone may better grasp and understand what and how our people teach and preach.

18 In the first place, it is taught among us concerning those who are inclined to marry, that all those who are not suited for celibacy have the power, authority, and right to marry. For vows cannot annul God's order and command.

19 Now God's command reads (1 Cor. 7[:2]): "But because of cases of sexual immorality, each man should have his own wife and each woman her own

20 husband." Not only God's command urges, compels, and insists upon this, but also God's creation and order direct all to the state of marriage who are not blessed with the gift of virginity by a special work of God, according to God's own Word (Gen. 2[:18]): "It is not good that the man should be alone; I will make him a helper as his partner."

22 What objections can be raised against this? People may praise the vow and obligation as highly as they want, but they still cannot force the abrogation

23 of God's command. The teachers say that vows made contrary to papal law are not even binding.[189] How much less should they be binding or have legal standing when they are contrary to God's command!

24 If there were no reasons for allowing the annulment of the binding vows, popes would also not have given dispensation and release from them. For no human being has the right to break an obligation derived from divine laws.

25 That is why the popes were well aware that some balance should be used in
26 regard to this obligation and have often given dispensation, as in the case of the king of Aragon[190] and many others. If, then, dispensations were granted for the maintenance of temporal interests, how much more fairly should dispensations be granted for the sake of the souls' needs.

27 Next, why do our opponents insist so strongly that vows must be kept without first ascertaining whether a vow has integrity? For in matters within human
28 power a vow should not be forced but voluntary.[191] However, it is well known

---

188. For example, Thomas Aquinas, *STh* II, 2, q. 186, a. 1. The words *Stand* and *Stände* are translated "state" and "walks of life," respectively.

189. Gratian, *Decretum* II, chap. 20, q. 4, c. 2, states that a vow made by a monk without the consent of his abbot is without effect.

190. Ramiro II, a monk, was released from his vows after the death of his childless brother so that he might assume the throne. The story is told by John Gerson, *Concerning the Counsels of the Gospel and the State of Perfection* (*De consiliis evangelicis et statu perfectionis*), in his *Opera* II, 678c.

191. See Thomas Aquinas, *STh* II, 2, q. 88, a. 8. "A vow is a promise made to God. However, no one can obligate himself or herself for something in the power of another, but only for what is in his or her own power."

unnecessary to present an account of what is well known. In former times they were suitable places for learning. Now people pretend that this kind of life was instituted to merit grace and righteousness. Indeed, they proclaim that it is a state of perfection, and they greatly prefer it above all other kinds of life instituted by God. For this reason we have recounted these things, while exaggerating nothing out of malice, so that the teaching of our people concerning this matter may be better understood. 16 17

In the first place,[192] concerning those who marry our people teach that this is lawful for all who are not fit for celibacy, because vows cannot abrogate the institution and command of God. Moreover, this is the command of God [1 Cor. 7:2]: "Because of cases of sexual immorality, each man should have his own wife." Not only God's command, but also God's creation and institution drive those into marriage who, apart from a special work of God, are not exempted according to Genesis 2[:18]: "It is not good that the man should be alone." Consequently, those who comply with this command and institution of God do not sin. 18 19 20 21

What objection can be raised to this? No matter how anyone exaggerates the obligation of a vow, it still cannot be made to abrogate the command of God. The canons teach that every vow is subject to the right of a superior. How much less valid are the vows that are contrary to the commands of God! 22 23

Now if the obligation of vows could not be changed for any reasons, the Roman pontiffs would not have granted dispensations. For it is not lawful for a human being to repeal an obligation that is plainly a matter of divine right. However, the Roman pontiffs have prudently decided that such an obligation should be treated with fairness. That is why we read that they often granted dispensation from vows. Indeed, the story of the king of Aragon, who was recalled from a monastery, is well known, and there is no lack of examples in our time. 24 25 26 27

Furthermore, why do our adversaries exaggerate the obligation or effect of a vow while remaining silent about the nature of this vow, which should be in the realm of possibility, voluntary, and chosen freely and deliberately? Yet it is 28

---

192. The second argument begins in par. 36.

29 to what degree perpetual chastity lies within human power and ability. Moreover, there are few—men or women—who have taken monastic vows on their own, willingly and after due consideration. They were talked into taking monastic vows before they understood what was involved. At times, they were

30 also forced and driven to do so. Accordingly, it is not right to argue so rashly and insistently about the obligation of vows, in view of the fact that everyone confesses it is against the nature and integrity of a vow to be taken by force, but rather it should be taken with good counsel and due consideration.

31 Some canons and papal laws annul vows made under the age of fifteen years.[193] For they take into consideration that before this age a person does not have sufficient understanding to decide how possibly to determine or arrange

32 an entire life. Another canon concedes still more years to human frailty, for it

33 forbids taking monastic vows before the eighteenth year.[194] This provides an excuse and reason for a great many to leave the monasteries. For a majority entered the monastery in childhood before attaining such age.

34 Finally, even if the breaking of monastic vows might be censured, it could not be concluded from this that the marriage of those who broke them should

35 be dissolved. For St. Augustine, cited in *Marriage Matters* (q. 27, chap. 1),[195] says that such a marriage should not be dissolved. Now St. Augustine certainly does not have a low reputation in the Christian church, even though some have subsequently differed from him.

36 Although God's command concerning marriage frees and releases many from monastic vows, our people offer still more reasons why monastic vows are null and void. For all service of God instituted and chosen by human beings without God's command and authority to obtain righteousness and God's grace is contrary to God, the holy gospel, and God's decree, as Christ himself says (Matt. 15[:9]): "In vain do they worship me, teaching human pre-

37 cepts as doctrines." St. Paul also teaches everywhere that righteousness is not to be sought in our precepts and services of God contrived by human beings, but that righteousness and innocence before God come from faith and trust, when we believe that God receives us in grace for the sake of Christ, his only Son.

38 Now it is quite evident the monks have taught and preached that their contrived spiritual status makes satisfaction for sin and obtains God's grace and righteousness.[196] What is this but to diminish the glory and praise of the

39 grace of Christ and to deny the righteousness of faith? It follows from this that the customary vows have been improper and false services of God. That

40 is why they are also not binding. For a godless vow, made contrary to God's

---

193. Gratian, *Decretum* II, chap. 20, q. 1, c. 10.

194. Gratian, *Decretum* II, chap. 5.

195. *Nuptiarum.* Augustine, *Concerning the Goodness of Widowhood* (*De bono viduitatis*), chap. IX.12 (*CSEL* 41:317–18; *NPNF*, ser. 1, 3:445f.), cited in Gratian, *Decretum* II, chap. 27, q. 1, c. 41.

196. See Thomas Aquinas, as cited above, n. 187.

not known to what extent perpetual chastity is within human capability. How 29 many have taken the vow voluntarily and deliberately? Girls and boys are persuaded—sometimes even compelled—to take the vow before they are able to judge. That is why it is not fair to debate so narrow-mindedly about obligation, 30 when everyone concedes that it is contrary to the nature of the vow to make a promise that is neither voluntary nor deliberate.

Many canons annul vows contracted before the age of fifteen, because 31 before such an age a person does not seem to have sufficient judgment concerning the rest of his or her life. Another canon, conceding more to human 32 frailty, adds a few years, since it prohibits taking a vow before the age of eighteen. But whether we follow the one or the other, the overwhelming major- 33 ity have an excuse to leave the monastery since many took vows before they reached such an age.

Finally, even though the violation of the vow could perhaps be censured, 34 still it does not seem to follow immediately that the marriages of such people ought to be dissolved. For Augustine (cited in c. 27, q. 1, chap., "Of 35 Marriages") denies that they should be dissolved. His authority is not inconsiderable, although others have subsequently differed from him.

Moreover, although God's command concerning marriage appears to free 36 many from their vows, our people offer still another reason why vows may be invalid: every service of God instituted and chosen by human beings without the command of God, in order to merit justification and grace, is ungodly, just as Christ says [Matt. 15:9]: "In vain do they worship me, teaching human precepts as doctrines." Paul also teaches everywhere that righteousness is not 37 to be sought in our observances or acts of worship devised by human beings, but that it comes through faith to those who believe that they are received by God into grace on account of Christ.

However, very clearly the monks have taught that their humanly invented 38 observances make satisfaction for sins and merit grace and justification. What is this but to detract from the glory of Christ and to obscure and deny the righteousness of faith? It follows, therefore, that such customary vows were 39 ungodly acts of worship and are invalid for that reason. For an ungodly vow 40 command, is null and void, just as the canons also teach that an oath should not bind a person to sin.[197]

|1 St. Paul says in Galatians 5[:4]: "You who want to be justified by the law have cut yourselves off from Christ; you have fallen away from grace."

|2 Therefore, those who want to be justified by vows are also cut off from Christ

|3 and fall away from the grace of God. For they rob Christ, who alone justifies, of his honor and give such honor to their vows and monastic life.

|4 No one can deny that the monks also taught and preached that they become righteous and earn forgiveness of sins through their vows and monastic life. In fact, they have contrived an even more useless and absurd claim,

|5 saying that they imparted their good works to others. Now if someone wanted to take all this to an extreme and bring accusation against them, how many items could be assembled that the monks themselves are now ashamed of

|6 and wish had never occurred! Besides all this, they persuaded the people that these humanly contrived spiritual orders were states of Christian perfection.[198]

|7–48 Surely this means to praise works as the means of becoming righteous. Now it is no small offense in the Christian church to present to the people a service of God, which human beings have contrived without God's command, teaching that such service of God makes people innocent and righteous before God. For righteousness of faith, which ought to be emphasized most, is obscured when people are bedazzled with this strange angelic spirituality and false pretense of poverty, humility, and chastity.[199]

|9 In addition, the commands of God and proper, true service of God are obscured when people hear that only monks must be in the state of perfection. For Christian perfection is to fear God earnestly with the whole heart and yet also to have a sincere confidence, faith, and trust that we have a gracious, merciful God because of Christ; that we may and should pray for and request from God whatever we need and confidently expect help from him in all affliction, according to each person's vocation and walk of life; and that meanwhile we

|0 should diligently do external good works and attend to our calling. This is true perfection and true service of God—not being a mendicant or wearing a black

|1 or gray cowl, etc. However, the common people form many harmful opinions

|2 from false praise of the monastic life, such as when they hear the state of celibacy praised above all measure. For it follows that their consciences are troubled

|3 because they are married. When the common people hear that only mendicants may be perfect, they cannot know that they may keep possessions and

|4 transact business without sin. When the people hear that it is only a "counsel" [of the gospel] not to take revenge, some will conclude that it is not sinful to

---

197. Gratian, *Decretum* II, chap. 22, q. 4, c. 22.

198. Cited above, n. 188.

199. By the later Middle Ages the monastic vow was centered on three things: poverty, chastity, and obedience. See Thomas Aquinas, *STh* II, 2, q. 186, a. 7. "The religious state . . . comprises three vows of obedience, continence, and poverty, in which vows religious perfection consists."

made contrary to God's command is invalid. For no vow ought to be a bond of iniquity, as the canon says.

Paul says [Gal. 5:4]: "You who want to be justified by the law have cut 41 yourselves off from Christ; you have fallen away from grace." Therefore those 42 who want to be justified by vows fall away from Christ and are cut off from grace. For those who ascribe justification to vows, ascribe to their own works 43 what properly belongs to the glory of Christ. It cannot be denied that the 44 monks taught that they were justified and merited forgiveness of sins through vows and observances. In fact, they added greater absurdities to this when they boasted that they could transfer their works to others. If anyone wants to 45 exaggerate this out of hatred, how much could be collected about which the monks themselves would be ashamed! Moreover, they persuaded people that 46 their humanly invented observances constituted a state of Christian perfection. 47 Is this not ascribing justification to works? It is no minor scandal in the church 48 to propose to the people a certain act of worship invented by human beings without a command of God and to teach that such worship justifies human beings. For the righteousness of faith, which ought to be taught in the church most of all, is obscured when these astonishing angelic observances and this pretense of poverty, humility, and celibacy are blinding people.

Furthermore, the precepts of God and true worship of God are obscured 49 when people hear that only monks are in a state of perfection. For Christian perfection means earnestly to fear God and, at the same time, to have great faith and to trust that we have a gracious God on account of Christ; to ask for and to expect with certainty help from God in all things that are to be borne in connection with our calling; and, in the meantime, diligently to do good works for others and to serve in our calling. True perfection and true worship of God 50 consist in all these things, not in celibacy, mendicancy, or shabby clothing. On 51 that account, the people form many pernicious opinions from such false commendations of monastic life. They hear celibacy praised without restraint, and 52 so they live in marriage with a troubled conscience. They hear that only mendi- 53 cants are perfect, and so they keep their possessions or engage in business with a troubled conscience. They hear that it is an Evangelical counsel not to take 54 revenge, and so some are not afraid to take vengeance in their private lives, since they are told that this is prohibited by a counsel and not by a precept.

55 take revenge outside their office. Still others think that revenge is not right for Christians at all, even on the part of political authority.[200]

56
57 Many examples are recorded of people leaving wife and child—even their civil office—and putting themselves into a monastery. This, they said, is fleeing from the world and seeking a life that is more pleasing to God than the other life. They were unable to realize that one should serve God by observing the commandments he has given and not through the commandments con-

58 trived by human beings. Now the life supported by God's command is certainly a good and perfect state, but the life not supported by God's command

59 is a dangerous state. It has been necessary to keep people well informed about such matters.

60 In former times, Gerson also rebuked the errors of the monks about perfection. He showed that it was an innovation in his day to speak of monastic life as a state of perfection.[201]

61 There are so many ungodly notions and errors attached to monastic vows: that they justify and make righteous before God; that they must be Christian perfection; that through them a person may keep both the counsels of the gospel and the commandments; that they contain works of supererogation,

62 beyond what is owed to God.[202] Since, then, all of this is false, useless, and humanly contrived, monastic vows are null and void.[203]

[XXVIII.] Concerning the Power of Bishops[204]

1 Many and various things have been written in former times concerning the power of bishops. Some have improperly mixed the power of bishops with

2 the secular sword, and such careless mixture has caused many extensive wars, uprisings, and rebellions. For the bishops, under the guise of power given to them by Christ, have not only introduced new forms of worship[205] and burdened consciences with reserved cases[206] and with forcible use of the ban, but they also took it upon themselves to set up and depose emperors and kings

3 according to their pleasure. Such outrage has long since been condemned

4 by learned and devout people in Christendom. That is why our people have

---

200. A veiled reference to the teaching of some Anabaptists and others not allied with the reformers. For par. 54–55 see *CA* XXVII.12 and n. 188.

201. See John Gerson, *Concerning the Counsels of the Gospel and the State of Perfection* (*De consiliis evangelicis et statu perfectionis*), in his *Opera*, II, 680.

202. Works in addition to those that every Christian is obliged to perform, such as the "counsels of the gospel," which earned a higher degree of merit.

203. The 1531 *editio princeps* contains some variations of the text of this article without, however, varying in substance. See the variations in *BSLK* 110–13.

204. Based on an earlier draft entitled "Concerning the Power of the Keys." See the text in *BSLK* 120–24.

205. *Gottesdienst*, literally, service of God. See above *CA* XXVI and XXVII.

206. Cases in which absolution was reserved for bishops or the pope.

Others err still more, for they judge that all magistracy and all civil offices are unworthy of Christians and in conflict with an Evangelical counsel. 55

Cases can be read of people who, deserting marriage and participation in the administration of the state, withdrew into a monastery. They called this "fleeing from the world" and "seeking a holy kind of life." They did not see that God is to be served in those commands he himself has handed down, not in commands invented by human beings. The good and perfect kind of life is one that has God's command. It was necessary for people to be instructed about these matters. 56 57 58 59

Before our time, Gerson, too, reproved the error of the monks concerning perfection and testified that it was a novelty in his day to say that the monastic life was a state of perfection. 60

So there are many ungodly opinions attached to vows: that they justify, that they constitute Christian perfection, that monks keep both the counsels and precepts, that they do works of supererogation. All these things, because they are false and without substance, make vows invalid. 61 62

[XXVIII.] Concerning the Church's Power

In former times, there were serious controversies about the power of bishops, in which some people improperly mixed the power of the church and the power of the sword. Tremendous wars and rebellions resulted from this confusion, while the pontiffs, relying on the power of the keys, not only instituted new forms of worship and burdened consciences with reservations of cases and violent excommunications but also attempted to transfer earthly kingdoms and to take away from emperors the right to rule. Devout and learned people have long since condemned these vices in the church. That is why our people 1 2 3 4 been compelled, for the sake of comforting consciences, to indicate the difference between spiritual and secular power, sword, and authority. They have taught that, for the sake of God's command, everyone should honor and esteem with all reverence both authorities and powers as the two highest gifts of God on earth.

5   Our people teach as follows. According to the gospel the power of the keys[207] or of the bishops is a power and command of God to preach the gospel,

6   to forgive or retain sin, and to administer and distribute the sacraments. For Christ sent out the apostles with this command (John 20[:21-23]): "As the Father has sent me, so I send you. . . . Receive the Holy Spirit. If you forgive the sins of any, they are forgiven them; if you retain the sins of any, they are retained."

8   The same power of the keys or of the bishops is used and exercised only by teaching and preaching God's Word and by administering the sacraments to many persons or to individuals, depending on one's calling. Not bodily but eternal things and benefits are given in this way, such as eternal righteousness,

9   the Holy Spirit, and eternal life. These benefits cannot be obtained except through the office of preaching and through the administration of the holy sacraments. For St. Paul says [Rom. 1:16]: "The gospel is the power of God

10   for salvation to everyone who has faith." Now inasmuch as the power of the church or of the bishops bestows eternal benefits and is used and exercised only through the office of preaching, it does not interfere at all with public

11   order and secular authority. For secular authority deals with matters altogether different from the gospel. Secular power does not protect the soul but, using the sword and physical penalties, it protects the body and goods against external violence.[208]

12   That is why one should not mix or confuse the two authorities, the spiritual and the secular. For spiritual power has its command to preach the gospel and

13   to administer the sacraments. It should not invade an alien office. It should not set up and depose kings. It should not annul or disrupt secular law and obedience to political authority. It should not make or prescribe laws for the

14   secular power concerning secular affairs. For Christ himself said [John 18:36]:

15   "My kingdom is not from this world." And again [Luke 12:14]: "Who set me

16   to be a judge or arbitrator over you?" And St. Paul in Philippians 3[:20]: "Our

17   citizenship is in heaven." And in 2 Corinthians 10[:4-5]: "For the weapons of our warfare are not merely human, but they have divine power to destroy strongholds . . . arguments and every proud obstacle raised up against the knowledge of God."

18   In this way our people distinguish the offices of the two authorities and powers and direct that both be honored as the highest gifts of God on earth.

---

207. The original title of this article. See the Torgau Articles.
208. *Gewalt,* otherwise translated "power."

have been compelled, for the sake of instructing consciences, to show the difference between the power of the church and the power of the sword. They have taught that because of the command of God both are to be devoutly respected and honored as the highest blessings of God on earth.

However, they believe that, according to the gospel, the power of the 5 keys or the power of the bishops is the power of God's mandate to preach the gospel, to forgive and retain sins, and to administer the sacraments. For 6 Christ sent out the apostles with this command [John 20:21-23]: "As the Father has sent me, so I send you. . . . Receive the Holy Spirit. If you forgive the sins of any, they are forgiven them; if your retain the sins of any, they are retained." And Mark 16[:15]: "Go . . . and proclaim the good news to the 7 whole creation. . . ."

This power is exercised only by teaching or preaching the gospel and by 8 administering the sacraments either to many or to individuals, depending on one's calling. For not bodily things but eternal things, eternal righteousness, the Holy Spirit, eternal life, are being given. These things cannot come about 9 except through the ministry of Word and sacraments, as Paul says [Rom. 1:16]: "The gospel . . . is the power of God for salvation to everyone who has faith." And Psalm 119[:50]: "Your promise gives me life." Therefore, since 10 this power of the church bestows eternal things and is exercised only through the ministry of the Word, it interferes with civil government as little as the art of singing interferes with it. For civil government is concerned with things 11 other than the gospel. For the magistrate protects not minds but bodies and goods from manifest harm and constrains people with the sword and physical penalties. The gospel protects minds from ungodly ideas, the devil, and eternal death.

Consequently, the powers of church and civil government must not be 12 mixed. The power of the church possesses its own command to preach the gospel and administer the sacraments. It should not usurp the other's duty, 13 transfer earthly kingdoms, abrogate the laws of magistrates, abolish lawful obedience, interfere with judgments concerning any civil ordinances or contracts, prescribe to magistrates laws concerning the form of government that should be established. As Christ says [John 18:36]: "My kingdom is not from 14 this world." And again [Luke 12:14]: "Who set me to be a judge or arbitra- 15 tor over you?" And St. Paul says in Philippians 3[:20], "Our citizenship is in 16 heaven," and in 2 Corinthians 10[:4]: "For the weapons of our warfare are not 17 merely human, but they have divine power to destroy . . . arguments. . . ."

In this way our people distinguish the duties of the two powers, and they 18 command that both be held in honor and acknowledged as a gift and blessing of God.

19   However, where bishops possess secular authority and the sword, they possess them not as bishops by divine right but by human, imperial right, given by Roman emperors and kings for the secular administration of their lands. That has nothing at all to do with the office of the gospel.

21   Consequently, according to divine right it is the office of the bishop to preach the gospel, to forgive sin, to judge doctrine and reject doctrine that is contrary to the gospel, and to exclude from the Christian community the ungodly whose ungodly life is manifest—not with human power but with

22   God's Word alone. That is why parishioners and churches owe obedience to bishops, according to this saying of Christ (Luke 10[:16]): "Whoever listens

23   to you listens to me." But whenever they teach, institute, or introduce something contrary to the gospel, we have God's command in such a case not to be

24   obedient (Matt. 7[:15]): "Beware of false prophets." And St. Paul in Galatians 1[:8]: "But even if we or an angel from heaven should proclaim to you a gos-

25   pel contrary to what we proclaimed to you, let that one be accursed!" And in 2 Corinthians 13[:8]: "For we cannot do anything against the truth, but only

26   for the truth." And again [2 Cor. 13:10]: ". . . using the authority that the

27   Lord has given me for building up and not for tearing down." Canon law also commands the same in Part II, Question 7, in the chapters entitled "Priests"

28   and "Sheep."[209] And St. Augustine writes in the letter against Petilian that one should not obey bishops, even if they have been regularly elected, when they err or teach and command something contrary to the holy, divine Scripture.[210]

29   Whatever other power and jurisdiction bishops have in various matters, such as marriage or tithes,[211] they have them by virtue of human right. However, when bishops neglect such duties, the princes are obligated—whether they like it or not—to administer justice to their subjects for the sake of peace, in order to prevent discord and great unrest in their lands.

30   Furthermore, it is also debated whether bishops have the power to establish ceremonies in the church as well as regulations concerning food, festivals,

31   and the different orders of the clergy. For those who grant bishops this power cite this saying of Christ (John 16[:12-13]): "I still have many things to say to you, but you cannot bear them now. When the Spirit of truth comes, he will

32   guide you into all the truth." They also cite the example in Acts 15[:20, 29],[212]

33   where the eating of blood and what is strangled was prohibited. They appeal as well to the transference of the sabbath to Sunday—contrary to the Ten

---

209. *Sacerdotes* and *Oves.* Gratian, *Decretum* II, q. 7, c. 8, 13. Compare Luther, *That a Christian Assembly . . . Has the Right . . . to Judge All Teaching . . .* (1523) (WA 11:408–16; LW 39:301–14).

210. Augustine, *Concerning the Unity of the Church* (*De unitate ecclesiae*) 11, 28 (*MPL* 43:410f.; CSEL 52:264). This is his second response to Petilian.

211. The payment of one-tenth of the gross income from all lands and industries to the church. Such obligation was also part of Mosaic and Roman law, and it first became an obligation to the church in Ireland in the sixth century.

212. These passages were cited by John Eck, *Enchiridion of Commonplaces* (*Enchiridion Locorum Communiorum*) (Grand Rapids: Baker, 1979), chap. 1 (pp. 9, 13, 14), chap. 2 (p. 19), and chap. 4 (p. 46).

If bishops possess any power of the sword, they possess it not through a 19 command of the gospel but by human right, granted by kings and emperors for the civil administration of their lands. This, however, is a different function from the ministry of the gospel.

So, when asking about the jurisdiction of bishops, one must distinguish 20 political rule from the church's jurisdiction. Consequently, according to the 21 gospel, or, as they say, by divine right, this jurisdiction belongs to the bishops as bishops (that is, to those to whom the ministry of Word and sacraments has been committed): to forgive sins, to reject teaching that opposes the gospel, and to exclude from the communion of the church the ungodly whose ungodliness is known—doing all this not with human power but by the Word. In this regard, churches are bound by divine right to be obedient to 22 the bishops, according to the saying [Luke 10:16], "Whoever listens to you listens to me."

However, when they teach or establish anything contrary to the gospel, 23 churches have a command from God that prohibits obedience. Matthew 7[:15]: "Beware of false prophets." Galatians 1[:8]: "If . . . an angel from heaven 24 should proclaim to you a gospel contrary to what we proclaimed to you, let that one be accursed!" 2 Corinthians 13[:8, 10]: "For we cannot do anything 25 against the truth, but only for the truth," and, "Using the authority that the 26 Lord has given me for building up and not for tearing down." The canons 27 require the same thing in Part II, q. 7, chaps. "Priests" and "Sheep." Augustine 28 also says in the letter against Petilian that one should not agree with catholic bishops if they perchance should err and hold anything contrary to the canonical Scriptures of God.

If they possess any other power or jurisdiction in deciding certain cases 29 (for example, concerning marriage or tithes, etc.), they have it by human right. Wherever these overseers leave off doing such things, princes are compelled— even against their will—to administer justice to their subjects for the sake of maintaining public peace.

Moreover, it is debated whether bishops or pastors have the right to insti- 30 tute ceremonies in the church and make laws concerning food, holy days, ranks or orders of ministers, etc. Those who attribute this right to bishops cite 31 this testimony [John 16:12-13]: "I still have many things to say to you, but you cannot bear them now. When the Spirit of truth comes, he will guide you into all the truth." They also cite the example of the apostles [Acts 15:20, 29] who 32 commanded abstinence from blood and from what is strangled. The sabbath, 33 which—contrary to the Decalogue, it seems—was changed to Sunday, is also

Commandments, as they view it. No other example is so strongly emphasized and quoted as the transference of the sabbath. Thereby they want to maintain that the power of the church is great, because it has dispensed with and altered part of the Ten Commandments.[213]

34   Concerning this question, our people teach that bishops do not have the power to institute or establish something contrary to the gospel, as is indicated above and as is taught by canon law throughout the ninth distinction.[214] Now

35 it is patently contrary to God's command and Word to make laws out of opinions or to require that by observing them a person makes satisfaction for sin

36 and obtains grace. For the honor of Christ's merit is slandered when we take it

37 upon ourselves to earn grace through such ordinances. It is also obvious that, because of this notion, human ordinances have multiplied beyond calculation while the teaching concerning faith and the righteousness of faith have been almost completely suppressed. Daily new festivals and new fasts have been commanded; new ceremonies and new venerations of the saints have been instituted in order that by such works grace and everything good might be earned from God.

39   Moreover, those who institute human ordinances also act contrary to God's command when they attach sin to food, days, and similar things and burden Christendom with bondage to the law, as if in order to earn God's grace there had to be such service of God among Christians like the Levitical service,[215]

40 which God supposedly commanded the apostles and bishops to establish, as some have written. It is quite believable that some bishops have been deceived

41 by the example of the Law of Moses. This is how countless ordinances came into being: for example, that it is supposed to be a mortal sin to do manual labor on festivals, even when it offends no one else; that it is a mortal sin to omit the seven hours;[216] that some foods defile the conscience; that fasting is a work that appeases God; that in a reserved case sin is not forgiven unless one first asks to be forgiven by the person for whom the case is reserved—despite the fact that canon laws do not speak of the reservation of guilt but only of the reservation of church penalties.[217]

42   Where, then, did the bishops get the right and power to impose such ordinances on Christendom and to ensnare consciences? For in Acts 15[:10] St. Peter prohibits placing the yoke on the necks of the disciples. And St. Paul tells the Corinthians [2 Cor. 10:8] that they have been given authority for building up and not for tearing down. Why then do they increase sin with such ordinances?

---

213. Thomas Aquinas, *STh* II, 2, q. 122, a. 4 ad 4. "The observation of the Lord's Day [Sunday] in the new law succeeded the observation of the sabbath, not from the power of a prescribed law, but from the power of the church's constitution and the custom of the Christian people."

214. Gratian, *Decretum* I, dist. 9, chaps. 8ff.

215. A reference to Old Testament prescriptions, for example in the Book of Leviticus.

216. The canonical hours, or seven daily hours of prayer, prescribed for members of religious orders and often observed by other Christians.

217. See above, n. 206.

cited. No example is brought up more often than this change of the sabbath. Great, they contend, is the power of the church, that it dispensed with a commandment of the Decalogue!

However, concerning this question, our people teach, as has been shown 34 above, that bishops do not have the power to establish anything contrary to the gospel. The canons disclose this throughout dist. 9. Furthermore, it is con- 35 trary to Scripture to establish traditions in order that, by observing them, we may make satisfaction for sins and merit justification. For the glory of Christ's 36 merit is violated when we think that we are justified by such observances. 37 However, it is evident that because of this notion countless traditions have arisen in the church, while the teaching concerning faith and the righteousness of faith has been suppressed. For repeatedly more holy days were created, fasts were announced, and new ceremonies and orders were instituted, because the authors of these things imagined that they merited grace through such works. So the penitential canons increased in former times, and we can still see traces 38 of them in the satisfactions.

Again, the authors of traditions act contrary to the command of God when 39 they attach sin to food, days, and similar things and burden the church with the bondage of the law, as if, in order to merit justification, there had to be acts of worship among Christians similar to the Levitical ones, and as if God had commissioned the apostles and bishops to institute them. For some have 40 written this way, and the pontiffs seem to have been deceived in some measure by the example of the Law of Moses. From this came burdens such as these: 41 that it is a mortal sin to do manual labor on holy days, even when it does not offend others; that certain foods pollute the conscience; that fasting, when it is not natural but inflicts bodily pain, is a work pleasing to God; that it is a mortal sin to omit the canonical hours; that in a reserved case a sin cannot be forgiven without the approval of the person who has reserved the case, although the canons themselves do not speak here about reserving guilt but only of reserving ecclesiastical penalties.

Where did the bishops get the right to impose such traditions on the 42 churches in order to ensnare consciences? Given the fact that Peter prohibits putting a yoke on the disciples and Paul says that they were given power to build up not to tear down, why do they increase sins through such traditions?

43   Indeed, clear sayings of divine Scripture prohibit the establishment of such ordinances for the purpose of earning God's grace or as if they were necessary

44   for salvation. St. Paul says in Colossians 2[:16-17]: "Therefore do not let anyone condemn you in matters of food and drink or of observing festivals, new moons, or sabbaths. These are only a shadow of what is to come, but the sub-

45   stance belongs to Christ." Again [Col. 2:20-23]: "If with Christ you died to the elemental spirits of the universe, why do you live as if you still belonged to the world? Why do you submit to regulations, 'Do not handle, Do not taste, Do not touch?' All these regulations refer to things that perish with use; they are simply human commands and teachings. These have indeed an appearance of

46   wisdom. . . ." Again, in Titus 1[:14] St. Paul clearly prohibits paying attention to Jewish myths or human commandments, which obstruct the truth.

47   In Matthew 15[:14] Christ himself also speaks of those who drive the people to human commandments: "Let them alone; they are blind guides of the

48   blind." And he rejects such service of God, saying [Matt. 15:13]: "Every plant that my heavenly Father has not planted will be uprooted."

49   If, then, bishops have the power to burden the churches with innumerable ordinances and to ensnare consciences, why does divine Scripture so frequently prohibit the making and keeping of human ordinances? Why does it call them teachings of the devil? Could the Holy Spirit possibly have warned against all this in vain?

50   Inasmuch as it is contrary to the gospel to establish such regulations as necessary to appease God and earn grace, it is not at all proper for the bishops to

51   compel observation of such services of God. For in Christendom the teaching of Christian freedom must be preserved, namely, that bondage to the law is not necessary for justification, as Paul writes in Galatians 5[:1]: "For freedom Christ has set us free. Stand firm, therefore, and do not submit again to the

52   yoke of slavery." For the chief article of the gospel must be maintained, that we obtain the grace of God through faith in Christ without our merit and do not earn it through service of God instituted by human beings.

53   How, then, should Sunday and other similar church ordinances and ceremonies be regarded? Our people reply[218] that bishops or pastors may make regulations for the sake of good order in the church, but not thereby to obtain God's grace, to make satisfaction for sin, or to bind consciences, nor to regard such as a service of God or to consider it a sin when these rules are broken

54   without giving offense. So St. Paul prescribed in Corinthians that women should cover their heads in the assembly [1 Cor. 11:5], and that preachers in the assembly should not all speak at once, but in order, one after the other [1 Cor. 14:30-33].

55   Such regulation belongs rightfully in the Christian assembly for the sake of love and peace, to be obedient to bishops and pastors in such cases, and to keep

---

218. A reply was called for since John Eck had attacked the Lutherans for erroneous views of the Lord's Day in his *404 Theses*, nos. 177–79.

Nevertheless, there are clear testimonies that prohibit the establishment of 43 traditions for the purpose of appeasing God or as if they were necessary for salvation. Paul says in Colossians 2[:16, 20-23]: "Therefore do not let anyone condemn you in matters of food and drink or of observing festivals, new moons, or sabbaths," and, "If with Christ you died to the elemental spirits of the universe, 45 why do you live as if you still belonged to the world? Why do you submit to regulations, 'Do not handle, Do not taste, Do not touch'? All these regulations refer to things that perish with use; they are simply human commands and teachings. These have indeed an appearance of wisdom." Titus 1[:14]: "Not paying atten- 46 tion to Jewish myths or to commandments of those who reject the truth . . ."

Christ says in Matthew 15[:14], concerning those who require traditions: 47 "Let them alone; they are blind guides of the blind." And he rejects such acts 48 of worship [Matt. 15:13]: "Every plant that my heavenly Father has not planted will be uprooted."

If bishops have the right to burden consciences with such traditions, why 49 does Scripture so often prohibit the establishment of traditions? Why does it call them teachings of demons? Did the Holy Spirit warn against them in vain?

Therefore, it follows that it is not lawful for bishops to institute such acts 50 of worship or require them as necessary, because ordinances that are instituted as necessary or with the intention of meriting justification conflict with the gospel. For it is necessary to retain the teaching concerning Christian freedom 51 in the churches, that bondage to the law is not necessary for justification, as it is written in Galatians [5:1]: "Do not submit again to a yoke of slavery." It is 52 necessary to retain the chief article of the gospel: that we obtain grace through faith in Christ, not through certain observances or through acts of worship instituted by human beings.

What, therefore, should one think of Sunday and similar rites in places 53 of worship? To this our people reply that it is lawful for bishops or pastors to establish ordinances so that things are done in the church in an orderly fashion, not so that we may make satisfaction for our sins through them or so that consciences may be obliged to regard them as necessary acts of worship. 54 Thus, Paul ordered that women should cover their heads in the assembly [1 Cor. 11:5] and that interpreters should be heard in the church in an orderly way [1 Cor. 14:30].

It is fitting for the churches to comply with such ordinances for the sake 55 of love and tranquillity and to keep them insofar as they do not offend others.

56 such order to the extent that no one offends another—so that there may not be disorder or unruly conduct in the church. However, consciences should not be burdened by holding that such things are necessary for salvation or by considering it a sin when they are violated without giving offense to others; just as no one would say that a woman commits a sin if, without offending people, she leaves the house with her head uncovered.

57 The same applies to the regulation of Sunday, Easter, Pentecost, or similar
58 festivals and customs. For those who think that the sabbath had to be replaced
59 by Sunday are very much mistaken. For Holy Scripture did away with the sabbath, and it teaches that after the revelation of the gospel all ceremonies of the
60 old law may be given up. Nevertheless, the Christian church instituted Sunday because it became necessary to set apart a specific day so that the people might know when to assemble; and the church was all the more pleased and inclined to do this so that the people might have an example of Christian freedom and so that everyone would know that neither the keeping of the sabbath nor any other day is necessary.

61 There are many faulty debates about the transformation of the law, the ceremonies of the New Testament, and the change of the sabbath.[219]

They have all arisen from the false and erroneous opinion that in Christianity one would have to have services of God that correspond to the Levitical or Jewish ones, and that Christ commanded the apostles and the bish-
62 ops to invent new ceremonies that were necessary for salvation. Christianity has been permeated with these kinds of errors because the righteousness of
63 faith was not taught or preached with purity and sincerity. Some argue that although Sunday cannot be kept on the basis of divine law, it must be kept almost as if it were divine law; and they prescribe the kind and amount of work
64 that may be done on the day of rest. But what else are such debates except snares of conscience? For although they presume to moderate and mitigate[220] human ordinances, there certainly cannot be any mitigation and moderation as long as the opinion remains and prevails that they are necessary. Now this opinion will persist as long as no one knows anything about the righteousness of faith and Christian freedom.

65 The apostles directed that one should abstain from blood and from what is strangled. But who observes this now? Yet those who do not observe it commit no sin. For the apostles themselves did not want to burden consciences with
66 such bondage, but prohibited such eating for a time to avoid offense. For in this ordinance one must pay attention to the chief part of Christian doctrine which is not abolished by this decree.[221]

---

219. For example, Thomas Aquinas, *STh* II, 1, q. 103, considers such questions as whether the ceremonies of the law antedated the law, whether they ceased when Christ came, and whether it is a mortal sin to observe them subsequent to Christ's coming.

220. *Epikeiziern*, a German verb, from the Greek noun *epieikeia*, meaning "equity." Aristotle used the term to describe the sensible fulfillment of a law. See above, *CA* XXVI.14, n. 168.

221. The so-called apostolic decree in Acts 15:23-29.

Thus, everything may be done in an orderly fashion in the churches without confusion, but in such a way that consciences are not burdened by thinking 56 such things are necessary for salvation or that they sin when violating them without offense. Just as no one would say that a woman commits a sin by leaving the house with her head uncovered in an inoffensive way.

Such is the case with the observance of Sunday, Easter, Pentecost, and 57 similar festivals and rites. For those who judge that the necessary observance 58 of Sunday in place of the sabbath was instituted by the church's authority are mistaken. Scripture, not the church, abrogated the sabbath. For after the 59 revelation of the gospel all Mosaic ceremonies can be omitted. Yet, since it 60 was necessary to establish a certain day so that the people would know when they should assemble, it appears that the church designated Sunday for this purpose. Apparently, this was even more pleasing because people would have an example of Christian freedom and would know that it was not necessary to keep either the sabbath or any other day.

There are still tremendous debates concerning the change of the law, con- 61 cerning ceremonies of the new law, concerning the change of the sabbath, all of which have arisen from the false assumption that worship in the church should be like the Levitical worship and that Christ commissioned the apostles and bishops to devise new ceremonies that were necessary for salvation. 62 These errors crept into the church when the righteousness of faith was not taught with sufficient clarity. Some argue that the observance of Sunday is not 63 "in fact" of divine right, but "as if it were" of divine right, and they prescribe to what extent one is allowed to work on holy days. What are debates of this 64 kind but snares for consciences? For although they try to bring equity to[222] the traditions, fairness can never be achieved as long as the opinion remains that they are necessary. This opinion necessarily persists where righteousness of faith and Christian freedom are ignored.

The apostles commanded abstention from blood, etc. Who keeps this com- 65 mand now? Those who do not keep it certainly do not sin, because the apostles did not wish to burden consciences through such bondage. They issued the prohibition for a time to avoid scandal. For the general intention of the gospel 66 must be considered in connection with the decree.

---

222. *epiikeizare.* See note 220.

67 Hardly any of the ancient canons are observed according to the letter. Many of their rules fall daily into complete disuse, even among those who observe such
68 ordinances most diligently. Consciences can neither be counseled nor helped unless we keep this moderation in mind: that such ordinances are not to be considered necessary, and even disregarding them does no harm to consciences.

Bishops could easily foster obedience if they did not insist on the obser-
69 vance of ordinances that cannot be observed without sin. However, now they
70 engage in prohibiting both kinds of the holy sacrament or prohibiting marriage for the clergy; they admit no one to the ministry who refuses to swear an oath not to preach this doctrine, even though it is undoubtedly in accord with the holy gospel. Our churches do not desire that the bishops restore peace and
71 unity at the expense of their honor and dignity (even though it is incumbent on the bishops to do this, too, in an emergency). They ask only that the bish-
72 ops relax certain unreasonable burdens which did not exist in the church in former times and which were adopted contrary to the custom of the universal Christian church. Perhaps there were some reasons for introducing them, but
73 they are not in tune with our times. Nor can it be denied that some ordinances
74 were adopted without being understood. Accordingly, the bishops should be so gracious as to temper these ordinances, since such change does not harm the unity of the Christian church. For many ordinances devised by human beings have fallen into disuse with the passing of time and need not be observed, as papal law itself testifies.[223] If, however, this is impossible and permission can-
75 not be obtained from them to moderate and abrogate such human ordinances as cannot be observed without sin, then we must follow the apostolic rule which commands us to obey God rather than any human beings [Acts 5:29].

St. Peter prohibits the bishops to rule as if they had the power to force the
76 churches to do whatever they desired [1 Peter 5:2]. Now the question is not how
77 to take power away from the bishops. Instead, we desire and ask that they would not force consciences into sin. But if they will not do so and despise this request,
78 let them consider how they will have to answer to God, since by their obstinacy they cause division and schism, which they should rightly help to prevent.[224]

---

223. For example, the penitential rules of the ancient church were supplanted in the early Middle Ages when the sacrament of penance was developed.

224. Of the variants in the text of the 1531 *editio princeps*, listed in *BSLK* 133, n. 1, these are most important. For par. 50–52: "For in the church this chief article of the gospel must be kept pure and clear: that we do not earn forgiveness of sins through our work and that we are not pronounced righteous on account of our self-chosen service of God, but instead for the sake of Christ through faith. Furthermore, the following teaching must be known and kept: that no such service of God, as is found in the Law of Moses, with its appointed foods and clothing and the like, is necessary in the New Testament and that no one should burden the church and create sins out of such things. For Paul says in Galatians 5[:1]: 'Do not submit again to a yoke of slavery.' " For par. 60: "They ordered Sunday so that the Word of God could be heard and learned. In the same way the festivals, such as Christmas, Easter, and Pentecost, were set up to teach the marvelous story of salvation. Thus, having a fixed time is helpful, so that people remember such things more firmly. It is not our opinion that such celebration must be held in a Jewish way, as if there were a necessary worship in the New Testament, but rather that it should be held because of the teaching."

But scarcely any of the canons are observed according to the letter. Many 67
of them become obsolete daily even among those who defend traditions. It is 68
not possible to counsel consciences unless this measure of fairness is preserved.
As a result, we know that traditions may be kept as long as they are not held
to be necessary and as long as they may not harm consciences, even if human
practice changes in such a matter.

However, the bishops could easily retain lawful obedience if they did not 69
insist on keeping traditions that cannot be observed with a good conscience.
Now they impose celibacy, and they accept no one unless he swears that he will 70
not teach the pure doctrine of the gospel. Our churches do not ask that the 71
bishops restore concord at the expense of their honor—which, nevertheless,
good pastors ought do. They only ask that the bishops relax unjust burdens 72
that are new and were accepted contrary to the custom of the catholic church.
Perhaps in the beginning there were acceptable reasons for these ordinances, 73
but they are not suited for later times. It also seems that some were adopted 74
by mistake. Bishops, therefore, could show their clemency by mitigating them,
because such change would not threaten the unity of the church. For many
human traditions have been changed with the passing of time, as the canons
themselves show. But if it is impossible to obtain a relaxation of observances 75
that cannot be kept without sin, we must obey the apostolic injunction [Acts
5:29] which commands us to obey God rather than human beings.

Peter prohibits bishops from domineering over and coercing the church- 76
es. The present matter does not involve bishops abandoning their exercise of 77
lordship, but only one thing is requested, namely, that they permit the teaching of the gospel in its purity and relax those few observances that cannot be
kept without sin. If they do not do this, they will have to see to it how they will 78
render an account before God, given that they provide a cause for schism by
their obstinacy.

INDEX

Subject Index

(This Index does not include references in the Appendix.)

Name Index

Living by Faith: Justification and Sanctification, by Oswald Bayer (2003).

Harvesting Martin Luther's Reflections on Theology, Ethics and the Church, essays from *Lutheran Quarterly,* edited by Timothy J. Wengert, with foreword by David C. Steinmetz (2004).

A More Radical Gospel: Essays on Eschatology, Authority, Atonement, and Ecumenism, by Gerhard O. Forde, edited by Mark Mattes and Steven Paulson (2004).

The Role of Justification in Contemporary Theology, by Mark C. Mattes (2004).

The Captivation of the Will: Luther vs. Erasmus on Freedom and Bondage, by Gerhard O. Forde (2005).

Bound Choice, Election, and Wittenberg Theological Method: From Martin Luther to the Formula of Concord, by Robert Kolb (2005).

A Formula for Parish Practice: Using the Formula of Concord in Congregations, by Timothy J. Wengert (2006).

Luther's Liturgical Music: Principles and Implications, by Robin A. Leaver (2006).

The Preached God: Proclamation in Word and Sacrament, by Gerhard O. Forde, edited by Mark C. Mattes and Steven D. Paulson (2007).

Theology the Lutheran Way, by Oswald Bayer (2007).

A Time for Confessing, by Robert W. Bertram (2008).

The Pastoral Luther: Essays on Martin Luther's Practical Theology, edited by Timothy J. Wengert (2009).

Preaching from Home: The Stories of Seven Lutheran Women Hymn Writers, by Gracia Grindal (2011).

The Early Luther: Stages in a Reformation Reorientation, by Berndt Hamm (2013).

The Life, Works, and Witness of Tsehay Tolessa and Gudina Tumsa, the Ethiopian Bonhoeffer, edited by Samuel Yonas Deressa and Sarah Hinlicky (2017).

The Wittenberg Concord: Creating Space for Dialogue, by Gordon A. Jensen (2018).

Luther's Outlaw God: Volume 1: Hiddenness, Evil, and Predestination, by Steven D. Paulson (2018).

The Essential Forde: Distinguishing Law and Gospel, by Gerhard O. Forde, edited by Nicholas Hopman, Mark C. Mattes, and Steven D. Paulson (2019).

Luther's Outlaw God: Volume 2: Hidden in the Cross, by Steven D. Paulson (2019).

The Augsburg Confession: Renewing Lutheran Faith and Practice by Timothy J. Wengert (2020).